Rural craftsmen and their work

Rural craftsmen and their work

Equipment and techniques in the Mer village of Ratadi in Saurashtra, India

with a preface by Alfred Bühler

by Eberhard Fischer
Haku Shah

National Institute of Design
Ahmedabad

(India) 1970

All rights with National Institute of Design
Ahmedabad, India, 1970

Translation: Shamim Smetacek
Book Design: Hans Christian Pulver NID

Published by National Institute of Design
Paldi, Ahmedabad 7

Printed by Mr. R. K. Banerjee
at National Institute of Design
Printing Workshop
Paldi, Ahmedabad 7

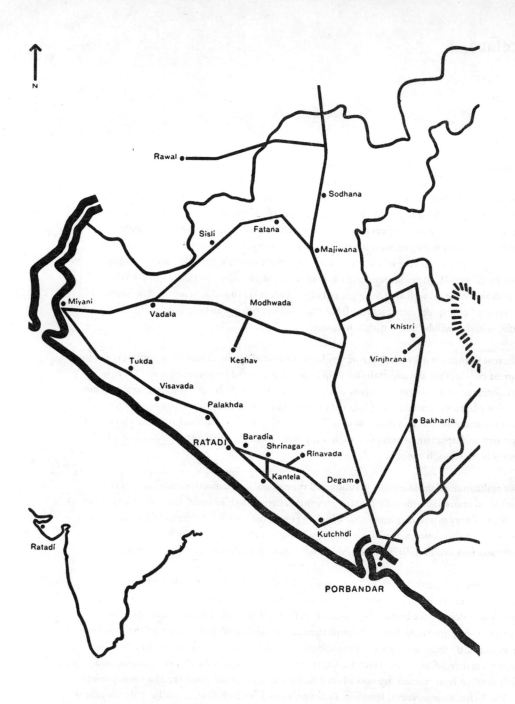

1. Location of the village of Ratadi in Saurashtra.

(Only villages and towns mentioned in the text are shown on the map.)

Preface

Indian arts and craft can be traced back to the third millenium B. C. and a great part thereof still exists today. In the course of those many centuries, unequalled times of bloom alternated with low marks that had to be overcome again and again. Conceptions of art and design have varied during this long time and very often foreign influences have strongly made themselves felt. In all these situations, however, fundamental attitudes and basic values of the Indian culture have been strong enough to preserve its continuity. Therefore the Indian character of arts and crafts has on the whole survived up to the present day. Strictly speaking, only since world war II, the influences take effect in the sense of a modernization and a levelling of craft and trade, as well as of an approach of the Indian art to modern tendencies. Especially with regard to arts, the estrangement from traditional forms has already begun. But for crafts, too, this will be only a question of time.

Whereas in India, works of the classic arts kept as national treasures and are accordingly held in great esteem, folk arts and crafts have up to now been payed little attention to. There is, therefore, the great danger that many of these latter works will disappear irretrievably before they have been sufficiently recorded. Yet this would mean an irreplaceable loss, not only from the scientific but also from the national point of view, as traditional arts (and also crafts) represent an important cultural foundation for every country, a property the value of which cannot be rated high enough.

This realization of the scientific, yet above all the cultural and national significance of the traditional crafts unfortunately has still very little asserted itself in India. It is true, there are a number of very interesting museums, which in connections with folklore and folk arts are to some extent also concerned with crafts; considering the abundance of the varied forms of crafts and folk arts in India, however, this is not much more than a drop in the ocean.

Of greater effect are the different, partly national, Indian organizations whose aim is to further the traditional crafts and to procure a ready market for them. In my opinion all these endeavours deserve the highest appreciation, as they not only increase the income of large groups of the population, but at the same time to a good deal support the traditional working procedures. By these widely spread organizations, which cover the whole country or at least large parts thereof, traditional techniques, motives and styles, specific of a certain area, and designs taken from abroad, are nowadays diffused throughout the country. The consequences will be an increasing general levelling, I dare say even a deterioration, as well as a development of completely new forms that are in no way determined by traditional patterns.

A modernization in economic fields and connected therewith in those of crafts and trade is necessary; for India it is a vital question. However, an accurate documentation, a collection of texts, illustrations and typical examples, of all still existing traditional crafts is to be desired. Such investigations would first of all be for the benefit of science. But what is more, with the help of such a documentation, one can at least save these national treasures and keep them alive in the memory of modern people. Furthermore, good products of craftsmanship from the various areas could, within the scope of technical development, serve as patterns for forms, styles and motives, for creations which, despite all their modernness, preserve the Indian character, and do not just represent mostly dreary everyday-forms as can be found everywhere according to the respective fashion.

Of the ethnographical research organized by the National Institue of Design, this book is the first result. On behalf of the Institute Dr. phil. Eberhard Fischer and Haku Shah carried on investigations into the arts and crafts in a village of Saurashtra, Gujarat. Being an ethnologist, Fischer has since his student days mainly concerned himself with problems of craft. He has done field work on this particular subject in West Africa and was, therefore, the very man to conduct this first documentation for the Institute. The painter Haku Shah with his extensive knowledge of the country, his open-mindedness and his artistic talent necessarily was an ideal colleague for Fischer. All the more so, as both were at work not only with their intellect but also with their heart, and both respected the qualities of well-performed craftsmanship.

The present book impressed me very much. In those many years, during which I have, within the scope of cultural anthropology, dealt with questions of crafts and technology I have hardly come across a treatise that has because of its profoundity and clarity such an enjoyable and animating effect on me. Both authors deserve the highest praise. Their publication can with full right be considered an example for similar future publications.

A small area of India, in fact only one single village, is treated in this work and already this has yielded rich material. It has, however, required hard work, too. From this it can be realized how immense the task is to carry through such research work for the whole of India. The difficulties are, however, also caused by the fact that today it is difficult to find anthropologists who are still interested in technology and ergology, i. e. the technical procedures and the material equipment. For most of them sociological and psychoanthropological aspects are by far uppermost. Because of this, organizations like the National Institute of Design are confronted with problems difficult to solve.

Together with my personal thanks, as well as those of anthropology in general, I therefore want to express the wish that the directors of the Institute may find ways and means and above all scientists to continue such documentation of arts and crafts in India. The beginning has been made and has been very successful. It would be a great pity, if further works of this kind were not to follow.

Basel, 12th February, 1968   Dr. phil. Alfred Buehler
Professor for Anthropology, University of Basel
Switzerland

Introduction

This treatise presents an ethnographical study of traditional rural design in a particular region of India. This has involved a description of various arts and crafts, an inquiry into the role of different craftsmen, their working condition and procedures. We have restricted this research to a limited area, so that the information may be as precise and condensed as possible.

The peninsula of Saurashtra was chosen because the existing conditions seemed ideally suited to subject of this kind of research. Saurashtra is noted for the variety of crafts practised not only in its towns but also in its villages.

The project involved the following programme :

(1) viewing the area in the course of a cross-country-tour through Saurashtra
(2) working out a report of the subjects to be treated as well as studying the relevant literature
(3) two months of field work in the village of Ratadi
(4) discussion of the information gathered and its presentation in this treatise form.

In order to gain a general impression of arts and crafts in Saurashtra, a cross-country-tour was plannned through the districts of Bhavnagar, Amreli, Junagadh and Rajkot. Villages were selected at random and the possibilities and conditions of extensive field work investigated. Our tour lasted from 27.10. 1965 to 7.11.1965 and led us to Bhavnagar, Sihor, Palitana (with the village of Bederada), Sava Kundla (with the village of Chakaradi and Nana Jinjura), Mahuva (with the villages of Katpura, Devalia and Vangar), Amreli (with the villages of Ishvaria and Varasada), Junagadh (with the villages of Valandia, Vipur, Bilkha and Umrala), Sasan (with some Nes-settlements), Veraval and Patan (with the villages of Jambur, Meraj, Inaj, Sonaria, Gorakhamadhi and Badalpara), Porbandar (with the villages of Chhaya, Bakharla, Degam, Kantela, Ratadi, Shrinagar and Visavada) and Rajkot (with the villages of Tramba and Gadhaka).

Our diary entries tell us that the village of Ratadi attracted us by the abundance of its traditional design, the many craftsmen working in and around the village, the relatively small number of households, and the friendliness of its people.

We stayed two months in Ratadi (from 10.12.1965 to 15.2.1966), and adopted our mode of life to the villagers while maintaining our identity as observers and interrogaters. We rented two houses directly in the village centre, and ate food cooked for us by a local family. During the time being, we were strict vegetarians and avoided everything that could annoy the villagers like drinking spirits, killing vermin or taking photographs of women. In the course of our field work we took some 3800 photographs, made a catalogue of 400 objects, drew ground plans of houses, and noted down in detail the function and significance of several objects and working procedures. The work was divided between us. Haku Shah organized our stay in Ratadi which was not always easy, and compiled the catalogue. He also undertook the description of the working techniques of women, while Eberhard Fischer observed and interviewed the craftsmen and farmers.

From Ratadi we undertook several short excursions to the following villages: Baradia, Shrinagar, Palakhda, Visavada, Miyani, Keshav, Modhvada, Majivana, Degam, Bakharla, Vinjhrana, Khistri, Patana, Sodhana and to the ruins of the fort of Gumli.

The information gathered during our field work led to the writing of this treatise, the German version of which was completed in Ahmedabad in August 1966.

We have tried to unify the chapters which deal with procedures working in special raw materials like stone, wood, clay, fabrics etc. by adopting – as far as possible – the same mode of description; in each case treating first the informants, the role of the craftsman, his traditional tools and materials, the conditions he works under, followed by a description of one or several typical procedures of work and finally a catalogue of typical examples of the objects under discussion. In the interest of clarity, a special mode of description has been adopted throughout. In the present "catalogue raisonne" a general *basic type* is first described. By this is implied not the historical basic model but a synthetically deduced definition of a cultural motif, including both functional as well as structural parts typical of the article described. In this sense a cultural motif which constitutes part of the equipment used by a community would be one species of tool, implement, furniture or part of the house construction which is characterized by homogeneous design and function, having further one common local name given it by its makers or users. As far as possible, this basic type will first be described in general outline, details of construction, with special peculiarities following later. This approach is intended to give as complete and detailed a description of the different basic types as possible.

Below this, the local term applied to it by its users is given. A typical example conforming closely to its basic type can be located in a specific household of Ratadi and is shown together with its measurements as far as they were available. A few remarks on the function of this kind of object have been added after each description. Finally, the most important variations of that basic type to be found in Ratadi households have been summarized and features of special interest described in detail.

All data given is the result of observations made by the authors. Information given by the villagers is printed in small type, the sign (//) standing for a question on part of the interviewer. The indigenous terms are given as we heard the villagers pronounce them. In several cases 'r' is equivalent to 'l' and 'h' to 's' in Gujarati. Orthography, however, is simplified, diacritic marks not being used.

The entire project was realized by the National Institute of Design, Ahmedabad, and generously patronized by the Government of Gujarat. We wish to acknowledge our appreciation of the advice given to us when planning our enterprise by Shri Vimalbhai Shah and his colleagues of the Tribal Research and Training Institute at Gujarat Vidyapith, Ahmedabad. We are also grateful to Shri Bechardas Madhavji and his partners of the Saurashtra Bharat Kala Mandir. We offer our thanks to C. V. Suchak, M. D. and Kausalyaben Suchak, M. D. in Porbandar for their constant help. In Ratadi we received assistance chiefly from the Sarpanch Shri Samadbhai Karsanbhai, the venerable Shri Vasabhai Bhojabhai and the Police Patel Ramabhai Jivabhai, to whom we are grateful. Above all, we wish to thank the old women who received us so warmly in their village, especially Rupiai, who devotedly cared for our daily comforts, the kind and brave Puriai, the artistic Makiai and the aged, venerable Vahaliai. In Ratadi we were given special help by Ranmalbhai, Parbatbhai, Vejabhai and Hiradas. Furthermore, we are much indebted to the Sarpanch of Palakhada village, Patel Hiradasbhai Bhayabhai and the Sarpanch of Baradia for their generous support. We were welcomed by the people of Degam and Visavada as well.

We are also deeply indebted to all the craftsmen of Ratadi and Baradia, all of them were most co-operative and gave us the opportunity to take glimpses of their craftsmanship. Our sincere gratitude is due to the carpenters Shri Maldebhai Khimabhai and his brothers Shri Mohanbhai and Shri Dhanjibhai, to the potter Shri Bhurabhai Dahyabhai, to the shepherd Shri Dahyabhai Nandiabhai, to the shoemaker Shri Keshavbhai Naranbhai, to the weaver Shri Amrabhai Parbatbhai, to the stone mason Shri Dahyabhai Khimabhai and to the quarryman Shri Rajsinhbhai Mepabhai.

We acknowledge with thanks the help of our colleagues of the National Institute of Design, Mr. S. V. Kar for having photographed the objects for our catalogue and the architect Mr. Subodh Dhairywan for having prepared the ground plans of some typical houses and work-shops. Mrs. Chaturlaxmiben helped Haku Shah in his write-up.

Warm thanks go to Shri Hamir Sinhji, the Darbar of Baradia, who rendered Eberhard Fischer invaluable service as an interpreter.

Ahmedabad, August 1966   Eberhard Fischer
                                                                       Haku Shah
                                                                       National Institute of Design

Many parts of the manuscript, written in German, were translated into English by Miss Shamim Smetacek, Bhimtal, U. P. The entire manuscript was finally revised by Eberhard Fischer and Mrs. Hannelore Meyer at the South Asia Institute in Heidelberg during the winter of 1968.

The paper for this publication has been donated by Internationes, Bad Godesberg and we want to thank Miss Magdalena Duckwitz (Embassy of the Federal Republic of Germany, New Delhi) very much for all the help she has rendered us in promoting this.

The lay-out for the book has been prepared by Mr. Hans Christian Pulver, the book-cover by Mr. Mahendra Patel and the book has been finally printed with great care under the supervision of Mr. R. K. Banerjee in the printing workshop of the National Institute of Design, Ahmedabad.

We shall not forget to mention with gratitude that one of us, Eberhard Fischer, was allowed to use some time during his appointment as the representative in India of the South Asia Institute, University of Heidelberg, to edit the manuscript and read the proofs together with Mrs. Asha Cariappa and Mrs. Yasmin F. Cambata. In this respect our thanks are specially due to Prof. Dr. Karl Jettmar, Head of the Department of Ethnology, South Asia Institute, Heidelberg.

Lastly we thank Prof. Dr. Alfred Buehler, University of Basel, for having contributed the preface to this book and encouraged us to work together, now and in future, on similar projects.

Ahmedabad, April 1970   E. F. and H. S.

Table of contents

Plans and Maps

List of photographs:

I. The village of Ratadi and its inhabitants

by Eberhard Fischer

I. 1. The location and environs of Ratadi

Ratadi is a village in the large peninsula of Gujarat formerly known as Kathiawar, now
called Saurashtra. It falls under the administration of the Porbandar Taluka (Municipality)
in the Junagadh District. The Indian Census 1961 (1964 : 120,175) gives the following report
on Ratadi and its inhabitants : The village of Ratadi extends over an area of 1489-22 acres
land and possesses a school and two wells. There are 132 households and as many houses.
The total population of 755 souls consists of 382 men and 373 women, of which only 81
persons belong to a scheduled caste. Only 139 can read and write. 346 work for a living. Of
these 155 men together with their 118 wives are independent farmers, while 10 men
are farm labourers. One man is a mason, 15 are craftsmen, 6 are traders and shopkeepers
and 41 are employees or servants.

Porbandar is a busy town with its own harbour, airport and railway station. From the city
a highway flanked by cinema houses, bazaars, factories and hospitals, leads out into the open
country across the sandy plain and along the coast northwards, past small, wall enclosed
fields beside which oxen draw water from wells under the shade of windblown trees, past a
vast, saltencrusted steppe upon which a Fata Morgana shimmers in the noonday sun, past
sand dunes and arid expanses dotted with cactus and dry scrub and the rock exposed here
and there by wind and weather. This is the face of the landscape in winter, when sharp gusts
of wind blow over from the sea; during the monsoon rain falls daily and the entire plain is
submerged. It then becomes one great lake out of which only the walls enclosing the fields
and the hillocks upon which the villages are built, remain above water-level. In the hot
season it is dry and a gentle sea breeze keeps the air clear.

Upon a slight rise of ground, set in the midst of the weathered limestone landscape, lies
the village of Ratadi, a flat expanse of grey houses with reddish-brown tiled roofs.
No special feature distinguishes it. The neighbouring village of Baradia, lying further
inland and visible from afar, is more imposing. It was formerly closely connected
with Ratadi, for it was in Baradia that the landowner and bailiff of Ratadi resided.
Baradia consists of a hill crowned by a fort, around which groups of houses are clustered.
The well at the base of the hill is shaded by the dense foliage of the surrounding trees.
The fields on the outskirts of the village are irrigated and are fertile.

The highway runs between both villages. A new school building with two classrooms
has been erected near the highway and the teacher is trying to grow a few flowers
and bushes in the front yard. The bus stops at a massive tree. Old men and idlers sit on
the stones placed in layers around the tree trunk and gossip or greet the newcomers.
Between the highway and the village is an uncultivated, open stretch of ground, at the
edge of which are two small shrines on platforms. Here also small stone posts have
been dug in for the rope-maker. Every morning the cattle of the village is herded together

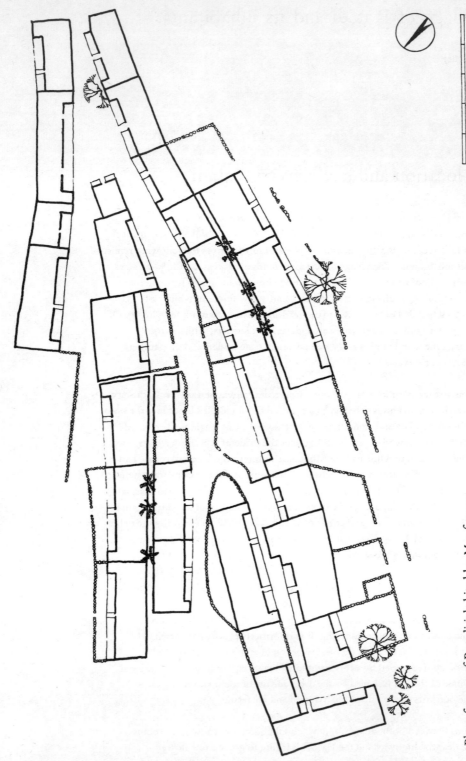

2. Plan of a part of Ratadi inhabited by Mer-farmers.

2

here and driven to the pastures. On festive occasions this stretch of ground is used for
dancing. On the left it is bounded by an enclosed rectangular yard in which the bull kept
for breeding purposes is stalled. Beyond this stall lives the community of the Rabari
shepherds, separated from the dwellings of the craftsmen (carpenter and tailor) and the
Muslim barber by a narrow path leading to the centre of the village. In front of these
houses is a modern farm. In the centre of the village are two small white Shiva temples
built on platforms. Close by are the two small shops in which one can buy cigarettes,
bidis, matches, tea, sugar, salt and other commodities. One can also sell one's cash crops
there. From this point the roads leading to various parts of the village diverge. The
eastern, northern and western areas are inhabited chiefly by Mer farmers, the Harijan
quarter lies southwest and the Rabari shepherds occupy the southeastern zone.
Near the centre stands the *choro*, assembly house, in front of which several memorial
stones have been set up.

The roads, which in some cases bifurcate, are flanked on both sides by rows of houses.
There is invariably a roofed verandah in front of every house. Small trees sometimes grow
in the narrow passages running between the back walls of the houses, although the
passages are more frequently laid out with stone and brick rubble. There are very few
large trees in Ratadi and these are usually found near small shrines.

In recent years the village has been gradually opening up. Since ramparts are not
necessary any more, farms can be established on the outskirts of the village, each farm with
its own stretch of ground for livestock, haystack, etc. Or else, the ruins of a broken-down
house in the village itself can be cleared away and the space used for stacking hay,
implements, and such. These are doubtless modern tendencies, for in the past people lived
crowded together, as the back walls of the houses had to serve as ramparts in case of
attack. Each street has one *falian*, a patri-lineage segment, or one *ari*, extended family, which
formerly constituted a defence unit in times of war. In our age the rules are more lenient
and outsiders who have married into the family as well as distant relatives live together.

The village is girded by a belt of land which is divided into plots and enclosed by walls.
Here each farmer keeps his haystack, fuel and dungheap. The premises are guarded at night by
the farmer or one of his sons. There is a small hut built on each plot for him to sleep in.

The fields are mostly small, scattered and divided into several plots as the result of
inheritance. Between the fields lie vast, unarable stone wastes. Bumpy, sandy paths lead to
the fields. Most of the fields are irrigated.

The village well, which lies beside the highway outside the village, yields brackish
water which can be used for washing and for watering the animals, but not for cooking and
drinking purposes. The women of Ratadi therefore fetch water several times a day in
large earthen pitchers or bronze pots from Baradia, a kilometre away. The cistern there is
broad and deep and contains clean, fresh water. The Ratadi villagers are therefore
economical with drinking water and this is also probably the reason why water is kept inside
the house and not on the verandah, where it would be accessible to everybody.

The village roads are swept daily by the women. There are no modern sanitary arrangements
and villagers have to use their own fields or go outside the village. A thorough bath is taken
once a week at the mouth of the channel leading from the well to the field. Daily
morning ablutions are carried out on the verandah in a squatting position, the water
being allowed to run onto the street. Since this region is dry most of the year
round and is kept clean by the people, there are no mosquitoes and few flies as compared

with other Saurashtrian villages. However, the village is ridden with bed-bugs to which the
people seem to have accustomed themselves. The refuse then is either thrown on the
dungheap and left to rot, or else deposited on the land around broken-down houses. Small
pieces of metal are "hidden" in walls; earthenware fragments and the like are thrown
behind the house or swept up against walls. Larger articles are deposited outside the village,
the wooden parts being removed for fuel and the rest discarded.

I. 2. The inhabitants

The majority of the villagers of Ratadi belong to the Mer community, a Hindu caste of
cultivators that predominates amongst the inhabitants of the Porbandar Taluka. History has
proved them a warlike and valiant folk, loyal to their rulers, the Jetwa princes, with whom
they were gradually driven back to the periphery of Saurashtra in the course of the last
few centuries. An excellent monograph (Trivedi,1961) has been written about the Mer.
Stress is laid chiefly on the social structure and economic organisation. In addition, much
valuable information on marriage rites and religious customs, human relations and traditions,
is given. According to this author (Trivedi, 1961, pg. 38) the Mer community is divided
into 14 maximal exogamous patri-lineages, all of which have a male founder ancestor.
These patri-lineages are divided into various major segments which are living partilocal.
It may be mentioned that these 14 lineages are of different social status, the oldest tracing
its origin back more than 50 generations, holds a superior position. This Keshvara-Mer-
lineage which forms the bulk of the population of Ratadi, has special rites and ritual duties
(Trivedi, 1961, pg. 105).

Bilateral cross-cousin marriages are quite common (Trivedi, 1961, pg. 39). A widow is
allowed to remarry; divorce and separation are possible. During and after the wedding both
families exchange presents, the bride's family giving chiefly gifts while the groom's gives
money. The joint-family system still prevails today. The oldest man in the household is
responsible for the administration of the property and divides the income among the other
family members, while the sons work together on the fields, although each lives with his
family in a separate house.

The position of the *patel,* headman, is a hereditary one and borne by the most elderly
member of that family (Trivedi, 1961, pg. 24). He takes an active part in all religious
and secular functions. He is supported by the *panchayat,* a body of advisors or an
assembly of elders elected by the village. The *panchayat* nowadays appoints a *sarpanch,*
mayor, who is in turn assisted by a *police patel,* a civil servant, and, a recent innovation,
a *talati,* accountant or secretary whose chief task is to promote the co-operative system.

All of the Mer people are farmers. Their most important crops are *bajro* (Pennisetum),
javar (Sorghum) and *chino* (Panicum). Wheat grows only on the best land. Cotton
and peanuts are cultivated as cash-crops. The vegetables include chillies, clover, aubergines
and more rarely tomatoes, turnips, sugar-cane, castor-oilseeds and pulses. Though fish
and game are available in plenty it is of very little use since the majority of the farmers
are strict vegetarians.

However, milk and milk products like clarified butter, sour-milk, and butter-milk play
an important part in the diet. The farmers themselves bread cattle and water-buffaloes,
while the Rabari shepherds rear mostly sheep and goats. Riding-horses are rare and

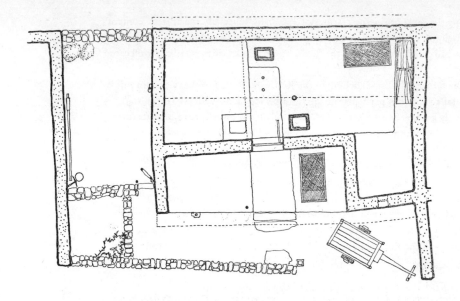

3. Plan of a traditional house of a Mer-farmer.

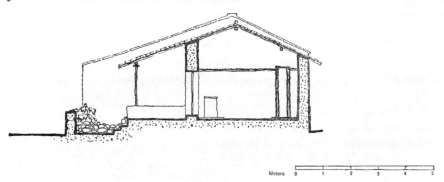

4. Cross-section of a traditional house of a Mer-farmer.

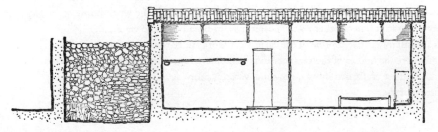

5. Longitudinal section of a traditional house of a Mer-farmer.

possessed only by the most prosperous farmers. Craftsmen, especially the potters, content themselves with donkeys. Bullocks are used to draw the heavy, two-wheeled carts and to lift the water-bags used for irrigating the fields. The bullocks are particularly well cared for·

Since most of the farmers of Ratadi belong to the Keshvara lineage of the Mer community, some further details about this particular group must be added. Trivedi (1961, pg. 105) gives the following particulars : "Members of the Keshvara lineage have regular features, and are light-skinned. A number of religious-minded and brave persons have come from the Keshvara lineage. The women of the Keshvara lineage are experts at wall-decoration and artistic clay-work in bas-relief. The favourite deities of the Keshvara lineage are *Shri Rama* and the goddess named *Khodiar*." It is furthermore stated that the Keshvara Mer assume to descend from *kesha*, a hair from God *Rama's* back, out of which the God created a man in order to safeguard the bridge between India and Ceylon, the story being told in the Ramayana. This tradition is still to be heared in Ratadi; some elders of the Keshvara lineage from Ratadi told Haku Shah the following sentences:

Keshvara e humai na didhel chho, Keshvara has been given by Mothergoddess Humai.
Ame bhagvan na runvada mathi niharya etvale ame hauthi unchha , we have come out of a God's body hair, that is why we are high (within) all.
Ame Raxasi maya chie amne hun gnan, we are "maya" of the *Raxasi,* giant, what knowledge (can we) have ?

The bard, Rajabhai Lakhabhai. the owner of the genealogical book for the Keshvara, stated in Ratadi that nowadays there are only five villages belonging to this lineage, Keshov, Visavada, Ratadi, Advana and Antroli. However, actually they possessed 24 villages (vide Trivedi, 1961, pg. 105). The fact that Keshvara did not spread out is emphasized in the following sentence common in Ratadi :

Keshvare timbo badlyo nath etle; vahani vadhati nath, Keshav has not changed the place; that is why it has not increased the generations.

Besides the Keshvara in Ratadi, there are a few Mer belonging to the Odedara, Kuthi, Kalavadra and Modvadia lineages. Most of these men came to stay in Ratadi as *gharjemai,* i. e. men who live in the houses of their fathers'-in-law, to take over their properties because there is no actual male heir. Often their brothers have joined them later. Some of these families in Ratadi came from Sodhana and from Baradia.

Since every village is a more or less independent economic unit, there must be besides the farmers a couple of *vasvaya,* craftsmen, the merchants and the barber. By the farmers they are sometimes called *rup,* beauty, of the village, nevertheless they most often live in a much lower economic standard than the farmers. In Ratadi there are the workshops of three carpenters and two cobblers, whereas the potter lives in Baradia where water, well and clay pits are suitably situated. One of the carpenters works in Baradia as a mason and near its small fort are the houses of the weavers and quarrymen. Since the living and working conditions of these craftsmen show quite some variety, more details are discussed within the specific chapters.

I. 3. The dwelling house

Within this chapter only a general background on the subject of housing will be provided; details such as fixtures, building materials and decorations will be discussed at length elsewhere.

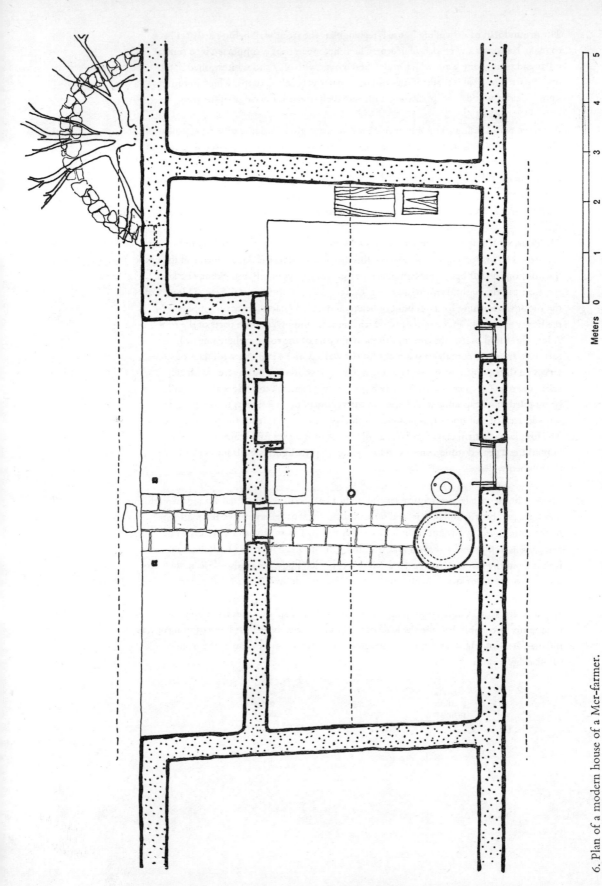

6. Plan of a modern house of a Mer-farmer.

The groundplan of a dwelling house is rectangular, the front wall being partly set back to make room for a verandah-platform. The simple span roof is supported by a central pillar and plain stone walls which are plastered over with clay and whitewashed in the upper part. The roof is made of tiles laid upon narrow bamboo strips, which in turn rest upon broader wooden strips. Stronger tiles are used towards the ridge of the roof.

A sunken path leading to the entrance door runs through the middle of the verandah-platform, dividing it into two. The verandah has a stone foundation plastered over with clay. In the hot season it is used as an airy sleeping place and during the day as a living room. Beside the path leading to the doorway, there is a pillar supporting the eaves rafter. Larger houses have several such supporting pillars. In some houses the anchor beam extends over the verandah as well, and is supported together with the eaves rafter by the pillar.

The door, which may have either one or two wings, is framed by a door case and swings inwards. The visitor steps over the stone threshold and enters the dark interior of the house; the floor on the left beside the entrance is not so clean, as young livestock may be kept there during the night. It is also used as a storage place for cotton, grain, etc. This part of the room is overhung by a loft built of beams and nailed boards. Its main support is the heavy anchor-beam or roof-tres, which connects and braces both parts of the roof. A low threshold marks the entrance to the main part of the room, where one or more earthenware grain containers stand against the wall. A niche laid out with slabs of stone serves on the opposite wall as a stand for water. The walls may be covered with clay relief-boards. The chest stands slightly higher, leveled against the side wall, the quilts being piled in a heap upon it. Adjacent to the verandah on one side, is the kitchen, with an arch of bamboo sticks plastered with clay separating it from the rest of the house. The fireplace is a firm clay structure; a hole in the roof serves for a chimney. Sometimes a grated stone window, which admits a little light, is built into one of the kitchen walls.

Modern houses are larger, require several anchor beams, have cemented verandah-platforms, block-shaped boards and beams, and sometimes even steps leading up to the platform. In the latter case, the room is on a higher level too, and no livestock are kept inside. Most modern houses also have a rear window, which can be used as a back door and is shut from the inside by a wooden latch. Two-storied houses may also be seen, the stairs leading to the upper storey being built against the outside wall.

A glance at a row of adjacent houses, reveals that the roof ridge varies from house to house, most probably because the level of the houses varies as well. A layer of stone covers the tiles. An ornamental ridge plate mounted between two stones covers the front of the ridge-beams.

verandah	*otlo*
platform	*padathar*
penplace	*dhor bar*

II. Farming implements

by Eberhard Fischer

All farming implements and similar equipment may be divided into two categories,
according to their function in the two most important aspects of a farmer's work:
cultivation of land, and livestock breeding together with animal husbandry. In addition
there are the basic fixtures required for both the above activities, namely fences,
sheds and stalls, the threshing floor and finally the well and irrigation system. Agricultural
implements fall into three categories: drawn vehicles (bullock carts), cultivating
implements (plough, harrow, etc.) and tools operated manually (hoe, rake, etc.). Animal
husbandry requires little equipment other than what is needed for feeding, tethering
and keeping the livestock clean.

All wooden implements are made by the village carpenter and repaired by him according
to fixed rules (vide VI. I. 2.). The metal parts are produced in the smith's forges at
Porbandar, but are assembled and repaired by the local carpenters. Jobs such as sharpening
the blades and fitting sickles into handles, are carried out by the carpenters. Plaited
implements are as a rule purchased from the Vagri tribes or at Porbandar. Some men
even make their tools themselves.

Thanks to the dry climate and the care with which they are handled, the tools and
implements have a long life. One of the villagers informed me that his harrow had
survived three generations of use! Implements not in use are kept in a roofed shed
near the house, care being taken to ensure that as little of the wooden surface as possible
touches the ground, to protect them from termites.

Wooden implements which cannot be used any more are burnt as fuel in the kitchen
fire, while the parts made of fabric, leather or iron are simply thrown away, swept into
broken-down houses or hidden in cracks in the wall. Rubbish heaps to receive common
refuse are unknown.

II. 1. The structures on the fields

Walls about one metre high and made of field stones enclose the fields; sometimes a
hedge of thorns encircles the wall. Occasionally cacti are planted along the wall to keep
thieves at bay. A cactus hedge of this kind is impenetrable, and in regions where there
is no danger of the monsoon rain washing away the soil, a stone wall may be dispensed
with altogether in favour of a cactus hedge. A gap in the wall provides access to the
field, and a thorny branch or a wooden beam may be temporarily laid across the gap
to keep out stray cattle.

Where ever hay is stacked, on the field or near the village in an enclosed plot, a little hut is
built for the watchman. Six or more forked poles are stuck into the ground to form a

rectangle, beams being laid across them. Bundles of straw are laid on this framework and from the roof. The walls also consist of bundles of straw placed on end and held in place by a horizontally suspended central beem. Should the hut be exposed to strong winds, one wall at least is built of stone. The side facing away from the wind is left open, thus affording an unrestricted view of the hay-stacks and the field. In the centre of the hut there is a manger, consisting of two rows of stones, behind which the bullocks are tethered, particularly in winter, when harsh winds blow from the sea. The rope around their necks is so short that the bullocks cannot reach up to the roof or the wall with their mouths. The man on watch sleeps in front of the manger or parallel to one wall. Throughout the night a fire is kept going in front of the hut.

irrigated field	*vadi*
enclosed hay plot	*vada*
watch hut	*oth*

Asked about the watch hut and the nightly duties of the man on watch, Rangmalbhai Karsanbhai of Baradia gave the following information :

//*Oth*, the hut is used as a sleeping place for the man who has to watch the fields during the night and as a shelter for the bullocks. The bullocks are kept in the middle of the hut so that they cannot reach the hay on the side walls or the roof.
//We keep them in the shelter only during the winter season to protect them from the cold winds.
//Somebody may steel the hay. //I myself sleep here every night. In some households the sons are sent out as watch. //During the night I have to get up two or three times to give fresh hay to the bullocks.
//If I give them all the hay for the night at one time, they will spoil it. They cannot eat all at once, but need many hours to chew the hay. During that time it comes under their legs and in their dung. They will not touch hay once it is spoilt. This is the reason why we have to feed our cattle three times during the night.
//Otherwise they are not strong and healthy.

II. 2. The threshing floor

Threshing may be carried out on any clear space in front of the field. However, all the village farmers usually thresh their grain on an unarable stretch of ground favourably situated near the village. In Ratadi the threshing floor lies north of the village on a flat, infertile, wind-swept plain. Years of threshing have smoothened out the rough stone ground completely.

In the morning, before threshing starts, a large circle is thinly plastered over with a mixture of cowdung and water. The warm wind quickly dries the floor, which is then swept ready for the threshing to begin.

threshing floor	*karun*

The following is a brief account of how the threshing is done. I had the opportunity to observe how *bajra* (pennisetum typhoideum) and *banti,* finger millet, were threshed together. The farmer Vikrambhai commented as follows:

//The *bajra* is cut near its roots when the grain is ripe. The whole plants are carried in bundles to the house, where the clubs or heads are cut and collected to be threshed some months later.
//These crops were harvested at *vadmer*, the period around *Divali*, the Hindu New Year (November).
//This morning we cleaned the place with dung and water. After that we started threshing and we will continue till the late afternoon. Tomorrow morning we will have to thresh again, and after lunch I will winnow the grain. (This programme of work resulted in two and a half bags of grain).

The millet ears are transported to the threshing floor in a bullock cart spread with canvas. On reaching the threshing floor the bullocks are unyoked and the load emptied.

10

Muzzles made of string are fitted over the mouths of three bullocks, which are then driven around the threshing floor in circles. The guide-rope runs from the muzzle of the outermost bullock, around the horns and muzzle of the middle one, to the muzzle of the bullock describing the innermost circle. From here the rope runs along the bullock's flank and over its hindshanks, ending in the hand of the driver, who trots behind the outermost bullock. The team is driven round in circles for hours on end. At intervals the bullocks are allowed to rest and eat some hay from the bundle which has been brought along and placed just outside the threshing floor. After this short respite, threshing is resumed. A helper keeps raking together the millet and spreading it out under the hooves of the bullocks. The driver, displaying great presence of mind, manages to intercept the droppings with his hand before they reach the ground and throws them on a heap beside the threshing floor. The bullock urine, however, falls on the millet and is evenly sprinkled over the grain by the wind.

Already during the threshing process, some of the chaff is blown away by the wind. In the evening the millet ears, grain and chaff are swept together, gathered up in baskets and bowls, and thrown into the cart over which a cloth quilt has previously been spread.

Finally, when the millet has been thoroughly threshed, the chaff is separated from the grain. For this, all the grain is raked together into a heap on one side of the floor. Next, the grain is shaken out bowl by bowl in the strong midday wind. The bowl is lifted up to chest level and held towards one side. Now the grain is shaken out of it, that is, the bowl is held at a slight slant and the grain shaken out a little at a time by tilting the bowl backwards in a series of rhythmical jerks. The amount of grain poured out at a time depends on how strong the wind is at the moment. The grain and the heavy ears fall to the ground after a flight of three metres or less while the chaff, which is light, is borne much further.

While the two elder sons alternately hand their father filled bowls for winnowing, the younger boys extricate the millet ears from the heap and sweep the grain yet to be winnowed together. The millet has to be winnowed several times before the grain is thoroughly separated from the chaff. Next, the grain is sieved in order to remove ears, and to let the wind blow away the last particles of chaff. The sieve is rhythmically shaken by two persons. Lastly, the grain is filled and tied up in gunny bags. The empty ears, which can be used as fodder, are loaded in the cart; even the chaff, which can be used as fodder or mixed with wall plaster, is sometimes collected in bags and carried to the village by women. The bags are piled on top of the cart and the farmer makes his way homewards.

Some words in threshing:

threshing	*halavu*
winnowing	*vavalvu*
full ears of millet	*dunda*
empty ears of millet	*picha*
chaff	*dunsa*
muzzle	*sikla*
small rake	*khapari*
sieve	*charana*

II. 3. The well and the irrigation system

In the present chapter we shall describe the traditional types of wells which to this day are used for the irrigation of fields. Water for domestic use is drawn in buckets from a simple, large cistern. These cisterns sunk and built under the supervision of the Indian Government, are cemented and possess frames of iron with a set of pulleys.

3. 1. The stone foundation

The well on the field is a simple shaft of rectangular section, the measurements 8, 9, 10
depending on the situation. A low wall of stone blocks encloses the upper edge of the
well. The water is drawn up in a leather bag on two ropes running over two pulleys,
and emptied into a short channel embanked on each side by a long stone slab (1), the front
edges of which project into the wall opening. The channel-bed is lined with a rectangular
stone block (2) and a large flat slab (3). At the other end opposite the mouth of the channel
lies another stone block (4) which dams the rush of water and deviates it into a simple
unlined furrow running out into the fields. Adjacent to the well shaft there is often a small
drinking trough (5) for livestock or a simple pit dug in the ground and lined with stone slabs.

well	*vao*
(1) embanking slabs	*dhonia*
(2) stone block	*osika* (lit cushion)
(3) bottom slab	*thara*
(4) damming block	*fonkni chippar*
(5) trough	*khund* or *khundi*

Upon this stone foundation is placed a wooden structure, with pulleys to draw up the
water. Holes are chiselled into the embanking slabs (2) at a point close to the end projecting
into the shaft. A post (6) is inserted into each hole and wedged in firmly. A cross beam
with several holes (7) is placed across these two poles and supported further by two forked
stakes (8) which are anchored in the ground next to the embanking slabs and weighted
down with stones. Two sticks (9) are stuck into the centre of the cross beam, which in their
turn support an iron axletree on two cogs (10). A large wooden sheave with a grooved
edge revolves on the axletree (11). The water bag is hauled up by this pulley with the help
of a thick rope.

This essential principle I found to be adopted in the case of every well I had the opportunity
to examine. The only feature which seems to vary is the position of the heavy second pulley
(12), on which the second drawing rope runs.

(6) pair of posts	*suja*
(7) cross beam	*tolia*
(8) forked stakes	*tel* (support)
(9) supporting sticks	*dangela*
(10) iron axletree	*dhari*
(11) wooden sheave	*paida* (wheel)
(12) wooden pulley	*garadi*

There are three distinct methods of installing the heavy pulley (12) above the edge of
the well shaft.

Two rectangular niches are chiselled into the inner longitudinal edge on the front side
of the embanking slabs (1) close to the edge of the well shaft; small toothed pieces
of wood are inserted into these niches and firmly wedged in. This forms a bearing in
which the iron axletree rotates.

Method of attachment	*pau*

Rectangular pieces of wood are set along the inner longitudinal edge of the embanking 10
slabs (1) and anchored in holes in the stone with wooden dowels. These wooden
pieces have a toothed or cogged edge cut into the front portion. The axletree rotates
in this bearing and with it, the pulley.

Method of attachment	*bardudia*
wooden dowel	*khili* (wedge)

Wooden beams are laid under the embanking slabs, the front edge being toothed to admit
the axletree. One of the beams generally projects at a slight angle from the stone, in
order to facilitate the axletree being rested upon it. The beams are fixed in place solely
through the weight of the stone slabs.

Method of attachment   garedia

3. 2. The drawing ropes and yoke

The leather water bag is hoisted up by means of a thick cable (13) made of three ropes   10
wrapped in rags and twisted together. A thinner and shorter rope (14) is used to lift the bag
so that the water is poured over the stone block. In order to prevent any of the ropes
from trailing on the ground, they are fastened together by a leather loop (15). Both ropes
are knotted to the water bag at different points, both terminating in a small cross-bar
(16); around this cross-bar is slipped a noose, which is fastened to the ox yoke.

The yoke is constructed for two draught oxen and consists of two pieces of timber with   11
the ends broadening out slightly (17). For the purpose of strengthening the two timbers, two
rods are tied to them immediately right and left of the centre (18). The heads of the oxen
fit into the spaces next to the rods. Finally a noose of rope (19) is slung around the two main
timbers and tightened. The short piece (20) joining the drawing ropes of the water bags
to the plough runs round the centre of both main timbers.

(13) large drawing cable	varat
(14) short drawing rope	varatadi or ras
(15) leather loop	maga
(16) cross-bar	karedho
(17) yoke	tarela or tarelu
upper timber or beam	dhunsari
lower timber or beam	hadiyu
(18) pair of rods	pisori
(19) rope nooses	ansekod
(20) joining rope	varlu
leather apron	ghansia
harness and waterbag	chodia

3. 3. The water bag

A detailed description of the leather water-bag is given in the chapter on leather. At this   9
juncture, suffice it to say that the water bag consists of a square frame constructed of strips of
wood joined by mortise and tenon, the rectangular bag being sewn around this frame.
At one side the bag continues in a tube, the length of which equals if not exceeds that of
the bag. At the end of the tube is an opening. The bag is dipped several times into the
well in order to fill it and than hauled up in such a manner that the tube is arched over the
frame. Only when the bag has reached the lower pulley and is being drawn over it,
the water flows out through the tube. This is accomplished simply by raising the water level
in the bag above that in the tube.

The path to be described by the oxen in order to hoist up the water bag depends on
the depth of the well shaft, in other words, upon the length of the drawing ropes.

The path is an open, downtrodden, rectangular stretch of flat ground. Every evening
it is cleared with a rake. Fresh dung is removed out of the way to the side of the track and
sequently carried to the fields. Wells are invariably shaded by trees. In the spot
exposed to harsh winds, a rough wall of rubble-work is constructed as protection. Either
the farmer himself, or one of his sons or workers conducts the water-drawing operation.

He sits on the drawing ropes and drives the oxen forward. He has a leather apron tied around him to protect his trousers. When the water bag has been drawn up above the level of the channel, the farmer curbs the oxen and transfers his body weight to the drawing rope in order to shake the water bag a little. When the bag has been emptied, the farmer rises and leads the oxen back to the well, the animals moving backwards in a sloping line, whereupon the water bag is lowered down the shaft and reaches water level. The farmer now gives a few powerful tugs to the drawing rope in order to dip the bag into the water, then waits a while to let it fill up before urging the oxen forwards once more with a loud click of the tongue. As the oxen plod along, the water bag is gradually drawn up.

The monotonous routine is repeated unvaryingly all through the day, although the farmer can smoke his pipe comfortably while discharging his duty and the younger boys may sometimes be heard singing at the top of their voices. At noon the oxen are unyoked, led to the shade and given a few bundles of hay. Whenever the opportunity for a rest arises, the farmer's first thought is for his oxen and he feeds them before starting to chat or turning to other work. The farmer takes his midday meal with his family, which has been weeding in the fields or laying the channels for irrigation. The customary meal consists of a roasted brinjal or egg-plant for each member of the family, child or grown-up, together with a flat cake made from unleavened millet flour. These cakes have previously been made at home, piled one on top of the other, wrapped in a cloth and brought along. This simple meal is washed down with a few gulps of butter milk from an earthenware pot.

When the day's work is over, the farmer loads the dripping wet water bag, both pulleys, the ropes and the draught yoke on the cart, yokes the oxen and drives home. The water bag is first hung on the door beam to drip dry and then taken into the house and slung over a hook.

II. 4. Drawn vehicles

4. 1. The traditional bullock cart

To give a lucid description of the traditional, two-wheeled, bullock-drawn cart, it will be expedient to divide it into the following parts : yoke, shaft, lower structure, cart floor, wheel attachment, the two wheels and applied metal ornaments.

bullock cart	*gadu*

The yoke-beem (1) is elliptic in section and widens at the two points resting above the necks of the bullocks. Very often, there is a slight projection in the centre of the yoke. At this point, the yoke is tied to the shaft by a rope (2). An intermediate layer is provided by an old shoe. Adjacent to the widened portions (3) above the bullocks' necks, a row of holes sloping towards the outer edge is bored perpendicularly to admit wooden pegs (4). The yoke-beam may be covered with a simple chip design, the widened portions being frequently embellished with a pattern of inscribed flowers. Even the wooden pegs are occasionally ornamented with a chip design.

(1) yoke beam	*dhunsari*
(2) rope	*naran*
(3) widened portion	*khandola*
(4) wooden peg	*sambal*

The shaft is composed of four timbers diverging in a fan-like manner, the two outer ones (5) being stout beams, while the two inner ones (6) are ordinary planks. Four transverse battens (7) support these timbers. The front end of the shaft (8) is encircled by a broad metal band; the first transverse batten being a stout, iron-mounted spike (9) that sets itself upright against the ground when the cart stands horizontal, thus ensuring that the shaft is kept as nearly horizontal as possible. A twisted wooden strip (10) is nailed behind the spike and may be used as a brace for the yoke. Directly in front of the floor of the cart, a narrow transverse lath (11) into which two circular iron-mounted holes are drilled rests on the shaft. The four timbers of the shaft run across the undersurface of the floor of the cart.

(5) outer timbers	*udhu*
(6) inner timbers	*maladiu*
(7) transverse battens	*maladiu*
(8) front end of shaft	*kagun*
(9) spike	*utedo*
(10) twisted wooden strip	*makli*
(11) transverse lath	*makli*

The two outer timbers of the shaft jutting out beyond the floor are abruptly cut off. Just before this, they are deeply notched, so as to allow the cart floor (12) a dip (13) followed by a gentle rise. The axle supports (14), a pair of triangular buttresses running alongside the wheels parallel to the side of the cart, are secured to transverse beams running under the shaft timbers' the butts projecting beyond the sides of the cart. The rods required to fix the wheels are fastened here. The axle supports consist of two timbers joined at right angles by mortise and tenon, iron plates being nailed over them. A strengthening of the joints is frequently effected by surmounting it with an angled reinforcement of wood. The rearmost transverse beem is concealed behind an ornamental board carved with a chip design (15).

The floor of the cart consists of planks (16) running transversely to the shaft timbers, an arrangement of crossing iron bands being nailed over the spaces where the planks are placed alongside each other. The sides (17) of the cart floor are enclosed by planks and the rear end (18) by a beam, the planks being joined to the beam by cogging.

(12) cart floor	*ochad*
(13) dip or notch	*tatu*
(14) axle support	*gudia*
(15) transverse beam and ornamental board	*tatani maladi, macheli* or *undar*
(16) first plank of cart floor	*supra*
(17) lateral planks	*ihota*
(18) rear end	*upri*

The axle supports, which transfer the weight of the cart to the axletree are pierced through the centre to admit two short straight iron rods of circular section which constitute the axle tree (19). The axle tree is fastened behind the supports at both ends by cotters. Adjacent to the wooden support there is usually a small separating strip of leather, a broad wooden disc (20), the wheel (21), then an iron ring (22) with a grease soaked rag, followed by the metal loops of two lathe-turned wooden rods (23), which are fixed into the laterally projecting butts of the transverse beams in such a manner as to move freely within them, and, finally, an iron rod (24) which is loosely hung by a loop on an iron pin at the side of the cart. These six parts are braced and held together by a horizontal bracing board (25). At one end, the board is attched by an iron ring (26) to two twisted iron rods (27) riveted together, which in turn are nailed to the transverse beam of the cart body by an iron ring. In front, the bracing board is joined with a rope to a pulley (28), which in turn is nailed to the foremost of the transverse beams. In order to prevent the bracing board slipping upwards and exposing the wheel on the axle tree, an upright barb is welded to the iron rod (24), which holds the bracing board firmly in place. All the individual parts, whether of wood or iron, are ornamented with a notch and groove design or else fluted.

(19) rods forming axletree	*dhari*
(20) wooden disc	*ungra*
(21) wheel	*paida*
(22) iron ring	*mora*
(23) wooden rods	*tarava*
(24) iron rod	*lundia*
(25) bracing board	*pinjali*
(26) iron ring	*kuda*
(27) twisted iron rods	*sanka*
(28) pulley	*tanavo*

The wheel (21) consists of a broad wooden felloe or rim (29) which is made up of five   13
arc-pieces of equal length joined together. The spokes (30) of more or less square section
are tenoned to each of these five arcs. The spokes are fixed to a very heavy hub (31),
which is originally cylindrical and encircled by a pair of iron rings (32), but subsequently
has its edges rounded off. A metal tube (33) is inserted into the hub as a lining;
the axle tree rotates in this tube, which is well lubricated with axle grease. The entire
wheel is encircled by an iron hoop (34). Parallel grooves are cut into the felloe and
the hub, and small metal plates are often nailed to the spokes for decoration.

(29) felloe	*patla*
(30) spoke	*ara*
(31) hub	*nai*
(32) iron ring	*mora*
(33) metal tube	*tarijela*
(34) iron hoop	*pata*

Pieces of iron with ornamental designs (35) are mounted on all visible edges of beams   15
and on all narrow sides of planks, flat-headed nails and small iron discs (36) being employed
for the purpose. Some surfaces have cut out copper strips with punched-in designs
nailed to them. At different points along the floor of the cart, circular and square holes
(37) are cut in and frequently lined with nailed-on strips of sheet iron. Wooden poles are stuck
into these holes and used to support a tilt or a length of basketwork (38), when the cart is
fully loaded. A number of projections (39) and small, broad-headed hooks (40) on the front
twisted wooden strip adjacent to the shaft, are used to fasten the ropes stretched across
the cart. Cattle or other livestock can be tied to the cart with the help of the holes along
the rear edge and thus trot in the wake of the moving cart.

(35) ornamental iron pieces	*fudla*
(36) ornamental iron discs	*naksi*
(37) holes in twisted wooden strip	*kataria*
(38) basketwork	*katarani*
(39) projection	*kanda*
(40) iron hook	*ankadia*

The measurements given below, of a cart belonging to Masaribhai Karsanbhai, may be
regarded as typical:
Total length 400 cm, breadth 126 cm, diameter of wheel 76 cm, length of bracing board
112 cm, width of transverse lath 17 cm, length of transverse lath 45 cm, width of yoke 156 cm,
length of iron spike 35 cm, length of shaft 220 cm, length of cart floor 160 cm, breadth
of cart floor 120 cm.

The traditional bullock cart is used by only very few farmers in their everyday work. It has
been practically completely superseded by the modern bullock cart. At present there are only
three old specimens existing in Ratadi, owned by Rangmalbhai Karsanbhai, Vikrambhai
Jesarbhai and Masaribhai Karsanbhai. There is not a single old bullock cart to be found in the
neighbouring village of Baradia.

I inquired of Harbhambhai Dudabhai the reason for the traditional bullock cart having been
replaced by the modern type. The reply was that :

// The *gadu*-cart is too heavy. Only strong bullocks can pull it. // Formerly, bullocks were strong and stout.   16
// Today the farmers don't feed them properly.

The Patel of Baradia, Hardasbhai Bhayabhai, gave a typical answer:

// Formerly I possessed a *gadu*-cart. What happened to it ? Some wooden parts were taken out and used for my new *gadi*-cart and thus the old cart became useless.
// Those carts were too heavy. The new *gadi*-cart was introduced and people liked it.

Rangmalbhai Karsanbhai, the owner of an old bullock-cart, stated :

// When my *gadu*-cart breaks, I will make *rotela*, bread, on it (i. e. will use it as firewood). Some parts may come in useful for the *gadeli*·cart. Our carts are differently built now.

Harbhambhai Dudabhai reports :

// The wheels of my *gadu*-cart were broken. I burnt them in the kitchen fire. Now the rest of the *gadu* is on the *vada*, hay stack. The next rains will destroy it completely. The last monsoon rains already did away with the *pinjali*, bracing board.

A bullock cart generally gives service to three or four generations of owners before being discarded as useless. For instance, the cart belonging to Vikrambhai Jasarbhai, an approximately forty-year old Mer-farmer of Ratadi, is still going strong, although it is extremely old, having been purchased by the present owner's grandfather Sidabhai Arjunbhai in Bakharla. It is the only vehicle used by the farmer.

Both types of carts, traditional as well as modern, are largely constructed in Bakharla, where the farmers from the surrounding region order and purchase them. The procedure is described by Rangmalbhai Karsanbhai of Baradia:

// The string and the shoe we take with us to Bakharla. The rest will be arranged for by the cartwright.
// The *murata joine lavava*, the ceremony of choosing a propitious time, will be carried out in the cartwright's workshop.
// For my new cart I paid Rs. 500 in cash a year ago. This was the money I received from selling cotton.
// The carts constructed in other villages are heavier. The carts from Bakharla are lighter.

As a rule, the price of a bullock-cart, which is paid for in cash ranges from Rs. 500 to Rs. 650, whereas the price of a traditional cart soars to Rs. 1200 and Rs. 1300. This enormous disparity in price itself explains why the latter carts are but little in demand. Nowadays the traditional cart has yielded entirely to the modern cart, but not unconditionally: the traditional cart still plays an important part in the wedding ceremony. The following statements are in accordance with personal observations; Harbhambhai Dudabhai, a farmer of Ratadi, reports:

// For the *lagan*, marriage ceremony, the *gadu*, traditional cart, is still compulsory. It is used at two junctures. One is when the family of the bridegroom gives *khajur*, dates, which come from Arabia, to the public. The bridegroom's mother sits on the *gadu* and distributes the dates in handfuls among the children of the village.-The second time the *gadu* is called into use, is to transport the women of the bridegroom's party when it visits the bride's home. This is called *jan*. At *anani jan*, when the bride is carried to her husband's home, the *gadu* is even more necessary because now the bride's parents will send with her one *tolia*, bed, and that does not fit into the smaller *gadeli*, modern cart.

Hardasbhai Bhayabhai Patel added:

// When the bridegroom's mother climbs on the *gadu*, cart, to distribute *khajur*, dates, she must first put her foot on the *pinjali*, bracing board.
// She always climbs into the cart from the right side.

In spite of this, very few traditional carts remain. For the wedding ceremony, they are borrowed. Nevertheless, all the people maintain that the modern cart will in due course also usurp the place of the traditional cart in wedding ceremonies.

4, 2. The modern bullock cart

16, 18

The modern bullock cart is also drawn by a span of two bullocks. The yoke and the
wheels are constructed in exactly the same way as for the traditional cart. The method of
attachment, the cart floor and the shaft, however, have been greatly simplified. The
entire vehicle is not only lighter, but far less complicated, more compact, less ornate and
composed of fewer individual parts. The shaft consists of only three diverging timbers,
the outer beams extending beyond the floor. The shaft together with the iron spike, the
twisted wooden strip and the transverse battens are mounted with several metal ornamental
pieces. In place of a simple transverse lath, a rectangular box with a hinged lid (1) is
fixed between the two outer shaft timbers where they terminate. A transverse plank and
several longitudinal ones constitute the cart floor, which is enclosed by a frame of
rectangular beams joined to each other by mortise and tenon. Massive walls, joined to the
beams by cogging, rise upwards from this frame. The frame is connected to the rear
wall by several pieces shaped into handles.

Each of the wheels rotates on an iron axle tree (2) passing under the vehicle and is
separated from the wooden axle support only by a strip of grease-soaked leather (3). The
wheels, which possess broad hubs, are nearly as high as the upper edge of the floor.
Adjacent to the wheel and fixed on the axle tree is a simple wooden disc (4) with an iron band
nailed to it. Finally, an iron pin broadening out at the points is inserted through the axle
tree. A length of cloth soaked in grease is wound tightly around the axle tree. A wheel
lubricated with the help of the smooth metal tube rotates on the axle tree. The cart always
needs to be thoroughly lubricated. For this purpose, a small calabash with grease often
hangs from the cart.

modern cart	*gadelo, gadeli* or *gadi*
(1) box	*peti*
(2) axle	*dharo*
(3) leather strip	*ungri*
(4) wooden disc	*ungra*

Dimensions of a modern cart in possession of Rangmalbhai Karsanbhai of Baradia are:
length of cart 395 cm, breadth of cart 104 cm, length of shaft 163 cm, diameter of wheel
85 cm, width of felloe 25 cm, length of box 44 cm, breadth of box 40 cm.

Lastly, it may be mentioned that the light cart was initially called *gadeli,* in order to
distinguish it from the traditional heavy cart or *gadu; gadeli* being a diminutive form of
the word *gadu.* Nowadays both carts are referred to as *gadu* or *gadi,* that is, "cart" in
everyday usage and it will soon be forgotten altogether that bullock carts used to look
different at one time.

4. 3. The drag prop

Two slightly concave pieces of wood are tenoned together almost at right angles. This
prop is placed over the harrow, which is placed in an inverted position, or over the sowing
machine, which is taken apart, in such a manner that the transverse timber lies on its
side upon the arms of the prop. The harrow is now secured by its shaft to the yoke and
dragged to the field. The ends of the arms of the prop bear the weight.

(example in the possession of Rangmalbhai Karsanbhai in Baradia)	
arms length	ca. 130 cm
space inbetween	180 cm

II. 5. Cultivating implements

5. 1. Implements drawn by bullocks

The plough
The plough consists essentially of a massive, lightly curved wooden plough-beam. The nose
of the beam terminates in a point below which the horizontal ploughtail is nailed. This is the
handle which the farmer holds. The lower end of the plough-beam is broad and square in
section. The plough-share is a long iron of rectangular section terminating in a coulter or
straight blade sharpened on two sides. The plough-share is affixed to the lower end of the
plough-beam. The point of fixation is marked on the rear surface of the beam by a tongue.
The plough-share is securely wedged in by a firm wooden plough-shoe of the same length as
the share. A little way up the beam the plough-tree projects, forming an acute angle with the
plough-share. It is attached to the ploughbeam by iron pins. Several holes are drilled into the
far end of the plough-tree at equal distances, thereby enabling the plough to be hitched to the
yoke at a variable height, depending on the hole into which the wooden peg is inserted.

plough	*har*
to plough	*kedva*
plough-beam	*tunga*
plough-share	*kas*
plough-shoe	*uvareta*
plough-tree	*hal*
wooden peg	*kili*
plough-tail or handle	*hal kili*

(example in the possession of Rangmalbhai Kersanbhai in Baradia)
height 95 cm
total length 300 cm

The plough is drawn by two oxen. The weight of the heavy beam suffices to press the
plough-share into the earth. The ploughman is therefore saved this exertion and must only
be careful that the jogging plough does not turn over on its side. Because the plough-share
is very narrow and the simple coulter does not turn over the soil, the furrows must be
drawn close together. The top layer of soil is uniformly thin. For this reason the plough-share
cannot be set at an upright angle or perpendicular to the ground.

Ploughing takes place shortly after harvesting. No special ceremony is performed to
mark the occasion. The task of ploughing the land is not restricted to any one member of
the family.

The harrow 25, 23
The harrow consists of a stout and heavy wooden beam, into which two wooden prongs
are wedged at a distance of a span, affording a foothold. Close to each other and immediately
right and left of the centre, two long shafts are tenoned to the beam and anchored firmly
with wedges. These shafts, which are unprepared thin tree trunks, are connected at their front
edge by a short wooden cross bar, by which they are affixed to the yoke. The tines are
surmounted at their ends by metal rings and continue either sloped on one side or hollowed
out so as to have provision for the upward curved ends of the blade. The straight edge of
the blade is coarsely ground on both sides.

harrow	*karia*
wooden beam	*lodio*
wooden prongs or tines	*data*
shafts	*sambida*
cross bar	*sagan*
anchor wedge	*punchelia*

blade	*ram* or *rap*
foothold	*steva*

(example in the possession of Rangmalbhai Karsanbhai of Baradia)

length	302 cm
breadth	147 cm
length of blade	118 cm
thickness of blade	30 cm

The harrow is used to break clods of earth on ploughed land and to cover the furrows in which seed has been scattered. During harrowing, the bullocks jog along at a fast pace over the dry, previously ploughed field while the farmer stands with legs apart on the beam, pressing the blade into the earth with his weight and expertly manipulating the harness so as to control the bullocks and yet prevent their coming to a halt. Before the field is sown, the farmer irrigates it for three or four days. He gives the topsoil one day to dry and then harrows the entire field lengthwise and crosswise once more. Now the sowing machine comes into play and seed is scattered over the damp earth. On the sower's heels, always one furrow behind and parallel to him, follows another farmer with the harrow, lightly covering the furrows with earth.

The drill plough or seed barrow   23, 24

This implement is composed of a sturdy beam, to which five wooden coulters are affixed. These coulters cut the drills or small furrows for sowing seed in and are placed at equal distances. They are of rectangular section and have holes bored right through their centres, thin triangular plates of iron being riveted to the ends. Two long shafts are attached to the beam equidistant from the centre and fastened by iron pins. A wooden cross-bar draws the ends of the shafts together and secures them. With this basic implement the drills are drawn. A sprinkler with five bamboo tubes is mounted on the apparatus described above and braced to the beam and the shafts with a rope. The wooden sprinkler consists of a carved funnel of conical shape. This funnel surmounts a wooden board into which five diverging holes are bored. This wooden structure, the edge of which is often reinforced and protected by an iron band, is frequently embellished with chip designs. The initial step in carving the funnel is boring a hole, which is followed and completed by chisel-work. The holes are partly bored and some are subsequently burnt out. The lengths of the bamboo tubes vary in accordance with their position and therefore with the angles they slope at. The nodes are pierced through.

drill plough or seed barrow	*dantad*
wooden beam	*lodio*
wooden coulters	*data*
shaft	*sambida*
cross-bar	*sagan*
iron point	*farvun*
bamboo tube	*dandua*
seed sprinkler with five holes	*orani*
with three holes	*vakadu*
bracing	*orani bandan*

 example in the possession of Rangmalbhai Karsanbhai of Baradia)

length	300 cm
breadth	160 cm
coulters length	37 cm
coulters width	8 cm
auxiliary tools used in sowing:	
a) sacking bag	*kobhaia*
b) scoring tool	*kharapia*

With the drill plough the seed is sown. The field must be previously watered and the soil loosened with the harrow. In a bag of sacking suspended in front of him, the farmer has a mixture of seed and dry crumbly earth. This latter is to ensure a sparse distribution of the seed. Nowadays farmers often use artificial manure in place of the dry earth as an admixture to the seed. In his right hand the sower holds the harness reins and the scoring tool, managing to keep a pinch of seed between his fingertips as well. With his free left hand he scoops up a handful of seed at a time, and while steering the harrow or drill plough across the field sprinkles it into the sprinkler, taking constant care to ensure that the seed is evenly distributed into the funnel holes. The situation becomes tricky when the left hand becomes empty before the end of the furrow has been reached. In this emergency the right hand must come to the rescue with what little seed it has until the left hand has succeeded in scooping up another handful from the bag.

Sowing calls for much skill and dexterity, for the sower has the twofold task of steering the bullocks and scattering the seed, the latter operation allowing of scarcely any intermission. Only after completing one furrow is there a minute's rest. This, the sower uses to scrape the coulters clean of earth, and to scoop up new seed with both hands from the bag of sacking in preparation for the next furrow.

Besides the five-holed sprinkler there is another with a similar exterior but with only three holes. This sprinkler may also be used on the five-coulter drill plough. There, therefore, exist four distinct methods of sowing:

(1) Drill plough with five-holed sprinkler
The seed is scattered over all five drills or rows. This method is useful only when vegetables are to be planted intensively in an area or when forage is sown. This method is not to be recommended, however, for wheat, millet, cotton and peanuts. The drills are so closely spaced that weeding can only be done by hand.

(2) Drill plough with three-holed sprinkler
The tubes are fixed to the five-coulter drill plough at regular intervals (1,3,5). The space between the drills is wide enough to permit the use of a narrow drill harrow. This sowing method is employed when the plants are to be given more growing space.

(3) Drill plough with three-holed sprinkler, the central hole being blocked
This method, whereby two tubes are attached unsymmetrically (2,5) to the five-coulter drill plough, is termed *ponia*. This system is employed primarily when millet, cotton and peanuts are sown. The wide spaces between the drills can be worked with a double drill harrow.

(4) Drill plough with three-holed sprinkler, the central hole being blocked
This system, known as *motebatel,* leaves the widest possible space between the drills or seed rows and is predominantly suited for the sowing of wheat, cotton and peanuts. The tubes are attached to the outermost coulters (1,5) of the drill plough.

It is generally said:

// Plants which have the most space grow most healthy.

A ceremony takes place before the annual sowing starts. Hardasbhai Bhayabhai, the Patel of Baradia, gives the following description:

// Before we start sowing, we hold a ceremony in front of the house. We adorn the bullocks with a *chandla,* red dot and some rice grains. We polish their horns, too. The man who will go to the field to sow also receives a *chandla,* mark. The *dantad,* drill plough, is carried in front of the house and a *satia,* swastika, drawn on the ground. The grain to be sown is placed in the centre and a *sopari,* betelnut, on top of it. The *satia,* swastika, is drawn with *kanku,* red coloured earth.
The man who will drive the *dantad,* drill plough, immediately takes the *sopari,* betelnut, and puts it in his pocket. If he meets within the village an unmarried girl from the village carrying water vessels, he must stop

the bullocks, take out another *sopari,* betelnut, from his pocket and put it into the girl's vessel. Then he proceeds to his field. // That is a good omen. // In the field itself nothing will happen. // The *satia,* swastika, was drawn by the women.
/ Is a bad omen possible? Because we are careful to take precautions well ahead, the omens must turn out favourable, there cannot be a bad omen. The main point, however, is that the nut is not taken by a person who will not sow the field.

The drill harrows

Harrows of the type described above may be employed when the task of extirpating weeds is not done by hand. Weeding harrows are available in two sizes : one with a simple iron or blade and the other with a double blade. Furthermore, these blades are procurable in various widths.

drill harrow with a single small blade	*vakada*
drill harrow with two small blades	*belu*

(examples in the possession of Karsanbhai Rangmalbhai of Baradia)

length of drill harrow	300 cm
length of blade	33 cm

drill harrow with a single large blade	*dodia*
drill harrow with two large blades	*rapto*

(examples in the possession of Rangmalbhai Karsanbhai of Baradia)

length of drill harrow	290 cm
length of blade	79 cm

These harrows are used in drill husbandry for extirpating the weeds between the drills or seed-rows. This takes place when the plants are about 20 cm high. If the drills have not been drawn straight, that is to say, when the width of the drill is not equivalent to the distance between the blades, drill harrows with single blades have to be resorted to. Fields in which the drills run too close to each other to permit the use of a drill harrow have to be weeded by hand.

5. 2. Manually operated tools

The broad hoe 21

A broad metal scoop is fixed to a straight handle by means of a ring.

broad hoe		*pavada*

(example in the possession of Karsanbhai Rangmalbhai of Baradia)

scoop	length	22 cm
	breadth	20 cm
length of handle		77 cm

The hoe 21

A narrow scoop is fixed into a straight handle by means of a loop.

hoe		*kodari*

(example in the possession of Rangmalbhai Karsanbhai of Baradia)

scoop	length	22 cm
	breadth	8 cm
length of handle		110 cm

The rake 21

This implement consists of a handle affixed by a wedge into a cross-bar with wooden tines. The tines are usually six in number and are fitted with a row of tenons. They are rectangular, but slightly curved at their bases. The cross-bar is stout and straight.

rake	kheparo

(example in the possession of Rangmalbhai Karsanbhai of Baradia)

length of cross-bar	44 cm
length of handle	106 cm
width of tines	6 cm
length of tines	15 cm

The wooden mallet

A cylindrical wooden head is fixed into a wooden handle, which runs transverse
to its long side.

wooden mallet	modari

(example in the possession of Rangmalbhai Karsanbhai of Baradia)

length of hammer head	15 cm
diameter of same	10 cm
length of handle	110 cm

All these hand-manipulated tools are used for weeding, loosening earth clods and for building
up little mounds of earth in the fields. The latter operation is known as *kiara*, and the rake
and hoe are of particular importance here. The field is divided into quarters by about 15 cm
high earth walls, the water from the well being conducted to these earth-enclosed quadrangles.
This ensures a uniform distribution of the water and the fields are thus evenly irrigated.

The sickle

A lightly curved sickle-blade of iron is set into a cylindrical wooden handle which either
broadens towards the end or is indented. The edge of the blade is finely serrated.

sickle	datarada

(example in the possession of Rangmalbhai Karsanbhai of Baradia)

length	23 cm

The sickle is used to reap grain, fodder plants, etc. Scythes are unknown.

II. 6. Equipment used in animal husbandry

Cattle and buffaloes, that is, livestock not employed in tilling the soil, are driven to graze
in separate herds. Each herd is led by a Rabari - shepherd. Uncultivated land is used as
pasture. The only animals kept in the village and regularly fed are bearing and milch cows
and new-born calves. Bundles of hay are thrown to them.

The fodder containers

Special fodder such as minced clover and rape is poured into a fodder bag made from
gunny. This bag is slung around the animal's neck and covers its muzzle. Thereby the
special fodder is prevented from being wasted by lying strewn around to be trampled
underfoot. In addition, this method ensures that the animal for whom the fodder is intended
gets all of it. Moreover, the fodder is kept safe from incursions by stray animals wandering
through the village. The chief item fed in fodder bags to milch buffalo cows is cotton seed,
which has a high oil content. The animals kept in the village during grazing time are led
to the well twice a day and are also given additional water. Nearly every day water is poured
over the buffaloes, as there is no pool in the immediate vicinity of the village. The young

are fed with diluted buttermilk once they have been weaned. A large hollowed-out stone serves as a trough.

cotton seed	*kapasia*
fodder bag	*paura*
stone trough	*kundi*

The implements for threshing thistles

A diet of thistles helps to increase the production of milk. However, only camels, donkeys and water-buffaloes will eat thistles, and the latter only if the wooden stems have previously been removed. In the afternoon women armed with sickles go out into the stony, unarable waste land around the village, and there collect thistles, using small forked sticks as props. The thistles are gathered in baskets which the women carry back to the village on their heads, emptying the contents into one common heap to be threshed by several women, who swing their long poles to a regular rhythm as they work. The tilt supports from the bullock carts serve as threshing poles. The bruised flowers and the prickly leaves are then picked out and given to the buffalo cows while the hard stems are burnt in the kitchen fire. The farmer Hardasbhai Bhayabhai contributes the following supplementary information:

// This thorny plant is the best food for buffaloes. The women collect it from the wasteland around the village. Thistles form an extra-food for the buffalo cow, and increase its milk production.
// It is only given to milch buffaloes. Cows do not eat it and young buffaloes do not get it. Camels eat mort of it and therefore the plant is called *unt kato*, camels' food.

thistle diet	*untkato*
sickle	*datarada*
forked props	*soratadi*
threshing pole	*adun*

The wooden hoe

A bamboo pole is fixed or wedged into a rectangular board with rounded-off corners. This simple implement is used to clear away dung.

wooden hoe	*pavadi*
(example in the possession of Rangmalbhai Karsanbhai of Baradia)	
length of handle	110 cm
width of board	19 cm
length of board	29 cm

Other equipment used in animal husbandry is decribed elsewhere. It includes tethering blocks and textile articles such as baskets, cloths used to rub down the animals, muzzles and yoke straps.

III. Stone working

by Eberhard Fischer

III. 1. The stone-workers

In the villages, which are inhabited predominantly by Mer-farmers, stone-working as a profession is not confined to any particular caste or community. Quarrying, cutting and stone-working in general being physically taxing, it is left for poor men without any land to call their own to undertake this kind of work. Women only help in house construction and, more recently, in road building.

A stone-worker's labour is arduous, the wages low and injuries frequent. While this kind of manual labour does not imply any rise in prestige, it is not objectionable or contemptible on religious grounds, as is, for instance, the skinning of cattle or the production of leather. For this reason Mer-farmers and Rabari-shepherds are stone-workers too. The mason of Baradia, questioned on the laboriousness of his profession, said:

//As long as I am healthy I can do this kind of work. But I will have to stop when my body becomes weak.
//Oh, then I can still do some plastering work or I will shape stones. With that I can carry on.
//Carpentry and masonry - well, both are equally exacting. When the wall I am building has grown high I have to lift up all the stones that are given to me. I have to heave them up on the wall. And this work goes on till evening. Masonary is more strenuous (than carpentry). After some years it affects the chest.

In Ratadi, the caste of former untouchables known as the Dhed, traditionally weavers by profession, have adopted stone-quarrying for their chief occupation. Judging from the following account, given to me by the young Dhed Rajsinhbhai Mepabhai, of Ratadi and Baradia they seem to have turned to this profession quite recently:

//This quarry was opened in 1959 - at that time there was not a single quarry here. //The stones for building houses were extracted from wells or imported.
//I have never worked as well-sinker. //Formerly I used to weave *sad* canvas. I still have two looms at home, one is for *pankora* cloth and one is for *sad* canvas. //I wove the cloth for my trousers myself. If I have time I weave cloth, otherwise I go to town and buy it. //I have never worked anywhere else as a labourer. I just watched other people quarrying.
// It was my idea (to start the quarry here). A man came to this village and started quarrying. I watched him. Then I thought a while and started by myself nearby. But I never worked with him.
// I started on my own account.
// From the beginning my brothers worked with me.
// Formerly we were all weavers because we are from the *Dhed* community.

Although quarrying is, to a large extent, carried out by former untouchables, members of the Mer caste also join when they are not busy with their fields or when they are in need of ready cash.

In larger towns such as Porbandar, stone-cutting and masonary is the work of one special caste, the Khadia or stone-cutter-community. In the villages the farmers build their houses themselves, engaging the help of specialists only during certain stages of the work. These "specialists" are qualified as such by having more experience than usual in this particular branch. They may be from any community, but in general belong to a caste of craftsmen.

The stone-cutter Dahyabhai Kimabhai of Baradia states:

I am from the Kumbhar, potter community.
// *Mota bap,* my father's elder brother, took up masonary first.
// When I was a boy I learnt carpentry. // I was an apprentice in my own father's workshop. // Stone cutting
I learnt much later. I went to Palakhda to work as a labourer in the workshop of Vasram Ram.

The services of stone-workers are engaged on varying terms. Whereas the stone-cutter is
paid a previously fixed lump-sum for carrying out an order, the masons are paid daily wages.
The quarrymen, however, lease land from the government and extract the blocks of stone,
which they sell singly. Upon inquiry I was informed that Rs. 12 was the annual rent paid to
the government plus a tax of Rs. 1.65 per 100 blocks. The price of 100 building blocks
of superior quality is Rs. 32 and for the same number, but of medium quality, Rs. 20.
Rubble is sold at the rate of Rs. 1 per cart load. Sharpening the tools and instruments entails
further expense. This must be regularly carried out every fortnight. In a special workshop
at Porbandar, the charge for whetting a pickaxe is 15 paise; an axe or an adze, though,
cost 50 paise apiece. For this purpose, one of the quarrymen cycles to the town with the
tools strapped to the carrier behind him, while his fellow workers take the day off to
rest. One of the quarrymen estimated his monthly earnings at Rs. 80 to Rs. 90 and professed
to be *"ready chalso"* quite content with this amount. Yet he is the only earning member
in a family of seven.

Stone is sold in the following manner: the blocks of stone are stacked in a heap beside the
quarry. The customers come to the site and inspect the stones being quarried. They later
return with a bullock cart, load about 50 stones on it, try to obtain another two or three
free of charge and then depart for their building-site with promises to pay later. The
quarrymen of Ratadi say that their customers come chiefly from the villages of Baradia,
Ratadi, Modhvada, Keshav, Palakhda, Visavada and Kantela. There is only one other quarry
in the neighbourhood, not counting a small one at Tukda, and that is in Visavada. The
largest and most important quarries, however, lie southeast of Porbandar.

Wellsinkers undertake to carry out a certain project against a previously fixed sum of
money. In the case I observed two parallel cousins agreed to sink a well of certain fixed
measurements for a lump-sum of Rs. 800. Before commencing work, they inspected the
site. However, they did not conduct a trial boring. They then calculated the time required
as four months. All expenses for sharpening tools and the costs of the explosive required to
blast rocks have to be paid out of the initial fixed sum. The blasting-powder alone costs
Rs. 60, as an estimated 15 kg are required during a well-sinking operation. It may therefore be
calculated that, this extremely toilsome labour yields a maximum monthly profit of Rs. 90.

III. 2. Quarrying

2. 1. Place of work

The quarry lies between the village of Ratadi and the coast. The terrain, which slopes gently
upwards in the direction of the dunes, is bare and arid. There is no covering layer of soil and
the country is entirely devoid of vegetation. The landscape is one stretch of limestone,
eroded into little crevices and jagged shapes and covered with dark incrustations. Here and
there the limestone is interspersed with a few lichens and dry thistles.

Since the quarrymen lease a plot of land in an unarable region for the pit, they usually only ask for a small plot of an area of approximately 100 ft. by 100 ft. They dig out this plot and continue expanding it underground. They thus not only save money but much futile labour as well, since the porous limestone at the surface is full of holes and fissures through which water runs. This kind of rock can only be sold as rubble or at the best as "second quality" building stone. A further advantage is that the projecting roof of the pit affords the workers occupied in digging near the wall some shade. Real mines with tunnels running deep into the earth are not dug and worked by the quarrymen of Ratadi. In their opinion a venture of this sort is perilous. Nevertheless, they have seen the imposing stone labyrinths in the region surrounding Porbandar.

Before they could discover a plot of land suitable for a quarry, it was necessary to dig three or four pits in the area around Ratadi. These pits, which yield but little, remain unworked. Between the quarry and the sand dunes on the coast the workers have erected a rough wall of rubble, which they use as lavatory. Other structures such as shelters from sun and wind, fireplaces, huts or waterholes are absent.

2. 2. Working conditions

The gang of five young men I watched at work had planned a daily schedule of work from seven to eleven in the morning and three to five or there abouts in the afternoon. At noon the men return home to Baradia for a long siesta. Every fortnight they take a day off from work, since the tools have to be taken to Porbandar for sharpening. In winter the working hours are shortened, because "a cold wind blows in the morning". But work is continued throughout the summer and the rainy season. The workers stay at home only when it rains heavily.

The quarry remains undamaged during the monsoon, because the water is speedily absorbed by the limestone. – A working day of a bare six hours may appear comparatively short; however, it must be borne in mind that the quarrymen work in silent concentration during this period. Very rarely do they interrupt their work to smoke a pipe or *bidi,* a rolled tobacco leaf. However, if one of the men feels that enough work has been done, he persuades his fellow-workers to call it a day and it not seldom happens that the gang returns to the village in the early afternoon and may be seen loafing around, smoking and gossiping.

2. 3. The tools

As a rule, every quarryman possesses a set of the tools described below. Only the water vessel is shared in common. For the least strong among them, who is allowed an occasional rest, the workers take along an axe, with which he dresses and trims the extracted blocks of stone.

Measuring rod, *othi*
Two strips of wood 36 cm and 46 cm long are used respectively to measure the breadth and length of the stone blocks. The height is estimated without the help of a measuring rod. The shorter rod may be dispensed with and its length measured off as a double *vet,* hand-span. A hand-span is the distance between the stretched-out little finger and thumb.

Adze, *vansalo*
The iron head of the rectangular section terminates in a straight-edged blade transverse to the shaft. The head is attached to a square socket with a central round hole, through which the comparatively short wooden shaft is driven.

Axe, *kavada*

A triangular iron head of rectangular section is attached to a wooden shaft by means of a socket. The straight blade is sharpened on both sides and runs parallel to the shaft.

Triangular axe, *kasi*

A thick, triangular head is riveted to a broad iron band around the wooden shaft. The blade is parallel to the shaft, the sides are sloping and the section of the head is trapezoid. With this axe, pieces of stone are chipped off by a rapid succession of blows.

Small water pitcher, *bampli*

Water for drinking and working purposes is carried to the quarry and there kept cool in a small, black, spherical earthenware pitcher. It has a narrow, high neck and a broad lip. A cord, by which the pitcher may be carried, is looped around the neck.

Bowl, *vadki*

The water used for stone-cutting is keept in a little alluminium bowl. A tiny mop of weed is wetted in this bowl and water poured from it into the cut in the rock.

Weed mop, *kar*

Roots, leaves and grass are collected from the area around the quarry and bundled together into a little mop. The mop is used to prevent the blade of the adze from slipping when splitting the rock.

Drag mat, *sidia*

Ropes are tied to the four corners of a gunny bag. Stone blocks are hoisted up from the pit of the quarry with the help of such drag mats.

2.4. Working techniques

In order to reach the bottom of the pit, one has to climb down the walls of the quarry. There are good footholds along the face of the rock, as it is full of holes and crevices and yet firm and not too jagged. Tools are thrown in and out of the pit. The water-pot iseither lowered by rope or carried down. When I watched them, the quarrymen were working on a horizontal rectangular ledge alongside the main pit. The desired breadth of the block is marked off on two places with the help of the shorter measuring rod. A line parallel to the edge of the ledge is then drawn with the finger into the dust on the rock. The line is now cut in slightly by a series of strokes with the triangular axe. The worker next splits the stone down to the desired height for one block, and then works methodically downwards, stone after stone, until he has reached the bottom. He stands with legs apart, bending slightly forwards over the split in the stone. He does not swing his arm high, but nevertheless deals powerful blows. With the right hand above and the left hand below, he grips the end of the shaft of his tool, the triangular axe. He strikes roughly 45 blows a minute, and the rock is soon split to the bottom. The width of the split is approximately 3 cm. Now the length of the stone-block is measured off with the help of the longer rod. The line is next slightly indented with the triangular axe and the stone finally split through. Depending on his mood, the quarryman either cuts in all the lines running transverse to the first split and then hews out the stones or else finishes cutting them one by one. The quarryman said:

That depends on my mood. Sometimes I cut a row, sometimes I take the stones out one by one.

When the stone has been evenly cut according to the specified measurements of lenght,

breadth and height, the quarryman cuts a groove along the lower edge with the adze.
To do this, he stands on the stone and bends over to the groove, gripping the short shaft of the
adze with both hands. He first cuts in the groove to a shallow but uniform depth, then
halts a while and now, leaving the adze-blade stuck in the wedge, proceeds to sprinkle a few
drops of water from the aluminium bowl into the wedge, wetting the adze blade. He next
delivers several more blows into the moistened wedge, then takes a little weed, rolls it
between his palms to a bundle and inserts it into the groove. The weed receives the impact
of the blows. He frequently cuts only two holes into the lower edge, changing from one to
the other after ten blows. Very soon the adze-blade gets caught in the two cm deep cut and
the quarryman struggles with the adze to free it. A few more blows and the entire stone block
is freed from the rock bed. The quarryman takes hold of the corners with both hands, lifts
the block and rolls it over to one side. The surface from which the first rock was hewn is
levelled with the adze and the next block measured and indented. In this fashion, the blocks
are hewn out, one by one. Finally, the stone blocks are hauled out of the pit in a gunny bag,
to the four corners of which ropes are tied. The rectangular blocks are dressed and
trimmed with the axe, and arranged in double rows.Now the stones are ready to be sold.

At the end of a day's work the tools are collected, swung over the shoulder and carried
home. Only the little aluminium bowl and sometimes the axe are left in the pit,
hidden underneath some rubble.

2. 5. The quarryman's lingo

The pit or quarry is described as *kan,* pit and an abandoned quarry as *ban kan,* closed pit.
The longitudinal split is known as *vad,* the transverse split as *nako,* and the holes made with
the adze on the lower edge of the block are called *tip.*

The stone extracted by the quarrymen is divided into three groups according to its quality:

Dangedi, is evenly dressed stone of prescribed measurements and superior quality. It is
excellently suited for building purposes.

Nakodi varo, which is sold at half the price of *dangedi,* is also building stone of prescribed
measurements. However, the rock is full of cavities and hence of inferior quality.

Toda, fragments of rock, is used for field walls and as a filling-in for thick walls.

2. 6. The quarried stone

On the subject of stone for building purposes, the geologist Adye writes (1917, pg. 63) :
" Ratadi itself is built upon a foundation of limestone belonging to the Dwarka Group of
beds …which were probably formed continuously during the Pliocene period or after.
These rocks were found … all the way along the inland roadway via Baradia, up to
the confines of Shrinagar. "

This same limestone is quarried in large shafts and in underground pits in the Porbandar area
and is sold for building purposes under the name " Porbunder Stone ". It is probable that
the stone quarried in the neighbourhood of Ratadi is coarser and more liable to contain
cracks than the Porbandar stone. Nevertheless, the stone worked in the Ratadi area is well
suited for building purposes and large blocks can be fairly easily extricated.

III. 3. Well sinking

3. 1. Place of work

During our field-work in Ratadi, a large well was sunk in the south west of the village for the purpose of obtaining water for field irrigation. Here the plain is slightly undulating and there is a thin layer of topsoil. The wells in the vicinity yield brackish water. It was hoped, and this hope was later proved justified, that the new well, situated at the summit of a hillock and sunk through hard rock, would yield sweet water.

The ground chosen for the well site is composed of a thin upper layer of loamy soil under which lies a broad stratum of sandstone. Underneath is a zone of limestone, beneath which water has collected.

The shaft is roughly square in section and tapers downwards. A series of irregular footholds on one side of the shaft leads down to a ledge, from which the workmen jump about two metres down to the digging level.

3. 2. Working conditions

Two men are engaged to sink the well. They work regularly from early morning till noon, make a short break and then continue till dusk. Since the workmen are not paid an hourly or daily wage, but receive a lump sum for the entire well sinking operations, they are naturally anxious to complete the project as quickly as possible. For this reason they work with great concentration and perseverance. The farmer who has commissioned the sinking is also eager to use the well and therefore sends his two grown-up sons every evening to the working site to help hauling up the rocks chipped away during the sinking operations. The farmer engages the services of another man to trim and dress the rocks into slabs and building stones. This man is paid for his work by the farmer, who sells the stones. The farmer urges the well sinkers to take care that the stones they dig out possess some commercial value.

3. 3. The tools

The tools used in well-sinking are the axe, the triangular axe, the drag mat, the adze used by quarrymen and the broad hoe used by farmers. Other tools required are:

Sledge hammer, *gan*
A wooden shaft is fixed into the middle of a heavy cylindrical iron head placed on end. The iron head shows four deeply indented surfaces, for not only the two faces but the sides as well are used to drive in iron pegs.

Heavy pointed hammer, *guma*
A cubic iron head with one of the faces tapering to a point is attached to a wooden shaft. This hammer is used to break up large rocks into smaller pieces.

Pickaxe, *trekam*
This tool consitsts of an iron bar with a point at one end, the other being somewhat broader. A stout wooden handle passes through the middle of the bar.

Crowbar, *sanged* or *hangeli*

An iron bar about two metres in length and of a hexagonal section terminates in a point. The crowbar is used to break and lever up stone blocks and to bore holes.

Splitting peg or wedge, *sina*

This is a short cylindrical piece of iron sloped on one side; it often shows marks where an iron splinter has been chipped off. This peg or wedge is driven into crevices or into the prepared grooves to split the rock.

Sludger, *doili*

One end of an iron bar is hammered flat to form a kind of dipper. With this sludger the dust and debris which have combined with water to form sludge is lifted out of the excavation.

In addition the equipment includes a water vessel, blasting powder wrapped in a piece of white cloth, a few metres' length of fuse, cylindrical cartridges made of tin, matches, weed mop, water and clay. These are required for blasting operation. Furthermore there is a stone idol (pg. 32)installed on the edge of the well shaft.

3. 4. Working techniques

Blasting rocks

Massive rock beds cannot be lifted out by mechanical devices only. Explosives have to be used to blast them. For this purpose, the well sinkers use blasting powder, which they buy ready-made together with the fuse. First of all the rock to be blasted is exposed and a suitable point to load the blasting-charge selected. Now a hole is bored at the chosen point with the crowbar. At the start, both men work together : one of them kneels on the ground and directs the blows delivered by the crowbar, while the other stands and drives the crowbar against the rock in powerful rhythmical strockes. He grips the crowbar at the upper end with his left. With the right hand he gathers impetus and with his left he gives the crowbar a turn the moment it comes into contact with the stone. In this way the crowbar grinds the stone with its weight and simultaneously bores into the stone with its sharp pointed end. Water is poured into the hole to increase friction and to make it feasible to remove the accumulated dust with sludger by mixing it with water. For this, the crowbar is extracted from the hole and leant against the stone, while the sludger is used to scoop out the slush from the hole. The remnants of stone adhering to the crowbar are then scraped off.

Using the sludger as a measuring scale, the hole is tested for its depth. If it is sufficiently deep, the prepared tin cartridge is inserted and carefully filled with the blasting powder. One end of the fuse, which is half a metre long, is inserted into the powder with the aid of the straight handle of the sludger. Now the hole with the cartridge is blocked up with earth and finally firmly sealed with wet clay. Only the fuse hangs out. Everybody present now climbs out of the pit, taking along the rest of the blasting powder, the fuse, their tobacco and pipes. Only one of the worker stays back. He lights the fuse with an ember and hurriedly climbs out of the pit. Now all run a considerable distance out into the open plain and await the detonation. There is a loud explosion and smoke ascends from the pit. All run back to examine the result; in most cases the stone has not been split but a narrow crack may be observed running under the point where the blasting powder was charged.

Breaking rocks

The top layers of sandstone and soil are removed with the pickaxe, axe or triangular axe. The hard rock is cracked by blasting and the desired measurements then marked off by cutting in grooves with the triangular axe. A groove is now cut along the base of the stone with the adze. If the adze slips in spite of the weed mop inserted into the groove, a wedge is placed in it and driven in with the sledge hammer. If necessary a second wedge is employed. If the stone still cannot be cracked, the wedges are extricated with the pickaxe and driven into the upper surface of the stone with the sledge hammer or the pointed hammer until cracks appear. The wellsinker punctuates each blow with a puff on the syllable "ha". When the stone has finally been freed, the crowbar is inserted under it and the stone raised from its bed and tipped over. Later it is cut into smaller pieces. The stone blocks and the rubble are left lying there till the evening, when a third man comes to help heave up the large blocks. One man remains in the pit to load the stone blocks and rubble on to the outspread dragmat. Smaller stones he sweeps together with the broad hoe. The dragmat is now hoisted up on ropes in even rhythm. Parallel to the narrow sides of the mat, two ropes are stitched on, the ropes used for hoisting up being knotted to the middle of these ropes. The workmen grasp the rope alternately when pulling up the dragmat with its stone load. They stand above one corner of the pit. While the stones are being hauled up, the workman in the pit withdraws into the opposite corner. No other safety measures are adopted, although the dragmat is often extremely threadbare and is responsible for the frequent accidents that occur. The most laborious job is to drive the first hole into a rockbed in order to form a rising or a lower edge before blasting the rock. This is generally done by exposing the entire rock, then gauging the weakest point and cutting grooves around it with the triangular axe. This surface is then cut into individual pieces with the hammer, then chipped off in layers and finally broadened into a ledge which facilitates the rock being cut downwards in steps.

Testing the water
As soon as water is encountered trickling through the cracks in the rock or collecting in a depression on the floor of the shaft, it is carefully covered. The water may be used to work with, but is not tasted or drunk.
The testing is done by the owner of the well on an auspicious day at an auspicious hour. After consulting the *murat*, good omen, the owner comes to the well at a fixed hour bringing with him a pot full of *gur*, molassess, and a pile of green leaves. Everybody present is given a share of the molasses on a leaf. Even the stone idol, which is a rectangular block of stone painted red on the front surface and decorated with a chisselled-in zigzag line, is offered some molasses. It is sprinkled over with flowers and rubbed with vermilion powder. Now the owner descends into the well and scoops up water in a metal bowl. He first sprinkles a few drops on the idol, then pours a sip each into the cupped hands of the guests and the workers, drinking the rest himself. He tastes the water reflectively, trying to judge its salt content. In the case I observed, the water was unexpectedly sweet, with not a trace of salt. The owner beamed at his good luck, for sweet water guarantees a good harvest.

3, 5, The wellsinker's lingo

Wellsinking is described as *suran*, blasting. The hole bored with the crowbar, into which the blasting charge is inserted, is known as *dara*.

III. 4. Masonry and stone-cutting

4. 1. Working - conditions

The mason usually works together with the members of the household for whom the house is being built. They direct the work, distribute the various tasks and participate actively themselves. They lay the stones, ensuring that they are perfectly joined, fit the doors and windows and themselves trim and dress the stone slabs required for threshold and lintel. The working hours are laid down by the head of the household. He and his family generally praticipate in the work only if there is no urgent field work at hand. The working day then commences in the early morning and lasts till nightfall. The wages are paid on the following day and vary according to the reputation of the mason or stonecutter, from five to eight rupees a day. The "workshop" of the stonecutter, which is generally identical with that of the mason, is set up against a wall or under a tree beside the building site. The working material is transported to him and he prepares it on the spot.

4. 2. The tools

The following is an enumeration of all the tools required in building and stone-cutting:

Marking cord, *dori bandhi*
A thick white cotton cord made of several strands twisted together is used to measure off the thickness of the wall.

Jointing rule, *othi*
The thickness of the wall is marked off by pencil strokes on two small pieces of rectangular wood, which are laid on the edges of the wall and weighted down with stones. The marking cord is then stretched between them according to the wall.

Compasses, *kompas,* engl. deriv.
These simple compasses have two straight tapering legs riveted together at one end. They have to be hammered in order to be properly adjusted.

Square, *katkua*
This is an ordinary iron try-square marked with the inch scale and used to measure the wall thickness and to measure out the right-angled corners.

Water pot, *tori*
This is probably a flat pot with a flat bottom, which is filled to the brim with water and placed on the wall; if it overflows on one side, it is an indication that the wall is not level. Another method of ascertaining whether the wall is perfectly horizontal is to lay a flat board on the wall and sprinkle a few drops of water on it. The wall is inclined in whichever direction the drops run off.

Plummet, *orabho*
This is a length of ordinary string with an imported sounding-lead attached to it. The mason Dhayabhai Kimabhai comments as follows on the plummet :

// Formerly for *uchan nichan jovanu,* to see high and low, to test the perpendicularity, we looked down from the top of the wall. We picked up the method of using *orabho,* plummet, from an engineer who explained it to us. He showed us the level too.

Level, engl, term adopted
This modern instrument is made of steel and glass and contains a yellow liquid. It is imported.

Axe, *kuada*
The ordinary axe, identical with that used by other stone workers and by carpenters, consists of a tringular head of rectangular section with a straight edge inclining slightly

towards the shaft. A rectangular socket is welded on to the head and a short, straight shaft driven into it.

Large-sized and small-sized chisels, *takna* and *pania*

These steel chisels consist of a straight blade sharpened on both sides and tanged into a narrower cylindrical handle. The small size is used predominantly by the sculptor, while the coarser and larger variety is employed to dress and trim stone blocks and slabs.

Rasp, *kanas*

This imported coarse file is of a hemispherical section and is used by sculptors to smooth over the stone and particularly to file over crevices.

Hammer, *hathod*

A wooden handle passes through the centre of a cylindrical metal head. The hammer head shows signs of wear, that is, dents, on all four surfaces.

Shallow bowl, *tagara*

This basin-like vessel, which is made of zinc, is used to transport rubble. It is bought in Porbandar.

4. 3. The working techniques

Building a wall

30, 31, 32

The building materials required are piled in a heap beside the site, which is levelled and the soil grubbed up and cleared. The lenght of the wall is then marked off with stakes driven into the ground and strings spanned between the stakes. It is essential that the bottom layer of the wall be of superior-quality stone and set in somewhat below the ground surface. Now the measuring cord is stretched from one corner to the other. The corners are always built up first; jointing rules marked with the wall thickness are placed on the corners and weighted down with stones. The marking cord is stretched from one mark to the other between both rules; thus the outer edges of the wall are measured off. The wall is built up in layers. The mason begins by joining the stones forming the outer edge. He points out to his helpers the stones he needs from the pile and bends down to lift them up himself as long as he can. He first places them on the wall and then trims them, using both the blade and the back of the axe. He lays the stones, working in layers, raising the level of some stones by inserting another underneath them and trimming them to fit into each other. Sometimes he lays the stones from above on the wall and at other times he fits them under a projecting side stone. As soon as the outer edge is ready, the mason lays the inner edge, after completing which he proceeds to "conceal" the large lumps of stone on the inside of the wall by filling it in with rubble and fragments of limestone. The "filling-in" is carried to the spot by women workers in large basin-like vessels of zinc. It is also the job of the women or other household members to distribute the rubble evenly and to ensure that no cracks and chinks remain. The rough wall structure is now complete. The topmost layer of stone is plastered with a mixture of cowdung and clay, for the woodwork of the roof will later be set upon it.

Stone-cutting

The slabs of limestone to be set in adjacent to the doorcase, as door or window lintels or base of niches, etc. are trimmed with the axe in a series of light strokes sloping towards the surface. The waste stone is thereby chipped off. Different chisels and hammer are used for more precise and detailed work, such as sculpturing or the carving of stone reliefs. The rasp is used to polish and smooth over the surface. I did not observe this kind of work, though. It may be mentioned here that the stencils used by the temple sculptors in Saurashtra are unknown.

4. 4. The mason's lingo

The following types of stone are used in house-building:

Dangedi, carefully dressed blocks quarried in the stone pits, find their place chiefly in the house facade flanking the doorway and in the corners.

Toda, rough building stone, have only one side dressed. The stone is generally silicated sandstone known as *bhuka* and is not very solid. It is the most commonly employed stone for wall construction. The large rocks are trimmed to the described shape one after the other by the mason while he lays the wall.

Kapsi, rubble, and waste fragments of stone are used as filling-in for walls.

Apart from pillars, lintel slabs and other features of the building conspicuous through workmanship or design, the supporting stone, i. e. the stone layers under walls and pillars, have a distinctive name. They are termed *sib.* The outer corner of the doorway is known as *kona* (engl. deriv.), while the inside corner of the doorway near the room is called *moska.* The wall is plastered with a mixture of cowdung, millet chaff and clay stirred with water and kneaded to a *garo,* heap, in front of the building site.

4. 5. Ornamental designs

The geometrical ornaments carved on stone lintel slabs, on memorial stones and on niches, resemble those carved in wood, although the rang of ornaments used in stone carving is more restricted. However, as far as my investigations permit me to judge, there are two designs used in stone carving that are absent in wood.

ladudia, sweetmeat
This represents a row of raised chiselled out circles (bead moulding), the name *ladudia* signifying a row of *ladu,* a ball-shaped sweetmeat eaten at festivals.

ful, simple flower
Simple as well as 24-petalled flowers composed of segments of a circle may be observed on stone carvings.

krasinu ful, inscribed flower
This open flower is constructed with compasses. It resembles a wheel, the number of spokes being variable.

kangri, zigzag
This simple zigzag pattern is either formed by simply cutting v-shaped grooves or as relief by lifting out the notches on one side.

chokedi, rhombs
The rhomb which is placed on end, may occur singly or as a border. The latter may also be termed *chokeda.*

karkaria, serrated saw-blade
The rows of sloping parallel notches can be arranged either following the same directions, or running in opposite directions, the latter forming a herringbone pattern.

35

vankia
The simplest form of this design is a relief border of single triangles placed in a row. In most cases, though, they are arranged crosswise.

toran, scarf with corners
This is a row of pentagons standing at right angles to a common base. The vertices point downwards.

eka
This is a series of hearts, named after one of the four suits of cards and bearing the same design.

kinar, frame
This is an elevated frame enclosing the motif carving on memorial stones and is generally a simple unadorned moulding.

thambheli, pillar
These are carved pillars, analagous in shape to wooden pillars, and are frequently employed as interstices separating relief designs.

4. 6. Stone fixtures, utensils and sculpture

Not withstanding stone structures such as houses and agricultural constructions like walls and wells, worked stone occurs in the following forms that are divided up in the author's own catagories:
(1) as stone fixtures in houses, such as lintel slabs, consoles, niches, etc.
(2) as stone utensils such as feeding trays and tethering blocks
(3) as sculpture i.e. memorial stones, idols and other religious symbols, reliefs, etc.

Apart from these articles, stone is used in conjunction with wood for pillar bases, mill-stones, wheels of chests, etc.

4. 6. 1. Stone fixtures in houses

Stone is used for the construction of walls and verandah platforms, the doorway is framed in stone and the floor laid out with stone slabs. In addition, there is the lintel slab, the stone console above the entrance door-way, the wall niches, the wall ledge, the perforated window, the ornamental ridge plate and the large niche inside the house.

The lintel slab
A white washed slab of limestone is fixed horizontally into the wall above the doorway.
It projects from the wall and is supported by two stone consoles. The lintel is carved from an oblong stone block. The narrow side facing towards the front may be covered with ornamental borders. In nearly every case, the upper longitudinal edge has been partly sloped; only very occasionally can symmetrically arranged zigzags, semicircles or floral and spiral designs be discerned. The undersurface of the slab projecting beyond the doorway is embellished with flower designs.

33

lintel slab	chhajali
(example in the possession of Avadabhai Samadbhai)	
length	189 cm
height	16 cm
breadth	32 cm

The lintel slab may be used to hold all kinds of articles, for instance a lamp is placed on it. Nevertheless, it is regarded primarily as a decoration of the house facade.

The console

A pair of consoles are fixed into the wall as suports for the lintel slab above the door. Each of the consoles is carved from a stone block and consists of a flat base and an s-shaped support below. This basic form occurs in three variations together with their combinations:

nag fani, snake – head   40

The s-shaped support is of uniform width; its front is fluted or decorated with a herringbone pattern. The support terminates in a carved flower in which pointed oval petals are arranged around a central hemispherical elevation.

sudo or *hudo,* parrot   37, 38

The contours of the s-shape are not identical, the lower curve being deeper than the other, and broad at the point where it joins the wall. The upper curve ends in a point that is directed downwards to the lower curve. Large discs are carved into the sides of the upper curve. This s-shaped support, which may be ornamented with a reed moulding, tori or other design, is obviously intended to represent a wild parrot. This is deduced from the following three characteristics typical of the bird: an arched chest, a hooked beak and large eyes.

ghorla, horse   39

The s-shaped support is of more or less uniform width, the upper curve extending right down to the commencing point of the lower curve, this extended portion resembling a cylinder with a band across the middle. This band representing the harness stretches across the s-shape, right up to the upper corner of the console. It is carved partly in relief, partly as a strap. Details such as eyes, nostrils, mouth and ears may be indicated by cuts.

(example in the possession of Hansabhai Muljibhai)	
height	33 cm
thickness	8 cm
breadth	30 cm

The consoles support the lintel slab above the door and decorate the facade of the house.

Besides these basic types, which may be varied through ornamentation, there exist other forms, for instance one in which a small parrot is carved in front of the s-shape. The s-shape is only rarely abandoned in favour of simple straight supports.

The niche   35, 36, 40

Niches are sunk into the wall straight under the consoles on both sides of the main doorway. The niches frequently have a rectangular frame resembling a miniature doorway, which is either modelled from clay or carved from a stone slab and then white-washed. In the latter case, it consists of four parts: between the threshold covered with an ornamental border and the lintel board decorated with ornamental interminiature posts in the shape of pilasters, columns or ornamental interstices. A bell-shaped knob often hangs down from the lintel of the frame.

niche	gokhlo
(example in the possession of Hansabhai Muljibhai)	
hight	35 cm
breadth	26 cm
depth	6 cm

The niche serves as a repository for the padlock when the door is open. As it affords shelter from the wind a small oil lamp may be placed on it and kept burning through the night.

The frames enclosing the niches vary in respect of the ornamental devices employed in each example. There are frames with little domes and creeper designs mounted on the lintel, calling to mind the facade of a temple. In one case the top of the niche was sloped and flanked on either side by a peacock bearing the lintel on its back and wings.

The wall ledge

Occasionally a projecting stone may be sunk into the varandah wall; on top of it is level and tapers downwards. The wall ledge is frequently ornamented with a reed or tori design.

lamp stand	*diveliu*
(example in the possession of Hansabhai Muljibhai)	
height	12 cm
diameter	8 cm

These stone ledges serve as lamp stands. They are usually set so high as to make reading by lamp-light possible.

The window

34

The kitchen window, roughly square in shape, is closed by a perforated stone slab. The purpose of this window is to keep out big animals. In Ratadi, the simple rectangular window is, with rare exceptions, the only one employed.

stone window	*gokhlo aryavaliyu*
(example in the possession of Puriai Lakiben)	
height	38 cm
breadth	46 cm
thickness	4 cm

The large niche

79

This is a large rectangular recess on the inside of the front wall. It is lined with thick stone slabs projecting beyond the wall surface. The slab lining the floor of the niche often has depressions hollowed out to receive two or three water vessels. The slabs rising up on the sides are joined to the floor slab by simple tenons. Sometimes an ornamental border is carved into the front edge of the top slab; more frequently, though, it is surmounted by a relief border of clay. The rear-wall of the niche is often covered with paintings.

niche for water vessels	*paniharun*
(example in the possession of Parbatbhai Shinabhai)	
height	123 cm
breadth	147 cm

The niche is used as a repository for vessels containing drinking water. The upper slab is used as a stand for unused articles, containers for sugar, salt and spices, kerosene-cookers, etc. In the rare cases where a stone water stand of this kind is absent, it is replaced by a wooden table. Rectangular niches with the short side horizontal and the long side vertical are also seldom to be seen.

The ornamental ridge plate

6

This is a circular stone slab with a rhombus on one side and on the opposite side a triangle or a recumbent sickle. The surface is ornamented with floral and spiral designs.

ridge plate	*ful*, literally flower
height	50 cm

No information could be gathered as to the function and significance of this unusual stone ornament. It was explained that it was merely a decoration of the roof. This stone slab, which is fixed between two stones by the rhomb, hangs on the side wall and covers the end of the ridge-beam. It also protects it from becoming wet.

4.6.2. Stone utensils

The feeding tray

An easily workable and porous block of stone, already hollowed out slightly by natural processes, is hewn to form an irregular bowl. According to their natural shape, these bowls may be of rectangular or oval section.

feeding tray	*kundi*
(example in the possession of Virambhai Arjunbhai)	
height	20 cm
length	41 cm
breadth	58 cm

These feeding trays usually lie in front of the house near the entrance, where the domestic animals are tethered. These trays serve as troughs for cattle as well as for dogs. All waste from the kitchen and excess butter-milk is poured into the trays for the animals to drink.

The tethering block

A block of stone, mostly with a naturally formed hole through it, is sunk in the ground beside the wall and used to tether animals. A stone slab with a hole through it is used as a hay-rack.

tethering block	*nanaguru*
(example in the possession of Virambhai Arjunbhai)	
height	9 cm
breadth	22 cm
thickness	10 cm

4.6.3. Stone sculpture

The memorial stone 41-55

This is usually pentagonal in shape, that is, a rectangle surmounted by a triangle. It is placed vertically and sunk into the earth. The rectangle is divided into a narrow base, into which is sometimes carved in Hindi or Gujarati the date, place and circumstances referring to the event depicted above in haute-relief. This event is represented by the following symbols: a rider with weapons, a rider with a snake, a woman with a snake, a woman with water-vessels, a hand, and a snake. The triangle above the pictorial representation frequently contains an inscribed flower (sun-symbol) and an encircled recumbent half-moon or else spiral or floral ornaments on either side of the central point. An elevated moulding runs round the entire carving. The memorial stones are mostly weather-beaten. The figures are also usually worn out by constant handling and smeared with vermilion paste.

memorial stone	*khambha*
(example in the possession of Parbatbhai Virambhai,	
carved by Dahyabhai Kimabhai in 1964)	
height	117 cm
breadth	56 cm
thickness	15 cm

In Ratadi the memorial stones, are arrayed in front of the assembly in the centre of the village. 50
Furthermore, there is a *pedha,* platform, on the west outside the village, on which stand the 49
three *khambha,* memorial stones, carved in remembrance of the Luhana or merchant caste settled in Ratadi. There are in addition several other memorial stones scattered singly through out the village. The memorial stones are arranged in rows or in echelon formation. If the surroundings permit, the carved front faces east. In many villages, the majority of the memorial stones are to be found outside the village itself on the eastern side.

There is but little to be gleaned of the function of memorial tablets by viewing the rows of stones. Some are smeared with *sindur* a vermilion dye made from earth, and others are painted with a chalk solution. The ground surrounding the stones is not kept particularly clean. A tile with a sooty hollow lying beside the memorial stone is a rare sight. More prosperous people, however, frequently arrange for a cement platform into which their memorial stone is set.

Trivedi (1961, pg. 78) informs us that memorial stones are installed to commemorate male ancestors who fell in battle, women who became *sati,* and all those who died by accident or by their own hand. It is believed that the spirit of such ancestors haunts the place of its birth and death, and that the descendants must appease the ghost. The ceremony of appeasing the ghosts takes place every New Years's Day (*divali,* the 30th day of *ashvina,* in November-December). Coconuts, boiled rice and other offerings are made and a lamp lit and placed in a small clay vessel before the idol. These idols of family ancestors are also anointed with *sindur,* the vermilion lead-powder, and oil.

The memorial stones therefore belong to certain patrilineages who worship them at least once a year. Unless a memorial tablet of this kind has been recently erected or unless a famous warrior is thereby honoured, the details regarding the deeds and fate of the worshipped ancestor have long since sunk into oblivion. Even the village elders of Ratadi knew very little about the men in whose name the memorial stones were erected. They said :

Khambha, memorial stones are erected for *surapura,* men who died bravely in battle. Later on a stone was also set up in memory of a person who had been bitten by a snake or had committed suicide.

The following is reported about the memorial stone erected in 1964 and dedicated to the memory of Parbatbhai Virambhai:

Parbat Viram burnt himself. He is not living anymore.

// His family moved to Jamnagar. They are farmers. // The stone was set up in memory of Parbat Viram. // Dhaya Kima of Baradia carved it.

The sculptor Dhaya Kima himself had the following to say about this particular memorial stone :

// That was the first *khambha,* memorial stone, I ever carved. // Jeta Viram, the brother of the deceased, ordered it. // I had never watched a stone-cutter carving a memorial stone. // At that time I was engaged in building the house of Rangmal Karsan, the house in which you are staying. Jeta Viram lives nearby. Being a craftsman, I was asked to carve the *khambha,* memorial stone. We fixed the price and I did the work.

This story is told about another memorial stone :

// The woman for whom the *khambha,* memorial stone is set up was bitten by a snake and died after that. The spirit of such a person enters the body of one of its relatives, who all of a sudden starts shouting, trembling and beating the ground with his hands. Somebody will ask him: "Who are you !" and the trembler will utter the spirit's name and the wish of the deceased.

This story is explained by the following information (Trivedi, 1961, pg. 79): "When a member of a family, or a cow, or buffalo falls ill or dies, it is conjectured that the spirit of an ancestor is annoyed because of neglect. The spirit of a dissatisfied ancestor possesses (*ghataman ave* meaning "comes in the body") one of the kins, and speaks through him or her, and mentions the cause of his discontent. When someone is thus harassed by a spirit, a professional medium of Vachhada Dada is consulted. The medium is powerful enough to evoke other spirits, from whom he learns the name and whereabouts of this spirit. If a malignant spirit tries to conceal its identity, the medium threatens the spirit concerned with punishment by Vachhada Dada. As a last resort, the reasons for the mischief are revealed through some other persons in whom the spirit is compelled to enter. At times the spirit in a medium is symbolically beaten to extract the truth.–The most important thing to be noted about invoking the spirit of an ancestor is that the head of the family conducts the performance in the presence of the kins within a range of five to six generations. For the spirit and its descendants are mutually linked and owe allegiance to one another."

I had the chance of witnessing an invocation of the ancestor spirit before a memorial stone 51-55 on the occasion of a wedding : On the wedding, the day before the processions leave for the bride's village, the entire family with their two sons, both of whom are to be married the next day, makes its way to the memorial stones. The party is accompanied by musicians and guests. It is late in the evening. The afternoon has been spent smoking and gossiping at a *daira,* tea party. As the procession with both bridegrooms in the middle approaches the memorial stones, the musicians strike up a wild strain while the members of the party seat themselves in a semicircle in front of the memorial stones and on the steps of the assembly house. The paternal grandmother of the bridegrooms now steps forward and lays a white scarf on each of the two memorial stones of the family. Earlier in the day, these stones have been smeared red. Between the stones she places a tile with fire from which smoke rises. The musicians play louder and the grandfather, a wizened little man, steps forward and commences to execute a clumsy dance with his arms stretched out from his bowed body. He then seizes the chain hanging on his shoulder, lashes about him with it and then starts to scourage himself. Hesitantly at first, he finally grabs the white scarves, waves them about and sinks forward to the ground, whereupon his grandsons, the bridegrooms, rush to him, lift him and humbly touch his knees. The scarves are then placed over the bridegroom's shoulders and the procession makes its way to the temple with the carved stone horses. The fire in the tiles placed before the memorial stones, continues to smoke.

It may therefore be safely asserted that in addition to their significance as mnemotechnic symbols, these memorial stones are places of ancestor worship or the means whereby the dead still exert their influence on society. It is explained that through this rite "the consent of the ancestors to the planned wedding was obtained."

The most common motifs depicted on memorial stones are riders, women with water vessels, and snakes. If men shown astride horses, the memorial stones belong to the Mer or Bava farmers, or the Luhana merchants; the Rabari shepherds show their heroes riding on camel.

It would be possible to classify one group of stones as the work of one special craftsman, for 47, 48 the observer will find that some stones, usually three or four in number, are so similar to one another as to be almost identical. Whether the reliefs are "realistic" or "simplified", is in this case irrelevant. But we must content ourselves with this statement. We shall now describe a few memorial stones to illustrate these two tendencies.

Standing somewhat remote from the main group beside the assembly house is a row of four 45 stones exceptional for the precise and detailed nature of their relief-carving. These stones have been dug out from their original places and transferred to this spot. They are neither painted nor adorned, most probably because they have lost their religious significance. The upper third of the base, the greater part of which was probably sunk in the earth, bears an inscription that is hardly to be deciphered. Above this is a high rectangle, the upper edge of which is covered. The whole is framed by a decorative moulding with herringbone patterns on the sides and a row of squares on top. The rider is carved in profile. Both arms are raised, for in his right hand he brandishes a lance and in his left he holds the reins. The rider apparently wears a coat of chain-mail. A round shield hangs on his right hip. The horse seems to be standing still, although it has its left foreleg raised.Saddle, bridle and reins are worked out in great detail and embellished with designs. The figure is drawn closely within the frame, but it never overlaps its. Above the figure in the middle is a bundle of lines and a standing triangle flanked by spirals terminating in floral desigs.

A specimen of this "realistic" type of memorial stone has the following measurements :

height	138 cm
breadth	54 cm
thickness	13 cm
depth of relief	3 cm

The most original of the less realistic memorial stones is the one standing in the middle of the 46
second row in front of the assembly house. The base is narrow and bears no inscription.
A rider is carved within a pentagon. The head is represented by a recumbent ellipse, the body
by a triangle and the arms and legs by narrow bars. He is mounted on a decrepit horse with
unformed legs, a swan like neck and a narrow head. A snake is shown lying curled up between
the horse's legs and biting the rider on his heel. The relief is enclosed by a border, partly
adorned with a herringbone pattern and slightly broken into on one side of the overhead
portion by the point of the rider's sword. The stone is whitewashed and the head of the figure,
which is probably depicted en face, is smeared red.-This memorial stone, which may be taken
to represent the "naïve-simplified" mode of depiction, has the following measurements:

height	110 cm
breadth	61 cm
thickness	14 cm
depth of relief	2.5 cm

Beside the narrow side of a house in the centre of the village, is a stone in memory of a 44
widow who committed *sati*, self-immolation on her husband's funeral pyre. On the
roughly shaped rectangular block a hand with outstretched fingers is depicted in haute relief
on an almost square ground. The ground surrounding the relief together with the rest of the
stone block is painted red. Only the frame around the relief-ground has been irregularly
whitewashed. Details such as finger nails or the lines of the hand have not been carved. But
the fingers are naturally proportioned. The base of the square cuts through the wrist.
This memorial stone, which shows one part of the body as a symbol for an event, has the
following measurements :

height	113 cm
breadth	55 cm
thickness	15 cm
depth of relie'	2 cm

A memorial stone near the assembly house depicts a female figure carved into a simple 43
hexagonal slab with a flattened top. The woman shown en face, carries two disc-like vessels on
her round head. Ears are indicated by two small circles. Between head and the triangular
lower body is a straight stick-like upper body above which the arms are arched. The arms end
in lumps for hands. The legs are thin bars with the feet turned outwards. A curled-up snake
is shown on the right of the picture. It is biting the woman's hand. On the narrow base, the
words *"maki dosi"*, probably the woman's name, may be deciphered. The stone is whitewashed and the figure painted red. The dimensions are as below :

height	82 cm
breadth	57 cm
thickness	11 cm
depth of relief	0.5 cm

The only memorial stone in Ratadi, displaying a camel rider, is to be found in the left corner
of the square in front of the assembly house. The slab itself is pentagonal. The relief-ground
is rectangular and framed by a moulding adorned with a herringbone pattern. The base bears
no inscription. The upper portion as divided by a central axis. In the space on the right a 42

recumbent half-moon is cut into a disc-shape and on the left an inscribed rose of equal size is carved. The inscribed rose is encircled by a hatched design. The largest portion of the relief ground, is taken up by the huge body of the dromedary, which rests like a mountain on four clumsy vertical legs. The joints are indicated by lumps (no doubt meant to represent tufts of hair). The rider sits on the centre of the back holding a curved sabre in one hand and the reins in the other. His head is painted red and the details are therefore not discernable. The narrow upper body continues downwards in a trapezoid skirt, the folds of which are respresented by paralled grooves. From the skirt juts out an extralong leg, which reaches below the belly of the dromedary. The spaces between the legs of the animal and the upper corners of the relief ground are covered with a design of discs and rosettes. This memorial stone has the following dimensions.

height	104 cm
breadth	50 cm
thickness	15 cm
depth of relief	2 cm

The stone images and idols
Apart from the usual images and idols such as the *lingam* and the blue-painted *fotia*, Nandi bulls, both of which may be seen in Hindu temples of the *Shiva* cult, and apart from the geometrically carved and sometimes merely red-painted stone symbols such as the idol of the stone workers and the symbols of the smallpox deity, there are several other stone figures in Ratadi. One of them is the figure of a standing woman conspicuous through her greatly shortened legs. The figure has been worn away by much handling. Another stone-carving is a fragment of a slab showing the engraved outline of the front portion of an advancing animal.

In another temple in Ratadi a row of horses carved in stone may be seen. The horses are carved out of square blocks half-a-metre high and are characterized by massive, globe-like heads, bulging bodies and short stumps for legs. With the exception of the bridle, no details are carved. The information given to me regarding these images of horses was very scanty and gave me the impression of being a modern "re-interpretation". The information I had hoped for could have also explained the use of ornamental horse-heads in houses and in various other articles. Hardasbhai Bhayabhai, the Patel of Baradia, stated:

The actual name of the horse is *Dada* or *Vashhada dada*. We are told that such horses represent the god *Vashhada dada*. // The man associated with the *dada* is called *bhuva*. The *bhuva*, medium, from our village Baradia is the young man who showed you the farming implements this morning.

// This religious practice has been handed down from generation to generation. Yet nobody knows the origin. The horse-carvings were brought very recently to Ratadi, whereas the ones in Baradia are old. I cannot remember who brought them.

An old relation of the Patel who happened to be present was questioned next. He told the following story of *Vashhada dada,* which I have somewhat condensed :

Formerly robbers used to raid our villages and steal our cows. We used to have to fight for our cows. Once a Rajput fought so bravely, that even when his head was cut off from his body, he continued fighting with the outlaws. Later, he fell from his horse and the body died. This incident rook place near Gorana. There is still a *khambha*, memorial stone, to this famous warrior depicting a headless man sitting on a horse and holding a sword in his right hand. Sometime later a Vanjara, merchant, came there and spent the night next to the *khambha*, memorial stone of *Vashhada dada*. During the night some outlaws came and tried to rob him of his goods. Suddenly, the warrior emerged from his *khambha*, memorial stone, and started fighting the robbers. When the merchant awoke in the morning, he found the warrior resting in front of the stone. He had overthrown all the outlaws. The merchant asked the man : "Who are you ?" The merchant had hardly heard the name when the warrior disappeared. The merchant cleared the ground and built a *pedharan*, platform, for the memorial stone,

// The *kadhia*, masons, carved the horse only, because the idea of carving a headless warrior repelled them. So the practice of representing *Vashhada dada* as a horse, came into existence and has persisted ever since. The original *khambha*, memorial stone, showed a headless man.

According to another version of this story, the faithful horse carried the body of the dead warrior back to his native village, and thereby earned the privilege of pictorial representation.

Vikrambhai told this story:

A Rajput from the Solanki community called *Vashhada dada* was to be married. The marriage ceremony had just started when news was brought that a cow had been stolen. He rose and left the wedding and his village to go out in search of the cow. He fought bravely and the cow came back, but his head was cut off and only his body continued fighting. He died on the field.
// The name of the outlaw who tried to rob the cow was *Asram*. He was a Muslim.
// Acutally the *khambha*, memorial stone, shows a headless rider on a horse. Later on, only the horse was shown, because it had brought back the corpse to the village. Therefore it became an important figure.

However, it is obvious, that these stories have been invented at a later date to explain the significance of an ancient cult symbol.

The influence of *Vashhada dada* on the people is thus set forth in Trivedi (1961: 81): "He is renowned for curing hydrophobia and serpent-bite. In fact, this deity in general may be called a multi-purpose deity, whose mediums have the power of curing numerous diseases.
.. Such a medium is said to be able to persuade the deity to do anything he wants. The deity has to come to the medium's rescue, because of the utter devotion and fidelity he shows to the deity."

Besides the curing of afflictions and diseases, the medium of *Vashhada dada* is asked to find out why a certain person is haunted by a ghost and to communicate to the people the advice of the god in certain important matters. Hardasbhai Bhayabhai, the Patel of Baradia, describes how this last consultation of the oracle takes place. In this case the medium does not fall into a trance:

// As far as horses are concerned, *lapsi*, sweet meats, are prepared and offered to them. At the same place they perform *dhup*, i. e. they pour *ghee*, clarified butter, into the fire. After this has been done, the person who is the *bhuva*, medium, dances special steps called the *dhunvo*. If a person is unhappy or has difficulties he asks the *bhuva*, medium, for his advice. The *bhuva*, medium, will consult the *chapti*, oracle, using for this purpose a few grains of *javar*, sorghum millet.

// There is one *bhuva* in Ratadi. Every monday evening he goes to the horse-carvings outside the village, opens the shrine and uses *ghee*, clarified butter, which the people have offered to light the lamps. If somebody has offered a coconut or sweetmeats, it is shared by the people who have gathered together.

// About the *chapti*, oracle, I can tell you this: if a person is in difficulties he will request the *bhuva*, medium, to help him. The *bhuva* will ask for the man's consent to do whatever may be required. However, the *bhuva* has first to give proof that he will speak the truth. // First you must know that there are two kinds of *chapti*, oracles. In one case the number of grains is odd; this is called *vadhava*. The second kind of oracle is called *vachha*, and here the number of grains is even. The grains are counted to ascertain whether their number is odd or even. By this, the *bhuva*, medium, is proved correct and the person will accept the conditions laid down by the *bhuva*.

At a marriage, I watched how the *bhuva*, medium, consulted *Vashhada dada*. The following 56–62 took place immediately after the rite before the *khambhas*, memorial stones: The company seat themselves in a semicircle before the shrine of *Vashhada dada*. The men are on the right and a few women on the left. The bridegrooms sit on the steps beside the entrance and the most important family members on the other side. The musicians (two trumpeters and a drummer) take their place opposite the entrance. The door to the little temple is open and the father of the bridegroom is inside. The people outside attentively watch him lighting incense sticks and oil lamps. He then removes his turban, crouches down and starts to dance. All of a sudden he steps out from the temple with a theatrical gesture, straightens himself up and then crouches again. He now turns around, seizes a chain with both hands and begins to scourage himself with it. He steps down and dances for a few minutes in a circle, whipping himself every time he turns towards the temple. Before he finally breaks down, laying the chain on the temple steps, his sons rush up to him and bow down before him, clasping his knees.

The father lays his arms upon their backs. He starts to dance once more, this time without the chain, for his brother has put it back inside the temple. Suddenly, the stepmother of the bridegrooms starts trembling; she separates herself from the crowd and dances with her head bent forward. Her head cloth falls in front of her face and covers it. After a few seconds of frenzied ecstacy she returns to her place exhausted and sinks into the arms of another woman. The grandfather of the bridegrooms squats inside the temple. The father reappears dancing. Without warning he fixes a stare upon one of his male relatives, who emits a soft cry and begins to tremble. He snatches the chain away from the father, turns around and whips himself lightly. But he is stopped from further self-castigation and lays the chain down. The bridegrooms keep stepping forward to receive blessings. The man who has been stopped from whipping himself returns to his place without displaying the slightest trace of emotion on his features. But the woman continues to weep and tremble. I could not help asking myself whether a large part of these "ecstatic performances" were not merely acted in order to fulfil a certain role in society. Finally the door of the temple is shut and the company returns to the house of the bridegrooms' father. The consent of *Vashhada dada* has been obtained.

IV. Clay relief working

by Haku Shah

IV. 1. The informant

Makiai, an elderly widow of about fifty-five, a Mer by caste, belongs to the Modhvadia lineage, while her husband Samatbhai Laxmanbhai to the Keshvara lineage. Makiai spent her childhood in Baradia, the village adjoining Ratadi; since her marriage she has settled down in Ratadi. She used to live in an old-fashioned house with a tiled roof in a small narrow lane in the north east quarter of Ratadi. After the marriage of her younger son Arasibhai, she divided her house and possessions, a small field of about four acres and house-hold goods, between her two sons. Her sons built a shed for her to live adjacent to the house which they now occupy with their families.

Though Makiai lives in the annexe, she still has control over the family, and her judgement in various problems, domestic or social, on marriage, the spending of money, attending parties etc., is still taken into consideration. She still has the right to interfere and command in family-quarrels between her sons. She has herself erected her own *kothla* for storing her own grain, and she has her own buffalo. Though she lives all by herself in the shed, Makiai's daily routine is associated with that of her sons. Apart from her own household duties, she goes out daily to work in her sons' fields, where she makes *panite*, channels for the irrigation of the fields; she helps in looking after the buffaloes and the cows belonging to her sons. If she has to stay at home she takes care of the grandchildren, cooks for the family, and sees that everything is clean and orderly.

When I first saw Makiai I was impressed by her personal appearance. She is tall, has long slender arms and legs, and long tapering fingers; the face is sharply outlined with an eagle nose and a pointed chin; the eyebrows are thick and black. The wrinkles on her face enhance the strength of her personality and you can easily tell she must have been a beauty in her youth. She still wears the traditional widows weeds of the Mer caste. The *dhalavo,* the knee length red cloth of about two metres is wrapped around her waist. With it she wears *kapadun,* a red blouse with sleeves covering the elbow. The *odhana,* red cloth of about a metre and a half with black dots printed on it serves as the head-covering. Whenever she goes out of her shed she takes up the extra fine *odhana* hanging on the peg and puts it on, removing the old one. Apart from her social status as an elder guide of the village folk, she is especially respected and much in demand for her skill in wall decoration, clay reliefs and paintings, and also for her singing. She is a born artist, one who works for the sake of the art rather than for monetary considerations. Though she cannot utterly disregard the material aspect of life, to her, her art is a labour of love. In the early days, when living was cheaper, she was paid six paisa a day, today she gets two rupees a day. Unlike many villagers she is scrupulously punctual and once she gets started in her work, she will not cease until she has completed it to her satisfaction, nor will she brook any interference from others. Thus her whole mind is focused on the work in hand. Naturally, unlike the others, she refrains from the inevitable chitchatting of the village folk, the drinking of tea or taking time off on some pretext or another. Her only indulgence is the taking of snuff which has become a habit. It was a delight to observe Makiai working, whether the task she was engaged in was difficult or elementary; Makiai enjoyed every bit of her work, e. g. the laborious preparation of the requisite type of clay, or the splitting of bomboos into long short or flat pieces as necessitated by the work, was as much enjoyed by her as the making of the clay ornaments.

She said once :

Jibh didhi chhe paisa vinani avle hane vaparie havali vaparie, the tongue has been given free; why use it wrongly, let us use it rightly. (She meant by this not only the tongue but the other limbs as well.)

Being a skilful craftsman, she knew the value of her work without being proud or self-laudatory about it. She knew :

Ho johi ne ek dohi baraber, one old woman is equal to a hundred seers.

So engrossed did she become in the performance of the task in hand that she disregarded all else until the completion of her work. Experience had made her aware of the exact time her work would take and so without any preparation of a time-table she planned her work to fit in with her other duties. Another noteworthy characteristic was her attitude towards the chance shortage of the raw material she needed. It was an attitude of matter-of-factness rather than of boredom or complaint or irritation. If she found a shortage of water for the clay mixture while working on it she would just say:

I shall now have to go and bring the water.

In this way she took the unpleasant facts of life. Her immediate concern was not the botheration of fetching water, but the amount necessary for the mixture. Another instance of this was to be observed when she broke the bamboos to the right length. She unconsciously made use of her knee for this purpose, obvious of the scratches and the consequent pain. Her son gently reminded her to stop, but her only retort was:

You do your work and I shall do mine. The work must be completed properly in time at any cost.

It naturally follows that she was never afraid of spoiling or tearing clothes, or risking a fall from the ladder. Now and then some village folk would drop in to watch her and many of them praised her saying :

Maki to bakhadi chhe. Kothiyun ghade chhe ne kalaja tode chhe, Maki is an able woman; she makes grain storage jars but breaks her ribs.

Makiai herself, absorbed in her work, ignored these observations. Similarly, any suggestion for the change of the clay ornaments or technique was disregarded. But I could realize the high regard the people had for her. Though so engrossed in her work, she was quite aware of the going-on in the house; if an important visitor came along, she offered him a seat, if one of her grand-children started crying she consoled it; and she remembered the time for untying the buffalo to let her go to the pastures. To her, all this was part of her days' work and not an interruption.

IV. 2. The tools

2. 1. Implements for preparing clay-mixtures

Hoe, *pavada*
A broad iron blade is fixed by a socket to a straight wooden handle about 40cm long.

Pickaxe, *trikam*
It consists of an iron bar with a point at one end, the other being somewhat broader and flattened. A straight wooden handle passes through the middle of the bar.

Cart, *gadu*
It is the usual kind of bullock cart used for transportation of goods.

Basket, *hundo*
A hemispherical basket is made of interwoven bamboostrips.

Waterpot, *hando*
A large clay pot is used both for fetching and storing water.

Brass pot, *kalasio*
The small brass jar with the circular edge turned outwards is used for taking water out of a container.

Sieve, *charani*
An iron container has a flat bottom with holes.

Winnowing fan, *supadu*
The horse-shoe shaped flat container is made of interwoven bamboo-strips.

Aluminium pan, *tapeli*
The cylindrical aluminium pan is used for boiling water.

Brass vessel, *beidu*
The large cylindrically shaped metal-pot with a narrow opening is used for fetching water at the well.

Cover, *dhaknu*
Flat clay dish or conical shaped lid is used as a cover on vessels to protect water from dust.

Vessel support, *indhon*i
A ring of cloth or straw is placed an the head for balancing a water-pot, and to break the weight of the burden.

2. 2. Construction implements

Iron bar, *naraj*
About a one meter long iron bar is bent at the end like a blade for the purpose of digging.

Sickle, *dataradu*
The lightly curved iron blade is fixed in a wooden handle.

Ladder, *nisarni*
A wooden bamboo-ladder has six steps.

IV. 3. Working materials

Unbroken bomboos, *akha vans*
The long bamboos are used as pillars.

Bamboo clips, *khanp*
Split bamboos are used for filling up the construction.

Jute string, *sutli*
For tying bamboo chips soft jute string is used.

Clay, *mati*
Dark clay which is fetched from the Baradia tank. It is naturally clean and not as rough
as clay from other places.

Sandy clay, *moram*
This is a redish clay mixed with white particles of sand. It is found on the road to Palakhda,
two miles away from Ratadi.

Ashes, *vani, rakh*
For the ornamentation work the clay is mixed with ashes from the fireplace in the kitchen.

Millet husk, *ghavar no kucho*
The husk is mixed with the clay.

Horse dung, *lad*
Horse dung was brought from a neighbor's place free. The dry dung is cleaned by rubbing
it with the fingers and thus removing longer particles.

Cow dung, *chhan*
The dung of a cow or a buffalo can be used instead of horse-dung.

Water, *pani*
Water is fetched from the Baradia tank.

IV. 4. The working techniques

4.1. Working conditions and working schedule

To Makiai a *tak,* clay arch, *toda* and *kandhi,* ornamented clay boards at the kitchen wall,
constitute a necessary part of a house; no house could be complete without them. When her
own house was divided between her two sons, her old *tak, toda* and *kandhi* passed into the
possession of the elder son as his family received the kitchen. The younger son Arasibhai, with
the help of Makiai constructed an archway in the new kitchen on the other side and Makiai
wanted to furnish it with *tak, toda* and *kandhi.*

Makiai had to do the clay work in between her daily duties whenever she could snatch the
time; she could not fix up her time schedule, but she calculated it about seven days. On the
whole the work took about forty hours in seven days time :

Quarrying the clay with the help of her son	2 hours
Bamboo-work with the help of her son and his wife	4 hours
Actual clay work with the help of her daughter-in-law	30 hours
White-washing the whole site by Makiai's daughter-in-law	4 hours

4. 2. Digging and fetching clay

One evening Makiai's younger son Arasibhai left the fields earlier than usual under his mother's
instructions for the purpose of fetching the clay. His bullock cart was also spared. He drove
the cart to the Baradia tank where Makiai had told him that good clay was to be found. The
place was dry then, but during the monsoon it is flooded. The requisite type of clay was to be
obtained on the top of a mound. Arasibhai dug with his hoe and threw the lumps of dry clay
into a basket. He carried this basket to the cart and overturned about fifty basketfuls until
the cart was full in an hour's time. Then he drove the cart back to unload it on his side of the
house. He stopped the bullocks outside the lane. Makiai, who was waiting for her son to
return, helped him unload the cart inspite of her son Arasibhai's remonstrances that she keep
away from the more laborious task, and merely give instruction as to which place he was to
dump the clay in. In her youthful days Makiai used to fetch the clay herself as a head-load.

That very day Makiai had gone to the village in search of bamboos but in vain. So she had
to work with whatever was stored in the house. These bamboo pieces had been used in the
ceiling before the tiles had been replaced. Arasibhai carried the best and longest pieces of
the split bamboos to the *havada*, animal pond, at the entrance of Ratadi. He arched the stricks
to the size of the tank and left them in the water over-night.

4.3. Preparation of the clay

Makiai had to make three different qualities of clay mixture to be used for different purposes:

The first clay mixture
Makiai laid special stress on the preparation of *paheli gar*, the first clay mixture, and was
careful to get the right proportion of the ingredients. This mixture would have to be used as
hethe chandavu, the bottom-most layer, for a strong foundation. It contained: two *hunda*,
baskets of *lad*, horse dung, one basket of clay, one basket of *dunha bajara*, millet husk, and two
pots of water.

The mixture was prepared in the courtyard. She arranged the clay in a large circular shape
and she made the inner circle of *dunha*, husk, against the clay. The third circle again was out
of husk. After pouring water over it she stood with her legs wide apart over the pile, bent
down and started to mix the clay with the fingers of both her hands, kneading it. When the
ingredients had been satisfactorily mixed, she began to trample on it with the heels of her feet,
taking care not to dig her toes in, because not only would the clay stick to them and make
the work laborious, but the weight of the heels would help pounding the lumps and the clay
to a more smooth and uniform mixture. Whenever the clay mixture spread beyond her reach,
she put it back in a heap with her hands and resumed her trampling. Of course, she threw
away stones and large particles from the mixture. When this was ready she built the mixture
into the form of a flat cone and hollowed it at the top. She washed her hands above this hollow
and with her wet palms she patted the surface of the cone and made it smooth. When this
process had been completed, she washed her hands over the hollow into which the water had
collected and gradually soaked the mixture. Makiai described the qualities of the mixture
as follows:

Paheli gar, clay mixture, must have the following qualities: it must be *chikano*, sticky; *jadero*, coarse; *bhare*, heavy; and *kalo*, dark.

Thus the *paheli gar*, first mixture, was ready to be used as the ground-layer. It was prepared in a large quantity because it was also used to fill up all the gaps left in the bamboo construction. The more rotten the mixture the stickier it becomes. So Makiai did not use it immediately but left the wet pile aside for some time saying:

Garo sadava devo sade e saras, the clay mixture should be left to rot, as rotten mixture is better.

The second clay mixture

As the first mixture was not to be used immediately, Makiai used the time to prepare *biji gar*, the second clay mixture for *mathe chaudavun*, the top layer. This clay mixture consists of: two baskets of *mati*, clay, two baskets of *ghavar no kucho*, husk, and the water of two pots.

When preparing the second mixture, Makiai put the clay in the centre and the husk was arranged arround it in a circle. As in the first case, she mixed the two ingredients by trampling on it. When ready, she left it to rot. This mixture was reddish-yellow and as sticky as the first mixture, but the quality was finer as it had to be used as the top layer.

The third clay mixture

As there was no immediate necessity for the use of *triji gar*, the third mixture, Makiai prepared it later. The amount was very little as is was to be used as *naksi no garo*, mixture for the clay relief works. The ingredients were: *be khoba*, two handfuls of *vani rakh*, ashes; two handfuls of *mati*, clay; two handfuls of *lad*, horse dung; and two handfuls of *moram*, sandy clay.

Makiai took special care of the mixture, explaining that there should not be any *kacho kucho*, coarse particles in it. Hence she refined it by winnowing. She explained that:

// Ashes smoothen the mixture and its stickiness helps to fix it well. Horse dung prevents cracks. *Simna ghoda ni lad lavie ne ghas ma nakhi e to toda kandhi ma pan udhai thay,* if we bring horse-dung from the outskirts and mix it with straw, then the *toda ,tak, kandhi* will be devoured by the white ants. Sandy clay makes the mixture hard and unbreakable.

Makiai did not prepare large quantities at once, but made fresh stocks as each got exhausted.

4. 4. Bamboo construction work

Arasibhai remained absent from his farmwork one day for the construction of the bamboo work in his house. His wife Tamuben also stayed at home. First of all, Arasibhai dug two holes in the floor near the walls, where he wanted to fix the *khambha*, frame poles with the *naraj*, crow-bar.

He dug the holes about 25 cm deep and placed a *khambha*-pole in each. The *khambhas* stood touching the wall and ended in the lathes of the ceiling, but they were not fixed at the top. He took another strong bamboo pole and placed it horizontally under which the arch would be fixed later. These bamboos were tied tightly with a string, and to strengthen the binding, he tied three or four split bamboo pieces over them. These chips were cut to the right length of string or bamboo by measuring with *angala*, finger, and *hath*, ell. Makiai would say: "*Sindari no charek angal no katako le,* take about four finger lengths of thread". Whenever Arasibhai had to fix the bamboo strips over the arch he had to climb down the ladder to tie the other side. Soon the space between the lintel beam and the ceiling was filled with the strips. Under this he had to fix the arch.

4. 5. Fixing the arch

This was the arched bamboo which had lain in the water-pond for one night. Makiai gave careful instructions on the exact bend of the curve, where exactly to fix it, and what string to use and so on. Having done this, Arasibhai tied a vertical piece of bamboo at the top in the centre of the arch. Now he commenced the work of filling up the two spaces between the two ends of the arch, and the *khambhas,* with small bamboo strips. When this was completed, Arasibhai came down the ladder. Immediately Makiai rushed up and pushed some more strips on the top of the arch. Makiai gave two special instructions to her son: (1) Not to use thick bamboo strips, because if the surface of the frame-work became uneven, she would have to use more clay mixture to fill up the background properly, and as it was, they were rather short of bamboo strips. -(2) Where long strips were lacking, the short strips should be tied together with a string and made use of. Though some of the bamboos seemed useless, they managed to finish the work. Then she looked the whole thing over, discovered a gap, and inserted two small strips vertically on the two sides of the arch.

4. 6. Undercoating the arch

On this occasion Puriben, wife of Makiai's elder son Lilabhai, came to help. She brought the ready mixture inside from the court yard, while keeping a watch on the children. The mixture in the clay underwent *kahanavu,* kneading with her fingers, again. She made small handy clay balls with a diameter of about 17 cm which could easily be passed on to Makiai. Whenever Makiai wanted one, Puriben gave her one the size and quality asked for by the old lady. Makiai herself plastered the arch with the clay mixture and applied an undercoating for further work. By her side she had the *tapeli,* aluminium pot, filled with water. Before applying the mixture she would touch the portion of the bamboo in order to calculate the amount of water and clay that would be needed. The first thing that she did was to sprinkle water on that part. Her method was to hold the water in the crook of her fingers and splash it on that part. Then she took up the lump of clay handed by Puriben and kept near her, and applied it to the marked part with her right hand. She continued stretching the flattening lumps upwards on the bamboo arch. Her other hand moved parallel to the right hand to catch pieces of the lumps which had not stuck to the ground surface, but seldom did such lumps fall on the floor, which were collected by Puriben to be used again. If any portion of the lump was found to be a little dry, Makiai patted it with some water or dipped the whole lump into the water and kneaded it again. She was rather anxious to make the ground even with a smooth surface, so that the bamboo ground would reach the depth.

Makiai commenced her work from the right hand bottom corner, and little by little went up to the centre of the arch; then she commenced with the left side, until she again reached the top of the arch. She completed the central part of the arch; then carefully passed her hand over the whole coating. Now she commenced applying the clay mixture to the arched bamboo beam itself. The arch was neither high nor low for her to reach with, while standing on the floor. An other difficulty was that she had to look upwards while working, and whatever clay would fall fell directly on her. The moment she applied it, it fell off, even though she tried to retain it in position by holding it up with her other hand for sometime. Any way, she finally managed to complete it. The difficulty lay also in its being a rounded shape and jutting out of the wall. For this the clay mixture had to be kneaded again and again to get it properly wet for the purpose of sticking it. When the wall facing the main room was completed Makiai took the ladder to the side of the kitchen to plaster the other side of the arch from there. Here again she encountered two difficulties. (1) The kitchen being dark, she could not clearly see the other side. (2) She had to apply the clay mixture gently to prevent it from falling down while she tapped the clay from the other side.

For filling up the gaps that remained after the work had been completed, Makiai stood on the ladder and had to keep the pot and clay mixture on a step of the ladder for easy reach. She had to stretch herself appreciably in order to reach some of the hollows. Makiai stretched herself to the top on the far side; erect, balancing her body on the soles of her feet; again she bent her knees and commenced her movements far and near in this inconvenient sitting posture; she bent downwards to reach some of the lowest parts on the panel. The sight was pleasing to the eyes as this lady, dressed in her dark red clothes worked with the matching ochre coloured clay. It was not her habit to converse while working, unless it was urgent or she wished to convey some pressing thing which she had remembered. However, she conversed a little with me:

Once there was a man named Lakho. Lakho had daily to go to Porbandar for his job: this meant 13 miles to and 13 miles from the job, totalling 26 miles a day. He was paid one anna a day. His work was to carry a sack full of grass on his shoulder. It was so overloaded that Lakho had to be very careful not to drop any. His master's threat was, if he let fall any, he would be relieved of his job. One anna was sufficient in those days, as one could buy a pound of dates for one paisa, while the three were used for buying grain. Twenty six years ago, female labourers were paid six paisa, while the men received ten paisa. I myself had worked for six paisa doing clay work, painting, and such other works.

What she meant to convey was, that life was economically cheaper and easier in those earlier days.

During the work, she continued to instruct her daughter-in-law Puriben regarding the clay mixture. She said:

Khahane ne pindo vali e bapa, my dear, you should first knead and then make the mud balls.
Kunu kunu makhan jevun banavavu, go on kneading until the clay becomes as soft and smooth as butter.
Bhenhe bhenhe ne lapetavu, press it hard with the bottom part of your palm until it becomes soft and smooth and the use it.
Hetho nakhe ne kahanje nahi to fanh lagi jay. Don't knead in the basket, take the clay on the floor and then knead it, otherwise you may be hurt by a thorn.
Khapatyu mathe tanka daun chhu jem daktar tanka de tem, I am stitching up the bamboo strips as a doctor stiches after the operation.

4. 7. Coating the vertical panel and the arch

The second clay mixture was brought into the house in baskets and again kneaded and formed into lumps. This was done by both, Puriben and Makiai, according to convenience. First Makiai commenced her work on the *toda,* vertical panel, on the side of the arch against the wall. As the wall had already undergone a coating, Makiai could apply this second mixture easily. She started her work by scraping the wall gently with the sickle to make the surface a little rough. Then she splashed water over the place, and applied one lump of the clay mixture. She rubbed it very carefully on the wall. The panel was about 38 cm broad and its coating was about 1.5 cm thick. She worked her way upwards taking very great care to keep it straight and this she did without any measuring instrument. She made use of her hand to span the space to the right breadth. Having coated the *toda,* vertical panel, she applied a thin layer of the yellow mixture to the *tak,* arch, the under-coating of which had already dried a little. This time the clay mixture was quite wet so that her hands moved smoothly over the arch while plastering it. The mixture was sucked by the ground-surface, so that it became light and soft after drying. When Makiai finished coating the *tak,* arch, she commenced working on the *panihara,* water place. She moistened the stone and then began applying the clay mixture to it; while doing this Makiai informed me:

Pani chhante to gar behe jay, the splashing of water is good for setting the mixture. Pani bhunhe to gar havali thay, the splashing of water smoothens the mixture.

4.8. Forming reliefs

Makiai had no need of any assistance for the shaping of reliefs on the different under-coatings.

The *naksi no garo,* clay mixture for the ornamentation, had already been prepared and she brought it in a pot. She placed this and an aluminium pot with some water in it near her for the convenience of working. She started with the *toda,* vertical panel. She sat slightly to the left and not directly opposite to the panel. With the crook of her fingers she splashed water on the under-coating. She began at the bottom making three horizontal parallel lines each at a distance of two fingers from another, tracing them from the right to the left. She made use of her fingers and hands for the required measurements. She took little lumps of clay in her right hand and stuck them on to the panel, while with her left hand she made the desired shapes. She made use of both her hands in forming the relief motifs. She used her left hand for the left side and her right hand for the right side. She made particular use of her thumbs and forefingers.

Sitting on the left, she stuck some clay mixture to the bottom right hand corner and began pinching the clay mixture between her thumbs and forefingers and stretching it out with the other hand. Dipping her fingers in water, she smoothened out the rough surface, and wherever the line appeared to be crooked, she straightened and smoothened it. She made three such parallel lines at a distance of two horizontal fingers. This ornament is called *hal,* stalk.

68

On the bottom most line she made a border motif of *dolana,* flat circular knob pendants hanging by a small line. This was done by sticking the clay mixture on the under coating, and then pressing on the two sides with the forefingers of the two hands, and the thumb was used to smoothen the surface.

On the top, that is the third line, she made *nana tak,* miniature arches, and *toda,* a vertical curvilinear stiff motif, similar to the *toda,* anklet worn by the women. She made two such arcatures, side by side on the same line, leaving some space on either side and in between for the floral motif. These were recessed *taks,* the inner one parallel to the outer. In the space on either side and in between the pair of arcatures she stuck round knobs of clay. As before, she pressed these with the two fingers of her two hands for the desired shape, and wetting her fingers and thumbs she patted and smoothened the reliefs. She took some clay mixture, worked upwards on the middle knob from a narrow stalk broadening upwards to hold the flower.

69, 70

She dug her fingers into the bottom knob between the pair of tiny arches and moved her fingers to give a three-legged support to the stalk of the flower. On the two sides of the archlets, she made curved stalks slightly parallel to the arch curves, and these stalks ended a little above and slightly on one side of the archlets. Here she stuck two knobs of the clay-mixture, one on each side. A little lower between these two knobs, she put a third clay knob. She dug her fingers into these and moved them in one direction, making a spetifolious floral motif. She continued these motifs right upto the top of the panel at a distance of about 30 cm or more between each motif, except for the pendant flat knobs which she made only at the bottom-most line as a braid.

71

She then proceeded to decorate the *panihara,* a rectangular niche in the wall for water pots. She deposited the pots of the clay mixture and water on the stone shelf on the top of the pillars, and stood in front of it. She divided the right jamb into two parts by splashing water, and by applying short bulges of clay and stretching them to form a *hal,* line, from top to bottom. She shaped these bulges with her thumbs and forefingers. On the outer side she formed *vankias,* oblique lines in the same way as she had formed the *hal.* On the left-inner side she formed *badamiyas,* almonds, that is a vertical line of squares with convex sides. For this motif she pressed the lump of clay mixture on the ground surface and pinched it from the sides while using both her thumbs and forefingers. However, she pressed the first four *badamiyas* with her thumb to get a hollow shape; afterwards she gave it up commenting, *"dhul gari jahe*, dust will collect (and it will be difficult to keep it clean)"*. When complete she smoothened all the motifs by gliding her finger tips over them. She did the same with the left jamb, using the ladder for the lintel on the *panihara*, water place. Sometimes she had to stand with one foot on the ladder in order to reach the lintel, while the other one found support somewhere in the niche. The next motif was a *ful*, flower, with eight petals. First she fixed a large round lump of clay with a diameter of about 6 cm on the ground surface, shaped it round, and glided over it with the wet palm of her hand. Then she took a small bamboo stick from the floor, probably a stick from the broom. This she inserted horizontally and in this way divided the round lump of clay into eight sectors. With her thumb and forefinger, she shaped and smoothened each petal. After this was prepared, she fixed a small dot in the centre of the flower. The distance between the two flowers was measured by a span horizontally. In the space between the flowers she made irregular leaflike shapes to give the effect of a *vel*, creeper plant. She did not make any design on the bottom shelf, because water would overrun the clay.

The *tak*, arch, by this time being dry and strong, Makiai placed her ladder against it. On both the sides of the *tak*, arch, she made flower motifs. She began to make a pair of *vankia ful*, oblique flowers, of quite a large size, the diameter of each being about 35 cm; underneath this she made a pair of round flowers, *gol ful*, of the ordinary size with petals. She stood high up on the ladder and took quite a long time in the making of her first large flower motif. First, she fixed the round lump of clay as usual and began shaping the *hal*, lines, into petal shape. Suddenly I heard her exclaim:

Ah, I've got it. *Haiya ni ukalate avadi jay,* one learns by the unfolding of the heart.

I inferred therefrom that she had been slightly doubtful about the shape of the flower at first.

Makiai made relief forms on *kandhi*, the horizontal panel over the arch, similar to those she had made on the *toda*, vertical panel. When making *hal*, line, she had to stand on the ladder and stretch herself to reach the parts of two small *taks*, arch units. Underneath these she made the *dolana*, triangles with concave sides.

4. 9. Application of the chalk layer

Khadi, chalk, Makiai informed me, comes from the following places: Adityana, a village near Probandar with stone mines, from slopes near Palakhda, a village near Ratadi, from Bakharla about fifteen km from Ratadi. Earth from these places, she said, was sticky, soft, and white; applied to the walls, it made the designs clear and bright. Makiai applied this white-wash five days after the clay-reliefs had dried completely. This *khadi*, chalk, had been brought by Makiai from Bakharla. She instructed Tamuben, her younger daughter-in-law, to mix the lumps of chalk with the water in a *tapeli*, aluminium pot, and stir the milky liquid. Pebbles were removed. When this chalk had dissolved, Tamuben strained it into another pot through a piece of cloth. This clear liquid was now applied to the wall by means of a small cloth. Tamuben started at the top working downwards. Sometimes the liquid overflowed and Makiai instructed her to work more slowly and use less whitewash.

IV. 5. Architectural fixtures, furniture and implements from clay

The following gives a short outline of the typical clayfixtures and furniture of households in Ratadi. Walls and floors of houses are coated with a clay-mixture consisting of clay or mud, buffalo or cow dung and water. Sometimes the women of one lane assemble and make collectively a clay mixture and later on each one takes away the portion needed by herself. Though this work is done during leisure hours, it seems somehow to continue regularly. Everyday the floor of the house is swept, sprinkled with water and repaired with cowdung and clay if necessary.

clay mixture for coating	*garo*

5. 1. Architectural fixtures from clay

The arch
The kitchen is separated from the main room by a step and the arch. The arch is constructed from bamboo strips and beams, knotted together with jute string and plastered with clay. The facade to the main room is often decorated with clay ornaments or large open-work-holes. The entire surface is whitewashed with a chalk solution.

arch	*tak*

In Ratadi there are only very few specimens of arches to be seen; each of the houses of Makiai's sons is decorated with an arch and the house of Nathabhai Becharbhai as well. The main purpose in the construction of an arch, is to protect the main room from smoke, which is to disappear in the kitchen through a gap in the roof. Another reason was mentioned by a woman in Ratadi, saying that the arch gives her a kind of privacy when sitting in the kitchen.

The panels
In the main room next to the arch long panels of clay decorated with small arches, niches and flat relief work may be fixed at the walls. They are whitewashed.   74

vertical clay panel	*toda*
horizontal clay panel	*kandhi*
deep, nichelike reliefwork	*ubha*
flat relief work	*betha*

Each vertical panel consisted of about ten vertical sections, mainly decorated with arches or arcades and a triangular top. Its special place in a house is either on the left or right side of the kitchen, while the horizontal panel could be fixed at any wall. Formerly, these panels were of quite some depth and were used as receptacles for spoons, nails, clothes, small vessels etc. However, nowadays they became more or less decorative wall panels. Two reasons for this change were mentioned in Ratadi : flat panels are less difficult to make, and ready made wooden shelves are easily available on the market and are fixed without any difficulty.

The large niche
The rectangular recess on the inside of the front wall is bordered by stone slabs. On top of   78, 79
these sometimes clay ornaments are applied.

niche	*panihara*

The wall ledge
A projecting stone in the wall can be plastered with clay and ornamented with moulds and relief work.

ledge for placing a lamp	*diveliu*

Generally there are two places in the house on which lamps are kept, one at the arch between kitchen and main room, and the second between the cattle shed and and the main room.

5. 2. Furniture from clay

The granary receptacles   72, 75, 92, 93

These receptacles are cylindrical in shape, some of them narrowing at the top. However, cubical ones with a square diameter can be seen as well. Usually they are about three metres high and 130 cm in diameter; their outside is whitewashed in the upper part, whereas the lower half may be yellowish.

large receptacle for grain	*kothla*
small receptacle for grain	*kothli*

These granaries are standing opposite to the main entrance next to the back window, at the place where the cattle yard is separated from the living quarters. They usually have a small opening at the bottom. Whenever grain is wanted, it is taken out from this small opening which can be closed again by a mixture of cow dung and clay. Sometimes the large granary has an ornamented edge on the top or circular mouldings. In Ratadi, sand is arranged at the bottom within the granary, on top of a stone-slab, to keep the grain safe from insects and pests. The owners of these receptacles say that they can store about a hundred maunds of grain.

The receptacle for pulses
The smaller rectangular receptacles of clay usually have a small opening. Their top-opening is made air tight by fastening the lid with a clay-dung paste.

small receptacle	*kothi*

These receptacles are used for storing pulses such as *mung, math* and seasonal seeds. Before storing the grain, precautions are taken to prevent it from getting spoiled. Usually a cloth serves to separate two kinds of grain from getting mixed.

The larder
The larder consists of a large square box standing on six feet. All the walls and the feet are   76, 77
plastered with clay. At the front in the centre is a small opening through which articles are put and which can be closed by a swinging wooden door. The feet are decorated with mouldings and often connected by arches. The inside bottom has often six big and a small depression or hollows. Clay reliefs are moulded on the frontside.

larder	*hanjaria*

The larder is a receptacle for utensils containing milk, curds, purified butter, butter etc. Often there is a tiny pot, as well, for coins amounting to about one anna. On top of the larder, matresses and quilts can be piled up. These larders are not to be found in Mer houses, however, they still serve the poor people of the Harijan community.

The finest example is to be found in the house of Vahaliben. The owner made the following remarks when showing the larder:

I made it years ago. We still use it. We shall die but it will survive. We have to make a strong door. Otherwise the cat will get in. The decorations consist of elephants, sunflowers, a mango tree, a boy, sun, moon etc.

.53. Implements from clay

The hand mill box

There are some handmills with clay boxes. They have sturdy walls and four legs. The constructional details are similar to mills with wooden boxes (vide vi.6.2.).

hand mill box	*thalun* or *thala*

The cooking stove

Some of the cooking stoves are made by the women themselves, some are bought from the local potter (vide viii.6.6.).

cooking stove	*chula*

V. Wall painting

by Haku Shah

V.1. The painter

The walls of houses are still being painted by the women of Ratadi on festive occasions such as the celebration of a wedding, the birth of a son, his registration in the genealogical book etc. It holds as important a place as preparing food for the occasion, the selection and ordering of the bridal trousseau or the ornaments.

1.1. The role of the painter

No special occasion is complete without a wall painting. Consequently the wall-painters are highly respected by the house-holders who have invited them. These wall-painters, are considered members of the family, so long as they are on the job. They are not treated as paid professionals or detached outsiders; they are given every assistance they need by the members of the family, who now and then come out to praise the work. The other women of the village also come to render help in their leisure hours. These skilled painters are paid by the house-holders either in cash or in kind, according to their convenience, and the artists gladly accept whatever is given to them.

1.2. The informant

The most popular wall-painter in the village of Ratadi is Makiai, an old woman of about fifty five (vide iv.1.) For more than thirty years, she has in addition to her own household chores, devoted herself to wall painting. The second woman, equally esteemed is Puriai. On our visit to Ratadi, we saw many of Makiai's paintings, but most of them had faded; a good one was that at the house of the *sarpanch,* the headman of the village.   92

Once I had the opportunity of seeing Makiai actually at work at a the house of Jehabhai, a   86
leading villager who was celebrating the wedding of both his sons. She commenced with the outer walls with the assistance of a few women. As Makiai drew the outlines of the designs with a steady hand, the other women put in the requisite colours.

V. 2. The tools

The following are the tools which were used by Makiai when painting a house-wall:

Aluminium pot, *tapeli*
A cylindrical aluminium pot with the top edge curved outwards is generally used to boil water for mixing it with *khadi,* chalk.

Bell-metal dish, *kansa ni thali*
A flat dish with an edge curved vertically inwards is used as a tray for holding the powder colours wrapped in papers.

Small brass bowl, *vadko*
The bowl with a flat bottom is used to hold the liquid colours.

Brass saucer, *rakabi*
The flat saucer is used as a palette.

Chair, *sangamachi*
On this low wooden chair with a seat of cotton tape, a wooden back and carved legs, Makiai sits when painting the lower portion of the wall.

Twig from a date palm, *khajuri ni dali*
The small fresh twig with the size of an ordinary pencil is smashed at one end to form a brush.

Piece of cloth, *chitharun*
This rag is used for wiping the hands during and after the painting, and for mopping the ground if the colour has run over or drops have fallen.

String, *dori*
With the string dipped in colour lines are marked out.

V. 3. The painting materials

Water, *pani*
Water is used to mix the colours and to wash hands.

Colours, *rang*
Pigments of blue, red and yellow colours are brought in the form of powder from the market in Porbandar. They are cheap in price and wrapped in small pieces of newspaper. -Formerly, pure turmeric powder was used for yellow; *geru,* red was obtained from clay; *kanku,* red from turmetric; blue from the juice of *dhatura,* a white thorny flower; green from the juice of the *gholi*-plant, and black from the burnt and powdered coconut shell or the ashes of a cactus.

V. 4. The working techniques

4. 1. Place of work and working conditions

Makiai while working on clay, had often expressed her desire to show me her painting from start to finish, "Oh, how I would like to show you how I paint", she would exclaim. She decided to paint the wall on the right of the entrance door of her own house. This part of the house was occupied by her elder son, Lilabhai. As the outer wall on the right side of the door was part of the verandah, it had plenty of sunshine and Makiai experienced no diffculty with the lighting.

As Makiai worked, visitors came and went, but none disturbed her. The village children gathered round her to watch her working, but she was not disturbed by anybody. There were, however, a woman and her daughter-in-law who came from the neighbourhood specially to offer help to Makiai if she needed any.

4.2. Working procedure

Makiai commenced her work by dusting and smoothening the surface of the wall. The wall had a number of hollow parts and holes in it. Makiai filled these up with a mixture of cow dung and clay, and after one or two hours, when they were dry, she applied a smooth coating of this mixture to the wall where she was to paint. When the mixture was dry, Makiai white-washed the wall using a mixture of chalk and water. She applied this coating with a piece of a rag, which she dipped into the *khadi,* chalk mixture. She had to be careful to coat the wall to the required thickness; if too thick, patches of the coated plaster might drop off; if too thin, the cow-dung and the colour would mix together and that would not make a clean priming. Having applied the *khadi,* chalk, she left it to dry.

The wall having dried perfectly, Makiai took a piece of string longer than the breadth of the space she was to paint.

She dipped the string in a pot of blue paint. She held one end of the string between her forefinger and thumb, and gave the other end to her grand daughter to hold. Then simultaneously they held it horizontally against the wall to make a slight impression. Makiai then pinched the string from the centre with the forefinger and thumb of her other hand, and pulled it away quickly from the wall. The two halves of the string moved in a straight line as Makiai pulled it, leaving a blue line on the wall.

Then she drew in the same way two other parallel lines above this one, leaving a little space in between them; leaving a wider space she drew three other lines in the same way and with the same distance between them. She drew five other such outlines, but the intervening space was between two lines only. These spaces were made in accordance with the sizes and the shapes of the motifs she wanted. Thus the whole painting was pre-planned in her mind. For instance, for the direction of the small geometrical figures called *vankia,* crooked or bent, she left a narrower space that for than of the *ful,* flower, or for the broad braid to be drawn at the two ends.

She commenced her work with her home-made brush, and a cup with *gali,* indigo-blue colour in it. She began from the bottom row and moved upwards to each of the horizontal rows. The motif she drew on the bottom row was a horizontally running scroll. She painted the space between the bottom line and the scroll in indigo blue. In the two rows made by the border lines above the running scroll, Makiai drew six vertical lines thus making fourteen squares altogether, seven in the top row and seven in the bottom. She made a chessboard design by colouring the two alternating squares in blue, both at the top and the bottom. She left the rest of the space untouched to be filled up later on.

On the next row above, Makiai drew a *chopat* that is she drew squares and diagonals and also crosses in them. Then she commenced her next motif. She placed *vankia,* fish bone lines between the two parallel lines closest to each other. The top row was also filled up with the fish bone design. The inner space, flanked by these fish bone borders, was filled with a row of *badamda,* almond, rhombs. In the row above, she drew four flowers with eight symmetrical curved lines on each of the petals, and filled up the space between the petal and the curved line with leaves, thus drawing eight leaves on the top of each petal. These flowers were joined by a curved line running from the top of one flower to the bottom of the next and so on. Then Makiai left the two intervening rows and, leaving some space, she drew battlements, and on each of these battlements she drew a flower called *barasa vel*, twelve month creeper; under the battlement she drew a *pan vel*, leaf creeper, which contained a number of leaves. These leaves were longer on the double curved line. When she had finished the whole of the *pan vel*, leaf creeper, Makiai returned to the *barasa vel*, floral creeper, and completed her design by drawing flowers, and in between these flowers, a little higher, she drew little *chakali*, sparrows.

At the left end of the row, Makiai had kept a big blank space. Now she filled up the blank by drawing a large flower, on the top of which she drew *vinzano*, fan. Having completed the top, she returned to the incomplete chess-board design and finalised the chess-board.

Having finished the drawings, she began to paint them. She had five colours which she put in five open bowls of different sizes. The largest bowl contained the indigo blue powder, because this was the colour she used most. This bowl she kept at her left hand while the others were on her right. She poured water into each of these bowls while stirring the mixture of water and powder until she obtained the required thickness. She held the middle of the handle of the brush between her thumb and forefinger. She could easily handle her brush, horizontally and vertically for her upward and downward strokes, at both acute and obtuse angles. She held the brush carefully to prevent colour running down the wall or her elbow. In her left hand she held the bowl containing the liquid colour so that she could easily dip her brush into the bowl. As the bowl was light in weight, she could carry it right up to the brush in her hand, and could even smoothen out the bristles of the brush by rubbing them against the edge of the bowl. If a few drops did fall off from the brush, they safely fell into the bowl.

Makiai never made an experiment on this occassion; every line was final with her, and it had to be so, because of the difficulty in rubbing out a mistake or a stain on the mud wall. Thus not a single line remained unused.

Makiai painted the entire outline in blue and then started to fill up the gaps with different colours. When the blue mixture was exhausted, Makiai took up the red paint, leaving designs for yellow and green. When these were done, Makiaai left untouched some parts in the running scroll and the flowers which remained white. Thus white was considered an extra colour with the five others.

Makiai finally drew the motif of the sun. She did not use colour for the round outline, but merely placed a number of dots on it.

The work was over; Makiai washed her hands. The time taken from the start to finish for a design of 1.70 metres on the verandah wall was twelve hours distributed between three days.

V. 5. Sites for paintings

All the Ratadi paintings may be seen on house-walls and on clay articles. The plaster of the facade is usually divided horizontally into two parts. The upper, the major portion is white, and the lower portion or the narrow one is ocherish yellow or redish. The same uniform colouring is to be found inside, on the walls of the houses and on the *kothla*, clay jars.

In addition to these, uniform plain colour walls, paintings are to be found both inside and 92, 155 outside the houses. The paintings are mostly large strips of colour on both sides of the entrance to the house and also on *kothla*, the storage jar. A square decoration depicting an embroidered hanger like the *chakla*, may occasionally be seen. Some times a painting may be done on top of a doorframe and may be continued on both sides of the door extending to the walls; various coloured motifs may also be on the arch, the entrance to the kitchen, on the vertical panels extending from the arch to the floor, at the *panihara*, niche for a keeping water pots, and on the *kothla*, clay jar.

Wall paintings are most common in the Harijan houses. A painted *toran* is a horizontal 90, 91 garlandlike design drawn over the door. The *gokhala*, stone niche, is also surrounded by painted designs. On the wall opposite to the entrance a place called *chauri*, the square enclosure in which the bride and bridegroom are married is also painted.

This painting depicts a richly decorated *shamiana*, which is a square plot with four pillars 89 at the corners supporting a decorated piece of cloth. In such a *chauri* or *shamiana*, sit the bride and bridegroom for the marriage ceremony. Its pillars are decorated with motifs such as flags, pots, flowers and triangles. In the middle of the painting, the imprint of the palm and the fingers of the right hand of the bride are depicted. It is the custom for the bride when leaving her parental home to leave an imprint of her hand after dipping it in *kanku*, a turmeric mixture. In the left hand corner of the frame, one usually finds the word 'om'. Sometimes in the centre of the blank space the marriage date is written. The elephant god *Ganesha*, is worshipped before and after the marriage ceremony by the bride and the bridegroom; he is also drawn on the wall.

V.6. Ornamental designs and motifs

The following ornamental designs ore common in Ratadi :

adadiya, small slices of sweets made from black *adad*-grains
It is similar to a chess board design with small blue squares alternating with white ones.

khajurio, date palm
It looks like a palm leaf. Two straight lines join at an angle forming a fish-bone pattern. The angle is about 60° and therefore its other name is *vankia*, bent.

badamda, almond nut
This is a band of equal rhombus each touching the corner of the other. They are bordered by straight parallel lines.

chopat, game board
It looks like the board, forming a cross out of many triangles which are alternately coloured dark and light (vide xi.2.2.).

jhul, running scroll
This curvilinear horizontal meandering appears often in applique textile work as well.

ful, flower
Eight rhombus are connected at a central point; small spirals or halfmoon designs are drawn at the corner of each.

ful vel, creeper with flowers
Flowers are drawn with curved lines connecting each one from its top with the bottom
of the next.

pan vel, creeper with leaves
From a curved wave-like horizontal line leaves emerge at regular intervals. The upper leaves
are longer than the lower ones. Every fourth leaf is replaced by a small flower on a twig.

barasa vel ane kangra, creeper and a spire
A triangle is shooting upwards like a bud bud from two petals from either side, the left dark
coloured and the righ one light. On top of the bud a small flower called the *kangra* is drawn.

chakali, sparrow
The sparrow is depicted in its profile. The wing is shown spread out.

vinzano, fan
The handle of the fan is usually horizontal. The fan is in the shape of a three-fourth of a circle,
the edge being attached to the handle.

surya, sun
In the circle of the sun may be seen two eyes, a nose, a large moustache and a mouth. The
gaps are filled with dots. Around the circumference small rhombus are drawn.

hukkavalo manas, man smoking a waterpipe
The man is standing, his face in profile. He is smoking a waterpipe.

VI. Wood working

by Eberhard Fischer

VI. 1. The carpenter

1.1. The informants

In the village of Ratadi only one family does carpentry work, an old man with his wife,
and four of his seven sons with their families. By caste they are potters, *Kumbhar*. However,
they claim that they gave up their original craft some generations ago. They now
call themselves *Kumbhar-Suthar*, as opposed to the real carpenters, the *Vansh-Suthar*. Marriage
partners, though are still selected from the *Kumbhar* caste only.
The carpenter Mohan tells the following story:

// None of us is working as a potter, we are all carpenters. Actually my forefathers were farmers and not
potters. Ten generations ago, we abandoned the craft (of pottery). Nobody remembers when that happened. My
father's brother's sons are still farmers. They live in Shrinagar (a *brahmin* village near Ratadi.) When
my father and one of his brothers went to Africa (Uganda), the brother who remained in Shrinagar was told:
"You will farm this land and it will be yours". First my father worked at the workshop of Vasram
in Shrinagar. Vasram was a *Vansh-Suthar,* carpenter, but he went to Africa with his whole family.
Formerly they were the carpenters of Shrinagar. When my father returned from Africa we settled
independently and my father resumed work with Vasram.
// My father learnt the craft from Vasram. At first he went to Vasram as an apprentice to learn
carpentry, but later on, after returning from Africa he joined him and was paid for his labour. After some
time, however, my father settled here in Ratadi.

Kimabhai, the father of the carpenters working in Ratadi today, was the first one of the
family to take up carpentry mainly in order to develop some skill in a craft that could earn
him a living in Uganda. He told us that he had worked there together with his brother in a
small door-factory. But he returned after some time when his brother fell ill and took up
work once more in his former master's workshop, most probably for the purpose of
regaining his skill in making farming implements. He later moved to nearby Ratadi and
settled there with his sons as the village carpenter since Moraji, the former village
carpenter, had emigrated to Africa as well.
The old father is still working, although his eyes are now very weak. More exacting
orders he passes over to his sons, three of whom have their own workshops in Ratadi.
Another one goes to work at Porbandar or is employed off and on in the workshops of his
younger brothers. Of the remaining three, one works as a mason and does rough
carpentry jobs, while the others have their own workshops at Jamnagar. One of the three
village carpenters sometimes goes for a season to work in his brothers' workshops there.
All the grandchildren of the old carpenter are learning the craft. Two of the brothers who are
permanently in Ratadi are training their nephews, since their own children are still too young.

All the carpenters live near their workshops on the outskirts of the village. The father
lives with two of his sons in the southern part inhabited by the *Rabari,* shepherds and the
other two sons in the east at the entrance to the village where the barber, the tailors and
the merchants live.

The carpenters are independent of each other. Each one has his own workshop and his own set of tools. However, they generously lend out the tools among themselves. Each uses his own materials and has his own clientele.

To our inquiries Malde answered:

// Our father comes to our shops, but we, his sons, are all independent of him. My father stays with his third son, with the *Khadia*, mason. However, whenever our father has not enough tools for his business, he comes to my workshop and takes whatever he needs.
// Each of us brothers buys the timber he needs in Porbandar.
// Last winter, when we went to buy wood in Porbandar, two of us brothers, Danjibhai and myself, were together examining one log. Danjibhai said: "That piece is not to be selected"-but at that moment I was out of the compound. When I came back I bought the same log which Danjibhai had refused and which proved one rupee cheaper. After sawing, the wooden pieces which came out were the same as usual. Thus our ideas differ and we do not buy the wood together.

If one of the brothers has more work than he can cope with at a time and another brother is free, he transfers part of the work to him and they share the profit. Such agreements are arrived at especially when carpenters have neighbouring workshops.

1.2. The role of the carpenter

Carpentry is a man's work which requires not only skilful craftsmanship but also a fair amount of physical strength and perseverance. Women never help in this kind of work. If a carpenter needs help, he will engage a *sikaru,* apprentice, who addresses his master as *kaka,* paternal uncle. He is usually a close relative, a nephew or a younger cousin, and is called by his first name. In some instances the apprentice is trained in his own father's workshop.

There is no definite method of training in a term of apprenticeship, nor is there any fixed duration for it. I have had the opportunity to observe how a boy of about ten spent his first days in a carpenter's workshop. First of all he punched small circles out of a tin sheet, which were later nailed on a chest as decoration. This he did several hours at a stretch for some days. Later the boy was told to punch out with the edge of a chisel all the plain surfaces of animal reliefs on a lintel-board. The master showed him how to do it and then returned to his work outside the workshop. Since the little fellow worked clumsily, the older apprentice came to his help and guided his hand with the chisel. He also dealt the hammer blows on the chisel edge. Later he left the boy to himself. The child continued to wield both tools with great awkwardness. However, he first faithfully finished the piece of work given to him and then started to play with one of his master's children. An older and more experienced apprentice is able to carry out repair work independently and is given more responsible jobs. He must also help in the house. Even if he does not fetch water or does the washing regularly, his master has the right to assign to him any task he wishes.

The learning procedure consists in repeating a task until it can be proficiently performed before undertaking a new one. The apprentice starts with simple work and then gradually takes over jobs which require more technical knowledge and training. Throughout the term of apprenticeship, the master closely examines the apprentice's work to avoid waste of material, since wood is costly. The apprentice therefore always produces one article or part of an article in many replicas before he is given another kind of work. The master thus has a stock of prefabricated pieces for future use.

Usually each workshop has an apprentice who takes over the simple or rough work. Only the carpenter Mohan in Ratadi thinks that an apprentice would be too expensive for him to maintain because the cost of feeding the boy would exceed the value of the work produced

104

by him. However, when one observes how these small boys, little more than children, are made to work in their master's workshops, one would doubt Mohan's statement.

No special ceremony marks the end of a term of apprenticeship. If a lad feels capable of coping with his job, he will leave his master's workshop and seek employment elsewhere, or he will ask his master for payment in return for his skilled work. Apprentices receive no remuneration but only clothing and food. When an apprentice becomes a master he may open his own workshop and is not dependent on anybody's support or permission for this. Only a short and inexpensive ceremony is involved, which Malde described as follows:

// Actually the ceremony is very simple. We see whether the fixed date is auspicious or not. If it is, we dig the ditch for *ne,* the wooden anvil and we take one *supari*—nut and one silver twenty-five *paisa* coin. Both are put in the ditch and on top of them we fix *ne,* the wooden anvil with the hammer. // For this ceremony we do not gather a crowd. We may break a coconut on the *ne,* wooden anvil and divide it among the children.

According to the carpenters, there are no special rules of any kind to be observed by the carpenter, a member of his family or any person entering the shop. Nevertheless, all the carpenters emphasize their faith in their religious beliefs and their piety. Mohan said:

Before I start my work I think of *Visvakarma* every day.

Malde declares:

In the evening after my meal I go to the temple. Afterwards I continue with my work.

However, there is no temple of *Visvakarma,* the patron god of craftsmen, in the area around Porbandar and even in the small shrines in the houses of the carpenters we only found symbols for *Shiva, Rama, Krishna, Ganesha* and for the Mother-Goddess. Only Mohan has on the wall a gallery of colour prints called "photos of the gods" - one of which depicts *Visvakarma.* Mohan explains the picture as follows:

Visvakarma has in his one hand the book *shilp purana.* This precious book is kept in the Government library and is prohibited to everyone. All the crafts in the entire world are described in this book.

Nowadays the carpenters indicate their profession, that is, the fact of their being craftsmen and not farmers or shepherds, by their dress. This consists of trousers and shirts of white or khaki cloth. On their heads they wear a cap of felt or wool instead of a white turban. Their womenfolk do not wear skirts and veils of red, white and black coloured cloth, as is still the custom among *Mer*-women, but prefer multicoloured printed material. In contrast to the peasant women, they shyly cover their faces with their veils when a stranger approaches.

A farmer in the village of Baradia attempted to define the scope of a carpenter's work by saying:

// The *Suthar,* carpenter, is the craftsman who knows how to use wood.

This is indeed an apt definition, for a carpenter not only makes all the wooden fixtures and utensils for the household, and implements for farming and tools for other craftsmen, but he must be able to repair them as well. He is therefore a combined joiner, wood-carver and general handyman. Furthermore, he must be able to operate the lathe, in order to produce tortile designs on round timber. In addition, he constructs the roof trusses, window frames and doors for a house. A carpenter must also know how to handle metal, since a number of the articles he produces have iron parts fitted into them. He buys the main iron pieces from a *Luhar*-blacksmith. However, small-scale repairs and the joining of wood with iron are his duties. This is why a forge with bellows and a small anvil are to be found in nearly every carpenter's workshop. The carpenter always reserves the early morning, when it is still relatively cool, for any forging work.

The services of the carpenters are engaged on varying terms. They are occasionally hired on a daily basis. Mohan, for instance, charges seven rupees a day. This particular arrangement is resorted to chiefly when the work is to be done in the house of a customer, that is, when a roof truss has to be built or when furniture has to be repaired.

The carpenters work on order as well, charging a fixed sum for each order. If, for example, a carpenter receives an order for a new chest, the date of completion is fixed, details of the design discussed and the purchase price agreed upon. The customer then appears on the day fixed, takes delivery of the article and pays cash for it. The materials required are initially paid for by the carpenter. Important for the carpenters are customers who pay regularly in kind. These are the farmers, whose implements are kept in repair throughout the year by the carpenters. The carpenters agree to maintain *sathi*, a set of farming implements, and will repair them when necessary, receiving in return *hath*, payment in grain. Malde reports in this context:

// The customer pays 32 *palis* of grain for *hath*, out of which 8 *palis bajra*, pearl millet, and 8 *palis juvar*, sorghum millet, are given in the first half of the year, while 16 *palis* of *sinar* millet are given in the second half. // Yes, the farmers pay us twice a year. // I have 18 farmers paying me *hath* every six months. Eleven are from Ratadi. // Danji, my brother, has 18 customers, too. We all have an equal number (18) of farmers who pay us *hath*; most of them live in Ratadi and Baradia.

Bullock carts and household utensils are not included in *sathi*, and all repairs on them must be paid for in cash. It is also usual for the customer himself to provide the wood required for the repair work. It sometimes happens that a carpenter refuses to undertake a piece of repair work which appears to him futile and advises the customer to have a new article made. Should he receive an order for the latter, he is paid in cash. A customer may dispense with the services of his carpenter and hire another one provided he has paid his annual fee. As a rule a farmer will not do so even though he may be aware that another carpenter is more competent. This is because he realizes that the better man has more work than he can cope with and little time to spare for his *hath*-paying customers. In addition, such an action could cause him no little trouble, as the members of the trade are united by bonds of loyalty, however superficial. This is why even today, several years after making themselves independent of each other, the Ratadi carpenters have each the same number of *hath* customers.

For economical reasons, however, some farmers prefer to do minor repair jobs themselves and only summon a carpenter for major ones, for which he is paid in cash.

The prosperity of the Ratadi carpenters varies with each individual, the brother who frequently works at Jamnagar being considered by the others to be better off than themselves. One of the carpenters made the following remark:

// Oh, look at his stock of wood and you will see who is the richest !

1.3. Quality of work

The villagers assess each carpenter according to his skill, the richest one being naturally regarded as the best. This conclusion can probably be drawn from the fact that this carpenter does all the work himself and has no apprentice in his workshop, whereas elsewhere many orders are carried out by the apprentices, a deterioration in quality being an obvious consequence. However, a close examination of work done by one of the masters himself will scarcely distinguish it from that of his apprentice, for all carpenters indulge in an excessive amount of slip-shod work. Rotting wood is used for less conspicuous parts, boards are carelessly joined, nails hammered in crooked and clumsy ornaments made for poorer customers. The carpenters are well able to work carefully, conscientiously and dexterously. However, they are generally so poorly paid for their work that they devote as little time as possible to one order and stint on material as well. They therefore either assign the work to the apprentices or else make a careless job of it in order to complete it quickly and commence with a new order, which is no better paid than the last.

To my question whether a carpenter could recognize work of his hand, Malde answered:

// I think I would recognize my own hand. The designs change from workshop to workshop. The choice of ornaments will differ. Details regarding the inner construction will be found to vary i.e. the size and arrangement of the secret drawers. However, if it is a piece made a long time ago, I might not recognize it.

The "personal stamp" of a carpenter is thus less a matter of individual style than of certain technical features. It must be emphasized that among carpenters designs are handed down from master to apprentice. Malde says:

// I taught Govin this *ghorla*, horse-head, just as I learnt it from my father. // I prepare the same shape. // This is because I use the same technique.

Since a certain procedure of work is mechanically repeated once a principle has been learnt, the carvings of carpenters are stereotyped reproductions of designs passed on from master to apprentice (i.e. petrified designing), the work of master-carpenters, skilled apprentices or beginners being distinguishable as such at the most in respect of minor details or negligible omissions. I do not, therefore, believe that any evidence of a change in style is to be traced in the life's work of any of the Ratadi carpenters. There is no doubt that phases of good work may be found to alternate with phases of inferior, careless work (which may have emotional causes). The development of the personality is, however, not to be gauged in any measure from the style of the work.

Nevertheless, a comparison of pieces of work adorned with figures from different villages cannot fail to reveal appreciable differences in execution and representation, even in the case of simple motifs. From this it is to be deduced that each group of carpenters or workshops has in the course of time evolved a characteristic style to which it adheres. This is partly due to the fact that for decorations involving figures, stencils of metal or wood are used, which may be easily reproduced. Besides, they can be preserved for a very long time in the workshops, during which time the designs, at least in rough outline, are derived from them. The "repertoire" of designs will be found to differ even from workshop to workshop. In Ratadi, for instance, the ornamental motif of a squatting figure, whether monkey or human, has never been used by a local craftsman, whereas in Visavada, the next village but one, this very motif appears to be a popular one. This fact was pointed out to me by the carpenters of Ratadi. A few squatting figures are to be found on the feet of chests, all of which have been brought by brides into Ratadi. Asked about a chest in his house which displayed some tastefully carved ornamentations of this kind, Gigabhai Lakhabhai said:

// The chest was given by my grandmother's brother to our family. This lady was from the village Tukda. // The figures are *vandro*, monkeys.

The carpenter Mohan stated having carved squatting figures on a cradle ordered by a customer from Visavada. But he had never been required to use this motif for a Ratadi customer.

The use of motifs alien to the workshop repertoire is probably the result of copying. There is no special term for this kind of work. It is usual to say *"chevi banavi diyun"*, meaning "reproduce in similar fashion". On being questioned in this context, Mohan replied:

// Certainly, I have often prepared a copy of an old specimen. // The son comes and wants a chest which is like one belonging to his father. // If he pays the full price I will prepare a chest exactly like the old one without changing a single ornament. // Yes, I have done this. // In this village there is no sample.

When a carpenter is given an old broken chest to repair, he cuts out the parts which are intact with the help of a saw and pieces them together to form a smaller chest. He makes no additions of his own except for plain mouldings. There is a chest of this kind made by Mohan in the house of Fograbhai Noghabhai. The wooden articles are often not maintained well, i.e. they are seldom cleaned and even more seldom given a coating of oil. Worn-out implements are mostly left to decay. They lie for sometime in the yard and are subsequently burnt in the kitchen. A last point to be mentioned is that the carpenter Mohan buys old wooden pieces which he sells in the village as *vaparelu*, second-hand articles. The inside door in the house of Karsanbhai Munjibhai was obtained in this way by Mohan. The farmers often buy old-deal goods directly from the people selling them. These are for the most part pieces of furniture sold at reduced prices by families emigrating to Africa.

1.4. The workshop lingo

The terminology of the carpenter affords an additional insight into this profession.

The surface of a piece of timber may be either *lasu*, smooth, or *kharhat*, rough. *Kavar ukade*, a tough grain renders wood difficult to work, since plane and chisel work are inclined to jam. Knots in the wood are known as *dag*, stain or spot.
Thoroughly dry wood is described as *sukai gayela*, fresh wood as *tajo* or *kajo*, immature, unripe

If a part is to be removed from the side of a block of wood, the carpenter ensures that during work the surface is *uped*, slightly convex. Scoring the outlines of ornaments into a board is known as *khasarvu*, the setting-in of punched ornaments or chipcarvings being described as *tocha marvu*.
As a rule, ornaments are arranged symmetrically. The word *chodi*, pair, signifies symmetry.

VI. 2. The tools

With very few exceptions, all the tools described in the following are used in Malde Mistri's workshop. A few examples from Mohan's workshop have been included in order to supplement the list, which is by no means an exhaustive one. It comprises merely the most important, more or less traditional tools used by the carpenter.

2.1 Measuring and Marking Tools

Scribe-awl, *rekh*
This consists of a 7 cm. long steel bar fixed into a wooden handle of the same length. The steel bar tapers to a point.

94

Line-marking cord, *dori*
This is a strong, twisted cord of several strands, about 3 metres long. It is dipped into a vermilion dye, stretched across the wood and brought into contact with the surface across which a line is to be drawn by a light jerk.

Dye container, *gerudi*
This is a hollowed out wooden receptacle in the form of a square box, in which a vermilion
dye made of burnt earth is mixed with water.

Wooden beam-compasses, ('trammel point'), *harjorun*   94
This instrument consists of a hexagonal block of wood, into which an iron spike is driven.
Through a hole drilled slantwise through the block, a one metre long wooden shaft is
fixed by a wedge. The wooden shaft has provision for a stick being fixed at its extremity,
the fibres of which are separated at the end to form a brush. This instrument is used
to describe circles, the brush being dipped into the vermilion dye.

Compasses, *krasi* or *kompas,* (engl. deriv.)   94
This has two straight tapering legs of equal length riveted together at one end. They are
somewhat difficult to adjust.

External calliper   94
These instruments are similar to the common compasses, but have slightly convex legs.

Carpenter's rule   94
This imported steel rule is marked with the inch scale.

Squares, *kathkua*   94
These are imported and are procurable in two sizes, the back square and the try square.

Sliding-bevel   94
This is a type of adjustable square. An iron bar, movable on a pivot is fixed to a rectangular
frame. The iron may either be placed on the wood or fixed into a central slot in the frame.

Gauge-measure, *garmi*   94
A lathe, through one end of which a sharp nail is driven, is wedged into a rectangular wooden
frame. This "gauge" is used to strike and score lines parallel to the edge of the work-block.

Stencils, *khasarun*   94
Designs of figures and ornaments are cut out of rectangular pieces of tin. The inner contours
are joined to the narrow outer border by means of thin cross-pieces. (In the village of Degam
the carpenter uses wooden stencils.)

2.2. Percussion tools

Axe, *kavada*   95
This hatchet possesses a triangular head of a rectangular section sharpened on both sides to
a straight-edged blade. The head is forged to a square socket, into which a straight wooden
shaft is driven to a hand's breadth.

Adze, *vanslo*   95
This consists of a wooden shaft fixed into a square socket transverse to the face of a four-
cornered steel head. The head has a step on its underside and is sharpened on both sides to a
straight-edged blade.

There are three types of chisels, which are available in different sizes: 96

Firmer chisel, *panaru*
The blade is of a narrow rectangular section and tapers to a narrow tang which is fixed
into a cylindrical wooden handle. This handle is usually reinforced by two iron ferrules. The
end of the blade is straight and bevelled at an angle to form a cutting edge.

Mortise chisel, *vindani, sorsi* or *farsi*
This heavy chisel consists of a stout blade rectangular in section. In the smaller type the
thickness of the blade may be greater than its width. The bevel, however, is always ground
at a very short angle. The blades are usually shaped out of worn-out files and resharpened.
They are tanged and fixed into wooden handles.

Gouge, *haklo*
A blade rectangular in section has a flat, square end bent to a curve. It is ground to a cutting
edge on both sides. The particular blade I observed had been fashioned out of a worn-out file
fixed into a wooden shaft.

Planes occur in various designs. All of them, however, bear some resemblance to their
European counterparts. Most of the plane-irons are imported.

Shaving or bench plane, small type *tuko randho,* **large type** *lambo randho*
The stock of the common shaving plane may be of any length. The cutting edges of
the plane-iron are always slightly rounded. A top-iron is often replaced by a simple standing
wedge. The only feature that distinguishes this type from the simple German jack plane
is its frontal handle. A movable lathe is screwed to the stock and serves as a handle for driving
the plane, while a second person holding the wooden edge guides it.

Rabbet plane without fence, *bedariun*
The plane-iron, which tapers on one side, is wedged into the centre of a wooden stock. Its
straight edge is as broad as the stock itself. The outlet for shavings is at the side of the stock.

Rabbet plane with fence, *kani pata*
The plane-iron is centrally inserted into a wooden stock. However, the iron extends to
the edge of the stock only on one side, the stock being lengthened to form a fence on the
other. Here, too, the outlet for shavings is at the side of the stock.

Large moulding plane, *galto*
This plane is similar to a shaving plane, the iron being ground to a wavy edge. The planed
surface corresponds to the shaping of the blade.

Small moulding plane with fence, (bead plane) *bit* **(engl. deriv.) or** *kasariun*
The plane-iron, the edge of which is ground to a point, is inserted laterally in the centre
of a wooden stock. A fence that serves as a guide is fixed to the other side. Shavings emerge
through a slot on one side of the stock.

Fillister plane, *filfil* **(engl. deriv.)**
This is a complicated tool constructed like a European model. It is a rabbet plane with
an adjustable guide.

Saws
Handsaws usually have a wooden handle shaped to a grip at one end of the blade and a
horizontal bar on the other. When both handles are removed the blade can be fitted into
a wooden bow.

97

The serration of the blade is the same as that of a simple pit saw. Blades occur in three different shapes:

Rectangular blade, *karvat*
This stout blade is used to saw standing and squared timber.

Trapezoid blade, *adiyun*
This blade with one edge sloping upwards is chiefly adapted to the sawing of boards.

Blade with waisted edge, *chenitrani*
This blade, which gradually decreases in diameter towards the centre, is mainly suited for the cutting of curves, as it can be freely drawn through without jamming.

Two-section drill, operated either by means of a cord or by a drill-bow, *shiardi*   96
with *dori* or *kamathi*
The drill itself consists of a rectangular bore with a sharp-edged point. It is fixed into a cylindrical wooden drill-stock terminating in a globe on top of which a bowl-shaped handle is fixed.

A large drill is operated by means of a thick cord, wooden handles being knotted to both ends. The cord is wound five to seven times around the drill-stock and rotates the bore when one end is pulled. This drill requires two persons to operate it.
A small drill can be made to spin by means of a drill-bow, the string of which is wound several times around the stock, stretched and drawn backwards and forwards. The straight bow is of a round section with holes at both ends, through which the string is passed and knotted. This drill can be operated by a single person.

       96

Pump drill
Here the simple drill stock is replaced by a broad, heavy fly-wheel and a long shaft. Above the stock a board with a central hole is fixed, from one end of which a thread runs through a hole in the shaft to the other end. When the drill is turned, the string is wound around it. The drill is now made to rotate by pressing down the board. The spinning motion thus produced must be taken advantage of.

2. 3. Impelling tools

       95

Hammer, *hathodi*
A wooden shaft is fixed into the middle of a cylindrical metal head. Imported claw hammers are also used.

Iron bar, *dhan*
This is round in section and is used as a mallet.

       96

Punch, *subo*
This is an iron spike having engraved into one end an ornament such as a circle, a radiated ring or concentric rings.

       95

2. 4. Auxiliary tools and supporting structures

Files and rasps, *adatara, kansas*
These tools are imported. They occur in various shapes, square, triangular, rectangular or   *73*

semicircular and are chiefly used to grind and whet other tools. They are not used in wood-work.

Whetstone, *pathri*

112

The imported, rectangular whetstone lies in a hollowed out wooden box. Water is frequently used in the grinding or whetting process.

Saw buck, *kadamnu bidlo*

Two wooden legs are joined to form a pointed arch. Three equally spaced iron rods are inserted through each of these legs. A beam is laid across the arch and the piece of timber to be sawn passed through the vertex of the arch so as to form a tripod.

Screw clamp

This instrument made from cast-iron is imported.

Pincers, *jambur*

95

This is imported as well, the commonest type being the "Lancashire pattern".

Wooden board, *pavathu*

94

This is a rectangular piece of timber on the narrow side of which a lathe is nailed. Sometimes, though, a block of wood is chipped out to form this supporting board.

Mitre block

94

Two lathes forming a right angle are nailed on a wooden board in such a way as to preserve a space in the mitre formed. This serves as a guide for the saw in cutting mitre joints.

Turning wheel

The rotation of a large manually operated wheel is transmitted to the lathe by means of a cord of cotton, whereby the wood being worked upon is fixed to the lathe by an iron spike.

VI. 3. The timber

Timber is rare in the arid steppes surrounding Porbandar. Straight, firm logs seem to be unknown. All squared timber, logs for straight beams and posts, boards and mouldings are purchased by the village carpenters at Porbandar, where the wood is shipped, chiefly from South Gujarat. After purchasing the timber for cash, they arrange to have it sawn into flat boards, which they then transport by bullock-cart to their villages.

Besides this imported material, which is predominantly heavy hard wood, the timber obtained from the few trees in the neighbourhood is also worked. Trees are, however, planted for the purpose of affording shade and not for their wood. These trees, knotted and twisted by the sharp sea wind, supply wood chiefly used to make farm implements, where strength and resistance to climatic conditions take precedence over regular grain and smoothness. The ornate lintel-boards and door-beams are carved out of pali and kutch wood, whereas the front surfaces of chests adorned by relief work are made of rosewood. This latter wood is highly prized for its dull black sheen, its hardness and durability.

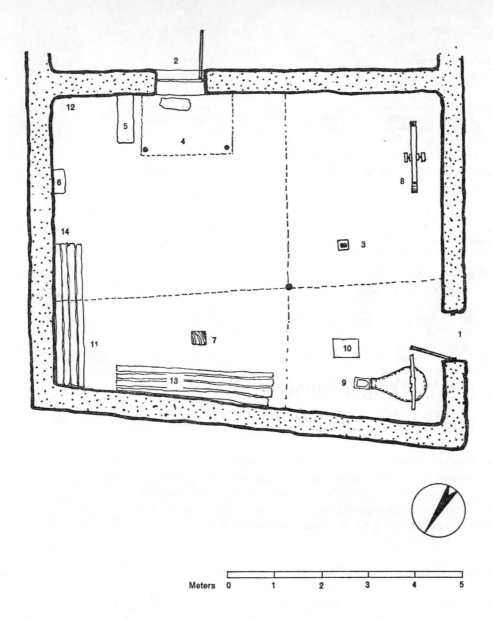

7. Plan of a carpenter's workshop in the village of Ratadi.

1 Entrance to the workshop
2 entrance to the dwelling house
3 roof post
4 shed
5 clay bench
6 small clay bench
7 wooden anvil

8 lathe
9 bellow
10 box for tools
11 table
12,13,14 wood storage
15 roof post

Names of types of wood

General terms used in India	botanical	local
Rosewood	Daibergia species	*sisham*
Kutch	Acacia catechu	*kacho*
Pali	Dichopsis species	*pali*

Wood must be thoroughly dry before it is worked. The drying process takes place
in the workshop of the carpenter and not in the timber-yard of the wholesale dealer. The
carpenter Malde gives the following comments:

// The wooden pieces I use are roughly three to five years old. I use fresh wood only when I am
short of dry wood. // Dry wood becomes hard and is difficult to work, whereas fresh wood is still soft. If you
carve fresh wood, the ornaments will crack. // After all, fresh wood gets cracks when it dries.
This is the reason why I insist on using wood that has already been dried.

VI. 4. The Working techniques

4. 1. Place of work

All work was carried out in Malde's workshop. To begin with, the master
squatted in a roofed over corner of his workshop and prepared the board. Later, he preferred
to work in the open, sun-warmed part of his workshop directly beside the entrance
to the house. While working he squatted on a folded gunny-bag spread on the floor of
plastered clay. On the second day, Malde chose the same spot in the sun to work.

4. 2. Working conditions

Malde worked with quiet concentration in spite of frequent visits from customers, family
members and acquaintances, besides the presence of the author and his interpreter.
When taking an order he noted down details in ink on the palm of his hand without
permitting himself to be detained long, for while at work he laboured without
respite. Malde neither allowed himself to be distracted by his children, nor did he gossip
with his customers. He did not smoke at all and drank tea only once in the course of
the morning. For the piece of completed work, the carpenter was paid a sum fixed on the
previous day. However, he worked on it only while I was present. At the period of our
visit, Malde had many orders to execute. He had enough work to cope with. The
evenings he devoted to other orders.

4. 3. Example 1 : Making a lintel-board

Working schedule
Malde makes the entire lintel-board himself. His apprentice is only once ordered to

whet the chisels. Constructing and decorating the lintel takes ten hours, and the work is distributed over two mornings and an afternoon (25th and 26th January 1966) as follows:

First day

9.40 – 10.00	preparing the board
10.00 – 10.30	marking out the board, spacing the relief-sections, carving the ornamental borders
10.30 – 12.40	carving eight vertical ornamental interstices
	seven minutes were required for the interstice with the triangle motif
	midday interval
14.00 – 17.10	carving five figure reliefs. 53 minutes were required for the piece depicting a peacock.

Second day

9.10 – 10.40	carving the sixth figure relief (the elephant to the immediate right of the centre)
10.40 – 10.47	outlining the figure of Ganesha
10.48 – 11.35	carving out the Ganesha figure in detail (central piece).

Working materials and tools

For the lintel-board Malde uses an unprepared plank of acacia wood which is neither rectangularly sawn nor planed. Its measurements were as follows: length 180 cm, breadth 20 cm, thickness 2.5 cm.

The final measurements of the lintel are: length 145 cm, breadth 18 cm, thickness 2.3 cm.

The following tools are used to prepare the board:
A scribe-awl, one large and one small square, a tenon saw, an adze, a stout firmer chisel, a small shaving plane and a square block of wood as a support.

For the chip-carving ornaments and for carving the reliefs the carpenter uses the following tools:
A scribe-awl, 3 metal stencils, a small squares, a gauge-measure, a rabbet plane with guide, two heavy mortise chisels of different size, a firmer chisel, a hammer, an iron punch, a nail and two wooden blocks as supporting structures.

Preparing the board

Before commencing with the work, Malde lays out the tools he will require and then fetches an unprepared plank from his wood-godown. The plank is planed along one length only. There is only one insignificant crack in the middle.

In order to mark out the desired length, Malde measures twice the long side and once the short side of the square on the surface, marking the point by means of a slight indentation with the edge of the square. He then saws through the board at this point with the tenon saw.

In order to measure out the width, he next scores out a line along the edge of the square with the scribe-awl parallel to the unprepared narrow side of the board. Grasping the adze low down on the shaft near the head, he chops away the superficial wood in rough chips. At first Malde adopts a standing position, which facilitates hacking away the waste wood from the top corner. Later he places the board on a support and squats in front of it, holding it with his left hand. With his adze he first cuts away chips and eventually, through gentle blows, fine parings.

98

Malde next kneels behind the board, holding it in position firmly with his knees. With powerful forward and backward movements of the arm he planes the edge of the board smooth with the help of a small shaving plane. He now sits on the board, fixing its position with his thighs and feet, and planes the front edge of the board. He grasps the plane with both hands, the right on the handle exerting a certain amount of downward pressure while the left guides the tool.

After checking the measurement of the board once again, Malde proceeds to plane the previously prepared longitudinal edge. Finally, the length is shortened to size by means of a chisel, the back of the adze serving as a mallet.

99

Now at last Malde begins to plane the surface of the board. But he soon discovers that in the meanwhile the blade of the shaving plane has become blunt. He interrupts his work, takes out the plane-iron, tests its edge with the ball of his index-finger and sharpens it on the whetstone. A few drops of water are used to moisten the stone. He then replaces the plane-iron, lightly hammering it in with the back of the adze. A final blow on the plane stock and the iron is fixed into position.

Malde crouches on the board, pressing it to the ground with his feet. He later reverses the position of the board, so that the unplaned edge, on which he has hitherto been squatting, is now before him.

While the master is thus engaged in planing the board smooth, he orders his apprentice to interrupt his work and whet the chisels he will now need.

Marking out the board and spacing the relief-sections

With a moulding plane guide grooves are cut parallel to the edge along both lengths. Further in, another groove is cut with the gauge, so that now two parallel grooves two centimeter apart run along both lengths.

With the square, Malde now commences to measure each of the different sized stencils and places them alternately left and right from the outer edges towards the centre. But he leaves a strip twice as wide as the short side of his square on either end before spacing the sections for the reliefs. Malde next measures out the stencil for the swan-motif and applies the measurements left and right of the board. He then reserves another narrower strip, the width this time being half that of the first one, and scores a vertical line. Working inwards, he now measures out the peacock stencil on either side. After this he once again leaves the same gap, then measures out the elephant stencil and applies the measurements to the board. He marks the space required by scoring in the outline of the section. The narrow strip is once more repeated, so that a more or less square space is left in the middle of the board. Because he does not place the stencils themselves on the surface, but spaces out the motifs merely by applying the measurements, his calculations go awry in one instance and all the marked lines have to be re-scored.

100

101

Carving the ornamental borders

While decorating both longitudinal borders of the lintel-board, Malde adopts the following three positions: as long as he works at one end of the board and the wood projects only slightly over the square support underneath, Malde sits on the floor with his right leg bent from the hip and his left knee resting on the board. As work progresses towards the centre and the board juts out considerably over the support, he changes his position. His right leg is stretched across the board, the calf holding it in position, while the left knee is propped against the edge of the board. The foot, though, is placed under the board. Once he reaches the centre of the board directly above the support he encloses the section being worked upon with his stretched-out legs, their weight serving to hold the board steady.

Malde begins by cutting a zig-zag line in one border with the ripping chisel. The chisel, which is held at a slight angle sloping towards the outer edge of the board, is given a sharp blow with the hammer. It is then turned at a right angle on its edge nearest the centre of the board and driven in the same fashion. A zig-zag sequence is the result, the rills forming angles at the outer edge being more deeply cut than those on the inner edge. In addition, the rills on this edge intersect, whereas on the opposite edge they coincide perfectly.

102

This zig-zag sequence is first cut in over the whole length of the border before Malde scoops out the triangular sections on the inner side of the board. He begins once more at the right edge of the board. The chisel is started at a slight angle to the surface of the wood with its edge parallel to one zig-zag rill and driven towards the opposite one. A second blow to lift out the chip is only rarely necessary. Should this happen, the carpenter, in order to smoothen the recessed space, uses the palm of his hand to drive in the chisel instead of a hammer. This light blow pares a fine shaving from the surface. When this type of chip-carving is done, Malde examines the work critically. Badly recessed notches are made to correspond with the others, while ragged edges are subsequently smoothed.

With the same ripping chisel, Malde cuts a hatching into the second border. He starts from the right edge of the board, which lies in front of him. The wide tool is held at an angle within the border, so that both edges line up with the previously planed grooves. The chisel is now held at an angle to the wood surface and a cut made with the help of a hammer. Another cut slopes towards the first and the chip comes away cleanly of its own accord, since the cuts meet the planed grooves. At intervals of about one centimeter about a dozen similar notches are cut parallel to the first horizontal one. Malde next cuts a line of notches above the first so that a row of small rhombic shapes remains elevated between both lines of notches. Malde then examines this sample. Satisfied with the spacing and arrangement, he now proceeds to cut a row of parallel sloping notches along the whole length of the board, finishing each notch individually. He sometimes runs the edge of the chisel along the notches and grooves in order to remove the splinters in the corners. When a row of equally spaced notches has been cut along the whole length, Malde reverses the board and cuts in the opposite row of notches. The border is now decorated with a line of small, upright, elevated rhombs intersecting the lower notches at right angles.

104

Carving the ornamental interstices

The vertical interstices separating the figure designs are now decorated with notch ornaments. During this process, the square support lies immediately underneath the part being worked upon, the board being drawn towards the front as work progresses in order to make the necessary adjustment. Malde hardly changes his position. His right knee rests on the board, while the left is either stretched across or bent under it.

To begin with, Malde decorates the edges enclosing the stencilled designs with simple vertical notches, whereby the chisel cuts overlap. After scooping out a notch, he runs the edge of the chisel through it. For this, he grasps the wooden handle with his right hand, while the left exerts pressure on the uptilted edge of the blade.

The first interstice to be ornamented is the one on the extreme right. Malde cuts in a vertical right-angled "W" with equal sides. For this he uses a ripping chisel, the double width of its blade corresponding to the width of one of these sides. He now cuts another groove running towards the right angles adjacent to the sides and alongside the notches. For this, the edges of the chisel facing outwards are impressed less than the ones facing inwards. With the chisel held at a slope from the wood surface, Malde scoops out the triangular forms set in facing the right-angles with two cuts parallel to one of the previously cut grooves.

The next interstice is first enclosed by two vertical notches. A perpendicular is then dropped to divide it into two equal sections. After this, rows of sloping parallel notches inclining towards the central perpendicular are cut into both sections. Finally, Malde guides the edge of the chisel along notches to remove chips and shavings.

The third interstice is also first divided by means of a central perpendicular, after which the opposite rows of triangles are cut. First of all, Malde cuts a series of zig-zag sequences on both sides, whereby the chisel edges nearest the outer lines penetrate deepest into the wood. He then removes the triangular pieces, scooping out the triangle pairs stepwise.

The ornamental piece adjoining the centre space is first divided into three equal, more or less square sections by means of two horizontal lines. Thereafter the diagonals are drawn in, dividing each section into four right-angled triangles. Now the same technique is used as for the first interstice with the "W" pattern. From outside the diagonal notches grooves deepening towards the angles are cut. The outer triangles can then be lifted out slantwise.

The order in which the triangles are scooped out varies each time. However, the triangles making up one square are first completed before work on another section is started.

The interstices on the left half of the board are decorated to correspond with those already completed.

Carving the figure reliefs

Malde now supports the board with another square block, so that it lies horizontally before him. This has practically no bearing on the position he adopts, for he remains sitting behind the board, his right knee steadying it while the big toe holds it in position. His left leg, which has no steadying or supporting function, is either bent at the thigh or else stretched across the board.
Malde first lays the metal stencil on the space reserved for it, adjusting it until he finds a satisfactory position for the figure. He does not seem to mind that the edges of the stencil and the space do not concur; he simply places the stencil in the space. He then presses down the stencil with his right heel and the finger-tips of his left hand, while the right hand grasps the scribe-awl and outlines the contours of the stencil. He now lays aside the stencil and regards the drawing after which some of the lines are deepened, corrected or retraced freehand. However, the gaps necessitated by the intervening crosspieces (which join the figure to the stencil frame) are often left without being closed, although they are no part of the design as such.

Before sinking the groundwork of the extreme left design just stencilled, Malde outlines the figures for the two adjoining spaces, working from the left towards the middle.

Since the stencilled figure reliefs for all the spaces are carved in the same fashion, it will suffice to describe the technique adopted in carving the most complicated one. This is a design depicting a peacock.

Malde uses a stout, heavy mortise chisel with which he cuts around the outline of the peacock's body. The bevelled edge of the chisel blade faces the design-outline, which is cut away on a slope. Malde accomplishes this by means of a sharp blow with the hammer on the upright chisel, which he then shifts, so that a continuous series of overlapping rills is the result. Where the outline is very short, Malde uses a mortise chisel with a correspondingly short edge. He has a whole set of chisels ready at hand. They are spread on his lap and he selects a suitable chisel as the nature of the work demands. In this way, he sets in the outline of the figure until he arrives at the border. By chiselling along this as well, he completes setting in the background for the design. This ground work is now sunk with the help of a heavy mortise chisel. This is done from a central point in downward cuts towards the prepared outline. After this, the outlines of the figure are followed up once more. This time, however, the bevelled edge of the chisel faces away from the outline of the design, which now stands up straight from the groundwork. Malde recesses the background once again, levelling down the central ridge by guiding the chisel in frequent light cuts over the surfaces. Only the palm of the hand is used to drive the chisel. The resulting shavings are extremely fine.

The board is now turned over and the shavings and wood-dust shaken out. The ground work is finished off with a narrow mortise chisel, ragged corners being cleaned up and the outline slightly remodelled, that is, the edges are sloped at points where the bevelled edge of the chisel made only a slight incision.

The plain surface of the design is articulated by means of patterns. The carpenter first traces a line following the contours of the peacock's body. A central groove is next cut through the tail, both sections thus formed being then decorated with parallel chip-lines. With a metal punch, a star-shaped ornament is next impressed on the head and on the fruit suspended from the beak. The two beaks formed by cutting out a triangular notch constitute the crest of the peacock. Malde next carves a row of little triangles along the groove outlining the body, using for this the corner of a wide mortise chisel placed on its edge upon the wood surface. He holds the blade with fingers and thumb and hammers upon the uptilted cutting edge. In this way, the entire inner surface of the bird-design is covered with small V-shaped patterns, which are only incised into the surface and not lifted out as the chips are.

As soon as one relief is completed, Malde commences with the next. In this way all six reliefs with animal and bird motifs are finished before the figure of Ganesha is carved into the centre space.

Like his fellow-carpenters, Malde does not use a stencil to outline the figure of the elephant-headed Ganesha, the god of luck, but draws it in freehand with his scribe-awl. So that the tool may better penetrate into the wood, he grasps it with his right hand, the index and middle fingers being placed on the top of the instrument, while the three remaining fingers hold it from underneath.

The figure is composed of geometrical shapes. Mentally dividing the space into three horizontal

106

107

108

109

110

111

sections, Malde first draws a small flat oval for the head in the topmost section. Now a larger oval, the body, is marked immediately below the first. Malde now attaches narrow angular pieces to the body so as to fill up the bottommost section. These represent the legs with the knees bent outwards, depicting the sitting position characteristic of Ganesha. Semicircular ears are now drawn on the sides of the oval head and a trapezoid crown on the top of it. Between the head and the body narrow split strips representing the four arms are drawn. These terminate in geometrically simplified emblems. Beginning where the ears touch the head, the eye-brows are now drawn in, intersecting in the middle of the forehead and continuing to form a trunk hanging down in front of the body.

The outline is now followed up once more with the scribe-awl. The right outline of Ganesha is next chiselled out, after which the ground work on this side is recessed. In the same way, the groundwork between the legs and finally on the left side is sunk.

Malde next cuts in along the previously drawn outline of the trunk and the eye-brows, hammers in a round point with a sharp nail as a forehead decoration and puts in two rhombs for eyes. Each rhomb is formed by two cuts with the corner of the chisel.

The lintel-board is now ready. The carpenter examines it critically once more, without, however, changing any feature. He lays the completed piece of work aside and turns his attention to a new order.

4. 4. Example 2: Carving wooden horse-heads

Working schedule

The work was carried out during the late morning and in the afternoon of the 26th January 1966 in Ratadi. The carpenter, whose apprentice helped him for a short while only in preparing the wooden blocks, required in all three and a half hours to carve the heads. The working hours were distributed as follows:

11.50 – 12.15	preparing both blocks of wood
	midday interval
14.10 – 15.55	carving the first horse-head
15.55 – 16.50	starting work on the second
16.50 – 17.15	work interrupted by sale of a chest and the accompanying transfering ceremony
17.15 – 18.00	completion of the second horse-head.

Working materials and tools

For the pair of horse-heads the carpenter used unplaned square wooden blocks, the scratched surfaces being due to their having served previously as supports. After planing, each block measured 39 x 12 x 7 cm. these being the final measurements of the block.

The following tools were used to shape and carve the block:
a small shaving plane, a moulding plane with guide, a gauge-measure, a mortise chisel in two different sizes, a ripping chisel in two sizes, a tenon saw, an adze, a hammer, an iron punch and different supports.

Preparing the blocks

The breadth of both blocks is checked with the square. The gauge is used to score a groove   113
parallel to one edge, preserving the breadth as far as possible. This measurement is then
transferred to the second block, so that both grooves are of the same length. The same method
is applied in measuring and scoring the thickness of the blocks.

The superfluous wood is now planed away with the small shaving plane. Here the apprentice
Govin helps by pulling the plane by the handle while Malde guides it. The moulding plane   115
is now used to run a groove along each length one centimeter away from the edge. With the
help of the square and the scribe-awl two lines each 5 inches (13 cm.) distant from the broad
edge of the block are drawn. These are then sawn in with the tenon saw to the depth of a quar-   114
ter of the block's thickness. After preparing the first block in this way, Malde hands it over
to his apprentice and commences to treat the second block similarly.

With the wide ripping chisel the side-pieces at the end of the block are chipped out, the   116
hammer or the back of the adze serving as a mallet. Malde takes care that the surface always   117
remains slightly convex. In the course of the work the apprentice asks permission to use
the hammer instead of the weighty adze. The exchange of tools follows tacitly. With the   118
adze, the final finish is given to the shaped part of the block. The instrument is grasped far down
near the blade with the shaft either resting on the forearm or terminating in the armpit. The
apprentice's block is less cleanly worked. Malde has therefore to remedy this by planing it and
filing along the shaped edge with the flat blade of the ripping chisel.

Carving the horse-head

Both pieces are carved one after the other. Malde follows more or less the same procedure
for both. While he works on the second piece, the first completed horse-head lies before him.
Yet he very seldom looks at it. The working procedure is apparently stereotyped. It will
therefore be sufficient to give a description of the carving of one head only.

The contours of the horse-head are first cut into the projecting part of the block. During
the following work, Malde places the wide end of the block upon a piece of square wood,
holding it steady with his left knee, while his right leg is stretched out. Or else he presses
with the toes of his right foot against the block, the leg being bent at the knee. When the
block is placed with its longitudinal edge uppermost, Malde holds it between the soles
of his feet. When it lies on its narrow side, Malde steadies it with the hollow of his knees,
the leg being stretched over the block.

Throughout the carving work, the block remains movable, each chisel-cut causing it to
give a slight jerk.

The wide ripping chisel is used to cut the front surface of the block into a series of different   119
shapes. An obtuse-angled triangle occupies the topmost quarter portion and a triangle with
one long sloping side and one short one forming a right angle with the edge fills out the
lower quarter portion. After reserving a narrow strap adjacent to this notch, Malde cuts in
once more at a right-angle and chisels out a slope from the opposite end to form a wedge.
At first all the edges are angular, the front surface of the block presenting a ridged appearance.
The edges are then rounded off first on one side and then on the other. Only the small
strap which will eventually form the harness is left projecting sharply. The chiselled surfaces
are now lightly hammered over.

The horse-head is now turned on one of its narrow edges. Through a chisel cut, the breadth
of the head is marked out longitudinally on the block commencing from the front and a
one centimeter deep cut made at this point. The sides of this cut are sloped downwards with
the ripping chisel. This is the notch separating the horse's muzzle from its neck. The block is
then turned around to stand on its other narrow edge. The ripping chisel is now used to
carve out a shallow indentation immediately behind the front edge so that one ear now stands
up from the head. At the point where the narrow horse-head starts to project from the
block, Malde saws in to about a quarter of the entire thickness and then slopes the cut in
three planes, working from the head downwards and using the ripping chisel. Thus a
curved neck with sloping sides emerges from the base of the block. He now goes over the
outline once again, rounding off all the edges except those of the neck. In addition, he
chisels the sides of the ear to shape and cleans and smoothens each corner of the block by means
of opposing chisel cuts.

Once the outline of the head has been completed, Malde turns his attention to the side surfaces.
He exchanges the ripping chisel, which he has been using in different sizes, for a narrow
mortise chisel. With this tool, he scores out a double-groove running from the headpiece
across the neck, this being the halter. Using the same tool, he chips in a triangular and
a square hollow above and below the halter respectively, thus separating the head
from the neck. This he accomplishes by first piercing the hole from one side, reversing the
block and then feeling for the perforation with his fingers, completing it from the other side.

A second pair of reins in the form of a double-groove bent at a right-angle is now cut into
the upper part of the neck. Both V-shaped grooves are worked one after the other by means
of cuts in opposite directions, one corner of the chisel being run along them to give a
smooth finish. At the junction of head and neck, a round radiating ornament is punched into
the end of the reins. The rule is to completely finish one side of the head before turning
the block and commencing with the other.

When both sides are carved, Malde stands the wooden block up at a slant, holds it between
the soles of his feet and saws two parallel slits into the ear. For this, the right hand works the
tenon saw, while the left index-finger lies adjacent to the blade and guides it. One blow with
the narrow mortise chisel and the sawn-in wedge is knocked out of the ear-piece. The
outlines of both ears are sloped away with the ripping chisel.

It is only at this stage during the carving of the first horse-head that Malde cuts in a zig-zag
border into the part of the rectangular block constituting the stand. Powerful blows on the
ripping chisel cut in the zig-zag line to half its intended depth, this operation being repeated
to penetrate down to the full depth. This time the chisel is given a slight twist at every cut,
which results in the wood chips coming cleanly away. The chisel is then passed with a
scraping movement over each peak. The first ornamental border completed, he turns the
block around and proceeds to carve the second.

As a final touch, Malde adorns the forehead of the horse with a chip ornament consisting of
a short herringbone pattern with two rhombs beside it carved with the mortise chisel. Now
Malde hammers over the entire surface of the wooden block, subsequently smoothing it
over with the ripping chisel which he drives forward with the palm of his hand.

He now critically scrutinizes the beam-piece with the horse-head, expresses his satisfaction
with it and smilingly hands it over to his customer for approval.

VI. 5. Ornamental designs and motifs

5.1. Geometrical ornaments

The following is a list of the commonest geometrical ornaments used in Ratadi to decorate the surfaces of boards, posts, chests, etc.

I found it most expedient to arrange the list according to geometrical principles : circular motiss and derived forms, chip motifs and derived forms, motifs based on the rill, and carved ornaments. It has not been possible to classify the ornaments according to their significance for the informants, as no reliable information could be obtained on this subject. Below is a classification of ornaments according to the meanings their names convey, this being the theoretical equivalent of the above:

(1) motifs derived from tools used to carve them: *subo, bhamarsiada, bid, toja.*
(2) motifs representing or symbolizing familiar implements or their parts: *karkaria, toran, karelia, chari.*
(3) motifs representing or symbolizing flowers and plants: *ful, vel.*
(4) motifs known by proper names and the derivatives of these motifs: *kangri, kangrini choda, vankia, kangri vankiun, chokedi, chokedi vankiun, kaniun, julun.*

The circle derived forms

These ornaments are punched in or scored with the help of compasses and drills. They may occasionally be cut as well.

kaniun, dots, spots
A row of points arranged in a straight or zig-zag line.
subo, punch
This is a punched or perforated design consisting of a simple or concentric circle, sometimes with a radiate design.
bhamarsiada, drill with serrated point
The drill is used to describe several concentric circles around a centre point. 153

ful, flower
This term embraces all chip ornaments cut on the surface which are characterized by complex patterns described within a circle. The most important forms are:

ful, simple flower 135
This is a common inscribed rose with twelve petals. This ornament is chiefly traced from a stencil and not constructed with compasses.
Pankhadiya chovis ful, 24-petalled flower 165
This is an inscribed rose with double petals for which the pattern for the common inscribed rose is most often used, rhombic shapes being inserted between the twelve petals.
krasinu ful, compass flower or *surej mukhi,* sun face or *surej mukhi ful,* sun flower 137
This design consists of an inscribed wheel with a varying number of spokes constructed and sometimes enclosed by a border of parrallel cuts.
krasinu char pankhadiya ful, inscribed rose with 4 petals
This is constructed with compasses as well. A type of Maltese cross is inscribed in a circle.
vel (1), tendril motif 163
This is a wavy line consisting of a series of semicircles curling to small spirals. The result is a continuous winding creeper.
julun 148
This type of meandering design is predominantly painted or used in applique work.

Chip ornaments and derived forms

These ornaments are made by two opposing chisel cuts, the wood chip between both cuts being lifted out. They are therefore examples of genuine chip-carving.

kangri, zig-zag. 143
This simple zig-zag pattern is formed either by V-shaped indentations or by lifting out either the upper or
lower row of zig-zags.
kangrini choda, double zig-zag 110
A double border of opposite triangles is described as "triangle-pair". In this ornament, only the corner
pointing outwards are deep-cut.
kangri vankiun, staggered zig-zag
This is a border consisting of a number of triangles with parallel sides arranged within each other. The effect
of an echelon formation is obtained either by light gradation or by notching the surface.
chokedi, rhomb 133
This designation "chokedi" is also used for one of the four suits of cards known to us as "diamond". It
signifies a rhomb standing on one corner.
chokedi vankiun, staggered rhombs 131
Here a border of rhombs placed on end is shown. The rhombs are segmented by vertical notches intersecting
both angles.
vankia
This motif depicts an elevated cross with arms of equal length decreasing in breadth towards the end. The
sides slope downwards towards the centre.
toran, scarf with corners 144
This represents a series of pentagons forming right-angles with common upper-edge. The inverted vertices
point downwards.
vel (2), creeper 165
This is a series of pentagons standing at right-angles to their common base. The vertices point upwards.
karkaria, serrated
These slanting parallel cuts are arranged on both sides of a central groove either uniformly or so as to form a 143
herringbone pattern. The name remains the same for both.

Rills, angular punches and carved motifs

This group includes all cuts which are punched, planed, scored or carved in without the
technique of true chip-carving being employed. Finally, two complex motifs representing a
leaf and a wrought-iron trellis are given.

toja 128
A row of small triangles punched in with the corner of the chisel blade is arranged either in a straight or
zig-zag line.
nar 144
This represents a set of vertical adjacent reeds carved with the moulding plane. Corrugated iron is known as
nar vala patra.
bid 144
This consists of a channel of V-shaped section cut in with a small moulding plane with guide and running
parallel to a side edge.
karelia
This embellishment named after the bulge formed by rolled-up trousers, consists of reeds falling away slantwise
from the centre on both sides.
vel (3)
A border showing a conventional representation of the palmetto leaf may sometimes be found adorning
chests and handmills.
jari, trellis 162
This consists of interlacing bars geometrically arranged. The design occurs most often on the front surface
of chests.

5. 2 Figure motifs

These are chiselled chiefly into lintel boards and the front surfaces of chests. I have only once
come across this kind of carving on the shaft of a column. Regarding figures modelled in
solid, the horse-head and the parrot-head are to be found decorating beam-ends at chests,
cradles and the capitals of pillars.

A characteristic of all figure reliefs is that they are placed against a rectangular ground,
narrow crosspieces called *teka* being used to connect the figures with the framing sides. This
striking point is to be explained only to a limited extent by the use of stencils. Since the
measurements of the stencil frame do not tally with the dimensions of the ground and since
the scored contours are always gone over once more freehand upon the stencil being removed

from the wood surface, it follows that dispensing with the crosspieces would be a simple matter. That several crosspieces are preserved, however, is presumably to be ascribed to an aesthetic principle, according to which they serve to articulate the empty space surrounding the figure. Viewed from a historical aspect, though, these crosspieces may be regarded as a relic of former intertwining designs. The most important motifs modelled in relief are:

Ganpati   137
The elephant-headed god *Ganesha* is represented in a sitting position. Both thin legs are curled inwards and the four arms stretched out. In his hands he holds *kuadi*, axe, *shankh*, a conch shell, *dhaja*, a triangular flag and *ladu*, a sweetmeat shaped like a ball. About this motif, Malde says:
// For *Ganpati* I have no *khasarun*, stencil. I have never seen a carpenter using one. This figure is prepared freehand.
It is therefore not surprising that this particular motif is represented in a number of different ways.
ghodo, rider   138, 140
This shows the upper torso of a man with outstretched arms astride upon a stepping-out horse. The rider holds a sword and a lance.
putli, girl   139
In contrast to the profile view most often presented in carved motifs, the girl-motif shows a front-view figure with water vessels balanced on its circular head. The body is composed of two triangles with thin bars for legs and arms. The feet are turned outwards, one arm being placed on the hip while the other is bent upwards to support the vessels.
morlo, peacock   133
With drooping wings and spread out tail a peacock is depicted in a posture adopted when courting, the tail plumage being delineated by means of hatching. A crest like a coronet is poised on the peacock's head and an oblong fruit is frequently held in its beak.
sudo or *hudo*, wild parrot   152
Characteristic of the wild species of the popat, or parrot, is a large eye, a stout, hooked beak, an arched breast and a pair of pointed wings.
hans, swan
This plump bird is shown with its neck arched backwards, so that the beak is buried in the back plumage of the bulky body.
hati, elephant   153
All four legs of the elephant, which is depicted stepping out, are always to be seen. A canopied howdah known as *ambadi* is often borne on its back or else *nar*, a chain, is suspended from its trunk. Both emblems suggest tameness. The bulky body of the animal is usually covered with chisel cuts. Elephants are not depicted in a natural manner. The mouth and tusks, particularly, frequently merge to form one mass. Upon inquiry, Malde, who himself carves such elephants, replied:
// When I was about ten years old, I have seen an elephant in the circus. Later on I never had the opportunity of seeing one again.
havaj or *savaj*, lion   148
The lion, which gives the impression of being stout, is drawn with its tail curved over its back and ending in a tuft. A long tongue may be discerned projecting from its large, open jaws. None of the carpenters in Ratadi has ever seen a lion in real life. Lions are supposed to have roamed the Barda hills at one time. However, today they are found exclusively in the Gir forest.

Although comparatively seldom, scenic representations and floral and foliage motifs may be seen decorating lintel boards in Ratadi. On a small coffer made of parts cut from an old chest, parrots sitting in a bush were depicted in one section and on another a cow was carved. I have observed a scene only on one lintel board in Ratadi though in other villages scenic representations seem to occur frequently.

Modelling in solid seems to be confined to horse-heads and parrots. Small wooden bell-like knobs may often be observed hanging from shelves and the mouths of carved horse-heads.

VI. 6. Wooden fixtures, furniture and kitchen utensils

These have a two-fold function: (1) They serve practical purposes, i.e. they are useful in a technical sense and (2) they serve at the same time as decorations by reason of design or embellishment, according to the quality of which they are regarded as symbols of prestige.

Certainly, there are among these some, such as the utensils and implements used in the kitchen or in farming, the designs of which are determined exclusively by practical considerations. However, no examples of the other extreme, works of art in the sense of "l' art pour l' art", which have either lost their practical value or else been originally produced as purely decorative pieces, could be found at Ratadi.

In the observer's point of view all accoutrements of a household which are constructed or carved of wood may be divided into three major categories:

(1)   wooden fixtures in houses such as pillars, doorways with doors, lintels etc.
(2)   wooden furniture such as chests, cradles, devices for suspension,devices serving as stands
(3)   wooden kitchen utensils such as mortars and pestles, handmills, bowls, vessels, etc.

Other wooden implements and tools used by the farmer or the craftsman will be described in their specific context.

6. 1. Wooden fixtures of the house

The door-way   126
The wooden parts consist of the door-case, the door wings, the door beams, the lintel-board and the grated door. Only the first three, being essential parts of the structure, are common to all door-ways, the others being either absent altogether or replaced by other features or materials. In the following only the main entrances will be described, but the descriptions given also apply to the smaller, undecorated, window-like backdoors to be found in some houses.

The door-case   127
The four pieces of squared timber forming a frame and comprising the threshold, the jambs and the head-piece are tenoned at their ends. The door-case is fitted into the stone wall and fixed to the two door beams.
The threshold piece is wedged between both jambs and lies upon a smooth step of stone-work. The jambs, which press closely to the wall on either side, are tenoned at right-angles to the threshold. All cracks are plastered over with clay. The upper ends of the jambs are mitred and fitted with a central mortise, so that the head-piece is not only firmly supported by the jambs but is fitted into both mortises by means of tenons terminating in the door beams in the wall, thus anchoring the door case in the stonework.

door-case	*barsankh*
threshold	*umro*

The wings of the door are attached to the jambs by means of hinges. The locking device consists of a chain attached to the door, which is looped over an iron ring fixed either in the head-piece (in the case of doors with one wing only) or in one of the jambs (two winged doors).
The outer surfaces of door-cases are often decorated with chip and groove designs. Either all four pieces are covered with the same design, or the threshold is patterned with pentagons pointing upwards, while the head-piece is adorned with pentagons pointing downwards, the jambs being decorated with various triangular designs.

The door-wings   126, 127
Doors may have either one or two wings. In the former case, vertical panels are hammered on to several horizontal strips with broad-headed iron nails. These strips are on the outside of the door. In the case of double-winged doors, the outside has vertical as well as horizontal strips, giving the impression of a pattern in squares. The horizontal strips are attached to the

jamb on one side. On the other side, the outermost strip of the right wing overlaps the corresponding strip on the left wing when the door is shut. The wings of the doors swing inwards on iron hinges.

door-wing	*barlun*
horizontal strip	*dhoka*
vertcal str ip	*veni*

Since the doors swing on hinges, they are easy to open and yet can be firmly shut. The strips reinforce the door. Besides this, they serve as footholds when climbing up to the attic.

Double-winged doors are to be found mainly in the houses of the more prosperous villagers, while the one-winged door is considered simple and in my opinion represents the traditional type of door.

These double-winged doors are shut from the inside with a cross-bar which consists of three parts: the sliding bar and the two bridges, each being constructed of a strong lathe under the end of which cubical wooden blocks are nailed. The sliding bar broadens at one end. In its middle part another conical block is fixed to prevent the bar from being entirely pushed out of the bridge.
The strips of door wings are occasionally decorated with carvings in contrast to the door panels, which are always left unadorned.

The door anchor beam   128
In place of a cornerstone, beams of rectangular section are inserted through the thickness of the wall on both sides adjacent to the upper corners of the door case. These beams terminate on the outside in a horse-head; in the opposite direction, however, they end short of the wall plaster. In the centre they are fitted with a mortise to receive the tenon of the head-piece.

The horse-heads on the ends of the beams are always carved two of a kind. They are modelled in two basic ways, angular and cylindrical. If an angular horse-head is to be fashioned, a   129, 130
notch is cut into the top edge of the rectangular beam at the point where it enters the wall. The part of the beam left projecting now measures about a span. Next the edges of the front surface are carved to the shape of small pyramids. Two short notches are often cut into the sloped lower edge and suggest the mouth of the horse.

The cylindrical horse-head with the arched neck is in most cases narrower than the beam and definitely separated from it. The cylindrical head hangs down from the neck, the harness running across the middle of it. Above the forehead, at the point where the head meets the neck, are the upstanding ears. Details such as the harness, eyes, nostrils, etc. are frequently indicated through cuts.

door-beam, horse-head	*ghorla*
angular horse-head	*ghorla nu sadu modhu,*
horse with smooth muzzle	
cylindrical horse-head	*ghorla nu naksi varu modhu,*
horse-head with ornamented muzzle	

As has already been mentioned, the door beams serve to anchor the door-case firmly in the stone wall. The carved horse-heads at their ends have, however, no technical function with regard to the construction of the door but are merely facade decorations.

I have observed these horse-heads being used as pegs to hold various implements and   135
articles, particularly bell collars and other pieces of oxen harness, wet water sacks, turban cloths and ropes. At dusk earthenware oil-lamps are placed behind the horse's ears and cast a dim light on the veranda.

No information could be obtained as to the significance of horse-heads. However, it was stressed that both types (angular and cylindrical) depicted stallions and never mares.

The simple modelling of the angular head permits very little ornamentation. Grooves may   129
be cut along the edges to accent them or else eye motifs may be punched in. Far greater variations in modelling may be observed with regard to the second type. A comparison between different examples occurring in the villages in the Porbandar area will reveal that a special style of modelling seems to prevail in each village. In *Sodhana*, for instance, there is a horse-head with an elegantly arched neck continuing downwards in harmonic waves to form the head; the wide space between head and neck is bridged only by a narrow harness strap. In *Kantela* the modelling is similar; however, the cylindrical head on the rectangular neck has a decidedly clumsier effect in this case. All horse-heads in *Ratadi* have one common trait: they are bulky and carved out of one block On the whole, these figures present a heavy, clumsy appearance. At the most, there is a row of perforations between head and neck. Although certain peculiarities of style are invariably evident in all the carved horse-heads belonging to one village, certain details identify each specimen as the work of a particular carpenter, generation or workshop. For example, horse-heads carved by the carpenter Kima are characterized by a broad, dome   130
shaped forehead and small pyramidical ears. Jesam's heads have crescent-shaped ears curved   132
inwards. The horse-heads of Morarji Laxman show long, narrow cylindrical heads and   131
close upstanding ears.

The lintel-board   133, 134, 135
The head-piece of the door-case lies under a stone transom which is occasionally covered with a rectangular board adorned with relief work. It is supported at its lower corners by levers cut into the anchor beams and is not firmly fixed to the wall. Sometimes it is pressed into the wall-plaster or stuck to the stone-wall with a mixture of cow-dung and clay.

This board is divided into sections by ornamental borders and interstices and enriched by figures or geometrical motifs carved in relief work. The figure of a sitting *Ganesha* occupies the central section of every such lintel.

lintel-board   *madhiyun*
(example in possession of Atiabhai Shinabhai)
height   14.5 cm
length   115 cm
thickness   2 cm

Malde had the following to say on the installation and significance of the lintel:

// (When the carpenter has finished carving the lintel) no ceremony is performed in the workshop, all is done in the owner's place. The day after bringing the lintel to the house the customer will apply *sindur*, red colour to the portrait of *Ganpati* (Ganesha). // That is not done by any special person, and may be performed either by a man or a woman. The woman of the house prepares sweetmeats which are offered to *Ganpati*. While offering it, they break a coconut and distribute it, the water and the whole fruit. All the people of the household eat the sweetmeats. // This is always the last piece of work to be done when a house has been built. They fix the lintel when the walls are all plastered and when the tiles are fitted. // They complete the house first and then they can wait even for a month—if the period is not auspicious (i,e. the omens are unlucky). // The ceremony has no special name.

The lintel with the central figure of *Ganesha* is thus a cult image enriched with decorative elements. This is further borne out by the fact that over some doors a stone idol of *Ganesha* is fixed into the wall plaster instead of a wooden lintel. However, I have seen lintels in Bakharla without the figure of a god.

The lintels, carved by different carpenters at different periods, vary with regard to the type of relief employed, the division of the board into sections, (i.e. the inside proportions, arrangements of motifs and symmetry) and the style in which the individual motifs are modelled. In Ratadi and in the neighbouring villages all relief-work is of the elevated type, i.e. haute relief, the ground-work around each motif being recessed or sunk. There is an exception to this rule, though: the carpenter Moraji Laxman of Ratadi, who has also carved a piece remarkable for its profuseness of motifs in haute relief technique, has employed the bas relief technique in one piece, the motif being recessed and the surrounding space elevated. In this extraordinary piece of work a figure of *Ganesha* occupies the central section, followed by a plant with leaves drooping to the side and little parrots perched between them. It is surprising to note that the veins of the leaves are raised. A very narrow groove separates this picture from a figure motif which, judging from its long tail, is obviously meant to represent Hanuman. This is also the opinion of the inhabitants of the house. The drawn sable of a walking man leading with his left hand a large horse with a small (headless ?) rider by its reins forms a counterpart to the upwards curved tail of *Hanuman,* the two motifs being separated by a narrow groove. The outermost motif in this series of relief carvings is another tree or bush. The motifs are arranged symmetrically towards the centre, the designs just described being carved to correspond on the other side of *Ganesha.*

140, 141

Particularly amazing and puzzling to the observer is the fact that certain parts of the outlines of some of the recessed figures are cut in deeper than the figures themselves. It is to be supposed that this is an unconscious and unintentional effect produced by the carpenter having cut in the outlines irregularly, which resulted in some lines remaining cut out deeper when the inner spaces were chipped out. Light falling upon the dulled, aged-grey of the lintel board, throws certain features into relief and obscures others, presenting herewith an astoundingly intricate picture-puzzle with seemingly abstract designs.

These lintel boards are often framed by a simple, unornamented border. Sometimes, one of the longitudinal borders is adorned with a carved pattern or both longitudinal may be decorated with the same or different patterns. A more or less equal number of examples for each of these various borders is to be found. But there was only one lintel board with the upper edge patterned with zig-zag chips.

The vertical interstices between the reliefs are decorated in the majority of boards with a carved pattern throughout. Different designs arranged symmetrically from the centre are seldom found. Occasionally two different designs alternate.

The relief-ground is invariably rectangular. Only one board shows two corresponding sections sloped to point towards the adjoining smaller central piece. The dimensions of the individual relief sections depend on the motif used and vary accordingly in width, while the height is determined by the board and always conformed to. Only in the lintel-board mentioned above the central piece containing the image of *Ganesha* is shortened below by a short ornamental border.

The motifs are usually arranged symmetrically on the board. This is the common order. (O standing for geometrical ornament, F for figural or scenic motif, P for naturalesque plant motif): O1, F1, F2, *Ganesha,* F2, F1, O1, or O1, F1, O2, F2, *Ganesha,* F2, O2, F1, O1. There are also lintel boards with exclusively figural or ornamental motifs. As far as symmetry is concerned it is to be noted that the carpenters will often only consider a motif as being either ornamental or figural without repeating the exact motif used. Thus the following arrangement occurs: O1, O2, F1, O2, *Ganesha,* O3, F1, O3, O1 or O1, O1, F1, *Ganesha,* F2, O1, O1.

The sole exception is a lintel-board made by the extraordinary carpenter Moraji Laxman, which shows an asymmetrical arrangement of motifs as follows: F1, P1, F2, F3, O1, *Ganesha,*

O2, F3, F4, F5, P2. This is at the same time the only piece of work of its kind where the order of motifs may be supposed to have some significance, for on the right side of the board a wild beast may be seen to attack a human being, who is separated from a lurking lion by a wild tree. After this a girl carrying water-vessels and a radiate flower are depicted. These last two motifs are repeated on the left side of *Ganesha*. Adjoining them, however, is the mild, flute-playing *Krishna,* beside him a cow and, closing the scene, a symmetrical, i.e. cultivated bush.

139

Designs in chip-carving often occur on the borders and vertical interstices of lintels, but only rarely decorate a whole section. Chipped-in circular designs are, however, used exclusively within these sections. Punched ornaments are used only to articulate the interior spaces of figure motifs. Figure motifs occur with varying frequency. In Ratadi a representation of *Ganesha* in the central section is never absent. *Krishna* or *Hanuman* as secondary figures in the side-sections are rare. The most popular animal or bird motif is doubtless the peacock, which is also delineated in pairs facing each other. Elephants and horses are just as common but the geese and swans, lions are rarer. I have never come across the sparrow motif. Human figures are the rider, less common the swordbrandishing, standing man and the water carrying girls. Landscapes are extremely rare. Outside of Ratadi, in the village of Sodhana the following motifs also occur: a row of dancing women, two women churning butter etc. Here lintels may also be found without the *Ganesha* motif. In the village of Degam, however, the God *Hanuman* is frequently carved on lintels.

137

138

The grated door

127

A feature of some houses is a two-winged grated door. It is hinged to the facade of the house immediately in front of the main door and is half as high. Both wings are symmetrical. Each consists of a rectangular frame joined by mortise and tenon, the ends of the posts projecting upwards beyond the joints. Strips of iron are nailed over the joints. Perforated boards, the breadth of each being a quarter of the entire space to be occupied by the grating, are fixed into the frame at both ends. These two boards are bridged by vertical battens, mostly three in number, the sides of which may be convex. The door is shut by means of a loop fixed to the end of one vertical post and closing over the other.

grated door	*pardo bhario*
battens	*garadh*
loop handle	*teba*

The grated door keeps dogs, cattle and other animals from entering the house whilst the main door is opened to ventilate the house and kitchen. Two-winged grated doors are found in combination with both one-winged and two-winged main doors. This practical contrivance is, however, not frequently found in Ratadi houses.

The pillar

142

The pillar consists of a wooden post fixed into a stone socket. A strong capital supports the roof-beam above the socket, which may be absent, if the pillar is anchored in stonework, is usually in the form of a slightly hollowed out square of a pyramid base. A wooden post of rectangular section is fixed into the socket. The pillar may be decorated with tori of various shapes. The capital is either placed upon the post or joined to it by mortise and tenon. It occurs in many different shapes, though its upper surface is always concave or shaped in such a way as to couch the beam.

pillar	*thambali*
stone socket	*fad* or *padaghli*
capital	*tibali* or *tibalun*
simple concave moulding	*kacho*
round torus	*trodo* (silver jewellery)
angular torus	*kareli*

The pillars stand on the edge of the veranda, mostly on either side of the path leading to the door, and support the eaves beam. The number of pillars required depends on the length of the veranda. The pillars are then all of the same shape and design. The large ridge-pieces within the house are fixed in the floor. They are unembellished and have no decorated capital. In the part of the roof truss projecting beyond the veranda a short template carved as a miniature of the main pillar is set as a support between the anchor beam and each of the main rafters.

The pillar post consists of a piece of squared timber and may be articulated by several tori. These most frequently occur in pairs, the first one generally quarter of the pillar length above the socket, the second quarterway below the capital. The concave mouldings may start with a sharp or a round edge. They may be simple or interrupted by round or angular tori. The four sides of the pillar post or shaft between the ornaments may be sloped, which results in the shaft having an octagonal section. These eight faces of the shaft are sometimes articulated by vertical rills, that is, they are fluted in the true sense of the word. They are very often decorated with ornamental borders of various designs, the designs being alternately employed in octagonal pillars.   143

Most richly decorated of all are the capitals. During its evolution (not necessarily a historical one) the capital may be presumed to have passed through the following stages:
(1) First of all, we have the square wooden block inserted between the eaves beam and the shaft or post. This roughly fashioned block may (2) have its upper surface hollowed out   144
to couch the beam, therewith presenting a longitudinal section of trapezoid shape. It is adorned with a carved pattern. (3) This unique capital is essentially derived from the one just   145
described, although other features of style and design have had their influence as well. Here the upper edges are curled to form small volutes, under which masks are carved into the rectangular surfaces in haute relief. On the longitudinal edges of the capital inscribed roses in chip-carving technique appear and, on the same pillar a carved female figure in haute relief may be seen adorning the top of the shaft. The commonest type of capital (4) to be   143
observed in Ratadi appears essentially geometrical. The shaft, of rectangular section, branches in such a way as to admit the eaves beam, which rests upon the concave bifurcation. Both sides of the capital end in a square parallel to the eaves beam. Below the squares on either side lie cylindrical shapes. A variation of this design replaces the squares through a second pair of cylinders. There are also instances of several cylinders piled one on top of the other. A modern capital (5) made by the carpenter Malde shows two pyramids placed on edge upon the volutes. On being questioned as to the significance of this capital, Malde replied that it was "mere decoration". An older man, Parbatbhai Shinabhai, who happened to be present declared positively that this type of capital was intended to represent *ghorlo pado,* a fallen horse. These capitals are, no doubt, a geometrical development of the horse-head motif, which was subjected to increasing variations once its original significance was forgotten. In neighbouring villages capitals clearly displaying carved horse-heads are to be observed. In some cases even the *paj,* forelegs are to be discerned. Examples of such pillars are to be found in the old village Keshav and also in Degam. In Modhvada an additional figural motif, the parrot head and its variation, appears as a decoration for capitals.

The boards
Very often, boards are fixed in front of or upon the eaves beams and anchor beams supporting the roof truss. A typical characteristic of these boards is that the lower edge runs in a line of broken waves. The board may also be carved on its surface with a simple notch or groove design.

board *movati* or *mohati*
broken wave form *tagbanaiva*

The boards are nailed to the round beams. When fixed to the eaves beam, the board shelters the veranda from wind and rain. Nailed on the anchor beam inside the house, it forms a cornice for the loft. In both cases, the board has a decorative function as well.

6. 2 The wooden furniture

The chest

The chest

146, 147

The chest resembles a square box resting on two pairs of wheels made of stone or wood. The front surface is divided into compartments by a system of crossing timberwork. Rectangular relief-plaques are set into these compartments. Carved horse-heads appear in all four corners and in the middle of the upper edge. At the level of three-quarters of the height, the chest is divided by an intermediate tray. The lower compartment is accessible through a winged door, the upper through a trap door. A secret drawer is often built into the upper right-hand corner of the chest. Other secret drawers may be hidden under the lid. The side panels of the chest are reinforced by crossing timber strips, the back and the lid having simple, unadorned board surfaces. A wooden frame forms the skeleton of the chest. The beams of the frame have mortises planed into them, into which the boards for the four sides, bottom, tray and lid are fitted. Squared timber is used for the construction of the frame. The horizontal pieces are joined to the mortised vertical ones by tenons. A wooden wedge is inserted into the lengthened, slitted tenons situated at the sides of the corners. At these same corners, the horizontal side pieces are joined to the vertical side pieces by mortise and tenon. The horizontal beams project beyond the front surface and are carved into horse-heads. On the front edge on either side of the centre two additional battens forming the door posts are tenoned to the horizontal frame beams. Inside the box, another batten is nailed horizontally at the height of the inset tray. Boards held together and reinforced by crossing timber strips are now nailed to the frame so as to form the side panels of the chest. Battens are now nailed to the inner surfaces so as to form a ledge running round the inside of the chest at a height of three-quarters of the measurement from the bottom to the lid. Upon this the tray made of boards is laid and nailed down. The side portions of the front, the back surface and the lid are made of nailed boards. Carved relief-plaques are fitted into the compartments formed by the crossing timberwork, framed by strips of wood and nailed down. Relief-plaques are also nailed to the door wings, the trap door and the drawer. Finally, wooden feet are fitted into the mortised lower horizontal frame-beams. These feet have holes through their bases, in which disc-shaped wheels rest on axle-bearings. Very often, these feet are concealed behind triangular pieces of wood.

chest	*majuh* or *majus*	
(example in possession of Parbatbhai Shinabhai)		
chest	height	1.20 m
	breadth	1.25 m
	width	60 cm

The chest is used to keep articles of value such as jewellery, trinkets, cloth, clothes and a few rarely used household appurtenances. According to their size and value, these articles are kept either in the secret drawer, the small upper compartment or the larger lower one. Heavy padlocks on the doors serve to guard against thieves. Pots, pans, mortars and pestles are often kept between the feet of the chest. Matresses, blankets and quilts are piled up on the lid in a high heap and fastened with cords. This pyramid makes the chest appear enormous. The horse-heads projecting from the front are used as pegs to hang ropes, tapes and clothes.

94

Besides the metal trunk and the bedstead, which is pushed into a corner, the chest is the only large piece of furniture in the house. For the casual guest the chest, according to its size, its solidity, the delicacy of the craftsmanship displayed in its carvings or metal appliques and its consequent costliness, already indicates the value of the treasures contained in it. The fact that a special ceremony marks the handing over of a new chest to a customer further stresses its significance as a symbol of prosperity and treasure box of the house. The following scene took place in Malde's workshop on the 26th January 1966:

The customer has arrived from the neighbouring village of Kantela. He is given a brief greeting and waits, his gaze directed towards the chest, until the carpenter interrupts his work, takes the calendar from the post and ascertains whether the hour is an auspicious one. If it is, the customer pays the carpenter the negotiated price of Rs. 160 and offers him in addition his bag, which contains *mag* or *hardar,* a green shawl, *sopari,* a few betelnuts, a little *sindur,* vermillion dye wrapped in newspaper, a few marigolds (calendula), a silver coin and a coconut. The carpenter spreads out the shawl, lays the marigolds, coin and nuts upon it, sprinkles a little of the dye over all and carefully knots the corners of the shawls crosswise. He carries the little bundle to the chest, opens the secret drawer, places the symbols promising luck and prosperity in it and closes it. He now breaks the coconut on *ne,* the wooden anvil, and lets the milk run into a specially prepared glass. With this glass he goes first to the customer, then to the grown-ups, to us and finally to the apprentices and the children, pouring a little of the coconut milk into the hollow of each one's hand. The liquid is sipped and the moist palm passed over the face and hair. The carpenter then orders his apprentice to distribute pieces of coconut. Therewith the brief ceremony is over. The carpenter knows no special name for it. Together the men carry the chest outside, load it on the bullock-cart, tie it down firmly with ropes and spread cloth over it as a protection against dust. The customer then urges on his bullocks and drives off with his new chest to his village Kantela.

149

The chest, in which chiefly women's finery is stored, is also in most cases part of the dowry brought by a bride to her new home. Possibly, the wheels are intended to point this out, for they make the chest appear movable. In practice, however, the chest is too heavy and the wheels too clumsy to allow of it being rolled. In the house, chests occupy a permanent place against the wall, mostly on an elevated step or in small stone sockets.

Chests found in one village are usually the product of workshops in the villages from where the women originally came. In Ratadi, old chests mainly originate from the villages of Modhvada, Sisli, Palakdha, Visavada and Ratadi itself. Since the chests have been made in various workshops, marked differences are to be noticed with regard to construction details and dimensions, the shape of the wood pieces covering the feet, the modelling of ornamental motifs and the arrangement and style of the relief-work. The number of relief-plaques on the front surface indicate varying dimensions. In the majority of examples there are four rows, each with six rectangular sections standing upright. Less frequent are three rows, each with six upright rectangular sections. The shape of the door also varies. Doors are usually found to have one wing rather than two, even if exclusively old chests are considered. The secret drawers are built in with particular care. A springed metal plate is attached outside to the side of the small drawer in the upper righthand corner of the chest. This plate snaps into a notch in the chest wall; a small rod may be inserted, which pushes the spring back. The drawer may now be easily opened. At the back of the upper compartment several more drawers are often built in and under the lid boards, which may be raised or shifted; still more may sometimes be found.

146, 147

The shape of the wood pieces covering the feet and the wheels varies exceedingly. The fact that each workshop uses a certain shape (with negligible variations) over and over again may be used as a rough guide to identify the Ratadi chests as to their origin and to verify the information of their owners. Older chests produced in Ratdi itself display sharp-edged triangular pieces adorned with groove and notch designs. Chests from Modhvada have triangular pieces with stepped edges, chests from Palakdha triangular pieces with slightly rounded vertices. In Sisli the shape is also triangular, the piece being embellished by concentric patterns parallel to the edge. In chests from Visavada Tukda these wooden pieces are absent altogether.

147
148

95

The crossing timberwork is also often decorated, more or less all known types of chip designs being evident. Even complicated designs such as the curvolineal meandering and the 148 palmetto motif occasionally appear.

A motif subjected to far greater variations of style is, doubtless, that depicting modelled horse-heads on the ends of the side horizontal timbers. These variations serve as a 150 guide in determining the origin of chests. Only cylindrical horse-heads of the type carved on the ends of the door anchor-beams, are used on chests. They are carved on a smaller scale naturally. The remarks regarding the individual styles of the different workshops apply here as well. Below the horse-heads extremely simplified parrot-heads frequently appear on the vertical timbers. Only one chest displays a crouching figure, which is carved out of the rectangular timber. This chest was made in Visavada Tukda.

The reliefs are divided into ornamental and figural motifs. They are symmetrically arranged in horizontal rows across the front surface of the chest. In the commonest arrangement, exclusively figural or ornamental motifs appear in the topmost row. In all other rows, ornamental motifs are employed for the spaces on either side of the door and figural motifs for the door itself. However, in some chests the front is adorned exclusively by figure reliefs. In others again pairs of ornamental and figural motifs alternate. A further arrangement shows the topmost and bottommost rows with figure, the rows in between with ornamental reliefs. Or else the central pair is always figural, while the side pairs are ornamental. These two variations may also be combined, the topmost and bottommost rows being figural while in both middle rows the outer pairs are ornamental and the inner ones figural. It very seldom occurs that the designs are not arranged in matching pairs, for example, a figural pair bounded on the outside by a mixed figural and ornamental pair is very rare.

As a rule, the individual motifs are repeated in the horizontal rows. Thus in a figural row there will be either six peacocks or six elephants or again two different ornamental pairs and a lion pair. Such pairs are generally depicted facing each other.

A relief section consists of four parts: first there is a wooden piece for the background, which, 152, 153 however, may be identical with the surface of the chest. This background is coated with mica chips or aluminum foil. Now the plaque with the motif carved in open work is placed on the background and fitted into the compartment it is intended for, the compartment being formed by the crossing timberwork. The plaque is now framed with a moulding and nailed in place. The plaques are invariably thin wooden boards with plain, grooved or notched surfaces. The outlines are sloped in order to make the relief-work appear modelled or "carved out". In some old chests, plaques of sheet-copper with the designs cut out of them are found instead of wooden plaques. In Ratadi such a chest is known as a pitrodia. In new chests, the wooden plaques are replaced by porcelain tiles and mirrors.

The individual figural motifs occur with varying frequency. The peacock motif is virtually never absent from any chest. Elephants appear just as frequently. The lion, sparrow, rider and swan are rarer. A female figure, plant designs with birds or images of gods have been seen only on one chest in Ratadi. I have never come across scenes carved on chests.

The cradle 154, 155
The cradle consists of a pair of vertical wooden supporting structures with a horizontal bar across. A piece of cloth is strung hammock-fashion on an iron hanger suspended from the horizontal bar. Each of the wooden supports consists of four parts. On the undersurface of the transverse piece of timber, which terminates in two horse-heads, a pair of divergent legs are tenoned at an angle. In the middle of the transverse piece a vertical support is tenoned so as to stand upright. This support has a hole in the middle, into which the horizontal

bar fits. The three joints between transverse piece, legs and support are reinforced by iron strips. Just short of the mortise set in the support, the horizontal bar continues in an extended tenon. Into a slit in this tenon a wedge is driven. The hanger consists of two bows made of iron wire twisted in the middle to form a loop. The bows bend downwards and upwards, ending in turned-up knobs. This loop in the hanger is joined to another loop by means of an iron ring. The unclosed ends of this upper loop are extended to pass through a hole in the horizontal bar and are hammered down sideways at the top.

Throughout Saurashtra and in Gujarat in general a second type of cradle also occurs. Its wooden parts are made of turned and painted round timber. These cradles are produced in larger towns such as Porbandar and are gradually superseding the village type described here.

The rectangular cradle-cloth is hooked to the hanger by means of slings stitched to the four corners. The cloth is tautly stretched between the two ends of the hanger.

cradle	*ghodiyun*
(example in possession of Puriai)	
height	about 100 cm
length	about 130 cm
pair of legs	*phaya*
support	*dhingla*
horizontal bar	*dandi*
iron hanger with two bows	*pangra*
iron ring	*kadu*
iron loop	*nakuja*
cradle cloth	*kodia*
rope for rocking	*dori*

The cradle is used as a bed for infants and as a swing for the small children of the family. For this reason there is often more than one cradle to be found in a house. Throughout the day the cradle stands near the mother who rocks the child by rhythmically pulling the rope while she busies herself with her kitchen work.

A cradle is not heavy and can be carried by the mother. It can therefore be comfortably pushed through the main door and out into the veranda. If the cradle is to be transported over a long distance, however, it may be easily dismantled by hammering out the wedges.

Very often the wooden surfaces of the cradles are decorated with simple chip designs. The outline of the support may be articulated by grooves running transversely. Sometimes one finds a pair of particularly delicately carved horse-heads at the ends of the transverse piece. The angular horse-head predominates in the simpler designed cradles, whereas the cylindrical horse-head seems to be preferred for the more ornate ones.

In Ratadi there are two cradles remarkable for their ornateness of design. Both were constuc- 155, 151
ted by Kima, one of the local Ratadi carpenters. Even today they are the pride of their owners. The execution and design of both cradles vary only very slightly. Distinctive features worthy of note are the following:

(1)   All wooden surfaces are covered with chip designs.
(2)   The transverse piece terminates in cylindrical horse-heads. The upper edge of the transverse piece has three ovolos of triangular section on each side of the support.
(3)   Each pair of legs is slightly convex. Six ovolos of triangular section pointing outwards adorn the legs to a height of about one-third of the length from the bottom.
(An interpretation as to the significance of this type of carving could not be gleaned. Cradles from Saurashtra very often have crouching figures at this point as well. Cradles decorated in this style are supposed to exist in the neighbouring village of Visavada.)

(4) Between the legs and the transverse piece a piece of wooden lattice work with small square holes is fitted in and bounded by a horizontal batten on which tiny, turned wooden knobs hang.

(5) At the base there is a carved panel at the corners of which four twisted columns stand. In the centre of the panel there is a fluted column of rectangular section.

(6) The support terminates in a square shape.

(7) The horizontal bar is of either square or octagonal section and fluted.

The natural suspension-hook 156

A naturally grown V-shaped branch is fashioned in such a way that a piece of an arm's length, pierced through at its upper end, continues at an upward angle to end in a point. Through the hole a cotton cord knotted together at its end is drawn.

hook	*ankedi*
(example in the possession of Hidibhai Karsanbhai)	
length	51 cm
breadth	15 cm
diameter	3 cm.

This hook, as well as the curved hook, swinging pole, suspended hanger and pegs driven into the wall etc. hold articles which are otherwise liable to be dirtied or destroyed by vermin. All projecting beams, whether on the sides of the door or on chests, are also used for this purpose.

The curved suspension-hook 157

Four upwards curving branches are inserted into the lower end of a vertical pole so as to be diametrically opposed to each other. This pole is suspended from a strong cord by an iron ring.

A typical feature of the curved hook is a lathe-turned projection below the point where the branches are set in. This is surmounted by a square block into which four rectangular mortises are cut to admit the branches. The middle section consists of four twisted columns spiralling upwards from the corners of the square. Halfway up, these columns meet to entwine in a kind of symmetrical knots. They end in a hemisphere with flattened sides carved in open work. This again is surmounted by a disc hung with knobs. An iron ring is attached above to this disc by means of a staple. The rope by which the hole is hung runs through the iron ring. The four branches are made of flat, curved pieces of wood and decorated with parallel grooves. Each branch ends in a horse-head, from the mouth of which a small wooden knob is sometimes suspended.

curved hook	*ankedi*
(example in Baradia)	
height	56 cm
breadth	53 cm

These two types serve principally as hooks for hanging up leather articles. I once observed a pair of women's shoes made of leather placed between two branches of a curved hook as described above. However, l was repeatedly assured that the chief function of these hooks was to protect the leather water-bags from rats during the monsoon, when the bags are not in use. Apart from this, onions and garlic are tied to the hooks as well, where they hang in a current of air.

These hooks are always hung inside the house and never on the veranda. The rope or cord is tied to the ridge-piece so that the hook is freely suspended, either above the loft or in the room.

In Ratadi there was only one natural hook to be found. In the neighbouring village of Baradia two curved hooks were found, both made by the same carpenter Kima of Ratadi and consequently similar.

The swinging pole

This consists of a pole, which may sometimes even be of bamboo, with a rill cut in at each end. Two pieces of rope are knotted around these and tied above to the ceiling so as to allow the horizontal pole to swing freely.

swinging pole   *olamani*
(example in the possession of Samadbhai Karsanbhai)
pole   diameter 4 cm
                                                       length approx. 160 cm
rope   length 55 cm

These swinging poles which occur in various sizes, are used to hold clothes and sometimes saddles. They are never decorated and are usually constructed by the house-owner himself.

The suspended hanger with a disc

A short wooden batten is knotted to the lower end of a double rope tied to the anchor-beam or to the ridge-piece. Several spans above the batten, the double rope runs through a pierced disc of wood or sheet-iron. This disc is fixed in place by a knot or a small wooden wedge.

suspension hanger   *koringadun or dhol*
(example in the possession of Vasabhai Bhogibhai)
disc   diameter about 30 cm
batten   length about 10 cm
rope   length about 150 cm

The wall peg

A wooden peg tapering to a point at one end is driven into a hole in the wall. The other end is either turned up to form a hook or notched. Sometimes it is even carved into a horse-head.

wooden peg   *khili*
(example in the possession of Parbatbhai Shinabhai)
length   35 cm
breadth   5 cm

Garments in use, ropes and strings or turban lengths are usually hung on these wall pegs. Occasionally a whole row of wall pegs may be seen. Examples of ornate design such as those with carved horse-heads are made by carpenters, while simpler pegs are whittled at home by men from naturally shaped tree branches.

The wall shelf

This consists of a board with a broad nailed-on moulding. It rests on several pegs which are sometimes carved to horse-heads. Occasionally, an ornamental moulding adorns the shelf. Its lower edge runs in a wavy line, wooden knobs being sometimes attached to it.

wall shelf   *kandhi*
(example in the possession of Samadbhai Karsanbhai)
length   140 cm
height   10 cm

This shelf is chiefly used as a place to keep or exhibit utensils made of copper, bell-metal or porcelain. Pieces of embroidery are often hung below the shelf. Frequently, framed photographs or colour-prints on religious subjects are put up between two parallel mouldings. Now and again several supported shelves are arranged one above the other, thus constituting a shelf-case.

The one-legged stand

A rectangular post is let into a square base, the post being surmounted by a disc. It is used as a lampstand in the house, especially during the evening meal.

lamp stand	padaghal
(example in possession of Atiabhai Sinabhai)	
height	41 cm
base height	13.5 cm

The flat trestle

The ends of two parallel bars are tenoned to two longer rectangular lathes to form a square frame. Large water vessels or milk pots during the churning process are placed on this trestle.

trestle	ghodi
(example in possession of Vejabhai Atiabhai)	
length	30 cm
breadth	26 cm

The four-legged stool-shaped stand   158

In the four corners of a trestle, divergent legs are fixed. These stands hold water vessels. For this reason, they mostly stand beside the stone niches.

stool-shaped stand	ghed machi or gola machi
(example in possession of Navadas)	
height	about 50 cm
breadth	about 38 cm

The four-legged table stand   159

A large board rests on four or more legs. A few slightly concave forms with the ring-shaped outline left standing high are cut out of the surface of the board. Besides the four corner posts, another post as support appears in the front centre of the table. Just above ground-level, a cross brace is nailed to all the posts. A plank is fixed in front across the upper edge. The side cross pieces of the frame terminate at the front in a pair of horse-heads.

table stand for water vessels	pani harun
(example in possession of Ramabhai Jivabhai)	
height about	80 cm
length about	120 cm
depth about	40 cm

The entire front surface of a table of this type may be covered with chip designs. Vessels for drinking water are rested on this type of stand, which replaces the wall niches lined with stone slabs.*

The knee-prop   160

A narrow stem carved with a tortile design rests on a broad base and is surmounted by a slightly domed top of the same diameter as the base. All knee-props are turned on the lathe from one piece and were originally painted red or yellow. All of them are made in larger towns such as Porbandar by special carpenters known as *Sanghadiya*, turners. Knee-props ornamented with chip designs, in fact, any kind of carved knee-props are altogether absent.

knee-prop	dhichaniyun or gothaniyun
(example in possession of Puriai)	
height	14 cm
diameter	10 cm

These short, lathe-turned cylinders are used to rest the knees upon when one has been sitting cross-legged on the ground for some time.

---

*In other villages in Saurashtra, wooden water-stands of this type are placed on the veranda, while the water required for cooking purposes is kept inside the house in stone niches. This custom is not usual in Ratadi, though, possibly due to the shortage of drinking water.

Four corner posts and four rectangular side pieces form the more or less square frame. The seat is made of string irregularly interlaced and tied with tape. It is stretched across the frame. The ends of the posts, which are tenoned to the side pieces, project beyond the frame.

stool	*machi*
(example in possession of Govindas Narandas)	
height	24 cm
length	43 cm
depth	38 cm

These stools are used by the women of the house to sit upon while they operate the hand mills. Unoccupied stools, therefore, mostly stand on the mills or beside the grain godown.

The corner posts are very often lathe-turned and painted. Sometimes they are only partly turned, thus being ornamented with tortile as well as carved designs. In design, they resemble bed posts, being, of course, very much smaller in size. Rarely, the side pieces are found to be fluted, the plane being used for this. Worthy of note is the fact that the seats of the stools are invariably in bad condition, for they either sag, are irregularly worked or have the interlacing cord broken in several places. When the turned or otherwise decorated corner posts break, they are replaced by roughly fashioned wooden posts. It is therefore to be concluded that this piece of furniture, which is used exclusively by the women, is less painstakingly repaired than the other pieces, which are used by the men or serve as symbols of prestige.

The chair

The wooden chair frame consists of four long side pieces of more or less equal length and four corner posts. The back pair of corner posts projects above the surface of the seat and continues upwards to form the side pieces for the back of the chair. Like the seat, the back is also nearly square and consists of horizontal wooden props, between which boards or posts in open work are fixed. Between these boards or posts, rows of wooden knobs are set. The seat is usually strung with a roughly woven cotton tape, ties being employed here and there with varying success.

chair	*sanga machi*
(example in possession of Rupiai)	
height 64 cm	seat height 24 cm
depth 44 cm	post diameter 8 cm
breadth 48 cm	

These little chairs are also used by the women while they grind their hand mills. Unused chairs are kept in the loft.

All the wooden portions of a chair of this type may be turned and painted in multi-colours, red, green and yellow. Such pieces are made in towns like Porbandar and Bakharla. The second type of chair to be met with has corner posts which are also turned, but are re-ornamented with carved designs instead of being painted. They are distinguished by their different shaped backs, for the posts are like those of the beds or stools. On the two back posts two sparrows often perch. They are carved cubical, the head being a sphere and the body an oval tapering to a point. The rectangular strip of wood forming the upper edge of the back may either be decorated by a chip design or be carved into irregular waves, which are nevertheless arranged symmetrically from the centre. From this hangs a row of knobs, which often alternate with a row of columns. After this comes a board carved in open work set in between two battens on the lower one of which wooden knobs are sometimes hung. The board constituting the chair back may be embellished with one or several of the designs forming the stock-in-trade of carpenters specializing in relief carving.

Besides lattice work and inscribed roses, the commonest designs are those based on bird motifs. The boards, the back surfaces of which are planed smooth, are carved in open relief-work, that is, the front surface is covered with chip designs, some of which penetrate right through the wood. The result is an interesting effect of shallow, light-intercepting surface cuts, where the chisel has broken through the wood and deep notches lying in shadow.

The bedstead

This consists of a rectangular frame formed by four corner posts and four lateral beams, across which a network of string or woven cotton tape is stretched. The lateral beams of rectangular section are tenoned to the corner posts, the mortises for the tenons of the shorter beams being always cut in higher than those for the longer beams. At the bed level, the corner posts are usually square in section but narrow downwards to end with a more or less circular section. They are very frequently adorned with tortile ornamentation.

bedstead	*dholani*
cornerpost	*phayo dholaniun*
(example in the possession of Atiabhai Shinabhai)	
length	260 cm
height	about 70 cm
breadth	about 90 cm

Beds occur in two different widths. The broad double beds have decorated corner posts, whereas the narrow bedsteads are undecorated and are used by a poor person or serve as a spare bed outside the house.

Besides beds with lathe-turned, red and yellow painted posts, a large number of bedsteads exist which display some fine carving such as tori or fluted designs. These later bedsteads were probably initially produced on the lathe as well and later carved. The part of the post into which the lateral beams are tenoned may be of either circular or square section. In order to prevent splintering, a ring of sheet bronze is sometimes hammered around the posts just above the mortises.

6.3 Wooden kitchen utensils

The hand mill

This consists of a wooden box of a flat cylindrical shape resting upon four legs and a central vertical wooden axle. The box contains the two mill-stones, both of them having a hole drilled through the centre. They are placed one on top of the other, the lower one being fixed to the bottom of the box, while the other, known as the grinder, is set to revolve upon it above the axle by means of a wooden handle. In order to prevent the powdery flour from rising upwards, the mill may be fitted with a spectacle-shaped lid.

The wooden box consists of four equal legs, four curved lateral planks, two crossing props across the undersurface of the box and a number of boards forming the bottom. The legs are strong boards placed on end, the portion of the sides continuing downwards from the box bottom being marked with indentations. The upper portion representing about a third of the length forms part of the enclosing sides of the box. In this part a mortise is cut into each of its sides, into which the lateral planks fit. Further, mortises are cut into the legs at the level of the box bottom to admit the lengthened and slit tenons of the bottom props, which are firmly fixed on the outside by small wooden wedges. The four lateral planks are slightly curved rectangular boards stretched between the upper portions of the legs. They are attached to the legs by mortise and tenon joints and by nailed-on iron strips. Into one of these planks a square opening is cut, which can be closed by a tiny hinged door. The bottom, which joints the lateral planks to the legs, consists of two crossing props. A hole is bored through the centre of the crossing point. Between the props and the lower rim of the box boards are tenoned so as to fill the bottom surface.

The lower millstone lies in this wooden box. It is stuck to it with a mixture of cowdung and clay. The part of the bottom surface projecting beyond the circumference of the millstone is plastered with clay. The lower millstone is a flat cylinder with slightly rounded edges and a hole through its centre. The second millstone is placed upon the first. It is also disc-shaped and has its centre pierced through, a kind of funnel being mounted over the hole. A wooden board with a dented metal piece is driven in crosswise through the hole. A handle prepared out of a piece of rounded timber is inserted vertically into the upper millstone and fixed firmly by small wooden wedges. A piece of round timber terminating in an oiled sphere-shape is inserted through a hole in the centre of the box bottom and the lower millstone. It is fixed tightly into the hole in the lower millstone with the help of a rag twisted around it. The upper millstone with its wooden strut inside the funnel revolves upon this centrally mounted wooden axle. Under the box, the axle rod is anchored in a small wedge-shaped board into which a little hollow is cut. The board in its turn rests either on a complementary wedge or on a stone, through which the entire lower mechanism together with the axle rod may be pushed upwards or pressed down. To what extent the upper millstone weighs on the lower depends on what height the axle reaches above the lower millstone. This means that the friction between the millstones is regulated by the height of the axle, that is to say, the grain may be ground to any quality, fine or coarse, as desired.

handmill	ghanti, thalun, or thala
lower millstone	be para
upper millstone or grinder	ghanti
wooden strut for grinder	makli
metal piece	adi
wooden handle	hatho
wooden box	thalun, or thala
leg	paya
side piece (lateral plank)	vankiun
opening	tarun
prop	mas
slit tenon	sona
wedge	khili
bottom boards	bharania
metal strips	chapla
wooden lid	dhakanu
stone base	osikun
wooden axel	khili
wedge-shaped board	patli
complementary wedge	patli

Further accessories are:

brush for sweeping floor	salun
winnowing basket	supadun
stool	machi

(example in the possession of the carpenter Malde Mistri)

wooden box	diameter 66 cm
millstone	diameter 38 cm
legs	height 30 cm
	width 12 cm
lateral planks	length 39 cm
wooden axle	length 25 cm
	diameter 2.5 cm
grinder	thickness 8 cm
breadth of funnel	2.5 cm
diameter of hole	8 cm

While at work the woman sits on a little stool beside the hand mill and turns the handle on the grinder (upper millstone) with her right hand. With her left hand she pours the grain into the funnel. The grain is crushed and ground between the two rough stone surfaces. The flour collects in the spaces around the millstones, where it is swept together with the brush and intercepted by a vessel placed in front of the outlet. The hand mill generally stands beside the granary and is plastered to the floor with clay. In most households there are several hand-mills. When not in use, the brush and the stool are placed on top of the box and the wedges under the wooden axle are loosened.

The wooden box enclosing the grinding mechanism can be constructed by a village carpenter. The millstones, however, are obtained from the village of Dhrangadhra, in the Surendranagar district, which lies close to the boundary of the Little Rann of Kutch. Whoever requires a new handmill must first buy the millstones in a shop at Porbandar and take them to the carpenter to order a box for them. The carpenters themselves do not stock millstones. The task of plastering down the lower millstone with clay is assigned to the women. Replastering must be undertaken every few years.

Since simple handmills have no wooden box but are cased in clay, most of the wooden boxes are artistically designed and decorated with groove and chip designs. Practically all geometrical designs may be encountered carved on these boxes. However, we did not come across any figural motifs.*

The mortar and pestle   163
The mortar consists of a cylinder carved out of one piece of wood and usually has a hollow channel cut around it. In newer pieces, the hollows are not very deep. An angular bar made of hard *sisham* (rosewood) or iron serves as a pestle.

mortar	*kathodun or khandani*
pestle	*dhoko*
(example in possession of Samadbhai Karsanbhai)	
mortar	height 19 cm
	diameter 18 cm
pestle	length 53 cm
	diameter 3.5 cm

Spices, dried chili pods, vegetables, tobacco, sugar and salt are crushed and pounded in the mortar with pestle. Besides these portable wooden mortars, there is a stone pit sunk into the kitchen floor in every house. For this, a broad wooden pestle with a rounded pounding surface is used.

Mortars may be of varying dimensions. There are flat as well as high cylindrical forms. Cube-shaped mortars also occur. Of particularly beautiful design and ornamentation are the *kava* mortars, which are at the same time used as receptacles for the ground powder, being stoppered with a plug of cloth. A vessel of this type may be in the shape of a chalice and ornamented with scrolls and interlacing designs.

The containers   164
These are hollowed out blocks of wood, either square-shaped or cylindrical. At the side a groove is cut, into which an iron nail is driven and on which a flat wooden lid with sloped sides and a handle pivots.

container	*kathodun, khandani* or *kathoda*
(example in possession of Puriai)	
length	17 cm
breadth	13 cm
height	9 cm

---

*Handmills carved with figures may be found in villages of the Amreli district in central Saurashtra.

These wooden boxes are mainly used as salt-containers, although salt is better preserved dry in clay vessels. Wooden salt containers are used chiefly on festive occasions, when they are passed around during the feast or placed before the guests. Salt cellars may be richly decorated with chip designs. If rectangular-shaped, the patterns are composed of triangles. The rounded types, which are rare, are frequently decorated with inscribed roses. As already mentioned, they are generally square in shape, although cylindrical and truncated cone forms are seen now and again. One remarkable piece consists of two bowls placed side by side upon two pairs of wheels and joined to each other by a bolt. The lids are fixed on the upper rim and slide in opposite directions. The whole is covered with chip ornaments. Both containers are used for salt.

The bowl

These round wooden bowls have a flat bottom, from which the sides rise at an obtuse angle. The upper rim has an angular edge. The entire bowl is carved out of one piece of hollowed out timber.

wooden bowl	*kathrota*
(example in possession of Atiabhai Shinabhai)	
height	7 cm
diameter	33 cm

These bowls are used to receive the freshly ground flour from the hand mill. They are also used to mix the dough made of flour and water, out of which the flat cakes of unleavened bread known as *rotli* are prepard.

Such bowls are very expensive and are replaced in poorer households by clay vessels, which are far cheaper. Because the village carpenters cannot procure timber of suitable size, these wooden bowls are always made in larger towns. These bowls vary only in respect of size and dimensions. They are never decorated in any way. Cracks are sealed with iron wire.

The receptacle

Receptacles with lids are of two kinds:
The first consists of a cylindrical vessel with a rounded base. It has a hemispherical lid with a broad rim, which fits into the inner cavity with the help of a tenon.

The second, smaller type is probably lathe-turned, as is the first. In this second type the base is much broader. The neck slopes down to continue in a cylindrical shape, which curves inwards abruptly almost at a right angle, to form the base. A hollow groove runs around the neck, which has a straight rim. A lid fits into the narrow opening. This lid is of a hemispherical shape broken at the sides and crowned by a lozenge-shape knob.

receptacle (1) *dablo*	(2) *kankavati*
(example (1) in possession of Bhimabhai Gigabhai,	
example (2) in possession of Bhimabhai Avabhai)	
(1) height 15 cm	(2) height 8 cm
(1) diameter 18 cm	(2) diameter 7 cm

Both types of receptacles are used by the women to keep trinkets and other small articles. Dyes and drugs are also kept in them.

The measuring cup

The rim of these wooden cups of cylindrical shape is encircled by a metal ring. They are decorated with horizontal grooves and rows of chips and are always carved out of one piece of timber. In the base, which is sometimes very thick, traces of broad drilled holes may frequently be seen, for the hollowing of the cup is first prepared by drilling holes into a cylindrical block and later scooping out the wood with the chisel. The iron ring, which is sometimes absent, is fixed below the rim of the measuring cup with broad-headed nails. This iron ring is frequently nailed on only after a piece of the rim has once been broken off. There are two measuring cups which differ from each other solely in respect of the quantities they hold.

large measuring cup (1)	*payali*
small measuring cup (2)	*pavaliun*
(example (1) in the possession of Atiabhai Shinabhai,	
example (2) in the possession of Hansabhai Nagabhai)	
(1) height 13 cm	(2) height 11 cm
(1) diameter 13.5 cm	(2) diameter 9 cm

These cups are used to measure out small quantities of grain. They are to be found in every household in spite of the fact that it has recently become customary to use tin cans for this purpose.

Wooden measuring cups are made by the carpenter. The various measures are not officially standardized. For this reason, a trader always uses his own measuring cup during his transactions in order to ensure that the right amount has been dealt out to him. The discrepancies in dimension between the measuring cups are therefore amazing. The following are the measurements of three large cups (height by diameter) 13×13 cm. 17×14 cm. and 15×12 cm. However, these external measurements by no means determine the capacity, for the width of base and sides varies considerably.

Old measuring cups are often found to be patched. Either a small piece of wood or the broken-off piece itself is set in and fixed in place with wire or an iron band. Cracks and holes are occasionally even filled up with clay.

On the outside, a groove running round the cup is often carved. However, this does not represent any unit of measurement.

The ladle

The ladle consists of a long wooden handle with cup-shaped bowls hollowed out at both ends. There is only this one type of ladle to be found in Ratadi. Generally, in Saurashtra as a whole, wooden ladles are rare, for iron ladles are used to stir food. The bowl is always hemispherical and the end of the handle indented or curved. Ladles have only one bowl with the handle expanding to a broad rhombus at the other end.

ladle	*chatavo*
(example in the possession of Puriai)	
length	55 cm
diameter	8 cm

These wooden spoons with long handles are used while cooking vegetables or to ladle out food. Since they are hollow and therefore difficult to clean, cheap metal spoons bought in the towns are gradually taking their place. The villagers eat only with their fingers. Sauces are either drunk or sopped up.

The moulding board and the rolling-pin

168

The board, which may be rectangular or disc-shaped, rests upon a short support. Carved out of one side of the disc-shaped board is a rhombic handle. The rectangular boards are fixed upon two strips of timber which run parallel under the two narrow sides of the board. The disc-shaped boards are either supported by inserting three divergent wooden legs of round section or by nailing on four radially arranged strips of wood.

The rolling-pin is a piece of timber of circular section, the diameter of which gradually increases towards the centre. It is often turned on a lathe.

(1) moulding board	*patalo*
(2) rolling-pin	*velano*
(example in the possession of Atiabhai Shinabhai)	
(1) height 6 cm	(2) length 34 cm
(1) diameter 27 cm	(2) diameter 3.5 cm

The disc-shaped boards are principally used to roll out *rotela,* flat flour cakes, whereas the rectangular boards also serve as a dish upon which the cooked cakes are piled and placed before the guest.

The churner

At the end of a thick bar a four leaved hemispherical churner is fastened which is chisseled out of a cubical wooden block. To cover the earthen butter vessel a centrally pierced wooden disc with two handles on both sides is driven through the bar.

churner	*ravai*
disc	*der*
(example in the possession of Parbatbhai Atiabhai)	
bar length	148 cm
churner diameter	9 cm
disc diameter	42 cm

With a string the bar is tied to a pillar if only one person rotates the churner by means of a thick cord wound several times around the churner. This cord has wooden handles being knotted to both ends. However, if larger quantities of butter are made, the churner is hung up at a beam and two persons pull the rotation cord.

VII. Articles from metal

by Eberhard Fischer

In the present chapter we shall describe the various types of weapons, household utensils and ornaments which are characterized by being made either entirely or mainly of metal. Since in Ratadi itself there is neither a Luhar-smith, nor a brass caster, nor an (active) goldsmith, all metal parts have to be obtained either from the smiths' workshops at Palakhda and Porbandar or imported from distant towns such as Kutiana, Sihor or Bhavnagar. I did not have the opportunity of observing a smith at work. The carpenters at Ratadi are capable of carrying out any repair work involving metal.

VII. 1. Weapons

The battle axe   170, 171

The triangular iron head is welded to a long socket, the base of which is straight while the upper edge is curved. The head tapers to a straight-edged blade parallel to the wooden shaft. The blade is sharpened on both sides. The socket is invariably engraved with different ornaments: hatched designs, parallel grooves, herringbone patterns, concentric circles, spirals and the curvi-linear meandering motif predominate.

The head is driven into the straight wooden shaft to about a hand's breadth. A bronze ring which fits snugly around the shaft prevents the head from slipping further down. Very often a bronze cap is also fixed to the handle-end, the old specimens displaying a pattern of pronounced elevated rings running transversely. A hilt of this kind is sometimes made of iron.

axe	*kavado* or *kuhado*
iron head	*halakun*
blade	*khrun*
wooden shaft	*lakdi*
metal ring	*kadiyali*
bronze cap	*kundali*
(example in the possession of Dahyabhai Natabhai)	
length of shaft	125 cm
thickness	12 cm
width of head	13 cm

The men of the Mer tribe constantly carry a battleaxe with them. A group of informants explained the versatile uses of this weapon: It serves as a tool for minor repair jobs. This weapon is moreover used to cut fruit from trees, to chop firewood, as a protection against vermin and snakes, to ward off one's enemies and for one's own amusement.. The battle-axe is the emblem of manhood. While explaining the significance of this weapen to me, the young men spoke mockingly of a young Bava farmer, remarking that the Bavas must be a peculiar type of men not to carry battle-axes with them.

The axes are well kept, painstakingly cleaned, the blade whetted to a keen edge and the head polished till it gleams. The smiths in Baupra have a reputation for making good axe-heads. Large cartridge caps, which bear the inscription PRAC, are frequently used instead of bronze caps to cover the end of the handle.

The sable

The slightly curved sable blade is sharpened to a cutting edge only on its concave side. The blade is couched in a bronze pommel, which is often richly ornamented and covered with a thin gold plate, or the blade may be welded to an iron hilt. A transverse iron bar broadening out at both ends prevents any slipping of the hand. On the end of the pommel farthest from the blade, is a plate surmounted by a central boss. These latter sables come from Rajasthan, whereas the ones described first were made in Sihor (Bhavnagar district). The sables are usually sheathed in leather scabbards with a tip of cast bronze and a bronze mounting around the upper edge. In the absence of a scabbard, the carefully oiled sable is kept wrapped in a large cloth.

sable	*talavar*
scabbard	*myan*
tip	*kholi*
mounting	*muth*
(example in the possession of Atiabhai Shinabhai)	
length	95 cm
width	9 cm

Sables are found only in prosperous homes, in the so-called *patel* families and in the houses of the former landlords like the *darbar* of Baradia. They are normally found hanging, well-wrapped and packed, on the walls of the houses, but are taken down from the wall when a marriage takes place. During the nuptial ceremony the sable represents the bridegroom in the village of the bride. The sable also forms part of the regalia of the bridegroom when he rides in the processions during the marriage-week.

The lance

A two-edged triangular head is fixed into a stout (bamboo) pole. The blade edges are slightly curved.

302

lance	*bhalun*
length of pole	roughly 180 cm
length of head	roughly 20 cm

The shaft is occasionally reinforced by a metal ring fitted over it. In my opinion, the lance was intended for stabbing rather than for throwing. Nowadays the lance has come to be regarded merely as an accessory for personal decoration and is borne by some men when they ride to the neighbouring village to pay a visit.

The gun

Some of the older men possess muzzle-loaders. These guns are usually of English make and date back to the turn of the century. I had the opportunity to examine a very dangerous gun, the ignition being effected by lighting a thick cotton cord and bringing it into contact with the gunpowder with the help of a bent metal wire.

The shield

169

The shield, which is slightly arched and circular in shape, is comparatively small in size. It has a straight edge and an umbo in the centre, around which four flower-shaped burls are arranged. A leather strap serves as a handle.

shield	*dhal*
(example in the possession of Puriai)	
diameter	29 cm
thickness	3 cm

Shields were formerly made chiefly in the village of Madhavpur, which lies in the environs of Kutiana. These small rider-shields are not used at all now a days. They were earlier supposed to have been used by martial men during the *ras*-dances.

VII. 2. Household utensils and other accoutrements from metal

The iron chest

These large rectangular chests are made from strong wood. They have lids attached to the box by hinges on one side. They have sheet iron mountings, the front surface of the chest being divided into several sections by the mountings. The designs are either punched in or stamped on the sheet iron, which is framed by traversing metal bands nailed on the iron pieces. The chest usually stands on two pairs of wooden wheels, which may be concealed behind semicircular plates. The slightly projecting lid, which is mounted with sheet iron, mooves on two broad hinges. When the lid is shut, the chest can be locked with the help of two metal studs on the front surface of the chest, through which a long transverse padlock may be passed.

chest	*patara*
(example in the possession of Vasabhai Bhojabhai)	
height	95 cm
length	145 cm
breadth roughly	50 cm

Cloth, costumes for festive occassions, jewellery and other valubles are stored in these strong chests and thus protected from thieves and vermin. These chests are extremely costly as they are imported from remote towns such as Bhavnagar.

The designs punched into the mountings and engraved on the traversing bands are exclusively geometrical. Figure motifs of the kind that may be observed on the beautiful, bronze-mounted chests of Central Saurashtra are not employed in the decoration of chests to be seen in Ratadi houses. There are, however, few wooden chests with copper plaques fitted into them.

The lock

A long padlock hangs in front of the chest. It consists of a horizontal elongated metal part with a hoop projecting upwards and a parallel piece which is passed through it. A long iron key opens a spring when inserted into the lock.

lock	*hachavanu*
(example in the possession of Puriai)	
length	35 cm
height	6 cm

The bowl

Such a bowl or a dish is composed of several pieces of sheet iron riveted together. The rim is cylindrical and the hammered dish-bottom slightly hollow. At the joints the iron pieces are cut into a fringe-like formation and the ends thus fitted together.

bowl	*kundi*
(example in the possession of Vasabhai Bhojabhai)	
diameter	24 cm
hight	10 cm

The bowls or dishes are chiefly used to carry small quantities of grain, molasses or chilli powder. They are more solid and durable than baskets and possess the further advantage of being easily cleaned, since there are no cracks in which grain, etc. are likely to stick.

In similar bowls, which sometimes can be up to two metres in diameter, at festivities the food for the guests is cooked.

The winnowing shovel
Three sides of the rectangular shovel are curved upwards. The edges are dovetailed
and hammered over.

winnowing shovel	*supadu*
(example in the possession of Govindas Narandas)	
length	32 cm
height	9 cm
breadth	28 cm

Nowadays winnowing shovels made from tin have largely superseded those made
from wood or of wicker-work.

The kitchen tongs
The two arms of the tongs are riveted together and hammered flat. Both arms are straight
and diverge outwards from the riveted joint.

tongs	*hansi*
(example in the possession of Atiabhai Shinabhai)	
length	28 cm
width	6 cm

With these tongs, pots and pans both of clay and metal are lifted and removed from the fire.

The scraping spoon
This consists of an iron rod hammered flat at one end into a shallow bowl with a straight edge.

scraping spoon	*tavetho*
(example in the possession Atiabhai Shinabhai)	
length	24 cm
width	4 cm

The scraping spoon is used for cooking and roasting.

The ladle
The wooden ladle has now been replaced by mass-produced metal spoons pressed out of tin.
The bowl is round and slightly hollow

ladle	*chamcho*
(example in the possession of Atiabhai Shinabhai)	
length	23 cm
width	7 cm

The nut-cutter
The nut-cutter, commonly used throughout Gujarat, consists of a simple handle with a wide
iron blade, the whole being riveted to a broad iron base which terminates in a handle.
Designs are sometimes engraved on the iron.

nut-cutter	*hudi*
(example in the possession of Puriai)	
length	15 cm
thickness	5 cm

The nut-cutters seen in Ratadi are generally simple and sparingly ornamented. All the
village people, especially the men, always carry a nut-cutter with them and use
it as a kind of pen-knife as well as to cut *sopari*-nuts into pieces.

The lamp stand
A disc-shaped horizontal shelf or bracket is welded to one end of a long iron hook. A small
oil or kerosene lamp may be placed upon this shelf. The lamp stand may be suspended
from a rafter or from a projection in the wall.

lamp stand	*divelu*
(example in the possession of Harbhambhai Rangmalbhai)	
length	29 cm
diameter	7 cm

The marriage lamp stand

173

This consists of a rectangular frame constructed of horizontal and perpendicular iron strips
riveted together. To the centre of the lower edge, a disc-shaped lamp stand is attached,
upon which a small oil lamp may be placed. The central perpendicular strip projects beyond
the frame to terminate in a hook, by which the lamp stand is hung. Sometimes cut-out
pieces of tin are fitted into the spaces between the compartments formed by the crossing iron
strips. But as a rule there are only simple iron strips, cut so as to taper to a point.

lamp	*jamarag divelo*
(example in the possession of Nathabhai Vitabhai)	
height	20 cm
breadth	13 cm

Lamp stands of this description are found above all in the homes of Harijans and craftsmen,
where they play a part in the marriage rites.

The grated window

Grated windows imported from Porbandar are a feature of some of the more prosperous
houses in Ratadi. The stout iron wires are twisted into a wavy line and run at right angles to
each other, being encircled by a ring at the points of contact.

grated window	*anjavaliyu*
(example in the possession of Samadbhai Karsanbhai)	
height	22 cm
breadth	19 cm

The vessels of copper-alloys and aluminium

Vessels of brass and bell-metal, such as are in common use throughout Saurashtra, are also
part of the kitchen inventory in Ratadi households. All of them are purchased at Porbandar,
but most probably manufactured at Sihor (Bhavnagar district.) By virtue of their greater
durability and lighter weight, vessels of metal are gradually ousting those made of earthenware.
It appears that only very few metal utensils were used in Ratadi households before the war.

The chief types of vessels are as follows:

78, 176, 299

small water pot	*kahelio*
large vessel for carrying water	*ghado kasho*
large dish	*thal*
small bowl	*tranhali*
lamp with cotton wick	*divo*

The bells

Bells cast in brass occur in two forms: they are either spherical in shape with a cross-cut in
the undersurface, a raised ridge along the diameter, an iron clapper inside and a ring to hang
it by, or else they are cup-shaped and have an iron clapper which is continued to form a
ring on the outside. These bells are procurable in two sizes. All bells are purchased at Porbandar.

spherical bell	*gugra*
large cup-shaped bell	*tokra*
small cup-shaped bell	*tokri*
bell-strap	*gugerma*

Seven to nine bells are sewn in a row to a leather strap, the large cup-shaped bell being
placed in the centre. On festive occasions, this bell-harness is hung around the necks of the
draught-oxen.

The censer

This is a shallow, chased bowl riveted to a tripod, one leg of which projects outwards like a handle. The bowl with its tripod is generally made of iron.

censer	dhupeliyu

When twilight falls, a little *ghee* is burnt in the bowl. Sometimes perfumes are added. The smoke "consecrates" the house. Nowadays the censer is often replaced by incense-sticks purchased at Porbandar.

The water-pipe

174

A large, hollowed-out African coconut serves as the water-container. It is polished black and is mounted with silver at its pointed end. A long wooden tube with a silver mouth piece is inserted into one side of the coconut which is surmounted by a clay funnel resting on a silver tube decorated with a fluted-design. In the clay funnel, the tobacco slowly burns under a layer of charcoal.

The silver parts are either chased silver plates or hammered silver threads. They are fastened 175 to the coconut with the help of silver rivets. In the costlier water-pipes, the clay funnel is of black earthenware and is more stable in quality. Inside, it has a built-in tray with an opening in the centre. The tobacco is filled into the lower compartment and pieces of hot charcoal are placed upon it. On its outside, the funnel is decorated with scored designs, which are sometimes painted with a chalk solution.

The water in the coconut is changed every day. Should the smoker wish to burn the tobacco slowly, he places a cover in the form of a circular piece of tin on the funnel.

water-pipe	hukka
(example in the possession of Atiabhai Shinabhai)	
length	75 cm
height	49 cm
funnel (chimney)	15 cm

With the exception of the chimney, which is made by expert potters at Porbandar, the entire water-pipe is made by the goldsmiths at Porbandar or Una Delvada. A water-pipe of particularly fine quality and workmanship formerly cost approximately 80 Rs. and hence represented an article of value. But even less well-to-do men such as the potter of Baradia permit themselves the luxury of a water-pipe. In this case the pipes are obviously less elaborately decorated and have practically no silver mountings.

As a rule, the pipe is pieced together and lit early in the morning, to be smoked by the group of old men who meet on the verandah at sunrise for their morning gossip. The pipe is passed around the circle. Many men smoke through their fingers, that is, they clasp one hand around the mouthpiece to prevent their lips from touching it. The owner of such a pipe will always gather a circle of friends around him. The tobacco is mixed with a large amount of molasses and stored in a bamboo reed.

The fire-striker

The fire-striker consits of an angular steel rod with one end turned up to form a handle, a piece of flint, reddish in colour and a piece of coarse dry cotton cord.

steel rod	kadi
flint	chemak
cord	kup
bamboo	bhugali
(example in the possession of Sangatabhai Kamabhai)	

A fire-striker of this kind is obsolete and used only by a few of the old men. Matches brought from dealers are in general use. To my knowledge, no other types of fire-strikers are used.

VII.3. Precious metal ornaments

by Haku Shah

In daily use are only gold earrings and some silver bangles and anklets. The full gold-treasure is kept in boxes and is only taken out during a marriage. Since the villagers are always suspicious if someone wanted to see their gold, we decided not to offend them. My information therefore is somewhat scanty.

3.1. Men's ornaments

The men usually decorate themselves with golden earrings and sometimes with a necklace.

The golden earrings
There are two kinds, one is a golden half globe on which concentrically gold wires are applied. This type is fixed through a hole bored in the upper part of the earring and kept in place by a spiral or a screw with a nut. The other type is a slight curve with a ball in the centre.

64, 302

half-globe earring	*hihoria*
earring with centre	*chapava*

The necklace
The necklace consists of four or five rows of rhombic beads which are alternatively golden or red corals.

necklace	*mala*

An old man wears only, *hihoria,* earring, whereas a young man may wear all the ornaments at the time. A boy of four or five years may wear ornaments like *pelo anhadi,* a small ornament on a string, *kandoro,* a silver band round the waist or *kankaliyu,* a silver anklet.

During the marrige ceremony the bridegroom wears the family treasures such as *mala,* a necklace and the large necklaces like *kanthali, tupiyu* etc. and silver armrings like *troda* and *bedi.*

352

The wearing of ornaments is now becoming rare. I was told that formerly there were different silver ornaments in use which have more or less disappeared. Save in the Rabari community in Ratadi, even gold ornaments are not worn every day. The only ornament still popular is the *hihoria,* earring.

3.2. Women's ornaments

The golden earring
On a ring is fixed a heavy gold ornament consisting of a body shaped to four rhombs standing on their points with triangles adjoining on all sides, and a small cylindrical band with points, arranged to form vertical strips, links it to the half globe with which the earring ends.

71, 80, 317

golden earring	*vedhala*

These earrings are worn by every grown woman whether working or merrymaking. They are fixed in the earlobe.

The rhombic earring

This golden earring is in the form of a rhombic shield and has at its centre a prominent dot with small dots spread over the entire surface.

rhombic earring   *pandadiyu*

The ornament is only worn on special occasions and is fixed at the top of the ear. One woman can wear many of them at the same time.

Other earrings

Besides these two earrings the *hihoria*, earring for men, and a *thoria*, another ear ornament can be worn by women.

The necklaces

Necklaces are mainly used on marriage occasions. There are different types, called *zumanu*, *kanthalia*, *mandaliya*, *mohanma*, *panamala* and *har*.

The nose-ornament is no more in use. Formerly woman used to wear *nath*, a large golden ring which covered the lips, too.

The silver ornaments

Only very little information can be submitted. *Haraliya* is a thin silver arm bangle with a curvilinear shape. *Chudi* is a solid cylindrical armring worn on the lower arm on special occasions like marriages. Other silver anklets are called *kambiyu* and *kadala*. All silver ornaments are worn by young women. Small girls wear *polariaya*, anklet, *hanakli* and *khelmana*, necklace, *chunk*, nose ring and *hihoria*, men's earring.

VIII. Pottery

by Eberhard Fischer

VIII.1. The potter

1.1. The informant

There is today no potter working in the village of Ratadi itself. The members of the Kumbhar or potter caste are either carpenters or stonecutters by profession. But there are potteries in the neighbouring villages of Baradia, Shrinagar, Kutchhdi and Tukda-Miyani. There were two reasons for our choosing the particularly skilled potter of Baradia for our informant: firstly, because the village of Ratadi and Baradia formerly constituted an economic unit and secondly, because the potter of Baradia continues to this day to supply the greater part of the earthenware required by Ratadi households.

The potter Bhurabhai Dhayabhai is a man about 45 years of age. He is married and has three sons and four daughters. Of these children, only the eldest daughter is married and lives with her husband in the village of Kalavad (Jamnagar District). The eldest son works in a ceramics factory in Junagadh, and has not visited his parents for a long time. The potter lives with his family in a small homestead on the borders of the village, near the well shaft. His sole possessions are his household goods, the tools and general equipment for his craft, three female donkeys and two goats. All the family members co-operate to help the potter in his business. The older children are sometimes sent out as help to the farmers. Two girls attend school irregularly.

The following account, in which the potter Bhurabhai relates the story of his life, has been pieced together from two interviews. The potter narrates:

// I was born in Kantela. My father had four brothers: one of these brothers was living in Kantela, one here in Baradia, one in Shrinagar and one in Palakhda. My father died when I was ten months old. I was brought up by my father's younger brother who lived here in Baradia and later became a tailor in Vansalia. His sons are not potters either. They are tailors. So I inherited my uncle's set of potter's tools.

// I was ten months old when my father died. If all the brothers die, even if all the sisters die, it does not matter. But if the parents of a boy die when he is still of a tender age, his plight is a pitiable one. He becomes homeless. True, he picks up a lot from the different people who take him in, but he is put to hard work and if he rebels, he is beaten; thus the orphan necessarily becomes a hard worker. This is because he is beaten wherever he goes and is never treated well.

Speaking of myself, I was with my uncle up to the time of my marriage age.

// I don't remember (whether he was kind to me). However, you will never love the children of your brother as you love your own children. Somehow I felt he was not quite the same to me as my parents would have been. // As long as I was with my uncle, I only knew how to make *kodia*, oil lamps and *kuda*, simple pots. I was not taught to handle the wheel. My uncle used to send me daily to fetch the fuel for firing the vessels. He did not teach me *kasab*, the craft.

After my marriage I lived apart from my uncle. At that time he made me an offer to stay with him. I was to receive a sum of 40 Rs. a year. I stayed one year in his house. My uncle had a special reason for wanting me to live with him: his own donkeys had died, while I had two sturdy donkeys at that time. So he thought that if I stayed with him he could use my donkeys.

When I separated from him, he told me that the expenses of my marriage would be shared by both, and since I had stayed with him one year, he owed me forty rupees. From this, thirty rupees were taken as payment towards my marriage and I left him with ten rupees wages for one year. I therefore became completely bankrupt. I started my own business and in the second year after leaving my uncle, I slowly began to acquire more skill in my *kasab*, craft. Through my own efforts I gradually learnt the tricks of the trade, and from then onwards I have been continuing this business.

//When my father died, he left very few possessions. Out of these the ceremony had to be paid for and the rest was taken by the family. I did not receive a single item.

// After leaving my uncle's house I went away from this village and moved to Vansalia. There I spent about ten years. Then I returned, and since then I have lived here continuously. My uncle was here and therefore I could not stay here too, for if two potters stay in the same village, neither of them is able to earn enough. My uncle now lives in Vansalia and I live here in his former house. // No, I did not pay him anything for it. I even use his tools. He does not care for this occupation any more. He concentrates on sewing. However, my uncle is a very good potter. He is far more skilled than I am. He is now sixty-five. Sometimes he comes here and helps us in our work just for pleasure's sake.

// I have no recollection of my mother. I never stayed with her. In our community a widow may take a new husband, this custom being known as *gharghvun*. She must remain a widow for about six months, but as there is nobody to give her food she must take a new husband.

Finally, it may be recorded that of all the craftsmen I interviewed in Ratadi, the potter was the one with the most extensive professional knowledge. He was also the most responsive during the interrogations and without reservation communicated to me every technique and every complexity of his *kasab*, craft.

1.2. The role of the potter

The manufacture of earthenware calls for the co-operation of the entire family of the potter. The principal work, that of throwing and moulding the vessels is confined strictly to the male members, while the younger ones are charged with supplying the raw materials and fuel. The wife assists her husband in mixing the clay, while the other woman of the household draw the required water and subsequently rub and polish the earthenware, when it becomes as hard as leather. The women sometimes also paint the earthenware, using chalk solutions and pigments in a variety of colours. The marketable earthenware is sold by the potter himself. He may also depute his children for the task.

Since all the family members have a share in the procedure of work, they imbibe some knowledge, however superficial, of the craft. An ideal family enterprise of this sort, where each aspect of the work is performed by a specialist in his particular duty, is to be seen in Shrinagar. Here, every phase of the potter's craft may be observed in one large working yard. In a large family concern of this kind it is likely, though, that a child eager to learn is sent for years to collect firewood instead of being taught the craft (vide pg. 116). However, the procedure of learning generally takes another course.

During my stay in Baradia the potter mostly works alone, helped in the afternoons by his wife. The older daughter retreated to the house because of my presence. The bigger boy tends the goat while the little girls play with their friends in the village or help in the households of farmers. The younger son, a child of about five years, plays by himself in the yard where his father works. The potter keeps a fond eye on the little fellow. When he starts to cry the father interrupts his work, fetches the little one to him and cracks a few peanuts for him to soothe his pain or appease his rage. Even while working concentratedly, the potter keeps chatting with the little boy. But the most remarkable thing is that the child plays all the time in the yard, chiefly with clay and potters' tools, imitating his father's movements or the driving of the wheel. He is sometimes given a miniature vessel to "finish" and is otherwise constantly occupied in kneading and moulding lumps of clay. When his mother polishes a vessel at the proper stage (when it has become as hard as leather) using a piece of sacking, the little boy

203, 266

wants to help her. He is at once handed a jute rag and a vessel which he proceeds to scrub with great zeal. The child is naturally no help yet, quite the contrary in fact; he merely worries his busy parents and distracts them from their work. Apart from my own home, I have never come across a father more devoted to the care of his children in everyday life. – The elder son of the potter is about fourteen years old, and therefore at an age when the boys soak their hair with oil and comb it in fancy puffs and waves. They regard childish games with contempt and gradually begin to make themselves useful around the house. Every day the boy tends the goats, carries water, searches with his father for fuel to feed the kiln fire, and sells vessels on his own. But he has not yet learnt the potter's trade.

Speaking of his own apprenticeship and how he learnt the craft, the potter Bhurabhai Dhayabhai says:

// I learnt the craft from my uncle through daily practice. Learning our craft takes twenty to twenty-five years. I cannot yet concider myself a perfect potter. The work done by the children is of mediocre quality. However that is how they learn the trade.

// My son is ten years old. He has just started learning pottery. After ten or fifteen years he will be able to do the work. When the child possesses a natural aptitude, he can learn in less time.

// The most difficult part of the work is using the wheel. // My son ? No, he cannot mould vessels.

// There was no special day to mark the end of my term of apprenticeship. I stayed some time longer with my uncle and we were partners. My uncle was the head, because I had no father.

There is no fixed term of apprenticeship and no definite method of training apprentices in the potter's trade. The various manipulations must be learnt by watching, imitating and experimenting. This is sometimes rendered difficult, because with the exception of their own sons, the skilled potters jealously guard the secrets of their craft from all, even near relations. After the interviews had dragged on for over a week, the potter suddenly remarked to me in the midst of explaining a complicated technical process:

How much knowledge you get ! If any person from the Kumbhar community were to come to my door and ask me to show him how to make a vessel step by step, I would not comply with the request. That would amount to divulging the secrets of my craft, *kasab*. The person who wants to see it wants to steal my knowledge. That is why I would strictly refuse such a request.

// O yes, there are many persons of my caste who know how to prepare clay and how to use the wheel - but they do not know how to lift the moulded vessel from the wheel.

The reason for not showing my work is this : suppose the other man is *kasab*, skilful and learns my trade, he might come here and establish himself as a potter, too. He would then prepare the same vessels as I do, and he might sell them at a cheaper rate.

It therefore follows, that not all the trained potters of Saurashtra possess the same elementary knowledge of their craft, and it is astonishing to observe, among potters belonging to the same marriage group, how greatly their working techniques vary, what a range of vessels of different shapes and sizes they produce, and how individually diversified the process of decorating their pottery is.

The social status of the potters is not to be easily ascertained. The Kumbhar potters belong to the class of Sudra craftsmen, and are therefore of a lower caste than the Mers, who are considered members of the Kshatria or warrior castes. Because they are financially worse off than other Sudra craftsmen like the carpenters and smiths, the potters are frequently looked upon as inferior to these; nevertheless, this drawback is amply made up for by the socio-religious prestige enjoyed by the potters, for they are called upon to perform special functions on various occasions. The form of address employed is *bhagat*, pious man, and indicates the particular prestige that is the potter's due. Bhurabhai gives an explanation of this flattering epithet :

It is the general custom that any person who is a stranger to the village, regardless of the community he belongs to, may come to our door for hospitality. We will give him shelter and keep him as our guest. This is in fact the duty of our caste and the reason why we are called *bhagat*, pious person.

Pavitra means a holy object and a pious person is called *bhagat*. //Piety implies praying often and using a *mala*, rosary.

This explanation of the concept "piety" provokes a taunting farmer to promptly make an ironic comment on the function of a rosary :

However, the potter uses a *mala*, rosary, not for praying but for polishing his pots...

A further indication of the religious superiority of the potter over other craftsmen is the fact that, the potters regard their working equipment as given by one of the deities. Bhurabhai explains this :

// All our tools are give to us by god *Shankar (Shiva)*. *Shankar* gave the tools to *Brahma* and *Brahma* gave them to the potters. When *Brahma* first gave the tools to the potters, the wheel used to turn automatically. We had to use the hand to stop it turning. But one day a potter in a fit of madness wanted to stop the turning wheel without using his hand and instead gave the wheel a kick with his foot. After that the wheel stopped forever, and since that day we have had to turn the wheel with a stick.

The comparatively close association of pottery with religious beliefs is borne out by the fact that the lump of clay placed on the potter's wheel before being moulded is called *Shankar nu ling*, *Shiva's lingam*, because "all the shapes and forms that the mind can imagine are capable of being moulded from the cone-shaped lump of clay". The potter thus draws analogy between himself and one of the creative deities.

There remains to be mentioned the following taboo aetiologically explainable :

// One must never touch the turning wheel with the foot. That is the only thing forbidden in the workshop.

It seems probable to me that, similar taboos existing for other craftsmen are also rooted in religion, and merely lack satisfactory elucidation.

To my question, whether he could also mould vessels without using the wheel, the potter Bhurabhai answered :

// No, pots can only be moulded on the *shankar no chakdo*, *Shiva's* wheel. It is an essential part of our equipment. Without it we cannot work. We cannot work *jadu*, magic.

This answer reveals the general attitude of the potters to their work : they believe their tools to be vested with a potent primordial power given by the gods. This power in combination with the skill of the craftsman, makes possible the production of earthenware. The potter uses the word *kala* to denote skill or the individual art, whereas the practised ability of a craftsman is known as *kasab*. This word is also used to describe craft in its connotation as a *dhandho*, trade.

The customs of the Kumbhar caste differ in some respects from those of other marriage groups. The potter Bhurabhai describes his wedding ceremony in the following manner.

First my betrothal took place. Some time later the marriage ceremony was performed. At that time my father-in-law said to me : 'If you wish to marry my daughter immediately, I will give her to you. We are ready'. Then we ate *gur*, molasses, together as a sign that our families were about to form an alliance. We became relatives. We consulted the Brahmin as to which time would be the most propitious for the ceremony, and he pointed out an auspicious date. He told us : 'After eight days you can come to be married'. On my wedding day, I wore new clothes and ornaments. I distributed *tam*. and some sweetmeats among my relatives. We called them all together, and gave them a feast. When the bridal procession went to the bride's house, there were twentyfive of my relatives with me.

We went to Ranavav, five miles away from Porbandar. The big ceremony took place in the bride's house. Twenty women were singing songs for the reception of the bridegroom, and they accompanied me into the house to wait for the arrival of the Brahmin. When the Brahmin, who is called *gor* came, he started to recite some *mantras*. He built an altar of clay, on which he lit a fire with cowdung and wood. He poured *ghee* into the fire. I placed my right hand on the right hand of my bride, and we went round the fire together. Next day we went to my house and the ceremony was therewith over.

// She was not chosen by me. She was chosen by my uncle. I had to obey him.

// He gave her to me because her family has *sari abru*, a good reputation, and because we are distantly related.

Widows are permitted to marry again. A re-marriage of this kind is known as *gharadvun*. Bhurabhai told me that he stayed back in the family of his father when his mother took another husband. That happened when he was still a small child. This is how he explains it :

// *Gharadvun*, remarriage is a frequent occurrence. However, it very seldom happens that the widow marries a widower. In many cases, purely financial considerations prompt a widow to marry again *(gharghe)*, or a single man to marry a widow.

// This kind of ceremony is very cheap and the expenses are met by the bride's parents, whereas *lagan*, a normal marriage is paid for by the bridegroom's family.

Speaking of *gharadvun*, the two parties are either friends or else the parents of bride and groom fix the sum to be paid to the bride's parents. After that, the bride will be sent to her husband's house. The procedure is very simple. *Gharadvun*, marriage with a widow, does not require the normally compulsory expense entailed by the bridegroom inviting his entire family, his brothers and uncles and their respective families for a period of about eight days.

// In the *gharadvun*,-ceremony the woman receives only a new *sadla*, dress, and a coconut. // No, she gets no money, whereas in *lagan*, the normal marriage ceremony, the groom's parents have to pay 51 Rs. to the bride's parents. // This amount is fixed by the community and in our case it is fixed at 51 Rs.

When his wife dies, the husband bears the expenses of the cremation and attendant ceremonies. Bhurabhai once more informs me:

// If the woman dies, they will wrap the corpse in costly materials, if they are able to afford them, and burn them with the body. It is lucky for a woman to die before the husband dies.

// Sometimes, they will preserve the ivory bangle in a bag and should the potter remarry, he will present the ornament to his new wife. If he is rich, he is expected to buy a new bangle, whereas if he is poor, he will have to make do with the old one.

If a realation dies, even if he or she is only related by marriage, the potter or one of his sons has to participate in the funeral rites. Bhurabhai for instance had to journey hundreds of kilometres to the village of Kalavad (Jamnagar District), when the grandmother of his son-in-law died. When interrogated, he replied :

// When *vodi vevan*, a relation of importance, dies in the family of *vevai*, the son-in-law's father, we have to attend the *kerea*, ceremony. I have to go for the ceremony of my *vevana*, son-in-law's mother or grandmother.

// There is no other event for which we have to be present in the house of the *vevai*.

// I am compelled to go. I will have to bear all the expenses, which will amount to about 25 Rs. and in addition I will have to give a piece of cloth costing five rupees, which is called *pot*. // They keep the cloth and use it. The material is *pachhedi*, the white cloth that is used for turbans.

// If I have no money ? Then I will have to borrow it from somewhere.

/ And if you do not go ? / Then I will be abused in the community and my daughter will be harrassed and rebuked by her in-laws because I did not go there. // I could send my eldest son and I would send him, if he were here. However, one may only send one's son if one happens to fall ill at the time.

There is another custom peculiar to the woman of the Kumbhar caste and not practised as strictly elsewhere :

// During *chhede beshvun*, menstrual period, the women must not work for four days. During this time nobody is allowed to touch her, not even her husband. She must rest in the house, sitting in one corner. The Mer women keep their hair open during this period. However, they continue to work and are not compelled to keep inside the house.

The dress worn by the male members of the Kumbhar caste is not remarkable for any feature : they generally wear baggy trousers, shirts and turbans made of coarse white cloth. The potter Bhurabhai says:

Most potters dress as I do : some wear a cap; some prefer to be bare-headed. Some wear *angadi*, waistcoat, some prefer *kamis*, shirt.

The women wear pleated skirts, bodices and head covers or veils of material printed in many bright colours. A special feature of the jewellery is a pair of broad ivory bangles. These bangles are decorated with a groove. The opening is fitted with a hammered silver piece which serves as a catch. The other metal ornaments are the same as those worn by women of other communities of craftsmen. The potter Bhurabhai relates :

|| *Balovan*, the ivory bangle, is given to the wife after marriage by her husband. || It is from Porbandar. The *miniara*, merchants specialize in these kinds of goods. || Usually the potter women wear only one bangle on each arm.

|| *Khadla*, is a hollow silver ring which is worn on the ankles.

|| When a potter's wife becomes a widow she breaks her bangles and they are thrown away. However, if she dies first, the husband keeps the ornaments in a bag and uses them again for a second marriage. || The silver catch of the *balovan*, ivory bangle, is called *jud* and it holds both ends together.

|| Nowadays the ornaments worn by all the castes are the same, but formerly they used to differ. I myself have no third hole in my ear, but we formerly used to wear *bunkri*, a golden conical ornament in these upper ear-holes. In the middle earhole we used to wear *toria*, which occured in two types, one with a screw which was made entirely of gold and one with *dhandhala*, a silver bar which was passed through the ear-hole and then rolled to a spiral. In the lobe of the ear we wear *sapva*, fixed with a screw or *markli*, a small flower-like design.

The actual working procedure involves searching for, digging out and collecting natural raw materials and then throwing, moulding, shaping, ornamenting, and firing the earthenware, the last processes which demand the skill of the craftsman. Finally, the vessels must be sold. The production programme is extensive, comprising approximately 30 vessels of shapes in common demand for households. Two methods of firing are employed, which also require different raw materials, the earthenware consequently varying in quality. Besides these earthenware vessels, the potter also makes cooking stoves, tiles, and bricks. In addition to the production of earthenware the potter is mostly called upon to attend religious ceremonies, at which objects prepared by him in his workshop play a part: the wedding ceremony and the funeral rites. The potter Bhurabhai gives the following information regarding the use of earthenware vessels in the wedding ceremony, among the Mer farmers:

|| For ther *lagan*, marriage ceremony, which we here more often call *vivah*, the people of the Mer caste use 36 vessels, which are divided into four piles, each made up of nine vessels. They are arranged around the fire. The exact kind and number of vessels we need are twelve *matela*, four *mateli*, eight *ghada*, which are usually called *muria*, four *pharka*, four *chakli*, and four *chakla*. Two *gatrida*, called generally *gadi*, are also required. All the vessels must be well painted with white, red and green pigments. || For green colour I use the leaves of any tree and mash them to make a green solution.

|| The colour is applied when the vessel has already been fired. || The colour can be washed away. || The person in whose house the ceremony is held, will keep and use the vessels. || If the colours fade, it does not matter.

At a marriage ceremony the role played by the potter is restricted to bringing the vessels to the bride's house, and arranging them around the fire. Furthermore he might help in preparing food and in serving it to the guests. But his function at a funeral ceremony is a far more impressive one, as the following detailed account will show, for he is here entrusted with actually performing certain rites.

First of all I will give an account of the *ghadasu*-ceremony which I witnessed, and thereafter cite the two explanatory interviews that followed. The ceremony was held in the village of Ratadi on the 22nd January, 1966. I witnessed the following scene :

Upon our arrival in the afternoon, we are greeted by the sight of a group of men sitting on the verandah of the house of the deceased. They are smoking and talking softly among themselves. Only one figure crouches immobile in one corner of the verandah without taking part in the general conversation. It is the son of the dead man. With the exception of one long lock, every hair on his head, including moustache and eyebrows, have been shaved off. His forehead bears a red mark shaped like a pointed oval. His entire apparel consists of a white cloth girded about his loins and a white cord running transversely across his chest.

The potter unloads the frame with the required pots from his donkey. While he arranges them in front of his house, his son drives away the animal. First of all he arranges the large *moria*, the brown baked pots decorated with red stripes. These he sets up in four parallel rows of six pots each. He takes care that they stand properly, propping them up with little stones when necessary. At present there are still two pots missing in the right corner. Another pot of the same description is now placed on each of those just set out. These in turn are surmounted by small *kurda* pots, which finally serve as sockets for flat *kodia*, earthenware oil lamps. Two *kurda* pots and a few other objects, from which I can manage to discern a piece of yellow cloth, are deposited to the right of the rectangular arrangement.

While the potter is thus engaged, the Brahmin arrives in the company of a man holding a dipper tied to a rope. Two women, each carrying two earthenware pots filled with water, are also of the party. They are clad in white clothes, but wear the usual gold earrings. They hold long reeds in their hands.

The women range the four water vessels to the right beside the rows of previously arranged pots, and the potter covers these too with earthenware oil lamps. The women now enter the house. The potter asks for white thread which he ties around the left corner pot adjacent to the outermost one. The thread is now spanned so as to encircle all the pots with the exception of the corner pot placed in the direction of the village. A separate thread is tied around this pot.

After a few minutes the women emerge once more, each with a dish in her hands. All dishes contain sweetmeats, little balls of sweet flour, ano ther flat cakes. Following the directions of the potter, the women place two cakes and one sweet ball in each oil lamp. Only in the corner pot standing apart from the others a single, large ball is placed, over which *ghee,* clarified butter is poured. A little water is poured from one of the water vessels into a small metal bowl. Red earth is now mixed with water. The Brahmin brings a little stool from the house, which is placed on the left beside the corner pot. The family members of the deceased now place two brass bowls with soot-blackened and scratched under-surfaces, a cotton bed cover, a water vessel and a pair of shoes on the corner pot. The potter folds a gunny bag and lays it on the floor in front of the tower of pots. The son of the dead man, who has hitherto been sitting immobile in one corner of the verandah, now seats himself crosslegged on the mat. He remains motionless, his eyes downcast. The potter now comes out of the house, carrying a piece of burning cow-dung in a metal pot. He seizes the two small vessels together with the yellow strip of material previously deposited there by the members of the household, and runs out on the road leading out of the village. Upon this sign the relatives step forward and lay white scarves on the shoulders of the deceased's son. Among them are two elderly sobbing women. The son now stands up. All the scarves but one are removed from his shoulders. He takes hold of one of the water vessels and dashes it to pieces on the left corner between the stool and the corner pot standing apart from the others. All this takes place in complete silence. Only the Brahmin gives instructions every now and then as to what must be done.

The potter now appears once more; this time he emerges from the house carrying a small lit oil lamp which he has placed in a large metal pot to shield from the wind. He now sets alight the thread which he has spanned around the pots, kindling it in several places. The thread does not burn properly but falls in fragments to the ground. The thread encircling the separate corner pot is not set alight. The Brahmin orders the man to rise. The potter takes food from nine pots and puts it into the gunny bag, while the Brahmin takes the food from the separate corner pot, the shoes, bed cover and metal pots for himself. The corner pots piled one on top of the other pass into the possession of the Brahmin. He is also given some coins. The rest of the pots save one are taken by the children of the house and the neighbourhood. After a lapse of a few minutes, during which time the conversation on the varandah is resumed, the son of the deceased emerges from the house and takes up his position on the road in front of the entrance. From a dish he picks up small pieces of sweetmeat and proceeds to throw them on the roof of the house, all the while crying *kadkad*, crow. As if in answer to his beckoning, several of the birds come flying over the house and carry away the titbits. This is followed up by the two elderly women, who distribute a few morsels in the same way. This marks the end of the ceremony. The one remaining water vessel is carried by the mourning son to a tree near the yard and deposited there. The Brahmin packs up the articles he has profited by, the potter loads the gunny bag with the sweetmeats on his donkey, and both of them make their way homewards to their village Baradia. The only objects left in front of the house are a forgotten oil lamp belonging to one of the corner posts, the fragments of the broken water vessel and a water puddle. The assembled mourners have again turned their attention to smoking and tea-drinking.

So much I was able to observe. The next evening I asked the Brahmin to explain the ceremony to me. From Premjibhai Javadjibhai of Baradia, for such is his name, I gleaned the following information:

The ceremony you were present at is called *khadsa*. Prior to it a *saramna* ceremony was conducted down at the seashore.

// While fetching water the women have to wear white clothes. // They have to keep a grain of *bajra*, millet in their hand to drive away the cow or bird that tries to drink out of the pots. // The dead man had only one son. // Shaving the hair is a sign to all the people who come from outside that he is the chief mourner. // This is done at the very start.

// For a women the same ceremony is performed.

// There is a special significance in burning the thread : the relations between the dead man and his family have come to an end. *Trakla*, the thread symbolizes the spirit of the dead man.

// The corner-pot is mine by right, for it is always given to the *gor*, village Brahmin. // Since its name is *gara saravni* they will not put *rotli*, flat bread on it. To make sure that the soul of the deceased will fly straight to paradise, some water is poured on the tail of a cow. If the family does not keep a cow, they give 25 paisa to the Brahmin instead.

// The Brahmin takes the corner pot with him. The *moria* is left under the *pipla* tree, where the son of the deceased also puts down the water pot. // The string around that pot was not burned. It was to show that these pots were mine.

// I always receive a fee of five annas and one paisa in cash, even if the family is very poor. At the end of the ceremony, I am also given some grain. So much will suffice. The family is not compelled to give me more. They are not required to give more cash to the Brahmin, but they can give him brass or copper vessels.

// If the Brahmin wears the shoes, the spirit will walk in paradise in them and will not be hurt by thorns. This is the reason why I receive shoes. // The blankets are for the same purpose. I can, and I will sell these objects.

// The value of these objects is about three or four rupees, and in cash I received 1.25 Rs. - that is all. Only the bell-metal dish is of particular value to me, for it is unused.

// Crows are said to be the descendants of the *rushis*. One of the *rushis* was called *kaglo*, crow and he could change himself into any shape he wished. Once he changed himself into a crow to help somebody. At that moment his enemy uttered a *shrap*, malediction and the *rushi* and all his descendants were thereafter doomed to remain crows for ever.

After this interview I also questioned the potter who had assisted at the ceremony. Bhurabhai told me the following :

The Brahmin is taken down to the seashore to perform the *saramna* ceremony, at which he is required to recite some verses. When the mourning party returns to the village the hair and moustache of the dead man's son are shaved off. If the deceased is a Mer by caste, four *kurdas*, four *kodias* and two *kundas* are the pots required for this ceremony. If the deceased is a Brahmin, one *moria* and one *kodia* pot are required. After the ceremony is over, the pots are destroyed and the fragments are left on the spot.

// At the *ghadasu,* lighting ceremony, the Mers need 48 *moria,* 26 *kurda,* and 24 *kodia* pots.

// All the pots are fired. The red stripes on the pots indicate that they were made for the ceremony. // They are just for decoration as plain pots do not look well. // The design depends on the potter and is not fixed. For example, the pots which were used in the other house for the *ghadasu* ceremony, came from Shrinagar and they were not decorated with lines.

// The ceremony is not performed when a child dies, but only when the dead person was more than 15 years old. If a person dies unmarried, I will have to paint a special design on the pot: between the lines I must paint *deradi,* a pattern of dots.

// The number of pots will be the usual. // In that case the pots are *chitarela,* ornamented.

// The pots brought filled with water from the well are part of the collection of pots required for the ceremony. Each of the women has two *moria* and one *kurda* pots. And the pot which is subsequently broken is one of the *kurda* pots.

// The scarves laid over the shoulders of the son are called *pot.* All pots used in the ceremony are called *beda.* The extra one in the corner is called *koru bedu,* because it is "completely dry". It may not be touched. It is so dry, that even water cannot touch it. The pots are not for household use, they are for the Brahmin. // The other pots have no names.

// At how many points I set alight the *trak,* thread, depends on me. Even once will do.

// The single thread cannot burn up. It is a holy thing and belongs to the potter.

// Besides the *beda* pots, I brought two *kurdas,* which are called *charodia.* In both of them I put rice, some money, and one *sopari* nut. I take a piece of white cloth twelve fingers in length and three in breadth and rub it in *halda,* yellow turmeric. The cloth is laid over the two pots.

// Before I burn the thread I take some fire from the house and carry the two *kurda* pots beyond the limits of the household. I also take along the money and the *sopari,* both of which I put into my pocket. I sprinkle the rice on the ground and leave the pots and the cloth over there. // All this must be done by me alone.

// There is no fixed spot for this part of the ceremony.

// The last part of the ceremony is conducted eleven days after the death of the person. Now the relationship between the deceased and the living family is severed.

// It is always done like this. – I myself interpret it this way: the *charodia* is taken far away before the thread is burned. This might be to ensure the spirit not being disturbed on its way to paradise.

// All this is the potter's work. // My son could go in my stead, because the Brahmin knows the ceremony and could instruct him.

// Nine portions of the sweet-meats are by right mine

// There is no reason behind the number. It has been so established for generations. // We eat our share, and what is collected by the members of the household is eaten by them.

// The price of the vessels has to be paid in cash. // The amount depends on the household, it can be ten, eight or twelve rupees.

// I always keep some of these pots in stock and if the need arises, I have to make some more to complete the number. // Sometimes I have about five hundred pots at home. That is always before the monsoon breaks. At this time of the year I have to possess so many, because when the rains come I cannot work.

These religious ceremonies, for which the potter not only supplies the pots required to conduct the rites, but himself participates in them, constitute for him an important though irregular source of food and income in cash.

However, his principal earnings are derived from the sale of earthenware kitchen vessels, for which the potter has fixed prices to be paid in cash or grain. These he specifies himself :

// I sell my products either for money or for grain.

// The kind of grain I receive depends on the buyer – he can make it half wheat, half millet, or only millet, as he likes.

// When selling pots I carry my own measuring cup with me.

// The quantity of grain fixed as the price varies with the kind of pot in question. I sell a *kathrot, tolio* and *tavali* for two *povala* measuring cups full of grain. For three *povala* full of grain I give a *gada* and *donia* pot, for one and a half *pali* a *matelo* can be bought and for two *pali* a *gorio*. Two *pali*, cups of grain are now equivalent to two rupees. // We are more frequently paid in grain than in money.

The following is Bhurabhai's report on the procedure of sale :

// Whenever I have a large number of vessels ready at home, I go out myself to sell them. Then I take my measuring cup with me. Just now my children have gone out to Ratadi with a load of vessels. // They will sell the pots. There are no orders. If they cannot sell them they will bring them back.

// They will bring grain. They have taken the *povala*, measuring cup with them. Of the different kinds of millet we appreciate *bajro*, most, then *juvar*, and lastly *chino*, which is the cheapest. It is a locally grown grain.

When the children return, the potter makes a calculation of what has been sold (all the pots were black baked and therefore of good quality).

With the children I sent today 16 *tavali*, one *kathrot*, one *tauli*. From these, nine *tavali*, the *kathrot*, and the *tauli* were sold. All with the exception of one *tavali* which was taken by a Mer without fields were paid for with grain. // All were sold in Ratadi village.

The potter however is not always so successful, for potters do not only supply their own villages with earthenware, but journey for several days together through the countryside, trying to sell their ware. In this case they must out-manoeuvre the local potters. Even so, Bhurabhai tells me that on such journeys it is usual for a potter to spend the night in the house of the local Kumbhar, potter-family.

At village festivals, potters are often engaged as cooks in Mer households. The women and children of the potter's household frequently work as helpers on the fields, so as to supplement their sparse income or obtain some small share of the harvest. Bhurabhai reports :

// *Dhud*, milk, and *ghee*, clarified butter, are the two items I have to buy. *Chhash*, buttermilk, one gets free in the village. And for that (he points to peanuts) I send all my family members to the fields to help. In the evening they receive their share.

A futher consideration is that the potter cannot practise his profession the whole year round, because during the monsoon the clay from which the vessels are fashioned does not dry, and firing in addition is quite impossible. During these four months therefore, his work comes to a complete standstill. The shed that normally serves as the workshop is coverted into a stable for goats to be tethered in and the potter is without work and consequently without income. Any field work for his neighbours is restricted to the beginning of the monsoon. Under these circumstances, even the most dexterous and hardworking of potters must needs be poorly off. Since the land reform, by which the farmers became free owners of the fields they cultivated, the social and economic situation of the potters has been aggravated, for it has only succeeded in widening the gap between potters and farmers. Questioned on his attitude towards a farmers' mode of livelihood, the potter Bhurabhai answered :

// You ask which I would prefer, pottery or agriculture, if I could earn the same money by either occupation ? Well, I would do both to raise my income.

// If I had to choose only one of these occupations, I would select agriculture and leave pottery, because slowly the demand for earthenware is sinking, day by day. // For instance *nalia*, tiles and *int*, bricks, are not needed anymore.

The potter therefore looks pessimistically into the future. Not only has the demand for earthenware considerably sunk of late, even the raw materials are not as plentifully available as they once were. The potter remarked in this context:

// Formerly, when there was a sufficiant demand for tiles, we used to makes tiles for about three months and vessels for four months. But now, since the demand has sunk, I can only make vessels. And even vessels are not as much in demand as they used to be at one time. It will take me a year to sell these ten *ghora*, large pots. // *Tavali* for baking *roteli*, are sold most. *Nalia* and *mobhia*, tiles are no more in demand.

// What do you want your son to learn ? / I want him to learn tailoring. Some relatives of mine are tailors and I will send the boy to them. It will take him three to five years to learn. However, if the boy is clever, he can master the craft within three years. // I would like to send him right now to my uncle's sons. // They have all given up the potter's craft because of the scarcity of fuel. // The trees have been cut down. // Nowdays *katara*, cactus is the best. // If I were to buy wood, it would be too costly. *Katara* does as well because it burns slowly and gives heat for a long time. // Cowdung cakes would also be too expensive.

Lastly, it may not be out of place to quote here a sentence uttered by the Brahmin Premjibhai upon perceiving the large number of curious onlookers that had assembled in the yard of the potter's homestead and who then greeted this remark with peals of laughter :

Nobody knew that there was anything to learn in the potter's house !

This pronouncement well reflects the utter ignorance of the farmers of craftmen's problems and knowledge.

VIII.2. The tools

The tools described in the following are those to be found in the workshop of Bhurabhai Dhayabhai of Baradia.   177, 178

2.1. Tools for digging clay

Broad hoe, *pavada*
A broad iron scoop is fitted into a straight handle by means of a hole at one end.

Narrow hoe, *kodari*
A narrow, trapezoid scoop has a hole at one end to admit a straight handle.

Pick, *trekam*
The pick iron has one pointed and one broad end. A stout straight handle is fixed to the centre of the iron.

Rake, *khaparo*
This consists of a cross-bar into which six wooden tines are fitted and wedged. The handle is straight.

Sadle-bag, *gun*
This is worked from coconut fibre, employing the technique of twining. In shape the saddle-bag is roughly triangular and is laid across the back of the donkey.

Basin, *tagara*
This is a common metal basin with a rusty undersurface and is used to carry clay. It is purchased in Porbandar.

2.2. Tools for mixing clay

Wooden mallet, *modara* or *tapla*
A cylindrical wooden head is fixed into a wooden handle, which runs transverse to its long side.

Basket, *hundo*
The hemispherical basket consists of a simple woven structure of bamboo strips running parallel to the rim.

Sieve, *havalo* or *chalano*
A piece of wire-netting (0.5 cm x 0.5 cm) is stretched across a large rectangular frame. The second type of sieve consists of a fine wire netting (0.2 cm x 0.2 cm) fitted into a cylindrically curved wooden frame and nailed down under an iron hoop.

Water pot, *ghoro*
A spherical, black-baked earthenware vessel serves to hold water.

Stone slab, *chlipar*
A smooth stone slab roughly rectangular in shape serves as a base for rolling lumps of clay.

2.3. Tools for moulding earthenware

Potter's wheel, *Shankar no chakdo* (*Shiva's* wheel)
This resembles a cart wheel, consisting of a broad, heavy curved felloe composed of several pieces tenoned together. The felloe is connected with the central hub or disc by means of ten spokes, which are also tenoned. The flat upper surface is used to mould or "throw" the earthenware vessels. A small, slightly concave piece of white flint enclosed in a frame of metal strips is nailed to the centre on the under-side of the wheel. It is at this point that the wheel rotates on the bearing. An aperture is cut into the curved felloe to admit the stick with which the wheel is made to turn.

The wheel is very heavy. In the potter's opinion it weighs 160 lbs.

central disc	*thala*
spokes	*ara*
bearing	*adi*
aperture in felloe	*khado*

Support, *chopti*
A rectangular piece of wood is fitted into the centre of an irregularly shaped stone slab, and wedged firmly in place by means of a chip of wood and rags of cloth. This rectangular wooden pin, which is fashioned from hard *kher*-wood, is tapered to end in a spherical point well lubricated with oil.

rectangular wooden pin	*khal*

Stick, *chabakani*
A straight wooden rod or bamboo stick about a yard in length is used to drive the wheel.

Cloth, *Shankar ni langoti* (*Shiva's* loincloth)
This is a piece of cotton cloth oblong in shape and of a strong texture. It is moistened used, to smoothen the rims of the vessels.

Cord, *dori* or *Shankar no kandoro* (*Shiva's* cord)
This is a cotton cord made of several strands twisted together. It is used to cut the vessels moulded on the wheel.

Pointed paddle, *datio*
This term generally embraces all wooden mallets (or paddles) employed to chase vessels into

shape. In a more restricted sense, though, it applies to one particular type of paddle characterized by its peculiar head, in which the narrow planes taper to a point. The cylindrical handle is sometimes decorated with a design of simple grooves.

Broad paddle, *khalo*
For the purpose of shaping the bottom of the vessel, a wooden paddle is used. The broad planes of the paddle head are slightly concave, the cylindrical handle may be ornamented with a simple groove design.

Narrow paddle, *pati*
A paddle with a narrow oblong striking surface is employed to shape the shoulders of vessels.

Counter support or anvil, *pindo*
A button-like handle is on top of a flat stone cylinder. All corners of the cylinder are rounded off. These anvils are available in various sizes.

Base, *pudgha*
An earthenware ring with a rounded rim is covered with a piece of sacking and serves thus as a base for moulding vessels. A hole dug in the ground and lined with sacking is sometimes employed for the same purpose.

Moulding box for bricks, *intia*.
A rectangular frame of boards, its dimensions being those of a brick, is used to press and mould bricks. Bricks are manufactured in two sizes: the large sized ones are pressed in individual mould and the small ones in double moulding boxes, the compartments in the latter being divided by a narrow partition.

Comb, *kanski*
A piece of a broken comb is used to decorate vessels when they have acquired the hardness of leather. Combs of horn and wood can be bought at Porbandar from Marwari traders from Rajasthan.

Pigment pot and stick for applying the colour, *rang*, pigment and *pichhi*, twig
The earth pigment is mixed in any handy vessel. The mixture is applied with a brush made from a *nim* – twig by peeling it and separating the ends to form a fringe. A piece of cloth is used to apply the chalk solution.

String of seeds used for polishing, *mala*
A long string which is arranged to form a manifold twisted chain is threaded with smooth *kachko*-seeds.

Piece of sacking, *kothro*
A common piece of sacking is used to rub vessels and to remove dust from them.

2.4. Tools and equipment for firing and selling earthenware

Axe, *kuado*
A common axe with a welded on socket and a long straight handle is employed to chop the fuel. Parts of the cactus plants are the fuel most commonly used.

Kiln site, *nibhando*
A circular, slightly hollowed stretch of ground serves as a site on which the kiln for firing the vessels is built.

Tongs, *chipio*
Two flexible iron rods are riveted together at one end and used to handle hot objects.

Poker, *saliva*
A simple wooden stick is used to poke the fire.

Potsherds, *thikara*
Large fragments of broken earthenware are used to plaster the ground and to form ventilation holes that can be closed if necessary.

Metal bowl, *penno*
The freshly fired vessels are dipped into a bowl filled with water; this renders them more durable and thus also decreases the chance of their breaking before they are sold.

Double basket, *tagara*
A basket frame is slung over the donkey's back. This consists of a pyramid-shaped basket resting on either flank of the animal. The frame is constructed from bamboo poles, between which an irregularly woven fabric (chiefly using the techniques of twining and knotting) is stretched.

Pack-saddle and pack-cord for donkey, *godla* or *athar* and *padhat*
The pack-saddle consists merely of a number of old quilts thrown across the donkey's back. These prevent chafing by friction of the baskets against the animal's flanks. The quilts are tied in place with pack-cord made of nine strings plaited together.

Measuring cub, *payali* (large), *pavalu* (small)
Cylindrical wooden bowls with a standard capacity are constantly carried by potters to measure the quantity of grain they fix as the price for their wares.

VIII. 3. The raw materials

An accurate analysis of the various clays and the different types of ochre used as slip has yet to be undertaken. In the meanwhile I reproduce here the report of the geologist Adye on the clay occuring in Shrinagar (Adye, 1917, pg. 116) This clay is used by the potter Bhurabhai for black earthenware : "Daya Lagdhir (i. e. a relative of the actual potter from Baradia), the Kumbhar of Kantela, having drawn attention to the unusual excellence of his earthenware, accompanied the writer.. to Shrinagar, to point out the site from which he was in the habit of digging out his supplies of clay. . .Alluvial clay, freely incorporated with dissocated grains of Gaj limonitic limestone to constitute a kind of dark grey, plastic marl, is deposited year after year upon the bed of the affluent to the talav, and when dry after the monsoon, forms a deep layer of potter's clay".

The same geologist writes on the subject of the yellow ochre which the potter Bhurabhai digs in Bharvada (1917, pg. 62 f): "One mile east by ESE of Palakra (i. e. near Bharvada). . an abandoned well-shaft was found, sunk into a depth of 15 feet through soil merging below greyish clay, followed by an unascertained thickness of bright yellow ochre of excellent quality. Up to the present this material lies hidden beneath a wide area of cultivated land, and has not hitherto been utilized in any way. . .(At the same place the author finds) sundry beds of compact, ornamental yellow limestone called Pindaralite; and the newly named, Bharwaralite, which is an indurated, fresh cinnamon-coloured ornamental stone, available in thick and larger slabs, 1 1/4 miles S. W. of the village after which it has been named".

We had a good opportunity of observing the digging of ochre clays near Bharvada, a village lying at a distance of 13 km. from Ratadi. Signs of digging are evident all over the undulating landscape. The potter makes his way to each hollow, where he crumbles clods of earth to ascertain the colour of the inside layers. He then widens a suitable hole, removes the top layer of earth and digs out lumps of damp yellow-coloured ochre with a pick. The ochre is collected in sacks. The yellow ochre material is partly veined with red. The men who heat the ochre for 15 days in a stone enclosure informed me that there was a copper mine in the vicinity. They sell the burnt ochre for 15 Rs. per ton.

The potter digs out the grey clay from small pits close by. He says that a depth of about five feet the clay is of very good quality. Even so, he merely scratches away the top soil and digs out a layer of plastic, friable, grey coloured clay, which is tinged with yellowish-white.

Clay, *mati*
This term is applied by the potter after the clay has been dug and collected, but before it has been prepared or tempered.

Prepared clay without temper, *ragad*
This clay is picked clean of impurities and mixed with water.

Tempered clay, *mati kadav*
This term applies to clay after temper has been added; the mixture is ready for the wheel.

Temper for clay, *ghasan*
This temper consists of a mixture of dung and ash.

Donkey dung, *lad*
Donkey dung collected from the stall is dried, crumbled, pressed through a sieve and finally added to the clay mixture. It has most probably the effect of rendering the mixture porous.

Ash, *rakh*
Ash collected from the fireplace, the residue of dried and burnt cowdung, less often of wood and shrubs, is also used for tempering. It is further employed to dry the floor of the workshop and to dust over the vessels while they are chased.

Sand, *mithi reti* (lit. sweet sand)
Quarry sand collected from the neighbourhood of Ratadi is used for tempering. The potter informed me that sand from the seashore could not be used for this purpose.

Cow dung, *chhan*
A layer of fresh cow dung may be applied to a chased vessel in order to keep it moist.

Ochre, *pili mati*, yellow clay
Ochre mixed with water is used as a pigment to paint vessels. When fired, the ochre turns red. This earth occurs in the neighbourhood of Bharvada.

Beige mud, *met* or *dholi mati*

This plastic light beige ochre is mixed with water to form a pigment which turns reddish-brown when fired. The beige mud is also found in the neighbourhood of Bharvada.

Chalk, *khadi mati*

Grey chalk is stirred with water and used for painting white designs on earthenware. Chalk is dug from the stone quarries near Adityana, which lies ten km. south of Porbandar.

Red mud, *gheru lal mati*

Small stone-gravel found in the neighbourhood of the village of Karpat yield this dark red mud. When subjected to pressure, the stones dissolve in water. Firing induces no change in their dark red colour.

Roots, *motha*

The roots of a special kind of reed are collected during the dry season and used to fire red earthenware.

Reeds, *dad, sanya* or *sach*

The reed stalks, which resemble grass, are cut in bundles with the sickle and used as fuel to fire red earthenware.

Chaff, *dusana*

The chaff of different grains is also used to fire red earthenware.

Sedge, *kucho*

Dry sedge serves as a bed on which black earthenware is fired.

Cactus pieces, *katara*

Pieces of dry cactus chopped up with the axe are used chiefly to fire black earthenware.

Goat droppings, *lindi*

In order to produce smoke in the covered kiln, that is to say, in order to cause the oxygen to burn, dry goat droppings are thrown into the fire.

Water, *pani*

Clean well water which is transported to the potter's working site in vessels is used to prepare the clay mixture and to stir the slime. It is further required during the throwing and moulding operation on the wheel and also to moisten the paddles. It is additionally used in building the kiln preparatory to firing the vessels.

VIII. 4. The working techniques

4. 1. Site of work

The potter's homestead lies west of the village of Baradia on a gentle slope, at the foot of which the village well is situated, behind a mighty embankment of earth.

Coming from the direction of the village, the visitor approaches the potter's homestead through a gap in the broad, unplastered wall, which is roughly constructed of field stones piled one on top of the other. On the left, beside the wall are three pegs driven into the ground, to which both female donkeys belonging to the potter are tethered at night. The wall then continues to form one side of the comparatively small, clay-plastered dwelling house (length 7.30 m and breadth 5.50 m), which though old is still in good condition. Through the low doorway closed by a single-winged door, the visitor enters a rectangular room in which vessels for sale are exhibited. Immediately opposite, there is a second door leading to the windowless, dark living room, which is furnished with three small urns for storing grain, beddings, a few boxes and a kind of cupboard made of clay. On the wall there is a shelf with implements and other odd equipment. Two ridge posts in the centre of the room support the span-roof, which is covered with tiles. The kitchen adjoins the front room and projects beyond it. Two fireplaces and a shaft stocked with kitchen utensils represent the sole inventory.

A small yard bounded by field stones adjoins the house on to the west. In the yard, large vessels ready for sale are set out, also wood for fuel. Disused articles of all kinds are also deposited here. Near the wall on the west there stands a beautiful shady acacia to which the milch goat is tied. There is a breach in the stonework, now largely crumbled away, after which the wall pursues a slanting course in a north-easterly direction. At this point a walled platform has been built against it, upon which a few bushes have been planted with the purpose of providing shade for the water vessels placed there. The wall next touches the front corner of the small shed (length 3.60 m and breadth 2.20 m), of which only the entrance is plastered. The almost flat roof is covered with straw thatching. The doorless entrance to the shed, which is so low that the potter cannot stand upright in it, is situated in the longitudinal wall on one side of the centre. The front portion of the workshed is strewn with ash, followed by a depression in the ground used to hammer and shape vessels. In the rear portion, the floor is stony, the ready shaped vessels being deposited here preparatory to being fired in the kiln. Heaps of sand and pigments are also deposited here.

The lower part of the transverse shed wall projects into the yard to form a bench and is plastered over with mud. The wall surrounding the yard, on the other hand, starts from the rear longitudinal shed wall and breaks off after turning sharply at a right-angle to the entrance. Clay and donkey dung are stored in this corner of the yard.

Outside this complex of homestead, yard and shed, there is a forecourt enclosed partly by low, crumbling walls and partly by cacti growing in close concentration. Here the vessels are fired, and here also dung-cakes are dried, washing operations carried out, and fuel, hay for livestock fodder, and broken earthenware fragments stored. There is also an old disused kiln in the forecourt.

The following features of the homestead complex play a part in the process of earthenware manufacture: adjacent to the dwelling house, in the shadow of the eaves, is the place where the clay mixture is prepared and subsequently kneaded on a stone slab. The raw materials for this procedure are either fetched from the workshed (ash, special kinds of clay and sand) or from the corner between shed and wall (clay and dung). Water is stored in large vessels in the corner of the house and on the stone platform in the wall opposite. Vessels are generally moulded in the centre of the place mentioned above, next to the spot where the clay mixture is prepared. After finishing his work the potter rolls the wheel against the wall of the shed. The spare wheel leans against the yard wall beside the west entrance. The moulded vessels are carried into the shed, where they are dried till hard as leather in the leeward shade before being chased. Later they are put out into the mottled shade of the yard before being fired in the forecourt.

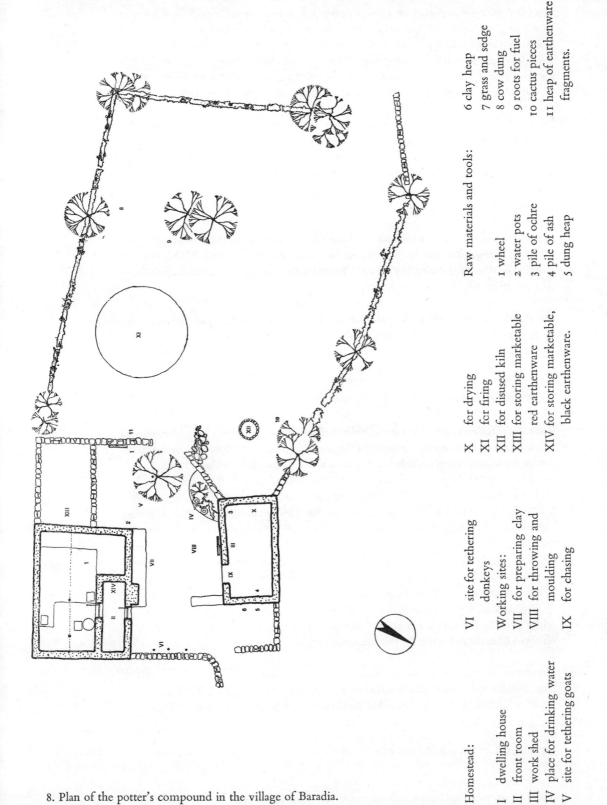

Homestead:

I dwelling house
II front room
III work shed
IV place for drinking water
V site for tethering goats

VI site for tethering donkeys

Working sites:

VII for preparing clay
VIII for throwing and moulding
IX for chasing

X for drying
XI for firing
XII for disused kiln
XIII for storing marketable red earthenware
XIV for storing marketable, black earthenware.

Raw materials and tools:

1 wheel
2 water pots
3 pile of ochre
4 pile of ash
5 dung heap

6 clay heap
7 grass and sedge
8 cow dung
9 roots for fuel
10 cactus pieces
11 heap of earthenware fragments.

8. Plan of the potter's compound in the village of Baradia.

4. 2. Working conditions

The potter Bhurabhai works with quiet assurance. All his movements bespeak confidence and are executed with practised skill and swiftness. At no stage of his work have I ever observed him dawdling or hesitating. Yet he is always at ease, interrupts his work frequently to indulge in a smoke and explains his working methods even during the most complicated stages of the procedure. As a rule he has few visitors during working hours, customers rarely come to him. But his yard is used by his neighbours as a thoroughfare to the village well.

The little boy who plays beside the working potter is the apple of his father's eye. Bhurabhai also puts up with prolonged interruptions of his work for the little boy's sake, fully aware that he must make up for the time lost in the night, because certain working procedures must be completed within a limited number of hours. On such days he works far into the night. Normally he ends his day's work, which commences early in the morning, as soon as twilight appears.

The terms on which the potter worked with me were the most favourable that could be expected: he engaged to prepare first one and then another set of differently shaped vessels, working on them only during my presence. In return, we promised to buy all the vessels for an appropriate sum of money. Each set consisted of about twenty vessels.

But also later, after our agreement was at an end, I spent many a pleasant and instructive hour in the potter's company, watching him work, smoking with him and chatting. As a sign of our appreciation for his co-operation, we tried to help him obtain a plot of land near Baradia.

4.3. Working schedule

Because, according to our agreement, a series of differently shaped vessels had to be prepared at one time, and because every member of the potter's family helps at one time or the other during the work, it is not possible to set up an exact table of working hours. The time required to mould the various vessels is stated in the section on the working procedure (vide 4.4.) As a rule, the potter digs the clay early in the morning, prepares the clay mixture before noon the same day and throws and mould the vessels in the afternoon. The following day he chases the vessels. Thereafter they are dried for a day or two, during which time their position must be changed, the vessels being carried from one spot to another. At least one whole morning is needed to collect fuel and a whole afternoon to fire the vessels and there with complete the manufacturing process. Vessels which are exposed to an open fire, in order to oxidize, can be taken out of the ashes on the same evening. However, good quality black earthenwere is fired in a sealed "ash-kiln", the preparation of which takes a whole day. The fire must be maintained the whole night through, and the earthenware is removed from the embers on the following morning.

However, only thirty medium-sized vessels were manufactured according to this theoretical plan. Firing is only worthwhile when about 150 vessels have accumulated. The potter therefore, normally spends considerable time in moulding before he can think of firing.

4.4. Example 1: The manufacture of red earthenware

Raw materials and tools
The basic material used for the manufacture of red baked earthenware, which is not very

durable, is yellow clay. The clay occurs nearby and is used in combination with donkey dung and ash. Roots, reeds, chaff and any dry donkey dung that may be lying about are collected and used as fuel. All the tools with the exception of the moulding box for bricks, comb and measuring cub, are employed in the making of this kind of earthenware.

Preparing the clay

9.50 – 10.15	walk to the clay pit, digging the clay and transporting it home
10.15 – 10.35	breaking up the clods of clay
10.35 – 10.40	pouring water over the clay, smoking interval
10.40 – 11.00	preparing the temper, smoking interval
11.00 – 11.25	crumbling the clay, sifting the ash, smoking interval
11.25 – 12.05	preparing the clay mixture
	midday interval
2.40 – 2.55	kneading the clay
2.55 – 3.05	cleaning the working place, setting up the wheel, smoking interval
3.05 – 3.15	preparing four rolls of clay.

The potter and his sons are ready to go to the clay pit. A few old quilts are laid over the back of the donkey and fastened in placed with a woven strap. The potter throws a double sack containing a metal basin and a narrow hoe over the quilts. The little boy sits on the donkey, while his father leads the animal. The older boy shoulders the broad hoe. They make their way past the well, skirt the horse-shoe shaped hillock and descend to the plain, walking in the direction of Ratadi village. In the midst of this bare and stony waste stand a few undecorated stones, as tall as a man. These menhirs have stood here for ages and in the potter's opinion date from the time "when the entire area was covered with primeval jungle."

The clay pit, a hardly distinguishable, hemispherical depression, is situated near the menhirs. 180

The older boy remains beside the donkey, while the potter clears away the rubble from the pit with the broad hoe. With the narrow hoe he digs out dry clods of clay, which he breaks into smaller lumps by pounding them with the back of the hoe. Earth that falls away in granules from the clay is pushed to one side, while the clay is accumulated in a heap in the centre.

He calls to his son to drive the donkey nearer and fills the clay into the slantingly placed metal 181 basin with the aid of the broad hoe. With a powerful swinging motion he lifts up the full basin, places both hands on its badly perforated undersurface and carries it to the donkey holding it in front of him. In emptying the basin, he places the rim against the middle of both sacks on the donkey's back, so that the contents of the basin are distributed evenly in both bags. He then shakes each bag, which causes the lumps of clay to settle at the bottom and the dust to fly in clouds through the gunny fabric. The last few lumps of clay the potter collects with his hands, placing them in the gunny bags. He spreads his shawl over the filled bags, puts both hoes into another and hoists the little boy once more on the donkey's back. The elder son carries the basin.

On arriving home, he empties the saddle bags with his usual verve. The clay falls on the space beside the house wall. The place has previously been swept clean.

Bhurabhai takes off his shoes, sends his son into the house to fetch a mallet, and himself goes 182 into the shed to bring his already lighted *hukka,* waterpipe. After a few puffs he lays it aside, and pounds the lumps of clay with the mallet, picking out any little stones present and throwing them into a tin. While doing this, he crouches beside the heap of clay and picks out the lumps one by one with his left hand, breaking them up with the mallet and then picking out little stones, roots, etc. with both hands. The crumbled and inspected clay he pushes forwarded with the palm of his hand. Thus a semicircle of pounded clay is gradually formed around the central heap. When all the clay has been picked clean, he empties the tin with the stone on one side of the yard.

184

With the broad hoe he now spreads out the clay. He next draws his fingers, which are spread to resemble a rake, through it. Any large pieces remain suspended between the fingers. These he collects in a mound near the house wall. With the palm of his left hand he scraps together the powdery clay and arranges it in a ring formation around the mound.

The result is a semicircle, with its 80 cm broad inner curve consisting of lumps of clay averaging 18 square cm and more in size, while the 20 cm broad outer rim is an accumulation of smaller clay granules, the size of the latter averaging a mere 4 square cm.

Several pots of water are now emptied over the clay, the stream being made to flow over the right hand, which maintains a continuous up and down movement. First the inner semicircle curve is watered and then, with special care, the rim. The water seeps slowly into the clay. Only at the beginning a few bubbles are formed. The potter now fetches his waterpipe and settles down to enjoy a comfortable smoke. Now and then he reaches forward and picks out stones or straw from the clay.

Finally he rubs his hands dry on the seat of his trousers and crosses the yard to the rear wall, where the donkeys are tethered at night. Here the dung has been swept into a heap in the corner. The potter spreads out the dung before him and crumbles it by passing his slightly outspread fingers, without using much pressure, over the dung balls. The dung is reduced to fibrous granules resembling chaff, which are subsequently further reduced to a fine powder by rubbing them between the palms. The potter finally dusts his hands clean by clapping them together several times and fills the dung powder into a basin.

186

The powder is now sifted through the rectangular sieve with the coarse wire-meshing, the sieve being leant against the shed wall. He places the basin against the wire netting, his right arm passing over the upper rim and his hand holding the basin in place. Through the gap the dung is sprinkled, the potter pressing it through the wire-meshing with his left hand. The dung that has fallen to the ground during the sifting process without passing through the wire meshing is gathered up and thrown against the sieve. Finally all the finely powdered dung has passed through the sieve.

183

The sifted dung is piled into a heap. The potter now returns to the clay. The water has, in the meanwhile, completely permeated the clay. He runs his slightly spread fingers through the middle of the mass and stirs and mixes it thoroughly, dissolving any lumps by squeezing them. He finally scrapes off the clay paste from his fingers, both hands being used reciprocally, and then picks out any remaining stones.

After this he also kneads through the clay paste on the rim of the original semicircle. The clay here is less moist and appears somewhat baked. He sweeps it from both sides to form a kind of second mound and sprinkles some more water on it. This part of the paste, which is made from the finer clay granules, is only kneaded briefly.

He cleans the sole of his feet by scraping them on the ground and washes his hands in preparation for smoking his waterpipe. After this interlude he also flattens out the mound of fine clay and mixes it with slimy water from a pot, into which he occasionally dips his finger while turning the wheel.

The potter's wife brings ash from the kitchen in a hemispherical basket. She also fetches a gunny bag and a cylindrical sieve. The ash from this and a second basket is sifted over the gunny bag. In doing this, the potter crouches with the gunny bag in front of him, his back to the wind, while he lifts and drops the sieve, following an up and down rather than a rotary motion.

He next fetches a basinful of donkey dung and empties it over the mound of clay. Over this he strews the ash and mingles both upper layers to form a uniformly thick crust over the clay. With his fingers placed close to each other he cuts out a corner of the mass. It is no problem to lift the slice from the ground, because the clay paste is easily distinguishable from the dry earth on the ground. He kneads this slice, throws it on the ground and forms it into a roll. He now takes another slice of clay with the surmounting layers formed by the temper and kneads the three ingredients together with both hands. The chief method is forcing the mixture through the arched and spread fingers of his hands. He finally picks up the clay lump from the floor and dashes it with considerable force to the ground. He now forms it into a roll. Before taking a third slice of the clay mixture, he dries the ground by strewing some of the ash and dung over it. He continues to knead the clay until he has about fifteen rolls beside him. He scrapes together the remaining clay from the ground and rolls it into a ball, which he throws to the other rolls. He then scatters a generous amount of ash over the ground, over which he piles up the clay rolls into a mound. Over this he spreads an old quilt, which, however, is not wet. He then decides to interrupt his work for the midday interval.

When I return in the afternoon, Bhurabhai has just woken up from his siesta and is winding his turban.

He rolls his narrow trousers up to the calves and then arranges the clay rolls in a circular shape. He now proceeds to tread and stamp on the mass with his feet. First of all he marks parallel lines across the circle with his right foot, working from the centre from right to left and standing firmly on his left foot. This he follows by transfering his weight to his right leg and impressing his left foot in a radial pattern along the circumference of the clay disc.

With his thumb he now slices off pices from the circumference, dislodges them from the ground and flings them down on the centre, thus forming another mound. He sprinkles ash on the ground around it. Then he stamps the mound flat once more. To do this he sprinkles a little more water on the clay and then stamps on it in clockwise direction, working spiral-fashion from outside to inside. This he accomplishes by standing in the middle on his right leg and treading with his left foot, its heel turned inward. The foot impressions on the clay are set close together. A second spiral formation follows the first, the potter working this time in the opposite direction.

After this he rubs his feet against each other to clean them. With his forefinger and the adjoining row of fingers, he again cuts sliced from the clay disc, this time not only from the circumference. The entire mass of clay is cut to pieces, which he throws together in a heap. These are subsequently patted with his palm, sprinkled with water and smoothed till the surface is quite even. The potter washes his hands and feet in a pot of water.

He scatters ash once more over the damb floor of the yard and then sweeps half of it with a broom.

He carries to the spot the support for the wheel. The stone slab does not rest firmly on the uneven floor and wobbles when the potter strikes his palm against its edge. To put this aright, he props up the slab here and there with fragments of earthenware gathered from the yard.

He now disappears into the house, reappearing with one oily finger. The oil on his finger, he smears first on the wooden pin fitted into the stone slab and then on the stone slab itself, along the path to be traced by the rotating wheel. He rolls the wheel to the spot and mounts it on the support. Beside the wheel he places a pot of water and a stone slab. He asks for a cloth and a length of cotton cord to be brought to him from the house. The latter he doubles, strings around his big toe and twists into a cord by rubbing it between his palms. He knots one end of the cord. He then trickles a few drops of water on the stone slab and on the centre of the wheel. The cloth and the cord are also wetted. The stone slab and the centre of the wheel are next scratched clean with the fingertips.

With his fingers pressed against each other, Bhurabhai cuts a three-cornered wedge from the clay mass and places it before him on the stone slab. With slightly spread fingers he draws furrows through the clay lump and then tears pieces from it, which he slaps down with force on the clay lump. He finally forms it into a roll about 25 cm in length and 10 cm in diameter, which he places upright on the slab in front of him.

191

The three other clay lumps are treated in the same way. The four rolls are patted and smoothed with the moistened palms. After this the potter washes his hands and reaches out for his waterpipe.

Throwing and moulding vessels

3.15 – 3.34	moulding vessels from one roll of clay
3.34 – 4.20	moulding vessels from three more rolls of clay
4.20 – 4.35	preparing four rolls of clay
4.35 – 5.15	moulding vessels from these four rolls.

In two hours twelve bowls, eighteen pots and four small earthenware oil lamps are moulded. For these, half the quantity of clay prepared is required.

The potter squats facing the wheel. The knees, which are drawn up towards the body, are separated, the elbows being frequently rested upon them during the work. – With the stick Bhurabhai dislodges some dry clay encrusting the wheel and then lays the stick aside. He inserts his right hand into the spokes and sets the wheel in motion. It commences to rotate with moderate speed. He places a lump of clay into the centre of the revolving wheel. To do this he clasps the clay in both hands and places it with utmost care exactly in the centre of the wheel. If necessary he adjusts its position before reaching for the stick, inserting it into the aperture provided for it in the felloe and then revolving the wheel with it. His left hand holds the end of the stick directly above the wheel centre, while the right grasps it in the middle and with it turns the wheel about twelve times with great speed. The wheel rotates in clockwise motion, and even when the potter is otherwise engaged, maintains its speed for a full three minutes before perceptibly slowing down.

192

The potter passes his moistened palm over the lump of clay and moulds it into a cone with slightly concave sides. He frequently sets the wheel in motion, particularly when a new lump of clay is placed on it. He then presses both thumbs into the cone, while on the outside the fingers are placed against the clay from the side. The result is a cup with broad sides. He now takes this cup between thumb and forefinger and draws it upwards and outwards in a slanting direction to form a bowl. The sides of this open vessel are now once more drawn inwards and pulled upwards. The vessel is now deeply rounded. In the next stage of work (the potter's hands are placed flat on the outside) the vessel is moulded to a cylindrical form and even made to taper towards the opening. The lip is then shaped curling outwards, two positions of the

193

hand being typical of this stage of work: first of all the left hand lies over the lip, that is to say, the forefinger is placed against the inner surface, while the thumb is busy shaping from outside. The thumb of the right hand lies with its nail downwards under the lip of the vessel, supporting the thumb of the left hand. The hands are then disengaged, the right thumb being placed on the lip, while the curled forefinger lies under it, the middle finger resting on the rounded body of the vessel. At the same time the forefinger of the left hand leans with its joint on the lip, the thumb of the same hand being placed below it.

195

It is only at this stage that the rounded belly of the vessel is further enlarged, Bhurabhai inserting his left hand into the vessel and pressing the walls outwards, while the tips of the right-hand fingers press from outside in the opposite direction. If necessary, Bhurabhai forms a small ridge along the shoulder of the vessel by pressing the clay at the appropriate point between thumb and forefinger, the thumb being held above.

194

196

The moulded or "thrown" vessel is finally smoothed over with the wetted cloth, this being usually done simply by stretching the cloth between the fingers and holding it against the rotating vessel.

197

Bhurabhai subjects the vessel to a short inspection, particularly noting the shape of the lip. He then takes the twisted cord and with it cuts the vessel from the block of clay on the wheel. He always cuts through the rounded belly of the vessel, so that it is without a bottom.

The potter cleans his fingers by rubbing off the mud from one hand with the other and vice versa. When necessary he stops the wheel for a while and then lays his right hand on the belly of the vessel, so that it comes to rest approximately on his wrist, while the hand encircles it. The left hand then also grasps the vessel from underneath and to complete the moulding process, the potter turns the vessel adroitly with his wrists. As may be imagined, this is an extremely complicated process, because the potter works with rather wet clay. Only one vessel broke during the manufacturing process, and that because the potter's attention was diverted by his stopping to explain a technical point to me.

When the day's work has been done, he scratches away any remaining clay adhering to the wheel, sticks the damp cord and cloth to it and rolls it towards the wall, against which it is left to lean overnight.

To mould a *donio,* a pot of medium size, the potter requires only two minutes and fifty seconds. This time is divided in the following manner : 0.00-0.15 forming the basic cone, 0.15-0.30 breaking apart the cone, 0.30-0.35 drawing up the vessel to a cylindrical shape, 0.35-0.45 drawing together the sides of the cylinder, 0.45-1.05 shaping the shoulder, 1.05-1.40 forming the lip, 1.40-1.45 cleaning the hands, 1.45-2.05 further forming of the lip, 2.05-2.15 forming the ridge along the shoulder line, 2.15-2.30 smothing the belly of the vessel, 2.30-2.40 smoothing the entire vessel surface with a cloth, 2.40 cutting the vessel with a cord, 2.50 laying aside the moulded vessel.

Speaking generally, all vessels are moulded in much the same way. The following are special features and techniques :

(1) The small flat *kodia,* earthenware oil lamps, and the *dhakani,* lids, are not cut with the cord but, as it were, twisted off. This the potter accomplishes by slowly squeezing together thumb and forefinger under the vessel and then jerking it up towards himself, as the result of which the earthenware lamp falls into his hand. Its symmetrical shape is largely preserved, because it is comparatively thick.

(2) The different shaped *zakua kunda*, flower pots, which are not subsequently chased with paddles and anvil and therefore have no bottoms, very often have a double lip moulded at their rims. The potter then halts the wheel and with his left hand proceeds to revolve the wheel backwards, at the same time pressing the lower lip against the upper at equidistant intervals with his thumb, the forefinger resting on the upper lip. The lower lip is thus formed into a wavy shape.

(3) A border of parallel grooves is sometimes scratched around the neck of a *goro*, water vessel. For this, the potter uses whichever fingernail happens to be longest.

Chasing vessels

9.25 – 10.20 chasing twenty vessels, previously dried in the sun, smoking interval
10.20 – 10.50 chasing several more vessels with sharp angular shoulders
10.50 – 10.55 carrying shaped vessels into the shade
10.55 – 11.25 chasing the remaining vessels, smoking interval.

After this other vessels are chased. Within barely two hours, in all thirty vessels of different shapes and sizes were chased.

The following morning some of the vessels moulded the previous day stand in the sun, while others are placed in the shade or in the shed. The potter tests the degree of hardness or dryness reached by the vessels by gently pressing the shoulder between thumb and forefinger. He then fetches seven paddles and two counter supports (anvils) from the shed, an old gunny bag and a bowl of water from the house, and seats himself in the middle of the yard in the warm morning sun. First of all he sits with both legs bent inwards, the knees resting on the floor and the feet 198, 199
tucked under his body. Later, when he works on the bowls, he changes his posture: the right leg is now bent with the knee up, while the left knee rests on the floor. The sole of the left foot now touches the right foot. The potter reaches out with his left hand for one of the moulded vessels and places it on his foot. With both hands he now frays the somewhat soiled under-surface. The dry, crumly bits of clay are thrown on the ground in front of him. In his left hand he takes one of the counter supports and in the right a narrow headed paddle. He dips the 198
point of the paddle into the water pot before him, rubbing the drops of water onto the anvil. First of all he closes the bottom of the vessel by pounding it with his paddle. For this, the vessel 200, 201
is lent against the slanting sole of his foot. All the fingertips of his left hand, the little finger excepted, grasp the anvil by the neck and press it against the spot being worked upon; with the paddle, the handle of which is held between thumb and forefinger of the right hand, light strokes are delivered, which bounce off the surface in a slanting downward direction. Several strokes of this kind are applied to one spot before the vessel is turned in an anticlockwise direction with the help of the outstretched middle finger. When the vessel bottom has been roughly closed, Bhurabhai exchanges the narrow headed paddle for the broad one, which he also moistens and then uses to smooth over the surface just worked. When this is accomplished, the bowl or pot, whichever may be the case, is ready and is accordingly placed on the side. The potter holds it diagonally across the top with both hands and lays it on its rim on the ground.

An average vessel with rounded shoulders measuring about 25 cm in height is chased in approximately two minutes. The separate stages are divided as follows:

0.00 - 0.15 scrubbing the under-surface, 0.15 - 0.30 moistening the narrow headed paddle, 0.30 - 0.50 chasing the vessel bottom, 0.50-0.55 moistening the paddle a second time, 0.55 - 1.30 closing the opening in the bottom, 1.30 - 1.37 moistening the broad headed paddle, 1.37 - 2.02 chasing the bottom and the shoulder, finishing the vessel.

In the case of bowls, the time required varies between one and a half and two and a half minutes.

It may be interesting to note that with the narrow headed paddle, usually less than ten strokes are delivered on one spot on the surface of the vessel, while when the broad-headed paddle is used, less than fifteen strokes on the same spot are thought sufficient.

This fact is particularly well illustrated in the case of a *tavali,* bowl:

Time	Stage of work	Number of paddle strokes delivered on the spot.
0.00 – 0.15	scrubbing	
0.15 – 0.30	moistening paddle and counter support	
0.30 – 0.50	chasing with narrow headed paddle	4,5,9,9,10,10,15,15,9,8,
	moistening paddle	
0.50 – 1.20	chasing with narrow headed paddle	3,6,9,9,5,6,3,3,3,4,4
	moistening the paddle	
1.20 – 1.45	chasing with narrow headed paddle diagonally across vessel bottom	10
	moistening the broad headed paddle	
1.45 – 2.10	chasing with broad headed paddle	10,9,10,17,15,15
	moistening the broad headed paddle	
2.10 – 2.35	chasing with broad headed paddle	20,10,15,17

It may be mentioned that the high figures quoted here are in reality probably higher. It was very difficult to gauge the exact number of strokes without a movie-camera.

Larger vessels with sharp-angled shoulders are chased on a ring-shaped support, over which a gunny bag strewn with ash is laid. In the case of these vessels with comparatively narrow shoulders, the paddle strokes are almost exclusively restricted to the rounded belly. The working procedure closely resembles that described on pg. 147 the only difference being that the clay used is a different one. The sounds produced by the strokes vary accordingly: in the case of the small thick-walled and relatively moist vessels manufacturd from Baradia clay a hollow sound is produced, whereas in the case of the large vessels made from Shrinagar clay the strokes sound high-pitched and metallic.

199

The chased vessels are first spread out on top of a bed, but removed to the shed the same afternoon. The next morning they are painted.

Painting red earthenware

9.15 – 9.20	first beige coating of ochre slip applied to small vessels
9.20 – 9.32	rubbing of large vessels
9.32 – 9.50	beige ochre slip coating applied to large vessels. First layer of yellow ochre pigment
9.50 – 10.15	interval, drying of vessels
10.15 – 10.20	second layer of ochre pigment
10.20 – 11.10	painting of vessels with red and white pigments.

Before my arrival, the potter has already prepared a solution of different coloured earth pigments in three small clay vessels. First of all he dips a rag into the watery, beige-coloured ochre solution and smears it on the surfaces of the vessels, particularly on the inner surface in the case of bowls and exclusively on the outside in the case of pots. He holds the vessels by the rim and applies the slip irregularly over the surface. The pigment dries quickly.

202

The large vessels which were strewn with ash during the chasing process are scrubbed on the outside with a piece of sacking. When all have been freed from dust, they are also given a coating of the ochre solution. During this operation, large vessels are placed with their rims on the botton surface of another inverted pot. He then paints the shoulder of the vessel first on one side and then, this time in the opposite direction, on the other side, finishing with a few smeers of colour across the bottom. The vessel is then inverted and placed on its bottom, the ochre now being applied to the lip and shoulder. Since the pigment is rapidly absorbed, a few of the vessels are immediately given a second thin coating of the ochre slip.

This first beige layer is now coated over with another layer of yellow ochre. Very often only the vessel bottom receives this second coating. Some of the pots display large dabs of colour, for the potter does not make a very thorough job of applying it. He then washes his fingers, fetches his waterpipe and settles down to half an hour of rest. In the meanwhile the vessels dry in the morning sun.

Later on the potter applies a second coating of yellow ochre to the vessels. When the slip has dried a little, his wife polishes the larger vessels with the cord string with seads (vide pg. 149). In the meanwhile the potter prepares some more slip. He elubriates lumps of chalk in an open bowl. In a small earthenware bowl he pounds some stony red earth with paddle. He adds water to it from a brass pot and stirs the mixture with a twig. With his penknife he then cuts a twig from the *nim*-bush nearby and peels off the rind. One end of it he chews till only the fibres remain, after which he rubs it between the ball of his thumb and his forefinger. This is the brush with which he will apply the pigment. Other brushes have been previously prepared.
The chalk colour is applied in short, slanting, more or less parallel strokes to the lip of some of the vessels. The potter always starts from inside the pot and paints outwards, ending on the edge of the lip. He comments:

It is not necessary that I paint *chitar*, designs on the whole pot. These vessels are small. Only large vessels need ornamentation.

Before dipping into the chalk solution, the potter always stirs the mixture briefly with the brush first and then charges his brush with the colour. When the colour trickles out and runs down the shoulder of the vessel being worked upon, Bhurabhai is not in the least disturbed by this. When painting a herringbone pattern he draws both strokes from inside outwards. He works in pairs, that is to say, he does not first make a row of parallel lines and the set of opposing parallel lines afterwards. When making a hatched design on the surface, however, he first draws all the parallel lines in one direction before crossing them with another set of parallel lines.

When all the white lines have been drawn and only the dots are left to be painted with the chalk solution, the potter charges a finer brush with the red earth solution and draws thin red lines between the white ones.

He finally draws a few leaf motifs, concentric semicircles and trapezoid shapes in red on the shoulders of a few vessels. While executing the designs, he holds the twig between thumb and forefinger against the middle finger, the same way we hold a pencil. A few dots are painted on these red designs with the chalk solution. To ensure the dots being small, the potter tears off half the point of the brush.

Lastly, the potter demonstrates how lines are drawn on large vessels : he suspends the vessel by means of a stick knotted to a string and fitted across the opening and turns it slowly, the brush charged with colour being leant all the while against it.

205

203

204

In comparison with other examples of painting on earthenware to be found throughout Saurashtra, the technique and designs of Bhurabhai are nothing remarkable. His own remarks will best supply the reason for this:

// Painting is her (Bhurabhai's wife's) work. However, she cannot see clearly. One of her eyes is very weak. If she could see properly, she would do the painting.

Firing red earthenware

Afternoon:

2.30 — 3.10	preparing the kiln, piling up the vessels
3.10 — 3.15	smoking interval
3.15	lighting the kiln
3.15 — 5.50	kiln fire left to smoulder
5.50	opening the kiln, the required temperature had been attained.

The vessels are left in the ashes to cool slowly overnight.

Morning:

9.20 — 9.45	clearing away the ashes and broken earthenware fragmente, sprinkling the vessels with water, removal of the vessels.

The painted vessels are left outside to be pre-heated in the scorching noonday sun. In the afternoon the potter puts on a pair of shoes and clears the kiln ground by sweeping the ashes left from the previous firing away from the center and heaping them in a ring (diameter roughly 1.40 metres) encircling the firing site. Under the tree nearby shrubs, roots and grass have earlier been heaped. All this fuel is thrown into the ash ring and distributed evenly with the rake. The potter sees to it that the layer is thicker on the edges than the middle. Finally, he treads on the shrubs to crush them. He asks his son to fetch him some bits of broken earthenware from the heap near the edge of the yard wall. These he spreads over the shrubs. On top of this layer he arranges the vessels, taking care that the openings show upwards and are left free. Again a layer of fragments is spread over the vessels. The resulting heap is not very high. He next proceeds to cover it with more shrubs, over which reeds are also laid. Finally he collects all the sticks, leaves, chaff and other fuel material in a basket, which he empties over the heap. With the hoe he piles up the ash all around. A vessel with a broken off bottom is placed against the pile facing the direction of the wind. The prepared kiln is later lit through this hole. On top of the vessels he places a broken pot with a broad opening, which serves both as chimney and peep-hole. In the meanwhile, though, the aperture is closed with another fragment.

206

When the rough kiln has been thinly covered with ashes and coal waste, Bhurabhai fetches a few burning coals from the house and inserts them through the opening at the side. The shrubs are at once set alight. The opening is then closed with another piece of earthenware. The fire is prevented from flaming by laying ash or slightly damp reeds over the spot where the flames rise. However, the potter is for the most part unemployed at this stage. He sits under a spreding tree, smokes his waterpipe and chats with passing idlers.

Later the wind changes direction and the increasing flames must be smothered. The potter covers the fire with a layer of crushed donkey dung.

Not before the kiln has been smouldering for nearly two hours does he open the peep-hole and sedulously inspects the colour of the broken pot fragments. Apparently dissatisfied, he closes the hole again and heaps ash over it. Ten minutes later he pokes holes left and right of the opening and widens them. He leaves these open, but throws more donkey's dung on the rear half of the kiln, where flames have manged to push their way. Through the openings in the front, the vessels can be seen. They are glowing red and show pink stripes, rather milky in colour. The potter carefully clears away the ash and professes the vessels to be *paki gaya*, ready. He does not remove the broken bits covering the vessels. 207

The fired earthenware is not taken out of the kiln till the following morning. The fragments, which were originally black in colour, have also oxidated along with the other vessels and turned red. Both, fragments and vessels are still warm. 208

Not one of the vessels is damaged. Only one pot is black over its entire under-surface, probably because it stood on a concave fragment. In taking out the vessels the potter knocks on each one, the resulting high-pitched sound indicating that it is sound and not cracked.

The potter's daughter brings water in a metal basin. One by one the vessels are dipped and briefly shaken in the water. They absorb the water and bubbles are formed. The porous and still warm earthenware dries at once. 209

Finally, the potter again overlays the kiln with ash and loads the vessels into the saddle bags thrown over the donkey's back by his son. First of all Bhurabhai places an equal number of large vessels in either bag. Later he picks up several vessels at one time with both hands, putting them into bags simultaneously. 210

Bhurabhai then wends his way to Ratadi with his load of vessels.

4.5. Example 2 : The manufacute of black earthenware

Of the multitude of vessels in diverse shapes and sizes produced by this process, I have chosen to describe *goro*, water pot, as a typical example. Its larger than usual dimensions lend themselves particulatly well to a clear elucidation of working techniques employed in the manufacture. A complete description of this basic working procedure is followed by notes on the manufacture of two vessels striking for their exceptional shape : *bampli*, pot for carrying water, and *donio*, the cooking pot with a multiple-layered bottom.

As far as the individual details of technique are concerned, the procedure in many respects resembles that described in Example I (for instance the preparation of clay, the moulding and polishing of vessels). For this reason details such as posture and position of the fingers will be largely omitted in the following account.

Raw materials and tools
Black baked easthenware, which is intended for everyday use in the household, is hard and practically nonporous. It is made from good-quality clay, dark grey or reddish brown in colour, which occurs in the area around the neighbouring village of Shrinagar. Ash, dung and sometimes also sand are added as temper to the clay. The reddish clay is used chiefly for bowls and cooking pots intended for exposure to the heat of the fire, the grey clay being employed to make milk and water pots of large size. The fuel chiefly used by the potter for firing all these vessels is cactus, although the kiln fire is also fed with roots, reeds, grass, chaff and donkey or goat-dung.

All the tools with the exception of the moulding box for bricks and the measuring cup are required in the manufacture of black baked earthenware.

Preparing the red clay
Time required 10.15-12.15
The heap of red earth stored in the corner of the work shed is emptied in the yard, crushed with the mallet and picked clean. The potter then pats the earth into a semicircle with his hands, collecting the larger lumps of clay in the centre and the fine powder earth around it. He sifts sand over it and sprinkles water on it as well. He lets the water permeate for about half an hour before kneading the clay and adding two basketfuls of crumbled donkey dung to it. When clay and dung are well mixed, the potter scrapes the mass together and smooths the surface of the heap with a wet hand. He now prepares his wheel, while his wife divides the mass into several rolls. It is apparently essential that the freshly mixed clay be at once moulded on the wheel.

Preparing the dark grey clay
Time required 9.30 — 11.20
The dark grey earth from Shrinagar is crushed and picked clean. Hardly any dust rises when it is pounded with the mallet; little stones must be picked out from the lumps of clay. The clay is once more formed into a semicircle near the wall of the house and then thoroughly watered. The potter sifts ash all round the clay heap so as to absorb any water that trickles out. The wet ash he then gathers up by rubbing and pressing his palms on the ground, throwing the ash thus collected out of the compound. He then spreads a layer of crumbled donkey dung over the clay, topping this with the same amount, a basinful, of ash. The three layers are then blended piece by piece, the potter taking care that the clayey ground is not ripped up along with the pieces he separates from the mass. For this reason, he always strews the ground with ash. The kneaded clay lumps are formed into balls, which he piles into a heap. Later on, his wife will work them on the slab prior to the moulding process.

The potter first lays out his tools. He wets the slab and the centre of the wheel, lets water trickle through the clay crust and then scrapes away the clay slivers with his nails. He then beats the clay, his wife later relieving him at this job. Bhurabhai takes a roll of clay, lays it on the wet slab and first kneads it by pressing his palm on the surface. He then withdraws his hand, at the same time pressing down the tips of his fingers. A piece of clay comes away in his hand, which he lifts up and dashes down against the flat cake on the slab. This kneading and beating process is repeated several times in quick succession, an interruption occuring only when the potter chances on a little stone, which he extracts from the mess with his fingers.

In the next stage, both hands, the thumbs stretched out, lie alongside each other on the clay surface. The thumbs are sunk firmly into the mass, thus cutting off a lump from the side of the cake. This is seized by the fingers, lifted up and flung down on the cake with force. Bhurabhai subsequently tears off large pieces of clay with one thumb only, grasping the piece with both hands and raising it above his head before casting it down on the mass. Both hands alternate in swift succession, beating the clay mass. When the clay has been sufficiently worked in this manner, the potter forms it into a roll, the hands being placed flat on the mass. He stands the resulting cylindrical shape upright in front of him on the stone slab and smooths over its surface with wet hands.

The beating process lasts six minuts for each roll of clay - three minutes for kneading, two for beating and one for rolling.

Throwing and moulding vessels
Bhurabhai now starts to turn the wheel with one hand, placing the smooth clay rool in the centre of the steadily turning disc with the other. In pressing it in place, he shapes it into a cone with a rounded top. After a short interval, he propels the wheel by turning it fortynine

211

145

times with accelerated speed by means of the stick, which he then lays aside. He now sinks both thumbs into the point of the cone, which yields to his touch and expands into a thick-walled, open bowl. The clay that has stuck to his fingers during the moulding process he later scrapes off. Now he wets his hands, places them inside the bowl and draws it upwards and inwards at the same time, the result being a tall vessel with a slightly curved belly. With both hands he once more encircles the base of the vessel and pulls it upwards, applying moderate pressure, into a narrow, smooth cylinder even in shape. The wheel must now be rotated by hand seventeen times, for the potter wishes to smooth the surface and remove ridges and other irregularities from it. He then accelerates the wheel once more by turning it thirtyfive times with the stick. The cylinder is now to be rounded. While the fingertips of the right hand press the wall of the vessel outwards, the back of the left hand lies against the exterior surface and exerts counter pressure from outside. Bhurabhai next shapes the lip. The rim of the vessel is held between the forefinger and the middle finger of the left hand, while the right thumb presses the neck inwards. A part of the thick lip is then turned downwards with the tip of the thumb into the middle of the neck, while the left thumb is extended over the lip, the fingers of the same hand being bent against the neck. The shape of the lip and the ring around the neck are then adjusted at length, the fingers of the left hand invariably supplying counter pressure from the inside of the vessel, while the thumb of the moulding right hand guides the process.

As a final touch, Bhurabhai forms a few grooves along the shoulder, using the nail of his right ring finger, the ball of the left thumb pressing from above so as to ensure an even spiral. The lip and shoulder of the vessel can now be smoothed over with the wet cloth. In the meanwhile, the wheel has retarded in speed and must be brought to revolve again with fifteen revolutions of the right hand. Now both hands with thumbs adjacent, encircle the base of the vessel and turn it slowly in the direction opposite to that of the rotating wheel, so as to twist off the vessel. The pot with its irregularly shaped bottom is placed on the earth beside the potter. After some time it is removed to dry in a safe place. Bhurabhai washes his hands in the bowl of water, rubbing each in turn with the other, before placing the next roll on the wheel. One large pot or two small ones may be moulded from one of these rolls.

Bhurabhai requires about eight minutes to mould the large *goro,* water pot. The individual stages of work are divided in the following manner:

0.00 — 0.20	setting the wheel in motion with the hand
0.20 — 0.50	placing the clay roll on the wheel; conical form
0.50 — 1.00	resting pause
1.00 — 1.10	revolving wheel with the stick
1.10 — 1.20	drawing out the vessel to form a bowl
1.20 — 1.40	cleaning fingers
1.40 — 2.00	drawing up the vessel to form a tall bowl shape
2.00 — 2.10	revolving wheel with the stick
2.10 — 3.00	drawing up the vessel to form a cylinder
3.00 — 3.40	revolving wheel with the stick
3.40 — 4.05	rounding the cylinderical form to a vase shape
4.05 — 4.15	forming the lip
4.15 — 7.10	adjusting the shape of the lip and neck
7.10 — 7.15	drawing grooves on the neck
7.15 — 7.40	smoothing lip and shoulder with cloth
7.40 — 8.00	revolving wheel with the hand
8.00 — 8.07	twisting off the vessel from the wheel
8.07 — 8.15	placing aside the vessel; washing hands.

A small vessel with a plain lip can be moulded in considerable less time and two such vessels can be made from one clay roll. To make a *matlu,* water pot, Bhurabhai requires about four minutes, while the first stage of a *bampli,* pot for carrying water, can be shaped in a mere two and a half minutes, because in the latter case a pronounced lip may be dispensed with.

Chasing vessels

The vessels are left to dry beside the wheel till they have become as hard as leather, after which they are removed, usually inside the shed. As a rule they can be chased already on the following day. In the case of grey earthenware, I observed the potter testing the degree of moisture present in the vessel with the palm of his hand. The vessels are chased in various ways depending on their shape and size.

Small pots such as the *bampli,* pot for carrying water, are placed on a ring to be chased. For this purpose a piece from an old quilts is coiled into a roll with the ends brought together, a cord being wound around this ring. A gunny bag is spread over the ring and ashes are strewn over it. The potter is not bound in his choice of a working place, because once chased the small vessels are simply inverted and placed on their rims to dry.

For chasing large vessels such as the *goro,* water pot, a pit is dug with the hoe in the sandy, ashy ground of the work shed, near the entrance. The earth dug out is neatly piled around the pit and, together with the walls of the pit, gently pounded with the stone counter support. The potter uses his slightly bent fingers to shape the rim to a rounded edge. He carefully lays a piece of sacking strewn with ash over the pit. The diameter of the pit is equal to that of the vessel to be chased and is accordingly adjusted, as the case may demand. This reason alone makes it advisable for the potter to work through a series of vessels graduated in size. The large vessels chased here must subsequently be placed at a slight slant in ash holes, to prevent the expanded bottoms from falling apart. The ash holes are dug with the hoe before the potter starts chasing the vessels.

No ash is used in chasing bowls. Neither are they fitted into a pit to be chased, but are instead laid with their rims resting on the potter's sole (vide pg. 140). They are dried in an inverted position, their rims on the ground.

Bhurabhai lifts up the *goro,* water pot, and lays it with its shoulder in the pit. He then scrapes
222–227
away the underface of the vessel so as to remove the dirtied clay fragments adhering to it. This he follows up by dipping the edge of the broad headed paddle in water and with it grinding away the drops of water on the stone counter support. He then expands, when necessary closes, and rounds the pointed oval vessel bottom where it was twisted off the wheel. He holds the paddle in his right hand and the anvil in his left. In chasing the undersurface, he arranges the paddle strokes spirally around the bottom. When a small spiral circle of this kind, beginning at the bottom of the vessel and terminating near the belly, is almost closed, the potter turns the vessel with his middle finger and overlapping the line, proceeds to chase an identical spiral closely following the first. Upon contact with the surface, each paddle stroke slides off in the direction of the centre of the vessel bottom. For this reason the individual impressions or dents made by the blows are not clearly defined. When the circle has been closed, the potter strews ash over the vessel and then chases the belly and shoulder up to the neck to expand them. The course followed by the paddle strokes now begins at the bottom, rises almost vertically up to where the neck begins and then turns at an acute angle to retrace their course in a second line next to the first, finally returning to the neck. Though the vessel is irregularly rounded and there is a fold near the neck, it has already been expanded practically to its full dimensions.

With rough blows dealt in chipping movements, the bottom is expanded so as to bulge out right up to the shoulder. Another fold is formed at about the level of the shoulder but soon dispelled by hammering on the spot. However, a sharp ridge persiststs, owing to the shoulder being more curved than the belly. After this, the bottom is once more expanded. In both cases spirals are traced above or below the shoulder, as the case may be, the main curve lying on the shoulder. The bottom is strewn with ash and chased a second time, the blows being now more forceful than at first. A double ridge is formed along the shoulder. Now the shoulder is chased again, so that it arches over the belly. This is followed by paddle blows in figures of eight on the shoulder itself. The shoulder now appears rounded and the pot is thus spherical. Its surface is quite smooth except for a few depressions or dents from the paddle blows. These, however, are scarcely discernible.

The potter then deposits the pot, which may for the time being be looked upon as chased and ready, in an ash pit. Later, after the clay has been allowed to contract by drying, it is subjected to a second chasing. This time the main purpose is to produce a smooth, even surface and not to further distend the vessel.

The potter requires roughly 20 minutes to chase the large *goro,* water pot. This time is divided as follows :

0.00 – 0.30	scraping clean the undersurface
0.30 – 0.45	chasing the bottom
0.45 – 2.30	chasing the bottom, shoulder and neck
2.30 – 5.00	chasing the bottom and up to the shoulder
5.00 – 7.20	chasing from neck to shoulder
7.20 – 8.10	chasing from bottom to shoulder.
8.10 – 13.00	chasing from bottom to shoulder
13.00 – 18.50	smoothing over the shoulder
18.50 – 19.20	laying aside the pot and preparing a place to deposit the next vessel.

Ornamenting and finishing the vessels

When the vessels have been chased for the last time and dried to the consistency of leather, an ornamental border is scratched around the shoulders of the large pots. A broken piece of comb, with a number of closely spaced fine teeth on one side and only two thick teeth on the other, is used for this purpose. As a rule the potter places the piece of comb against the shoulder and then turns the pot, which rests in the pit, on its own axis, concentric circles around the shoulder being the result. The pattern may be replaced by a running spiral, which is produced by describing small circles with the comb, while turning the vessel. With one thick tooth of the comb the potter cuts in a border with a herringbone pattern, the slanting lines being drawn in pairs.

240

Decorating a pot in this manner takes a bare two minutes.

Black baked earthenware is not painted. But all vessels made of red or grey clay from Shrinagar are covered with a coat of slip by the women of the potter's household just before firing. However, the coating is mostly restricted to neck and shoulder in the case of pots, and to lip and inner surface in the case of bowls. Only the large water pots are also coated with slip on the undersurface.

First of all the vessels are thoroughly scrubbed with a piece of sacking, after which dust from the ash is blown away.

The ochre slip has been prepared in a pot. The clean vessels are coated with the watery clay solution. This the wife of the potter does by placing each vessel on a clean surface, for instance a wooden board or a bed and turning it by the rim with her left hand, while the right hand applies a rag saturated with the ochre slip to the neck and shoulder. Lastly, the lip or rim itself is painted over with ochre. When the first coat has dried, the whole row of vessels is coated over a second time.

242

As a rule two women work together, for the vessels must be polished with the chain of strung seeds while wet. For this, the vessel is firmly laid in an unfired clay ring. The woman bends over it; several strands of the chain are wound around one wrist and held in the opposite hand. The chain is slung around the neck of the vessel, pulled taut and twisted around the vessel about twenty times under great pressure. The surface of the clay pot acquires a glazed appearance. The chain is then somewhat loosened and the shoulder polished with it. In the case of spherical water pots, the undersurface is also coated with slip as mentioned above. They are therefore inverted to rest on their rims, so that this surface may be polished as well. Bowls are only polished on the inside. Here the potter's wife twines the chain together and scours the vessel, as it were, with outstretched fingers, simultaneously pressing down the seeds.

243

It takes about a minute to scrub a vessel, fortyfive seconds to coat it with ochre slip and two minutes to polish neck and shoulder.

Preparing the kiln
Time required: 10.30 – 12.20
The kiln site, where the red earthenware was the last to be fired, is prepared the day before the firing is to take place. With the wooden rake the potter first clears away all the remnants of fuel from the preceding firing. Taking the broad hoe he next piles up the ash in a ring formation around the kiln site. He picks up broken scraps of earthenware and flings them in a wide arc out of the compound. His little son is instructed to bring him a basket from the shed. Assorted odds and ends that may still be burnt, such as charred chips of wood, leaves, etc. are collected in this basket. The ash floor has been baked black and must be dug up with the narrow hoe. First the potter collects the ash in a heap before him and then shovels it through between his legs in all directions, heaping it on top of the ash ring. For this the broad hoe is used. The work is strenuous and the potter sweats copiously. But after half an hour's work, a bank of ash enclosing the kiln site is ultimately built up. The top of the bank is flattened evenly with the rake.

245

After a short interval of rest, the edges of the bank are rounded in such a way that a ring shaped bed is formed, through which eight partition walls are drawn. All the children of the potter are now mobilized to fetch water, which is poured evenly into the compartments formed. The boys carry the water pots on their shoulders, the girls on their heads.

246

247

After a very large quantity of water has been poured over the bank and has thorouhhly permeated into the coal ash, the potter levels out the bank of ash with the back of the rake. Wet ash now surrounds the kiln site and can be used later to seal the kiln.

Including the bank, the kiln site measures roughly five metres in diameter. The inner circle itself measures only two metres across.

Firing black earthenware

Time required: approximately four hours collecting the fuel. In the afternoon:

2.45 – 3.15	preparing the fuel
3.15 – 3.45	piling up the vessels
3.45 – 4.30	enclosing the pots with earthenware fragments
4.30 – 4.50	surrounding the pile with straw
4.50 – 5.25	strewing ash around the pile
5.25 – 5.30	smoking interval
5.30 – 5.45	completing the ring of ash around the pile
5.45 – 5.55	smoking interval
5.55 – 6.15	piling more fuel on the kiln pile
6.15	lighting the fire
6.30	laying on more fuel
9.15	sealing the holes, adding of donkey dung
9.20	breaking though the layer of ash, spreading goat droppings over the kiln
9.35 – 10.10	covering the kiln with whet ash.

Following morning:

9.30 – 10.30	opening of the kiln
10.30 – 11.20	inspecting the fired earthenware.

The entire firing process thus demands roughly ten hours of work. In addition, the potter sleeps at night by the smouldering fire, so as to drive away any stray dogs that may venture near.

First of all, dry pieces of cactus gathered from the steppe-like wastes surrounding the village are chopped up with the axe and thrown into the centre of the kiln site. Then the mould is levelled out with the back of the rake to form an even layer, the potter being careful to leave a gap between the ash bank and the fuel. A layer of bulbous roots, of equal depth, is spread over the chopped cactus and compressed by pounding with the rake. This fuel layer is approximately 25 cm in depth. The vessels are next arranged on it. Following the curt instructions of the potter, his family fetches the vessels from where they have been warmed in the sun since late morning. First of all the large *gora,* water pots, are arranged on the layer of fuel, care being exercised to ensure that they stand at a slant on their rim, so that air may have access to the interior of the vessels. Four pots are first arranged in a square with their undersurfaces touching, four more pots being mounted on their shoulders. One large pot is then placed on each side, followed by four more on each side all round; a second layer of large pots is placed over the first so that in the centre there are three pots one on top of the other. All around and between these pots, bowls, dishes, plates, small vessels, etc. are laid, more or less systematically, the openings in every case pointing inwards. Bhurabhai now asks his daughter to bring him some bits of broken earthenware from the heaps piled against the wall. He first wishes for pieces broken off from the neck of vessels.

248

249

The potter now clears out the fuel from under the vessels on the side. Three basketfuls of fuel are carried away. He then places one ring-shaped neck fragment against the fuel, to which he holds another fragment almost equal in size, in such a way that the rims touch each other. He underlays both fragments with wet ash. Bhurabhai prepares altogether eight such openings. He then lays flat earthenware fragments all round the pile of vessels which is about 1.20 metres high. Bundles of dry grass are laid on this layer. The grass is partly wet, and the wet bundles are placed chiefly where sharp draughts of wind are frequent. When the supply of grass has been exhausted, reeds are used instead, the pile of vessels being covered with them as well. After a short while the potter builds up the bank of ash around the vessels. Here he works radially, the pit being first filled up. Bhurabhai then hacks free the wet ash and pushes it

250

against the straw with the broad hoe. He next directs his daughter to loosen the ash with blows, while he pats it against the kiln with his hands. He then orders water to be sprinkled over the loosened ash, after which he mixes the ash and water with the hoe and applies the mixture to the kiln. Both father and daughter work indefatigably, and at the end of half an hour a 10 cm thick layer of ash is laid 70 cm high around the heap that constitutes the kiln. Only the openings formed by the neck fragments are left free or, where they have been unwittingly covered, laid open again.

After a short smoking interval the cover of ashes is made higher. This is done by filling basins with ash and emptying them over the heap. The potter uses both hands to press the ash firm, particular attention being paid to the upper edge, which is patted thoroughly with the palms. Water from three large vessels is now sprinkled over the ash bank, which is once more patted smooth.

A short pause in the proceedings indicates that the preparation have temporarily come to an end. Chopped-up cactus is now thrown into each opening. With the purpose of making embers available, Bhurabhai next lights a small fire near the kiln site, using bits of cactus and half a bundle of reeds. In the meanwhile he collects two basketfuls of chaff, chopped straw and wood chops and one basketful of charred fuel, all of which he empties on top of the kiln.

With a stick he disperses the little blaze and carries the glowing embers to each of the eight openings. The fire does not catch readily but seems rather to flicker unsteadily. The potter extinguishes the first fire by spreading earth over the spot.

A little later, Bhurabhai pokes the fire in two of the openings and adds more fuel. Smoke rises reluctantly from the kiln, because the fire burns only in the openings directly exposed to the wind, which fans the flames.

The potter sits beside the kiln, smoking and chatting. With his visitors he drinks tea brewed together with goat's milk. At intervals he rises to see whether any holes have been formed on the kiln surface, in which case he stuffs them first with chaff and then seals them over with wet ash.

Shortly after nine o'clock, the potter empties several basketfuls of donkey dung over the kiln. The openings are closed with plate-shaped fragments, for the flames on the mound now flicker blue. Bhurabhai directs his daughter to scrape ash from the top of the kiln with the hoe, so that he can tip a few baskets of donkey dung into the fire. The dry, pebble-like dung rains down on the vessels, followed by several baskets of chaff, after which ash is once more spread over the kiln. For this he rolls up the legs of his trousers and then waters the upper part of the ash bank, slapping his palm in vertical movements over it. Basins of ash are then emptied over the kiln and patted to form a layer approximately four cm in thickness, the layer being subsequently watered several times. So as to reach the top, Bhurabhai supports himself by placing one leg against the kiln.

When the whole kiln heap has been evenly covered with a layer of ash and no flames or smoke may be seen to issue from it, the potter washes his hands and face and also sprinkles the washing water over the ash bank. I then take my leave. Bhurabhai says that he will spend the night sleeping beside the kiln, because it may be necessary for him to chase away dogs that are driven by the winter cold to seek warmth at the fire.

On the next morning the potter carries a hoe, a stick and a cloth rag to the kiln, which has been smouldering undisturbed through the night.

With the hoe he opens the kiln, breaking away the dry ash bank, from which clouds of
dust rise. He collects the fragments that had been arranged around the vessels and piles them
up in a heap. He grips the hot vessels with the rag, using the stick to keep the others from
tumbling out. He also pokes about in the ash, which falls between the vessels and helps to
support them. A few wisps of smoke issue from the kiln, for some of the chopped straw has
not been quite burnt up.

252

He takes out the pots and bowls one by one and heaps them around the kiln. Only one
bowl is perceptibly cracked. Nevertheless, Bhurabhai tests each vessel by holding it by the
rim and knocking on it with the flat of his hand or with the knuckle of his right forefinger.
When a dull, muffled sound is heard, the vessel is cracked. All such defective earthenware
is placed in an inverted position and later carried to the wall together with the other potsherds.

253, 254

Of the entire number of vessels fired, 234 are faultless and only 25 defective. Of these, 17
are *donia,* cooking pots with multiple-layered bottoms, and a few *bampli,* vessels for carrying
water. Bhurabhai had predicted earlier thet these last ones would not turn out well.

The black earthenware is stored in the potter's house and sold in the following week.

4. 6. Example 3 : The manufacture of a pot for carrying water

In the following, the process of moulding a *bampli* will be described, which is a small pot
for carrying water characterized by a narrower than usual neck.

Preparing the vessel
First of all a medium sized vessel with a flat neck and a roughly shaped lip is moulded from
grey clay. The pot is now dried as usual for a little while. It is then chased to a spherical shape,
ash being used in the process. The pot is allowed to dry overnight. The following morning
it is once more chased. The surface is smoothed with the paddle and the uneven thickness of
the pot regulated.

Bhurabhai asks his wife to bring him a basket of fresh, moist cow dung. The *bampli* pots
are collected around him. He takes up a piece of dung with the fingertips, kneads it lightly and
places it on the neck of the vessel. He lays seven more pieces of dung one beside the other
around the neck. He then wets his fingertips with water and raps them lightly over the dung
ring, after which he places the vessel with its rim on the ground.

228

During the midday break the humidity from the dung ring penetrates into the neck,
while the rest of the vessel dries. The pots first stand in the shade and are later carried into
the shed.

Preparing additional clay
Bhurabhai has prepared and watered a small heap of grey clay from Shrinagar. On the
heap he throws half the quantitiy of slippy ochre from Bharvada and strews crumbled donkey
dung and ash around it. All these ingredients are thoroughly kneaded together. Later he beats
the clay, adds a little more ash to it and finally dries his hands with crumbled donkey dung.

Moulding a pot base
The potter sets up the wheel, lubricates the wooden pin fixed in the support and inserts
small earthen ware fragments under it; he then fetches a bowl of water and the stick to revolve
the wheel. He once more sprinkles water on the mound of clay, wets the centre of the wheel

and shapes a piece of clay into a ball, which he throws down on the centre of the wheel. From this clay ball he moulds an open, hemispherical bowl with a rounded lip. He smooths the inside of the bowl carefully with the moistened cloth. The bowl, which is 9 cm high and has a diameter of 22.5 cm is then left to dry on the wheel. From the rest of the clay he shapes a large roll, the surface of which he carefully pats over with water. The roll is then carried to a shady spot and covered with a gunny bag.

Mounting the narrow neck
In the afternoon, Bhurabhai beats the already prepared clay once more on the stone slab. He then slices off a small piece, shapes it into a little roll and carefully washes it over with water.

He carries all the *bampli* pots out of the shed and deposits them in the middle of the still shady yard. He now prepares the clay roll, which he places on a piece of board, and also a knife, a basin, a bowl of water, a paddle, an anvil and a cushioning formed out of a piece of cloth twisted into a ring. The potter places a *bampli* pot on this ring. With his fingertips he scratches off the cow dung and throws it into the metal basin. Any remaining dung is   229 scraped off the shoulder of the vessel with the back of the knife. He washes the knife in the bowl of water and cuts off the top of the vessel at the neck by pressing the knife blade to the neck with his right forefinger, while the left hand exerts counter pressure from inside and at the same time turns the vessel. The knife is twice passed through the groove cut around the vessel before the neck ring is severed. The potter now moistens the broad paddle and the counter support and chases the shoulder. After this he trims the neck cut even.   230

The potter once more kneads the small clay roll. He then rolls it between his palms to a short   232 cylinder, through which he pierces the middle finger of his right hand. During this operation, the roll lies on his left palm. He now turns it around his middle finger, the edge being flattened out with the thumb. This pierced mushroom-shaped clay roll is now mounted on   233–235 the decapitated *bampli* pot, and the edges pressed to the thin neck, chiefly with the thumb. The thumb of the left hand later also comes into play, being used to stroke down the clay roll on the outside of the pot in such a way as to merge the two completely. Bhurabhai can then withdraw his middle finger from the interior of the vessel and smooth over the surface of the newly mounted neck.

Moulding the narrow neck
Bhurabhai sets the wheel in motion by turning it several times with his hand, taking care that   231 it rotates steadily without rocking. He then lifts up the *bampli* pot between both hands and   236 places it in the bowl-shaped base. This must be attempted several times before the pot sits right. Then he turns the wheel with the stick. His left middle finger is inserted into the neck of the vessel, while both hands rest on the neck cone and press it centrally down on the vessel. The left middle finger is kept inside the vessel to exert counter pressure, and is occasionally reinforced by the forefinger of the same hand. At the same time the other fingers, mainly the two thumbs and the right forefinger, shape the neck ring, the neck itself and the lip, working from the outside. The positions of the fingers during these processes largely resemble those already described (vide pg. 146). The now completed neck is smoothed over with the wet   237, 238 cloth. The pot is then removed from the wheel and placed on the previously cut off neck ring. When narrow necks have been moulded on to all the *bampli* pots, they are carried one by one into the shed and left to dry in the windless shade.

Later, these vessels are polished and fired together with other pottery made of grey clay. Of the seven *bampli* pots, only two are able to withstand the firing process without cracking. Already, while they are drying small cracks appear on some of the pots. According to the potter, the moulding of the second necks on the pots should have taken place only in a spot sheltered from the wind. It was I who had urged that the work be performed in the open yard.

Not regarding the time taken up in preparing the clay, drying the vessels and firing, the most important features of the time schedule (per *bampli*-vessel) are as follows:
Moulding two and half minutes; chasing six and a half minutes; smoothing with paddle two minutes; applying cowdung one minute; scratching off dung and cutting off neck three minutes; forming the clay roll for the new neck one minute forty seconds, and finally three to four minutes for moulding the second neck. Therefore, a total of seventeen minutes' work is required for each vessel without taking into account the preparation of clay, the collecting of fuel and the drying and firing of the vessels.

4.7. Example 4: The manufacture of cooking vessels

Cooking vessels, that is, earthenware intended for exposure to fire, are made of grey or red clay from Shrinagar. The distinguishing features of these pots are firstly, that their undersurfaces are lined with layers of different types of clay, and secondly, that they are given a coating of a special slip before they are fired. The cooking vessels are made from clay prepared in the normal way. They are also moulded, dried and fired like the other pots. The only differences are in the chasing process:

After moulding, the undersurface of the bowl is cut off, the opening being closed with the narrow paddle. Bhurabhai then shapes a ball of red clay, which he pats into a flat cake between his palms and plasters on the grey undersurface of the vessel, chasing it in. Seen in a longitudinal section, the undersurface is found to be equal in thickness to the walls of the vessel, that is to say, both layers of clay on the undersurface are half the usual thickness.

The bowl is then chased in the same way as other earthenware. When the vessels have been dried, polished and warmed preparatory to firing, the potter's wife paints them over with a watery solution of sand and red clay, using a cloth. Some of the vessels are smeared over with several layers of this mixture. Shortly after, they are piled up for firing. When the kiln was opened, a comparatively large percentage of these vessels was found to be defective.

244

4.8. Example 5: The manufacture of cooking stoves

Clay is dug from the nearby clay pit and prepared in the usual manner. However, it is not picked clean beforehand. Unsifted donkey dung is strewn over the clay mass, having been only mashed with a stick and crumbled before being added. While the first clay is mixed, the potter throws ash over it. Taken altogether equal amounts of dung and ash are mixed with more than twice the quantity of clay. The moist clay mass is thoroughly kneaded and ultimately formed into a large ball.

The potter cuts a broad slice from the mass with the flat of his hand. This he carries to the spot where the stove is to be made and left to dry, alongside the yard wall.

With his fingers pressed together, the potter trims the edges of the cut slice to a horse-shoe shape. The trimmings he throws back on the slice. He then gathers them up again and arranges them along the edges of the horse-shoe, concentrating on the front portion. He wets his hands, cuts the front portion straight and then smooths over it. In doing so, his hands always stroke downwards. He then traces round the horse-shoe cutline with his right forefinger, raps his

264

154

fingertips along the front line to make it straight, moulds both humps or elevations, and finally smooths over them. When he passes his wetted palms over the sides of the stove, the left palm simultaneously slides over the inner surface to provide counter pressure, while the right moulds and smooths.

Finally he presses the front pillars into shape, both of which incline slightly inwards.

The moulding of such a cooking stove takes barely fifteen minutes.

After the stoves have been left exposed to the sun for a few hours in the noon, they are 265 decorated. From the clay mass, which has been kneaded once again, the potter shapes little rolls and also balls, which he sticks to the still damp front of the fireplace with his thumb. He next squeezes them together again between thumb and forefinger at the sides. A wetted middle finger is passed over them by way of smoothing.

When several rows of clay rolls have been stuck to the surface, Bhurabhai begins to arrange them according to a regular pattern. He usually starts at the top of the left pillar, places roll after roll in a line going downwards and then starts once more upwards from the base of the right pillar ending at the top of it. When all the lines have been completed, Bhurabhai commences to press in the depressions with an outstretched middle finger of his right hand.

Although I voice no such wish, Bhurabhai decorates the front of the stove with various ornaments purely for my benefit. As a rule, all the stoves produced are uniform in shape and design.

The stoves must be allowed to dry for several days before they can be lifted from the ground and piled one on top of the other. At present there is a brisk trade in stoves because many new houses are being built and young women take little pleasure in working with clay.

VIII 5. Technical knowledge and workshop lingo

The following technical points were explained to me by Bhurabhai during the working procedure. In order to distinguish my observations from the technical knowledge of the potter, I have separated them, arranging them once more according to the various stages of the working procedure. I have followed the rough plan of quoting first information given by the potter and then the technical terms applied to the different stages of work or to individual manipulations.

5.1. Preparing the clay

The grey clay from Shrinagar must be mixed in the following proportion : four baskets of clay to one basket of ash. The red clay is prepared by combining four baskets of clay with one of sand, while for preparing clay from Baradia, about half as much ash as clay are required· Bhurabhai says :

// The proportions vary with the different kinds of clay.

// For *chula*, cooking stoves, I use clay from here; for red earthenware I also use clay from here, but it is dug at another site and therefore has other qualities. // *Chula* clay contains a larger admixture of sand, has also more stones and is less plastic than usual. Vessels cannot be moulded from this clay.

When the potter wishes to use a specially plastic clay, for instance when a second neck is to be moulded on a vessel, he mixes *met*, ochre slip, with the ordinary clay. He says;

Chiknai, plasticity, is destroyed by adding *rakh,* ashes. Mixing *met,* ochre with clay makes it more plastic. With *tadi,* clay-ochre mixture, very large vessels with very thin sides can be formed. Even so, a certain amount of *rakh,* ash, must be added even to the *tadi,* mixture.

// The ash is to help ensure that the vessel does not crack when heated. If I were to use only *met,* ochre, the vessel would burst in the kiln.

// The exact proportion in which the ingredients are to be added cannot be fixed beforehand. It depends on the plasticity of the clay. One must be taught by experience. I just estimate it every time.

The following expressions are used by Bhurabhai to describe the different phases in *mati bhelavavi,* preparing clay:

bhuko karvo, pounding lumps of clay to powder
kankari vinvi, picking out stones
muth thi cholvi, mixing clay with fist
mati kachravi, kneading and beating the clay
thapi, piling (the clay into a mound).

The semicircle in which the clay is arranged before being watered is called *aro* and the ring-shaped accumulation of powdery clay around it is *pari.* The act of mixing *met,* ochre, with water in a vessel is referred to as *dhovu,* stir, by Bhurabhai. Finally, I quote Bhurabhai's description of an alternative method of mixing clay :

// There is another method of mixing clay: I water the clay in a large vessel and pour it out over the clean floor, letting it spread out. After the water has been absorbed by the earth or by the sun, I collect the clay again. Now all the stones can be easily picked out. I add ashes and dung to the clay. By following this method, the clay can be thoroughly cleaned of stones.

5. 2. Throwing and moulding the clay

First of all the clay is beaten. Bhurabhai says :

// The clay from Shrinagar must be continuously beaten and can be moulded on the wheel only as long as it is fresh. When it becomes dry, the clay is useless. // It cannot be moulded.

Before the wheel is mounted on the support, the point of the wooden pin fixed to the latter must be sharpened. Bhurabhai calls this *khal ni ani kadhavi,* sharpening the pin on the support. The starting of throwing and moulding in called *murat.* Two expressions are used in connection with operating the wheel : *fer,* speed, turning and *tras,* revolving the wheel at an incline. Setting the wheel in motion is called *feravavu,* to impart speed.

The potter is not familiar with any particular technical expressions for the basic shapes of the vessel during the throwing and moulding process. Only the clay cone initially placed on the wheel is known as *Shankar nu ling* (Shiva's lingam). In its cylindrical state the vessel is *odvo,* hollow. *Lasvu* smoothing, means sliding the wet cloth over the surface of the vessel. When the vessel is twisted off the wheel with the hands and not with the cord, the potter describes it as *hath thi upadvu,* lifting up the vessel with the hand. Bhurabhai explains which vessels must be twisted off with the hands :

// Those vessel which are worked with the help of ashes must be lifted off with the hands, while those that should not come into contact with ash are twisted off with the cord.

5. 3. Chasing the vessels

Hori nakhvu, bringing into shape, chasing a vessel is possible as long as the article is *lilu tham,* fresh, that is to say, firm but still somewhat moist, before it has become quite dry, *suku*. The most important factor in this procedure is therefore time. Bhurabhai says :

// In chasing vessels one must keep strictly to a time schedule. The work must be accomplished at one stretch, regardless of whether it is day or night, otherwise all the preparatory work will have been in vain. The vessels must be chased within a time limit. Once one side of a pot becomes dry, there is no further remedy for it.

// Today we will have to sit up till midnight. I cannot leave the pots as they are.

It is risky to attempt to accelerate the drying process by placing the vessels in the sun. Bhurabhai explains:

// Just to speed up the work, I have put the vessels in the sun. Generally I keep them in the house. Then the vessels dry after two days or so. // The vessels which have dried slowly do not crack at all while they are being chased. If the pots are left in the house, they dry evenly.

// These pots here are still wet. I can enlarge them up to a certan point. Then the pots have to dry again in the ashes. Later on I can finish them.

If cracks appear in the vessel during chasing, the fault lies in its not having dried evenly. Only parts of the vessel remain *chikni* or *chikohni*, elastic like rubber. When vessels are chased for the first time, and are comparatively moist, they must be continually turned. Bhurabhai explains:

// Whan I chase a big vessel for the first time, I have to keep turning it, otherwise the pot will break. I cannot stop turning the pot for a single minute. This is possible only during the second chasing, when the pot is dry.

Large vessels can be chased in a *kund,* a pit in the ground, but very often the potter merely twists a piece from an old quilt into a roll. Asked about the difference, Bhurabhai answered:

// *Kund,* the pit in the ground is hard, whereas this here is *lambu tuku,* long and short. Vessels can never be damaged by it.

All earthenware pots must be chased more than once. The second chasing is known as *samaravu,* the third as *tranleva,* third taking. Bhurabhai says that some pots require to be chased no less than five times before they can be expanded to the right size.

5.4. Decorating the vessels

The designs, for which the potter knows no specific names, are either painted or cut in. Bhurabhai explains *chitrani,* decorating:

Black pottery can only be painted with white colour, because it has been fired in a special way. Yellow and red pots are fired in an open kiln. // I call all designs that are painted *chitar,* paintings. All designs cut in with the fingernail or the *kanski,* a piece of comb, I call *naksi,* ornaments.

5. 5. Polishing the vessels

The dry vessels are first scrubbed, *saf kari,* brushing off dust. They are then painted with a coating of ochre, this process being known as *met sathe potavu,* applying ochre. For this, the vessels are placed on a block of wood or a bed. The potter says:

// No dust must be allowed to touch the pot.

Only the water pots are given a complete coating of ochre. Bhurabhai explains:

// *Met,* ochre is very plastic in quality. It cannot be applied to pots that are intended for exposure to the fire. Therefore only water pots are given a thin coating of *met,* ochre.

As a rule, several very thin layers of ochre slip are applied to vessels. Bhurabhai supplies the following information on the difference between these layers:

// When I apply the first coat of *met,* ochre on the vessel, it will not look very white. The second layer should be very thin, otherwise the *met,* ochre, will chip off. With the third layer the surface of the pot becomes white. Now the solution can be even thinner; nevertheless, the whole *met,* ochre layer, will be thicker.

A *mala,* chain is used to *ghatavu,* polish, the earthenware. Polishing gives the surface of the vessel a glazed finish after firing. Bhurabhai expresses this thus:

// *Ghatavu,* polishing, makes the pots shine. They become quite smooth.

5.6. Firing the earthenware

Before commencing with the preparations for building the kiln, the potter explains the schedule he will follow:

// Three hours are needed to carry the vessels to the kiln site and to arrange the fuel around them. Another three hours are needed to heat the vessels. This last actually depends on the breeze. Then the kiln pile is closed and left for the night.

First of all the *tagariyu ghadavu,* kiln site is prepared. For this, a bank of moist ash is built up encircling the kiln site. Bhurabhai says:

// We wet the ash around the kiln site because we will later need it around it. To make only one pile would be easy, but then I would have to carry the wet ash around the fire. That would eventually prove more difficult.

// That you will see tomorrow. If I find the ash too dry, I will pour some more water over it. When the pots have become fully heated, they are covered with ash. At this stage, water is again required.

// A layer of wet ash seals the kiln, making it air-tight, *nabur karya.*

// In that ring of ash you see *pari,* walls and *kiara,* fields.

Later, the vessel are piled in layers on the *tagariya,* kiln site, this process being known as *khadakvu.* The built-up kiln ready to be set alight is called *limbhada;* the central opening which serves both as chimney and peep-hole is called *hari,* while the side openings are technically termed *bara,* windows.

On the subject of kindling the different types of flame, Bhurabhai says:

// The fire must catch very slowly. It should not spread quickly. No wind must be allowed to enter the kiln. Therefore I cover the openings.

// I make a little fire outside, the embers of which I divide into eight parts, one for each opening.

// If there is a strong wind, I cover the *bara,* openings, with a *tavali,* earthenware frying pan.

// First the flame is *kachu,* unripe or premature. Its colour is *lal,* red, or *pilo,* yellow. When the flame is *tuto,* blue, the heat has reached its most intensive point and I can cover the kiln. Firing can only be done during the night, because the potter must be able to see the flames.

When the fire is hottest the kiln is sealed, *paki chadvavi.* The potter says that at this stage no smoke must be allowed to escape. He first throws goat droppings into the kiln. He explains the reason for this:

// The *lindi,* goat droppings, produce a lot of smoke when burnt, which will blacken the pots.

// No smoke must be allowed to escape from the kiln. It must be completely air-tight.

The potter therefore identifies this firing process with the sooting of the pots. When the post are *paki gayu,* ready fired, the kiln can be opened; this is called *ukhedvu,* opening.

In making a distinction as to the quality of the pots placed in the centre of the kiln and those placed along the outer edge, the potter uses the word *kara*, black, to denote the former and *mora*, the latter. Bhurabhai explains:

// The *kara*, have been most thoroughly fired and are consequently of the best quality. The *mora* have been heated to a lesser extent, though still sufficiently. They are fit for use.

// You can see the difference : all the pots that were in the centre of the kiln have a white spot, *ankh*, eye, somewhere. Spots all round the pot indicate that it must have been placed in the centre. These are the pots which the women appreciate most.-This large white spot, however, was caused by the fact of the pot being near the *bara*, opening. When I covered the pile, something must have fallen on it and the spot therefore remained white. // It is the smoke from the goat droppings that blackens the vessels. Before the smoke could reach that vessel, some ash must have fallen on it and this cold part of the pot did not pick up the soot.

This somewhat confused answer seems to indicate that the potter ascribes the reducing firing process on the one hand to a fixed high temperature, and on the other also directly to the deposit of soot on the earthenware.

5.7. Special working techniques

Speaking of the manufacture of *bampli*, water pots, Bhurabhai says:

// This is the only kind of vessel that needs to be twice placed on the wheel. With tiles, though, it is the same.

// This *padagha*, base for the *bampli* pot I will afterwards remove carefully from the wheel and dry. I can use it again and again.

// I will fix it again on a wet clay layer in the centre of the turning wheel.

Bhurabhai spreads a layer of cowdung *gay nu chhan* around the neck of a *bampli*, pot, after it has been moulded and chased for the first time. He explains:

// I put cow dung on it. That will keep the neck moist. It will remain moist when the bottom is dry.

// *Lad,* donkey dung is dry, while *chhan,* cow dung is moist and sticky. It remains moist on the vessel. Cow or buffalo dung can be used here.

When the completed *bampli*, pots are polished, several cracks become evident. I quote Bhurabhai's explanation for this:

// These pots were standing in the wind. They could not dry slowly and evenly. Whenever the wind blows down from the Barda hills (inland), we potters stop making *bampli*, pots. But we can continue when the wind blows in from the sea.

// Actually a crack cannot be repaired, unless I want to cheat the customer. Then I can press some clay into the crack, so that it is not to be seen.

// The inland wind is warm and blows inside the pot while it is on the turning wheel for the second time. The pressure of the air bears on the joint and the new neck will not fit properly.

Regarding the vessels with the double-layered bottoms, Bhurabhai explains:

Pots with *be tar,* two bottoms, will not crack, even if they are placed over a very hot fire. The clay out of which the pot itself is made is plastic, but the *bandh* clay of the second layer on the bottom is not plastic. It is only red clay mixed with sand and dung. We call those pots *be tar be mati,* two bottoms two clays.

Before they are fired, another thin coating is applied over the bottoms of these vessels.

// For the *paka,* final solution I use two parts of *mithi reti,* sand to one part of *lal mati,* red clay and a lot of water. Out of these a *ragla,* very thin solution is stirred, which dries immediately on the pot.

Finally I add here a few remarks made by the potter concerning his tools:

// I possess about forty to fifty *pindo,* anvils, each one of a different size. They are from Junagadh, but I could make one myself too. // Some potters travel to Junagadh, buy the *pindo*, anvil there, and later on sell them to other potters. // A set of five in different sizes costs about ten to fifteen rupees.

// *Datio*, the paddle, was made by the carpenter. But all these tools have been here since my birth. I inherited them all from my uncle.

// The wheel was made by the carpenter, too. However, these wheels can only be made in big workshops, as *sanghadia*, lathe, is required to turn them.

I had one of my two wheels made to order in Vansalia, the village in which I once stayed.

VIII.6. The chief vessel forms

The following list gives only the most important earthenware vessels manufactured. For the nomenclature I have relied on information given to me by the potter Bhurabhai. In Ratadi I found that only very few people were able to define a vessel by its exact technical name, tending rather to generalize. The farmers, for instance, allude to all pots for holding or carrying water as *gora* or *matla*.

257

Every pot is composed of the following parts:

lip	*kantho*
neck	*dok*
shoulder	*dhal*
belly	*pet*
bottom	*talia*
interior	*polun*
neck ring	*dhar*

That a basic correspondence exists between the shape and the function of a vessel is demonstrated by the fact that pots with rounded shoulders are employed to hold water, whereas pots with angular shoulders are intended for use either as cooking or churning vessels or else to hold flour, butter-milk etc.

6.1. Water pots

The large water pot, *goro*
This is a large, practically spherical vessel. Only at the shoulders is there the merest suggestion of a break in the upward curve, designs being painted or scratched in at this point. The neck is short and terminates in a broad, rounded lip with a narrow groove.

example: maximum diameter	42 cm
diameter of mouth	22.5 cm
height	42 cm

This vessel is used to hold drinking water.

The medium-sized water pot, *matlu*
This vessel resembles the large water pot on a smaller scale and is more sparsely ornamented.

example: maximum diameter	50 cm
diameter of mouth	18 cm
height	33 cm

It is used to carry water.

The small water pot, *ghado*
The prominent features of this spherical vessel are an open, broad neck with a plain, pendulous lip.

example : maximum diameter	30 cm
diameter of mouth	11.5 cm
height	23 cm

This vessel is used to hold small quantities of drinking water.

The large water-carrying pot, *kupo* or *bambo*
A narrow neck is mounted on a spherical vessel. Below the simple lip is a pronounced ridge going all round the vessel. A cord is passed under this ridge and knotted, the vessel being carried by this sling.

example : maximum diameter	35 cm
diameter of mouth	6 cm
height	30 cm

This vessel serves to hold drinking water for the workers on the fields. It is used principally during the cotton picking season in the dry fields.

The small water-carrying pot, *bampli*
The small vessel is in every respect similar to the one just described, except that the neck here gives the effect of being somewhat larger. For a description of how it is manufactured, vide VIII.4.6.

example: maximum diameter	24 cm
diameter of mouth	6 cm
height	24 cm

In this vessel water is carried to the working site or taken along on journeys. Thanks to its well-rounded belly (surface expansion) the water remains cool.

6.2. Milk pots

The large pot for butter-milk, *gori*
The hemispherical bottom meets the flat, convexly arched shoulder at a sharp angle. A piece of comb is employed to cut in designs at the shoulder. The notched lip is drawn in considerably.

example: maximum diameter	40 cm
diameter of mouth	19 cm
height	27 cm

In this vessel warmed milk is curdled and churned. Later, the vessel serves as a receptacle for butter-milk.

The small pot for butter-milk, *pario*
The shoulder of this vessel is only slightly bent. A ridge runs round the broad, high neck. The lip is quite a plain one.

example: maximum diameter	25 cm
diameter of mouth	10 cm
height	20 cm
height of neck	5.5 cm

When the vessel is used to hold butter-milk or curdled milk for the midday meal of the field workers, a cord is knotted around the neck, so that it can be easily carried.

The pot for curdled milk, *donu*

The bottom, which is curved so as to be almost hemispherical, ends in a sharp edge, continuing upwards to form a broad, arched shoulder curved concavely. The shoulder may be ornamented with designs. A broad, plainly rounded lip emerges from the shoulder, a clearly defined neck being absent. Three protruding knobs are arranged horizontally on each of the two sides of the vessel. Only the shoulder and lip are polished, the bottom having the appearance of being covered with soot after being taken from the kiln. Under the black clay particles which can be easily scratched away, the grey clay employed in the manufacture is revealed. Several layers of different clays have been chased over the bottom of the vessel and the pot has been given a coating of a special ochre slip.

example: diameter of mouth	14 cm
height	17 cm
maximum diameter	26 cm

In this pot the milk is heated before being curdled or set aside to separate into curds and whey. The vessel is thus intended to be placed on the cooking stove.

The pot for butter-milk, *patardi*

This vessel is generally small. In most cases there is another ridge set above the shoulder, which later breaks away from the bottom at a decided angle and continues upwards in a slight convex curve, terminating in a comparatively high, open neck. The plain lip is sometimes ornamented with six knobs.

Like the *pairo-* pot, this vessel is also used to hold butter-milk. However it is hardly ever taken out of doors.

The milk pot, *donio*

The spherical belly merges into the shoulder at a curve, a ridge running round the pot at the shoulder. Above the ridge the shoulder dips into a slightly concave curve, continues in a relatively long neck and terminates finally in a plain narrow lip.

example: maximum diameter	17 cm
diameter of mouth	11 cm
height	13.5 cm

This pot is employed to hold small quantities of milk.

6.3. Cooking vessels

The cooking pot for rice, *tolio*

The deeply rounded belly ends above at a sharp angle, which may be further pronounced by a ridge running all round, continuing upwards in a steep, concavely arched shoulder. The rim, which lies in a horizontal plane and is bordered by a rounded lip, is ornamented on two sides by six (three on each) concave, triangular knobs.

example: maximum diameter	21 cm
diameter of mouth	18 cm
height	16 cm

In this vessel *khichadi,* a mixture of rice and pulses, is cooked slowly.

The pot for cooking vegetables, *tavali*
This bowl-like pot has a rounded belly which curves at a sharp angle to continue in a short shoulder. Here again the rim lies on a horizontal plane, the lip being a plain one. Sixteen slightly concave, triangular knobs are arranged around the rim.

example: diameter of shoulder	23.5 cm
diameter of mouth	25 cm
height	9 cm

In this pot different kinds of vegetables are cooked. However, this vessel has been largely superseded by metal pots.

The frying pan, *tavi*
A plain upright rim is moulded to a flat, very slightly upward curved plate. Six slightly concave, smooth knobs are arranged horizontally around the rim, three on each side.

example: diameter	25 cm
height	4 cm

In this frying pan sliced vegetables are fried in oil.

The roasting plate, *tavadi,* or *kadeli*
This is a flat plate turned up very slightly at the edgd to end in a plain rim.

example: diameter	24.5 cm
height	3 cm

Flat cakes of flour are baked on this plate, no fat of any kind being added.

6.4. Bowls

The bowl for mixing dough, *kathrot*
The sloping shoulder meets the slightly curved bottom at a sharp angle. The shoulder terminates in a simple, rounded lip. Inside the bowl the shoulder is rounded.

example: maximum diameter	31 cm
diameter of mouth	30 cm
height	10 cm

This bowl is sometimes also carved from wood. It is used as a mixing bowl in which flour and water are kneaded to a dough.

The eating bowl, *sapno*
This bowl has a curved bottom and a short, concave neck ending in a round lip which projects horizontally.

example: maximum diameter	22 cm
diameter of mouth	17.5 cm
height	9 cm

Food is eaten from this plate. However, this earthenware article has been almost entirely superseded by plates made of metal.

The feeding bowl, *kundo* or *kundi*
This bowl possesses a curved bottom and an inwards sloping rim. These vessels are produced in different sizes and their proportions vary as well.

Domestic animals and birds are fed from these bowls. Small bowls are filled with water and hung out in the yard for birds to drink from.

6.5. Other vessels

The small water pot, *kurdo*
This pot has a deeply rounded belly and a neck sloping outwards to end in a plain lip. The vessel is made from red clay.

example : maximum diameter	11 cm
diameter of mouth	9 cm
height	9.5 cm

In this pot water for washing is taken along when the villagers go to the toilet. *Kurda*-pots, are of special significance during the funeral rites (vide VIII 1.2.).

The flour receptacle, *zakadio*   259
The very slightly curved bottom meets the shoulder at a sharp angle. The shoulder slopes upwards. The wide mouth is encircled by a double ridged lip bent so as to lie horizontally. The ridges are sometimes pressed against each other, thus forming a wavy line.

example : maximum diameter	31 cm
diameter of mouth	25 cm
height	20 cm

This vessel serves as a receptacle for flour when it is collected in small quantities from the hand mill. Larger flour receptacles are found in the households of those communities that either beg or are paid for their labour with flour.

The can with spout, *vadhi*   261
A cylindrical spout slanting upwards is joined to the angular shoulder of a *patardi*, pot for butter milk. Above the joint a layer of clay is spread, upon which the fingernails have been impressed. A simple earthenware oil lamp serves as a cover.

example : diameter of vessel top	11 cm
height	20 cm

These cans with spouts are used to hold melted, slightly warmed *ghee* which is poured over *khichadi*, pulses and rice cooked together. These *vadhi* vessels are rare.

The pot for plants, *zad ni kundi*
These are simple cylindrical or also slightly rounded vessels of red earthen ware. The lip is pressed into a wavy line.

example : diameter	25 cm
height	10 cm

These pots usually stand on the roof of the shed. The two principal plants cultivated in these pots are *tulsi*, Basil – plant, the leaves of which are brewed to make a tea efficacious against colds, and *ajamo* plant, the leaves of which are cooked. Apart from their usefulness, a certain undefinable holiness is attributed to these plants.

The carthenware oil lamp, *kodiyu*
These are little bowls with thin walls and simple rims, made of red earthenware.

example : diameter across rim	8 cm
height	4 cm

Oil or *ghee*, clarified butter, is burnt in these little lamps, a wick made of cotton being used.

The pot lids, *dhakani*

A simple lid is conical in shape with a cylindrical or conical handle in the centre and a rim encircled by a high ridge. There are also arched lids with broad rims and handles decorated with grooves.

example : maximum diameter	23.5 cm
height	5.5 cm

Lids are used principally to cover pots in which vegetables are cooked.

The ceremonial pot, *chaklo*

This is a small vessel made of red earthenware. It consists of a horizontal base from which the walls rise slantingly. A closed cone is mounted on the sharply defined shoulder.

example : maximum diameter	10 cm
height	11,5 cm

This piece of earthenware is placed in the vessel described below during the marriage rites.

The ceremonial pot, *chakli*

This is also a small vessel made of red earthenware. Up to the sharply defined shoulder, the walls ascend following an outward sloping line. The walls then taper upwards and continue in a neck sloping outwards and indented at four points to terminate finally in a plain rim.

example: maximum diameter	10 cm
height	9 cm

This *chakli*, pot bears the feminine counterpart of the masculine name above and is employed in the marriage rites.

The ceremonial pot, *pharko*

This is a simply moulded deep bowl with a plain lip made of red earthenware.

example: diameter across rim	19 cm
height approx.	7 cm

Both the above ceremonial pots are placed in this bowl during the marriage ceremony.

6.6. Utensils from clay

The cooking stove, *chula*

266

This consists basically of a solid, heavy mass of clay arranged in a horse-shoe shape. In front and in the middle there are slight humps or elevations to support the coocking pots when they are placed over the fire. The facades of such stoves are frequently covered with designs. (For manufacture, vide VIII. 4.8.).

example: height	25 cm
breadth	20 cm
length	35 cm

The double cooking stove, *olaro*

This kind of stove is not to be found in Ratadi households. The potter Bhurabhai said that he had carried out orders for such stoves for customers from Porbandar. The distinguishing feature is a second, cylindrical compartment adjoining the main horse-shoe shape, over which another cooking vessel may be placed to simmer beside the main fire.

The tobacco pipes, *dhaturi*
Both black and red earthenware tobacco pipes are sold in Porbandar. In shape and design
they resemble the clay pipes that can be seen in markets throughout Saurashtra. They usually
have a cylindrical or cube-shaped bowl and a cylindrical stem tapering away from the
bowl to end in a rim without a lip. Men and old women smoke them.

The ring sockle, *kantho*
The horizontally severed neck of a broken pot is used as a sockle for the cooking vessels to
stand on.

6.7. Clay figures

The figure of a cow, with brown horns and blue painted udder is used as a decoration piece
in a house in Baradia. The figure is hung with trinkets and gewgaws that have temporarily
been laid aside.

Fragments of a terracotta horse are to be found at a shrine dedicated to *Vashhada dada* on
the border of Baradia. The horse is composed of a number of moulded tubes pressed together
and fired to a light brown colour. At one time, apparently several similar figures existed
which were arranged on a platform in the shade of a tree.

262

IX. Fabrics and textile techniques

by Eberhard Fischer

IX.1. The cotton spinning

The ripe cotton pods that have burst open are picked by hand from the shrubs and collected in cloths slung around the necks of the pluckers. They are transported to the village in carts. Children break the pods aud extract the fluffy cotton fibre. The woody pods are used as fodder for buffaloes, while the seeds are pressed through a ginning-instrument, which consists of two heavy rollers rotating towards each other. This operation is required in order to separate the seeds from the fibre. Where only small quantities of cotton are required for spinning, the seeds may also be removed by hand. The seed grains are used as fodder.

Spinning is done chiefly by old women, who enjoy sitting in the evening sun after the day's work, contemplatively plying the wheel.

273

The spinning wheel consists of a fly wheel and a spindle, both of which are affixed to a board and connected with each other by a cord. The wheel (1) consists of two discs, each made up of four tenoned or nailed boards tapering to an acute angle at their bases. These discs are mounted on the sides of a wooden cylinder, through which an iron rod passes. This rod serves as an axle. The axle rotates in two supporting posts (2) and has a club-shaped crank (3) attached to one end. The 32 corners of both discs are linked crosswise with each other by means of a cord (4). With the help of a taut cotton bracing cord (5) the large fly wheel drives a small wooden spool on an iron axle (6), which rotates next to a pair of short wooden posts and between two wooden cops (7) wound with yarn. The axle is lengthened to serve as a spindle being surmounted by a disc adjacent to the wooden post. Between both short posts there are also two upright wooden chips threaded through cords, above which a stock can be laid as a support for the turnstile (vide pg. 171).

spinning wheel	*retia*
(1) fly wheel	*jal*
(2) supporting posts	*godia*
(3) crank	*lat*
(4) linking cord	*chindri*
(5) bracing cord	*mar*
(6) iron axle	*trak*
(7) wooden cops	*chamarkha*
(example in the possession of Amrabhai Parbatbhai of Baradia)	
height	70 cm
length	95 cm

While spinning the woman sits on a small stool with the spinning wheel placed transversely in front of her. One leg is curled in while the other is outstretched. She turns the crank with her right hand. The unloosened bundles of unspun cotton lie before her. She attaches the cotton to the spindle, slowly separating the fibres while she winds them on it. In so doing she describes circles in the air with her left hand, in which she holds the cotton, until the entire bundle, now spun to thread, has been wound around the spindle. While spinning, she plucks the thread between thumb and fore- or middle finger giving it a little twist at the same time. After this initial stage, the thread is twisted with other similarly spun threads to form a thick yarn.

IX.2. The dyeing of cotton yarn

Since synthetically dyed yarns may be bought cheaply from the market nowadays, the weavers very rarely dye their yarn at home. For this reason I did not have the opportunity of observing the procedure. However, the weaver Amrabhai Parbatbhai has supplied me with the following detailed description of the dyeing process:

// To dye yarn black, we use *haldi* which is a kind of medicine and actually comes from a tree. The *haldi* is mixed with *parda* from the *baval* tree, the stems of which are used as tooth-brushes. These two ingredients are pounded in the mortar, stirred with water and put on the fire to heat. A very high temperature is required to prepare the dye.

This dye can be used equally effectively for wool and cotton. When the mixture starts boiling, the cotton or woollen yarn is immersed in it. To prevent the yarn from burning, the dye liquid must be vigorously stirred and the yarn itself kept in continuous movement. After some time the yarn is taken out and the liquid poured over it. It is kept in the dye-bath for half an hour. Subsequently, the yarn is wetted with plain water before being immersed once more in the dye. After another half-hour the yarn is dried in the sun for five hours. Now it is thoroughly washed in plain water, so that any dye not adhering firmly to the yarn is washed off. The black yarn is now ready.

// Coloured cotton yarn is dyed in Porbandar and we buy it there. This proves cheaper, whereas wollen yarn we dye ourselves.

// The beige-brown dye for cotton or woollen yarn is called *kesro* or *kesario*.

Before this dye can be used, *chuna*, lime must be applied to the textiles for a period of three days.

// This may be purchased in Porbandar. Formerly it was prepared near Shrinagar. Very little *chuna* is used. The yarn is covered with *avar*, which is the bark of a yellow blowing plant that blooms in the monsoon.

The bark of *runa*, a mountain tree, is used for the same purpose. A mixture of these three ingredients is required. The barks are thoroughly dried in the sun for two days before being pounded together. *Chuna* is also added.

The yarn is put into a vessel and cold water poured over it until it is completely soaked. Now the dye-mixture is added and well stirred into the water. The vessel is then covered and set aside. // For two days or so. During this time, the position of the yarn is changed by turning over the mass. The process of soaking the yarn may continue for five days. On the sixth day, the yarn is lifted out and dried in the sun. This is the way to thoroughly dye the yarn.

// Yes, this process does not require fire, for the mixture need not be heated.

// All the ingredients for the dye are bought in 'Gandhi-stores', (that is drug-stores) in Porbandar. Formerly we used to collect the barks ourselves.

// These two dyes were the main ones we used.

IX. 3. The weaving of cotton yarn

3.1. The weaver

Since there are no *vankar*, weaver, settled in Ratadi, that is to say, there is no person who follows this trade in the village, very little by way of information can be given about this profession.

Weaving cotton as well as woollen yarn is the traditional occupation of the Dhed - caste, the members of which are generally regarded as the " untouchables". After the Gandhi-movement, the term "Harijan" was applied to them collectively with other untouchables, with the result that these untouchables were henceforth treated as scheduled castes. In contrast to the inhabitants of other regions in Saurashtra, the Mers accepted the new laws that aimed at elevating the status of the untouchables and consequently renounced very many of their traditional customs. Nevertheless, the Harijans themselves have apparently not quite out-grown their deepseated consciousness of their "untouchability", as the following incident will demonstrate : While I was engaged together with my interpreter, Rajput by caste, in observing the working procedure of the weaver, his wife was busy preparing tea. With a regretful smile she apologized for not being able to offer us any. While the members of the family sipped their tea, we were obliged to go without.

In the village of Baradia, in which the present investigations were carried out, the Dhed live in their own, isolated community on the east outside the village. Their quarter is sepatated from that of the farmers by the mighty fort. The houses of the Harijan community present a mean and miserable appearance, despite the fact that the only modern cement house in the village is to be found in this quarter. They possess very little furniture and that but little decorated. In nearly every house a weaver's loom is set up. Where it is absent, the marks left by the treadles upon the floor may still be discerned. The loom is set up in most houses either beside the window or opposite the entrance doorway, so as to catch the early sun. The young men of these households have forsaken their hereditary trade, for the money it yields is scarce and irregular. I learned for instance, that a wollen blanket, which requires 32 Rs. worth of material and three days of labour cannot be sold for more than 42 Rs. From this may be deduced that three days' wages amount to a mere 10 Rs. although in this case at least one family member (usually the wife) works all the time beside the weaver, preparing the yarn. Another point to consider is that weavers do not receive regular orders and are unable to prepare goods to store by and sell later as ready-made articles, because they have no basic working capital.

3.2. The cotton loom

Under the large frame constituting the basic structure of the loom (1) is a pit which accommodates the treadles. The weaver squats in a narrow and shallow depression in the ground in front of the loom. Like the floor of the entire house, the pit and the depression are plastered over with a mixture of beige clay and cowdung.

274, 275

To the left of the weaver a post is driven into the floor, to which another post slanting towards the first is tied. Above the legs of the weaver, who squats in front of the pit, passes a transverse bar leading to another slanting post, which rests against a wedge in the wall and is tied to it. Two cross-pieces rest in two pairs of notches cut into the slanting post at a height just above eyelevel of the squatting weaver. The heavy guiding comb is fixed to the lower of these by two sticks tied to it, while from the upper cross piece the shafts and an open oil-pot are suspended.

The warp stretches under the loom and is fixed in front opposite the weaver to a rod (2) tied by two cords to the breast beam (3). The woven cloth is wound around the breast beam, which is of a square section and has a tenon projecting from both ends. These tenons rotate either in wooden forks (4) or in wooden rings (5) let into the ground. Two holes are pierced through the breast beam on the right to admit a wooden rod (6) being passed through slanting towards the floor.

The warp often runs over a transverse yarn beam (7) at the back of the pit. This yarn beam rests on two forks. The warp is finally gathered at the back wall of the room. A rope is tied around it. This rope runs first around a large peg driven into the earth (8) and then alongside the breast beam, where it is once more tautly stretched before being fastened to another peg. When this bracing rope (9) is loosened, the warp tension is relaxed and the woven cloth can be wound around the breast beam. The last third of the warp, however, is usually plaited and hung on the wall beside the loom.

The guiding comb (10) consists of two wooden battens, in the inner longitudinal grooves of which the reed is set (11), being made up of stout bamboo sticks. The number of these bamboo teeth constituting the reed corresponds to the number of threads in the warp. Stout wooden bars (12) as high as the reeds and fixed in the grooves of the battens confine the warp on either side. The teeth in the reed are therefore placed loosely between the battens. Both heddle shafts (13) are suspended from transverse bars fixed to the loom frame. These heddle shafts consist of cotton heddles suspended between two wooden loops. The straps holding the treadles are connected with the lower bars.

(1)	loom	sar
(2)	rod	nodhani
(3)	breastbeam	tara
(4)	wooden fork	khila
(5)	wooden rings	mundia
(6)	wooden rod	tarfani
(7)	yarn beam	khad khili
(8)	peg	ado
(9)	bracing rope	rasilo
(10)	guiding comb	hatho
(11)	reed with teeth	panchori
(12)	wooden bars	sambelu
(13)	heddle shafts	gara
(14)	transverse bars	lakadi
(15)	treadles	dingla

3.3. Accessories for the loom

The weft-thread (1) is shot through the warp (2) by means of a shuttle (3). The shuttle, which is of wood, has rounded sides and tapers to a point. The thread emerges from an eye (4) on one side of the shuttle. The spool (5) consists of a length of bamboo with a gently undulating outer surface. The thread is wound around the spool, which is placed upright in the shuttle. A piece of wire serving as an axle (6) passes through it, fitting into a rabbet at one end and into a notch in the other. Above the notch is a hole, which is stoppered with a quill or a piece of buffalo horn. The quill is folded and can be extracted from the hole by pulling a short thread tied to it, when the spool is required to be taken out of the shuttle.

In order to keep the woven cloth of uniform width, a stretcher (7) is employed. In wool weaving this is made up of two rods placed diagonally one over the other. At their upper ends they are fitted with iron spikes which flank and thus confine the woven cloth at either end. The lower ends are connected by a cord on which hangs an iron weight, drawing the ends of the rods towards each other. This, however, is prevented by a loop running laterally from the point of one to the end of the other rod. This loop checks the woven fabric from exceeding a fixed width determined by it.

A wooden knife (8) is employed to connect the heddles with their loops. A narrow cloth sheath (9) is tied to the knife. A wooden heddle hook (10) threaded with a string is used in conjunction with the knife. The wooden knife determines the height of the heddles. The heddle loop is inserted into the cloth sheath, in order to draw it through the heddle thread, while the hook is used to guide it.

In addition to these auiliary parts, the weaver also has three bundles of heddle and combs (11) which he uses to weave different types of cloth. The first bundle, tied together with a string, consists of a comb, four heddles, three heddles for special decorative effects and two shedding sticks. The warp threads, held together by a narrow strip of weft, still adhere to the heddles and the comb. This set of tools is used to weave coarse cotton cloth for cart tilts and woollen blankets with designs. In the case of the former, the special heddles for decorative effects are dispensed with. The second bundle contains four heddles, a comb and two shedding stick. This set is employed for the weaving of strong cloth for garments.-The third bundle is composed of a comb and two pairs of heddles with two shedding sticks. A warp of red thread is drawn through the comb. The red material used by women for their headcovers and veils and for fine wraps and shawls is woven with the help of this last set.

(1)	weft	*vano*
(2)	warp	*tano*
(3)	shuttle	*naro*, if large *gadelo*
(4)	eye	*moti*, lit. bead
(5)	empty spool	*tali*, lit. femur of a goat
	full spool	*nadi*
(6)	axle	*sari*
(7)	stretcher	*panku*
(8)	wooden knife	*karpo*
(9)	cotton sheath	*kotri*
(10)	wooden heddle hook	*suvo*
(11)	set of heddle and comb	*ras*

3.4. Measuring apparatus

For measuring the width of cloth the weavers use *hathio*, an iron rod, the length of which is one *hath*, ell. The weaver informed me that the length of the rod corresponded to the measurement of the distance between the elbow and the tip of an outstretched finger, and was divisible into 24 *angar*, finger-breadths. The width of a woollen shawl, for instance, was a double *hath,* ell, plus four finger-breadths for the border. I observed another measuring scale marked at the back of the iron rod, which the weaver Amrabhai Parbatbhai explained as follows:

// That *hathio,* scale has been in my family's possession for a very long time. Actually, there was another measurement which corresponded to one and a quarter *hath*, ell. // I do not remember the terms for its divisions. However, *gaj* was useful to shopkeepers who sold the cloth, but it was not useful here in the villages. *Gaj* was formerly used for weaving *choria*, a women's garment now out of date. We used to weave this cloth here too and therefore found *gaj*, yard, useful. Now - a days we use only *hath,* ell and *angar,* finger.

The weavers buy yarn according to weight, and sell woven canvas, which has a fixed width, also by weight.

3.5. The working procedure

Preparing the weft
For weaving canvas cloth, white cotton yarn packed in large bales (1) is purchased at the market in Porbandar. In the bales are tightly compressed hanks (2) of single-strand, coarsely spun yarn, four strands of which must be taken together to produce the right thickness for the weft thread (3).

The hanks are loosened and wrapped around the turnstile (4). These consist of a vertical wooden axle (5), into which two pairs of rods crossing each other diagonally are horizontally inserted and tied in place. Two cords (6) run in a zigzag formation between the eight corners. The wooden axle rotates in a naturally holed stone.

A hank of cotton yarn is wrapped around each of the four such turnstiles. The ends of the threads are gathered together and fastened to a fifth, somewhat larger turnstile (7) which is now made to revolve so that the yarn from the four turnstiles is wound on to it. After this winding process, the turnstile with the four-strand yarn is set up in front of the spinning wheel (8) suported by a slanting rod with a barb, against which the axle of the turnstile leans. A spool is now mounted on the spindle axle, and while the right hand turns the crank, the left hand places the yarn on the spindle. Subsequently, while the yarn is being rewound, it is twisted between thumb and forefinger. When the spool is full, the four strands of yarn are broken off, the spool removed and replaced by an empty one.

A large number of spools are wound at the same time. The full spools are collected and stored in a winnowing basket. The basket is placed beside the cotton loom, so as to be handy when spools have to be changed.

Simple weaving
The weaving of plain cotton cloth or canvas is a monotonous procedure. The shuttle is thrown through the shed. The weft thread just thrown is now drawn at its centre point towards the comb with the thumb of the hand that has just thrown the shuttle with the weft. As soon as the shuttle passes clear of the shed, the comb is brought forward, the weaver grasping it by its upper batten. By this the weft which has just been inserted is forced to its proper place. The weaver now changes the shed and throws the shuttle back with his other hand.

The weft is used in a dry state. The comb, however, is greased from time to time. This the weaver accomplishes by dipping his forefinger into the oil pot suspended before him and running his finger along the teeth of the comb. The bottom of the shuttle is also greased every now and then.

When the space between the comb and shed becomes too narrow, he loosens the taut bracing rope so as to be able to turn the breast beam. Should it be necessary, he spans the the bracing rope once more.

(1) yarn bale	*peti*
(2) hank	*antla*
(3) four-strand	*char tragu*
(4) turnstile	*charkhi*
(5) wooden axle	*sar*
(6) cord	*un*
(7) larger turnstile	*parto*
(8) spinning wheel	*retio*

3.6. The cotton materials for stitched garments and tilts

Plain cloth for stitched garments is woven in linen weave from cotton yarn. White materials are used for men's clothing and red or white materials for women's clothes. Some of these materials are also imported from far towns such as Ahmedabad.

fine cotton cloth	*pachhedi*
coarse cotton cloth	*pankora*
red cotton cloth	*kambi*

The canvas for tilts and similar purposes
When warp and weft consist of four-strand twisted cotton yarn, an extremely coarse fabric is the result. It is hardly possible to use this material for clothing. It is sold as canvas and for cart tilts.

| canvas | *sadh* or *sadhia* |

IX.4. The weaving of woollen yarn

4.1. The woollen loom

In its basic structure and principles, the woollen loom is the same as the cotton loom. The chief distinguishing features are described below:

The warp is stretched over a warp beam (1), to the ends of which a cord (2) is tied. This cord is then stretched and fastened to two pegs by means of a common rope. The comb is fitted with a lathe-turned handle (3), which is fixed in the upper batten. The comb is further suspended by two cords, the lengths of which are adjustable due to the presence of slip-knots and small wooden hooks (4). This mechanism ensures that the comb can perform its function of beating-up the pick of the weft – even in cases where the shed is at some distance from the comb.

The eye of each heddle picks two warp-threads. Two bamboo shedding sticks (5) keep the two thread systems of the warp separate. A flat wooden sword (6) is occasionally employed to aid the beating up of the weft threads. The sword normally lies beside the weaver, being called into play only when a design has been woven and the consequent bunching up of the threads is to be avoided.– The shuttle (7) for the woollen weft is mounted with iron at both ends.

(1) warp beam	*bajenia*
(2) cord	*parsan*
(3) handle	*koit*
(4) wooden hook	*ankado*
(5) shedding stick	*sarayu*
(6) sword	*patla*
(7) shuttle	*naro*
(example in the possession of Amrabhai Parbatbhai of Baradia)	
weave, breadth	59 cm
length	435 cm
comb, length	120 cm
height	23 cm
breast beam, length	123 cm
pit, depth	70 cm
sword, length	94 cm
width	7 cm
heddle shafts, height	14 cm

4. 2. Working procedure

Preparing the weft

The wool is purchased in hanks. The weaver's wife first soaks a hank in a basin of water, kneading it, so that the wool thoroughly absorbs the water. She then squeezes out the water, takes up the woollen yarn in both hands and wrings it by twisting it. She stretches the yarn once more between both hands and then wraps it around a turnstile from which the yarn is wound on small spools. The spools are then immersed in a basin of water.

Before inserting a full spool into the shuttle, the weaver passes it over the shed, therewith moistening the warp threads. He now uses the spool axle to thread the wool through the eye in the shuttle. Finally, he passes the axle through the spool, snapping it into place between rabbet and notch. The wool wound around a spool will last for approximately 18 weft picks.

Simple wool weaving

In picking the weft, one hand shoots the shuttle through the sheds, while the other catches it on the opposite side and deposits it on the floor beside the loom. With the same hand the weaver enters the shed and presses back the end of the woven fabric with fore- and middle fingers. With both hands he next takes hold of the comb left and right of the handle that is fixed to the upper batten and draws it forward once. Then the heddles are changed. This the weaver accomplishes by manipulating the treadles and drawing up the heddle loops with both hands. He then pushes the comb backwards and forwards twice, before picking in the new weft.

4. 3. Designs on woollen blankets

Woollen shawls are decorated at both ends with transverse stripes with designs. These decorative designs are woven in. The following are the commonest motifs :

ladula, a special kind of sweetmeat
This is a simple rhombus placed on end with a transverse dash in the centre. The weaver informed me that this design is also frequently employed in tatooing.

dakla or *damru,* drum
Two filled-in triangles are placed one on top of the other with their vertices touching.

gumedi
Short dashes run through both inner and outer planes of a border of rhombs placed on end.

vel, creeper, or *ardi gumedi*
Short dashes run through the triangles formed by a zigzag border.

jotar
This design consists of two pairs of right-angled triangles placed opposing each other. Then follow two vertical lines before the motif is repeated.

fatukia, firework, spark
This motif is composed of two vertical lines placed close together, each line being made up of several horizontal dashes.

deradia, shrine
A small triangle surmounts the vertex of a larger triangle.

vel, creeper, or *khajurio,* datepalm-leaf
This is a horizontal border built up from a simple herringbone pattern, the central horizontal line being dispensed with.

gumedi
This is a pattern of small checks, being made up of many small squares of equal size placed on end.

adadia, sweetmeat or a species of fish
This design shows parallel rows of dashes, the spacing of the dashes alternating in each row.

pandada, leaves
This woven-in pattern is made up of two pairs of trapezes that are placed as in a mirror image and therefore directly opposed. Both trapezes touch each other at the point of their central axis.

sandio, dromedary
This is a simplified representation of a standing dromedary.

There is no specific colour fixed by tradition for working a particular design. The name of
the design or motif remains the same whether it appears as a single motif or is repeated to
form a border. Similarly, no difference is made as regards terminology between 'broche'
and 'lance'. The only distinction made is with regard to patterns and designs that have to be
plaited in by hand (such as *dakla, sandio, pandada* and *deradia*) which are collectively termed
hathe banavavo. The remaining designs can be produced by adjusting the special heddles for
decorative effects.

4.4. The woven materials

The white woollen blanket
These blankets are made up of two identical pieces of woven fabric stitched together. Usually,
a broad stripe of warp threads in a dark colour runs along both selvages, to be crossed at the
opposite ends by a broad decorative border. All warp threads extend beyond this border
to form a fringe, or there may be instead a decorative border of multicoloured wool
twined in.

One square centimetre of this linen weave consists of seven warp and five weft threads.

light coloured woollen blanket	*dhabla*
decorative selvage stripe	*kor*
decorative border	*chhedo*
fringe	*okaru*
(example in the possession of Vejabhai Atiabhai)	
length	245 cm
breadth	140 cm

The dark coloured woollen blanket
Except for light-coloured warp threads along the selvages, these woollen blankets are
uniformly dark in colour. The ends of the blankets are decorated with woven-in stripes of
colourful design. Here too, multicoloured wool can be twined into the warp fringe.

dark coloured woollen blankets	*kambar*

Since they are made from the wool of naturally black-haired sheep and goats, these blankets
are reputed to be rather expensive. However, now-a-days they are frequently woven from
dyed wool.

Young men prefer to wear such dark-coloured blankets. But there are no strict restrictions
with regard to certain colours being worn by any particular age-group. These blankets are
used by the men like shoulder-cloths in the winter.

IX. 5. The stitched garments

by Haku Shah

Formerly all cloth used for costumes was produced in the village itself; the women spun,
while weaving was the craft of the Dhed-community. Now-a-days the material though
still handspun and handwoven, is purchased at the Porbandar market, and the clothes are
made and machine-stitched by the Sui, local tailor, who will be payed in cash for his work.

Men's dress

The costume for all men, young and old, is nearly the same : it is common that a young man will wear the garments of his deceased father. Personal variation in style is extremely rare ; the same costume is worn on every occasion. Even at marriages or mourning, a man will wear what he wears every day. There is, however, one difference between the costume of the old and the young. The young wear tight-fitting clothes as it is more convenient for heavy work in the fields: while the old men prefer loose comfortable clothing. Each man generally has three pairs of clothes, two of which are for daily use, while the third pair is folded in a cloth bundle called *potalu*, and kept in a chest. The pair of clothes that is not being worn is flung over the *olamani*, suspended bamboo pole. It is not flung haphazardly over the beam; it is put in its fixed place. There is usually a descending order beginning with clothes of the older people at one end and ending with those of the youngest.

301, 302

The turban

The turban consists of a rectangular piece of cotton cloth, which may have a thin border of red, green, or dark blue interwoven stripes. The length differs according to its use. Under the turban a cloth or a cap is used to cover the head.

turban	paghadi

The head-cover

284

A thick piece of cloth 90 cm long and about one metre broad is tied on the head, the knot being over the forehead. It is called a *latho*. The headcover keeps off the dirt from the head and, if used with the turban, keeps the oil in the hair from touching the turban. So it can be worn either by itself when the man is working in a dusty place, or inside the turban. For very poor people it is a substitute for a turban.

head-cover	melkholiyu, lit. dirt cover

The cap

A piece of white cloth is sewn up in the form of a cap to be used as a head-cover.

The short turban

The turban-cloth is a broad white cotton cloth and it often has at both borders small coloured weft-strips.

short turban	bathiyu
(example in the possession of Rangmalbhai Karsanbhai)	
length	360 cm
breadth about	100 cm

This turban-cloth can be tied in different ways, f.i. one end can be folded to stand erect over the turban like a crest, the other end hanging down on the shoulder, or it can be taken up and fixed inside the turban. The third way of fixing a turban is to fold one end around the cheeks and the chin to protect the face against the wind during the winter. This method is called *mahoriyu*.

The long turban

301, 304

This turban is generally white. However, if the turban is worn by a bride-groom or by a youngster on a special occasion it may be crimson red.

long turban	moti paghadi
(example in the possession of Rangmalbhai Karsanbhai)	
length about	600 cm
breadth about	120 cm

Usually these turbans are tied very neatly and have a central vertical braid in the middle over the forehead where the two ends meet and cross each other. The ends of the turban are fixed inside.-To tie such a turban is an art which is not known to every man. Young men especially will have the turban tied by their older friends or by their fathers. When the turban is fixed, it can be removed from the head like a cap and left in its form for quite a long period.— These long turbans have a prestige value and are worn only on religious or social functions.

The turban is the most personal thing a man possesses. He does not like to lend it or give it away. Wearing a turban is regarded as a matter of *amanya,* honour, and a man is expected always to have his head covered with it when he is out of his own house, though not amidst his close relatives. A man conscious of his status, will tie the turban whenever he steps out of his door, even in the early morning when brushing his teeth on the platform in front of the house. I observed that my neighbour, when he washed his face, he took the turban down; however, before walking into the house, he put it on again.

The waistcoat

This light shirt of strong white cotton material has long sleeves which always are rolled up at the wrist; it has a stiff quilted tight collar, and is knotted with cloth tapes sewn at left to the right on the breast. It falls in pleats down to the waist. Ornaments are quilted in white thread on the back.

301, 303, 349

| waistcoat | *angadi* |

The trousers

The loose trousers are fixed around the waist with a tape passed through the waist band. Down to the knee they are broad and loose. The long legs, however, are covered very tightly; they look like tubes. Waste cloth is rolled up in the legs. This is to show that the owner can afford to use much cloth for his dress.

301

| trousers | *chonrana* |

The shoulder-cloth

A white rectangular cloth of coarse quality is generally laid over the shoulder.

| shoulder-cloth | *pachhedi* |

This shoulder-cloth serves for two purposes. First of all it is used as *fant,* for carrying goods like vegetabley, grass, firewood etc. and is slung over the shoulders to form a bundle. The same cloth is used on formal occasions like dancing or on visits as *kamarbandh.* Now the cloth is slung around the waist hanging down on the left side. In the case of a young man its edge will only reach the knee, where as any old man can leave it hang down to the ankle. Further more, the shoulder-cloth can be spread as a cover, is used as a towel, can cover the face when a man is sleeping to protect him against the dust or flies, or is slung around the waist and knees as a ring when sitting.

Turban, waistcoat, trousers and shoulder-cloth are the parts of a mans dress made from cotton cloths. His costume will be completed with a woollen blanket (vide IX. 4. 4.), with shoes (vide X. 6.), ornaments (vide VII 3. 1.) and an axe or spear (vide VII 1.).

5. 2. Women's dress

The dress of the women-folk is as uniform as that of the men. Hower, there is some variation to indicate the social status and age group. We can distinguish the dress of married women, the dress of grown up, unmarried women staying in their father's village, and the dress of of small girls.

Dress of married women

The head-cover cloth
This black coloured woollen piece of rectangular shape has often some white strips on both ends.

head-cover cloth	*odhani*

This cloth is used by older women when they go out.

The printed head-cover cloth
The rectangular red cotton cloth has tree-like ornaments at the ends, and in the central part figurative designs printed in black. These cloths are handprinted with wooden blocks and are mainly manufactured in Ahmedabad city.

printed head-cover	*nagariya pachheda*, lit. head-cover from the town
tree-like ornament	*amba*
figurines	*putli*

The cotton blouse
The blouse has short sleeves reaching nearly to the elbow, the breast part has two pockets made of artificial silk in a different colour. The blouse has two pairs of tapes on the back to be knoted together. The blouse is tight-fitting. It covers just the breasts, the back being left quite bare. The blouse of uniform red cotton cloth is used daily for all occassions by everyone, young and old.

cotton blouse	*chadavo*

The silk blouse
Shaped like the ordinary cotton-blouse, the silk blouse is made from silvery shining brocade silk which is purchased in Porbandar. This blouse is used only during and after a marriage.

silk blouse	*kapadu*

The long cloth
A plain red cotton-cloth is slung around the waist falling down to the ankles. It is fixed around the waist by twisting the ends together in a knot.

long cloth	*dhalavo*

Dress of unmarried women and of small girls
Unmarried girls staying in their father's village wear instead of the long red cloth, a rectangular white cotton cloth together with the ordinary red head-cover and the red blouse.

white long cloth	*pankora*

The whith head-cover cloth
A rectangular white cotton cloth is placed over the head.

white head-cover cloth	*dhotali*

This cloth is not anymore in fashion.

The red-spotted black cover cloth
On the black cloth red spots are printed (most probably by a special kind of resist-dying). It is not anymore used and I could not find a single specimen.

cover cloth	*moyaniyu*

301

82

301

80

178

The blouse

A young girl's blouse is made of a thick white cotton cloth.

girl's blouse   *pankoru*

The skirt

A fringed skirt of red cotton is sewn and fixed around the waist with a tape passing through the tape-band. There is also one other kind of a pleated skirt which hangs down to the calfs.

skirt   *chaniyo*
pleated skirt   *kakani no chaniyo*

Besides the clothes a woman's dress consists of shoes (vide X. 6.) and ornaments from gold and silver (vide VII 3.2.)

IX. 6. Embroidery

In contrast to the people of Central Saurashtra, embroidery as a decorative art plays a subordinate role with the Mer-community. As an adornment it is altogether absent from stitched garments, except designs worked in white thread on a white background on the back of men's waistcoats. It has been asserted that the Mer of the Barda Hill region represent an independent school of embroidery, as it were, of which the predominant motif is the "sunflower" (inscribed flower) (Nanavati, 1966, pg. 26). This may well be so, for the few old pieces of embroidery existing in Ratadi are described as the handiwork of "mothers-in-law", in other words, women who were not originally residents of Ratadi. Several pieces, however, have been purchased at Porbandar and were made by tailors (or cobblers ?) in that city. There is but a small variety of embroidered articles to be seen in Ratadi, all of which are used either as wall hangings or as decoration for oxen. "Only a few colours such as yellow and white with an occasional insertion of red and black on a white or red ground are seen in their work" (Nanavati, 1966, pg. 26). As a rule, the thread used for embroidery is silk and the material cotton. Mirror-work is described as *abhla,* small discs of mirror glass being set into the design.

Embroidery as a leisure-time employment for girls has only in recent years come into vogue. Both chain stich and darning stitch are emploved to depict floral motifs (suggestive of European influence) and mythological scenes with figures. The most beautiful specimen of this kind of embroidery is, to my mind, the cloth worked by Jiviben, a girl belonging to Baradia. It is unfinished, for Jiviben was drowned in the village well in a tragic accident last year. The figure of *Krishna* playing his flute and leaning on a cow is the predominant motif embroidered on the rectangular cloth. In the upper right hand corner *Hanuman* is shown flying, in the corresponding, left corner there is an old woman with her prayer beads. The whole scene is worked in a variety of bright and contrasting colours. The original drawing of the scene represented in this touching piece of work was done by Jusub, the eldest son of the Muslim barber in Ratadi. Jiviben's mother describes him as "especially gifted in drawing. We sent him the plain white cloth and he drew on it what his fancy dictated".

It is probable that the boy drew some inspiration from prints, but the result is nevertheless surprisingly charming.

299

298

6.1. The wall-decorations

The square wall hanging

On a background of white cotton many designs are embroidered in a multitude of bright 299 colours. Among the motifs are the so-called inscribed rose, blossoms with oval petals surrounding a round centre, leaf designs, chessboards, v-shaped indentations and zigzag patterns. Larger spaces are sometimes filled in by means of an applique of cloth instead of darning-stitch.

wall hanging	*chakri* (or *chakla*)
(example in the possession of Hardasbhai Bhayabhai of Baradia)	
length	48 cm
height	49 cm

The round pillow

This is a round pillow case made of light coloured cotton and stuffed with cotton flock. It is embroidered with coloured silk, chain-stitch being used for the outlines and darning-stitch for filling in. The centre is the point of interest in the pattern; either rays are shown diverging in all directions from it or else it forms the centre of several concentric circles. Large and small mirrors are scattered across the work. A frill of gathered ribbon is sewn around the edge.

round pillow	*gol*
(example in the possession of Puriai)	
diameter about	34 cm

The lintel pannel

Pentagonal corners are stitched to the lower edge of a rectangular cloth. The main piece, that is to say the rectangle, is generally embroidered with dark roses surrounded with light garlands and framed by borders in geometrical designs. In rare cases, there are also vertical panels which hang down parallel to the door posts. These side panels also have a triangular piece pointing outwards attached to their lower edges.

horizontal panel	*toran*
vertical panel	*sakhiyu*

These panels may also be executed in applique work or in bead work.

6.2. Ornaments for oxen

The large cover

The large cover for oxen is as a rule ornamented with applique work and not with embroidery. 300 The designs worked by these two methods are not the same. Where embroidered, the designs are made up largely of multicoloured flowers, interlaced ornaments and bird motifs. The side pieces are more or less symmetrical. A piece specially designed to cover or make provision for the hump of the ox is worked in and in some cases even padded and quilted.

large cover	*ul*

The forehead strip

The forehead strip is in the shape of a broad rectangle, the upper edge of which is inflected, cords being stitched to the three corners. These cords are slung over the horns of the animal. The strip is usually dark blue in colour and thickly studded with little round mirrors sewn on with thread. Tassels or strings of beads fringe the lower edge of the forehead strip.

forehead strip	*makhiano*
tassels	*fumka*
(example in the possession of Puriai)	
breadth	24 cm
length	27 cm

The nose piece

There is yet another decoration which may sometimes be seen on oxen. This is a piece of embroidery covering the muzzle and ending above the nose. The nose piece ends in two long arms and is fastened behind the horns.

nose piece	*makhodu*

The horn sheaths

Two cone shaped sheaths are slipped over the horns of the ox. They are in some cases slit at the side and can be tied with cords. The sheaths are covered with embroidery, the design being either based on the peacock-feather motif or else corresponding to that on the forehead strip. A small sparrow made of silk stuffed with cotton is sewn to the point of each sheath.

300

horn sheath	*singda na kapda*
sparrow	*chakli devi* (goodess of the sparrows)
(example in the possession of Hardasbhai Bhayabhai of Baradia)	
length	44 cm
length of sparrow	6 cm

IX.7. Patch-work

by Haku Shah

7.1. The informants

Vahaliai is the oldest aged woman in the village of Ratadi. She is about eighty five years old, and lives with her husband Sangata in an old house in the western part of the village near its main entrance. The house is their own. It is shared by two families, one side is occupied by the aged couple, the other by Sangata's niece and her family.

Vahaliai and Sangata are outstanding personalities, the story of their lives is far from happy. Sangata was born in a poor family in Ratadi. The produce of the fields was sufficient for his needs, and there was even some to spare which he could sell. Unfortunately, however, his son wished to leave the village to seek his fortune elsewhere. In order to provide his son with cash, Sangata sold his land and gave his son the money. After this, he and Vahaliai had to accept any work that came to hand. One day he might be engaged as a daily labourer on a neighbour's fields; another day he might assist in driving the bullocks for drawing water from the well; or he might be seen carrying somebody's goods from one place to another, and so on. Vahaliai also accepted jobs suitable for women such as grinding grain, helping in making channels for the irrigation of the fields or sifting and picking pebbles from the grain.

Once Sangata had bought with the little cash that remained a camel which he named *Dhola*. This dromedary served him in various ways. *Dhola* was used for transport; it carried goods, grain and vegetables from one place to another, and it gave joy rides to people during the fairs. At the fairs, Sangata would pride himself that his camel could outrun any other in a camel race. During the wedding season, Sangata would start quite some time after the bridegroom's party had left, but would then race his camel so furiously that the wedding party would soon be overtaken and left far behind. Thus - according to his own words — *Dhola* was more than a friend and a brother to him.

After *Dhola's* death, Sangata fell into a slough of despondency and could not overcome his depression. Up to this day Sangata remembers his beloved camel with affection and pain. In this own words:

There never was and there never will be another camel like my *Dhola*. I must have used about hundred camels but my *Dhola* was the best. I have lived amongst camels for about sixteen years, and I can still say emphatically that none came up to my *Dhola*. The upper half of my *Dhola* was like a big round pot. He was better than even a man. Once I had to go a long distance to fetch a girl. There was a steady downpour of rain; the road was muddy. I felt rather doubtful about our journey but we went. We remained hungry for days together owing to the winds and the rain, but *Dhola* brought me safely home after twenty days. No one in the world could catch my *Dhola* if I let him loose. My *Dhola* was as high as a mountain and as white as an egg. Even today I dream of my *Dhola*. Such was my *Dhola*.

In honour and memory of his *Dhola*, Sangata has had a figure of a camel tattooed on one of his shoulders.

I learned from the other villagers that Sangata had a powerful voice which could be heard about a mile and a half away, and when they heard it in the distance people used to say "Sangata is riding home on his camel".

Sangata was a favourite singer with the villagers. He sang popular tunes like the *doha*, couplets, *chandrava*, quatrains. He could play the buffoon hilariously for the entertainment of the villagers and was also good at mimicry. He gave us a demonstration of his gift: as soon as he barked like a dog with his powerful voice, all the village dogs started barking in response.

Sangata however did not overestimate his gifts. He was a lover of the sea. Whenever he had time to spare, he used to go to the beach. It was not merely a walk for pleasure, since there he collected a number of things which would appear quite useless to us. Usually he walked along the shore from Kuchhedi to Visavada and back to Ratadi. He used to carry his pipe with him, and whether sitting on a beach watching the sea or the sun, or walking to collect the "treasures" of the beach, he invariably smoked his pipe. He showed some of his finds to me. Cuttle bones, shells, sea-shore vegetables, things thrown out by the sea such as a piece of fishing net, thread, a comb, a piece of soap, an empty match box, a bit of cotton, a rag for his pipe, a little piece of wax, a small piece of lead. His wife Vahaliai jokingly remarked:

Pitya, a badhi vahat to tu marhe tare tari khatali e bandhavani chhe, these things will be tied to your hearse when you die.

Then she told me:

Pityo akho dado dario dole chhe, poor fellow he churns the whole sea throughout the day. He specially collects sea-foam for trade. He is very easily satisfied and is too innocent to wonder whether he has been cheated by the trader. In fact, this is his one and only business now-adays. Whenever he gets hungry or there is need of money, he goes to the trader and sells his sea-foam. Hence he goes to the sea and addresses it thus: *"Jo hu tari pase avu chhu mane maru mul deje,* look I am coming to you, give me daily bread".

Naturally he has acquired a sound knowledge of the winds, birds, fishes, and sea-shore vegetables.

Vahaliai herself is respected not merely because she is an old woman of eighty five, but because she goes into trances. The villagefolk believe that the *Ai*, the mother-goddess, enters into her body and sends her into these trances. There are two specific things that marked her out as an *Ai*. One was *kadu*, a silver anklet and the other was her head covering *odhana*, a special kind of head-covering with some square tie-and-dye designs on it.

She is a cheerful woman who starts working early in the morning. She cooks a meal and she and Sangata take their lunch at one o'clock. Without any rest she resumes the work of sewing her quilt until about six o'clock. Thus from morning till evening, except for the lunchbreak, she is occupied with her quilt making. This wrinkled old woman, though erect, walks with a staff in her hand; she has fairly good eye-sight, but when she feels the strain she requests some one to thread her needle for her. As the well is at a distance, she sometimes requests somebody to get water for her, but generally Sangata brings the water. She loves singing, but, as she says, memory begins to fail in old age, and so she has forgotten many a song; yet she continues to hum in rhythm to the movement of the needle while sewing. Life is not easy for this poverty-striken aged couple.

7. 2. The role of the quilt-maker

As Vahaliai is an outstanding personality, I decided to watch her making the quilt. However, this work is done by any old woman in her leisure hours when she is free from household work or back from the fields. Nearly every woman in Ratadi makes quilts, but the younger of them make more and more elaborate ones with modern sophisticated designs. Some women even work as professionals making quilts on order. Vahaliai, however, does not sell such goods, she prepares them for her household only. It might be interesting to note that the women of the poor Harijan castes are especially skilled in producing quilts out of useless rags.

7. 3. The materials

Vahaliai gave me the following information regarding the material used for preparing quilts. For the two covering cloths the following pieces of the mens' garments are used : paghadi, the turban cloth of fine quality; kohiyu, the shoulder cloth, the shawl; angadi, the shirt with kotho, the chestpart; chorno, the trousers with charan, the upper part; gudia, the thigh portion and paichha, the leg portion. Except the turbancloth, all these garments are of rough thick cotton cloth called pankora.

From the womens' garments the following parts are utilised : dhalvo, the white skirt; ghiyu, the red skirt; ghaghro, the cloured skirt; odhani, the head-cover cloth; dhabalo, the black woollen shoulder-cloth; kapadu, the brassiere with elbow-long sleeves; and polkun, the blouse ef silk or coloured cotton. For the inlay of the quilt, any small rag or longish piece of cloth which is entirely worn out and useless for any other purpose can be used. It may be mentioned that strips of clothes such as those from the collar, the hems of sleeves etc. are not used for quilts, but for wicks and for strings to tie up rolls of quilts etc.

7. 4. The tools

Implements for washing the rags

Aluminium pot, tapeli
The light aluminium pot is used for carrying the cloths to the washing place. It is cylindrical in shape.

Iron trough, tagaru
This iron trough has the shape of a washing-basin.

Square piece of cloth, pachhedo
The cloth is used for making a bundle to carry the rags.

Wooden beater, dhako
The common beater is a long rectangular paddle with a cylindrical handle. Vahaliai used a wooden stick of about 30 cm length.

Pebbles, sticks and a staff, *pathar, dhefu, lakadi,*
These articles were used to weight the rags when drying in the sun.

Washing clay, *mati dhovani*
Grey clay from the neighbouring village of Adityana can be used for washing cloths.

Soda, *soda,* engl.
Washing soda is bought at Porbandar.

Implement used for quilt-making

Needle, *hui,*
A steel needle of about three cm length is bought at Porbandar.

Thread, *doro*
Three pieces of white hand-spun thread are twisted together to give it strength. – Machine made thread is common in Ratadi as well.

Sickle, *datardu*
The lightly curved iron blade is fixed in a wooden handle. The sickle is used instead of a pair of scissors.

Wooden pestle, *sambelu*
The wooden pestle, usually used for pounding spices and for beating rice, is used for rolling up the quilt over-night.

Cot, *charpay*
Vahaliai sits on the cot while doing the later part of patching up the quilt.

7. 5. The working procedure

It must be mentioned at the outset that all worn-out clothes are collected and tied in a *potalu,* bundle, before they are found sufficient for the making of an ordinary quilt. This bundle has to be hung in a safe place to prevent it being nibbled at by rats, squirrels and cockroaches. When the housewife finds that the bundle contains a sufficient number of garments and rags for making a quilt, she starts opening up the stitches carefuly. so that the garment may not be torn into an unwanted shape or size. Each bit of garment is carefully considered and then cut in accordance with the shape and the size which she wants. When Vahaliai had collected sufficient number of rags for making a quilt, she opened her bundle and got ready to wash them. She took a trough, put hot water in it and some washing soda and soaked the rags in the trough. After an hour or so, with her husband, she carried all the washing articles to the nearest well. There Vahaliai selected a special spot where stone slabs are kept for the convenience of washing clothes or for bathing.

305

306

The process of washing the rags was described by her as follows:

307, 308

The first process is called *cholavu,* rubbing, to loosen the dirt. I apply a special kind of clay to remove mud and dirt from the rags. To remove grease and sticky dirt I have to use soap. Next to follow is *dhokavu,* beating the watered cloths with a wooden beater. By *bhunhavavu,* kneading, I loosen the dirt again. While rubbing, I sprinke water on the rags. Now *taravavu,* rinsing, the rags in flowing water is necessary. For *nichovavu,* squeezing, I need the help of somebody. As for the quilt the two ends have to be held to squeez the cloth by rolling if round in opposite directions, when the cloth is clean, it must be squeezed and shaken for *hukavavu,* drying. While drying in the sun-shine on the ground they have to be weighted by pebbles or a stick to protect them from being carried away by the wind. When the rags are almost dry, they are *gothavavu,* arranged in a basket and carried home.

The quilt-making

Vahaliai prefered to sit in the privacy of her varandah with the sea breeze coming from one 315, 309, 310
side, and the front court yard hedged in by bushes. On the varandah floor she arranged the long
pieces of cloth which were to be used for one of the outer covers. For this she had to choose
the best of them. She arranged them in a rectangular shape to get the form of a quilt, though
she had not taken any measurements. Meanwhile Sangata sat at the other end of the verandah
tearing and cutting the old quilt into proper pieces. Now and then Vahaliai instructed
and guided her husband into making the most of the more endurable cloth and cutting it
accordingly. Sangata's method of cutting was to fix the sickle between the two soles of his feet 312
and cut the cloth carefully with a movement similar to the sawing of a log of wood. The
rags were arranged for a portion of the outer covering only. Vahaliai did not complete the
whole of the outer covering either, because the pieces would become disarranged or perhaps
because she felt it would be a waste of time to select the material for the whole covering at
one sitting.

Then she began to sew the selected pieces together with a needle and thread. Sometimes her
eyes alighted on a piece of cloth which she considered better for her immediate purpose than
what she had chosen. She instantly changed the piece. Sometimes she reflected a little before
changing her piece, wondering if it would not better serve the purpose in a different place such
as a square for the centre of the quilt where it might be better displayed. In the selection of
her pieces she considered the following points: (1) The durability of the cloth. She considered
that the centre of the quilt would be sooner worn out than the sides; hence a durable piece
of cloth was selected for the centre. (2) The colour of the rag. Though the outer quilt was
made of white pieces, yet the rags in question differed slightly in colour. There were the
near-whites and the off-coloured ones which had become either yellowish or rust-coloured.
Vahaliai selected the white ones and placed them in positions that would show up the quilt
to advantage. (3) The size of the cloth. Usually she selected the larger pieces for the centre to
help in the durability and its display.

Inspite of all the above points, Vahaliai had sometimes to forego her considerations for lack
of enough rags. It will be evident from the above points that Vahaliai considered the centre of
the quilt to be of the utmost importance from the point of view of both durability and
display.

She squatted on the floor and bent down to sew the quilt so that she need not displace the
rags. She began with the hem of the quilt.

She folded the rougher edge of the lower covering and put it on the upper covering. She
kept the folded edge in place with one foot, then placing her left hand under the quilt, held
up slightly the folded edge while hemming it with her right hand. Usually she threaded
the needle herself, but sometimes, after a hard day's work, if her eyes were more than usually
strained, one of the neighbours or one of her small childern threaded her needle. She sewed
horizontally, that is, the shorter side of the quilt from one end to the other.

Having arranged the pieces of the lower covering, she tacked them together. In order to keep 311
the lower covering straight and without creases, she put stones and also her staff on the edges
and in the middle. Then Sangata turned over the basket of rags on the floor from which she
began to select and arrange the smaller rags. It was difficult for her to keep the rags in their
places, both because they were small and because her fingers were stiff with old age. Having
completed this work Sangata helped her in spreading the longest piece of a turben cloth
and a shoulder cloth over the arranged rags. These large pieces of cloth were not stitched
together, they were just spread over the rags. On top of this Vahaliai arranged larger

pieces for the top covering. This time she had not sewn all the rags together; only the larger ones were tacked on to each other; on the others she placed stones to keep them in place. Now she started sewing the border. With her left foot she pressed the border to keep it intact and in place. First, she folded the hem of about one cm with her left hand. She pressed it with four fingers of the left hand underneath the quilt and her thumb pressed the border. With her right hand she hem-stitched the folded border. The stitches were widely spaced. As she went on stitching, she moved up along the quilt and then when she had reached the corner, she continued stitching the horizontal side. While hemming the border she often felt like changing a patch on the cloth, or putting in some more rags where the quilt seemed thin, or removing rags to make the quilt even where it was too thick. Once Vahaliai opened up the hem because she was dissatisfied with the shape of the quilt. When the quilt was arranged into a proper rectangular shape, Vahaliai resumed her work. When she had shaped the outline and fixed the top pieces together one by one, she selected small rags to mend outworn parts on the patches of the outer covering. After looking over the entire quilt and satisfying herself about the shape and size, Vahaliai began selecting coloured bits of rags for applique work. She turned their rough edges on the outer covering, and hemmed them on. She started from the left, went upward, then to the right, and finally down, fixing either a square or a rhombus shaped applique patch. This applique work on the quilt contained whatever coloured rags came to hand without much regard to symmetry, so that there would be perhaps one black square applique, or three or four blue rags with white floral designs, a brownish applique, and may be a few of bright red colours. As for the longish bits of rags, she placed two different coloured ones crosswise. There was no definite plan as is easily evident, but even while she did her applique work she would select, change, and select again. These rags were of various materials, satin, silk, cotton, wool, both fine and rough; again some were new and some were old. Not all these pieces were from her own outworn clothing. Some she had obtained by swopping pieces with neighbours, some were bought from the tailor and paid for in cash.

The usual designs are the square, the rectangle, the rhombus. But now-adays they have taken to flower shaped applique. Generally, as was done by Vahaliai, a large square piece is sewn in the centre of the quilt and at the four corners are placed four different coloured rhombus. Often crosses take the place of flowers at the four corners for the sake of variation.

When Vahaliai had completed one side of the quilt she requested her husband Sangata to help her turn it. Till now the quilt had not been moved from the floor. Instead, Vahaliai had moved around it to sew up the patches, to arrange the rags and to stitch the appliques. Now husband and wife took a hold of the opposite corners of the quilt, and with great speed, and yet carefully to assure that the rags were not displaced, crossed arms and the other side of the quilt had come upper most. Now Vahaliai commenced her applique work on this side, again with the same designs such as the cross, the flower-like design, the square and the rhombus. For the centre pieces she had to sit on the quilt, while for those on the sides she remained on the floor.

She cut her thread to the actual length of the smaller side of the quilt. She knotted one end of the thread and ran a tack along the hem on all sides. In this way each row was sewn with a fresh thread. Thus the two outercoverings and the small rags arranged between the two sides were all stitched firmly together. After having stitched about a quarter of the quilt Vahaliai changed her method. Now she took in hand the middle part of the quilt and stitched through it in an irregular rectangular spiral. But the old lady could not move easily over the quilt, so she lifted it in her hand slightly and carefully so that the rags would not be displaced. After this was done Vahaliai could fold the quilt. If was completed, ready to be stored in a *mali*, quilt-bag, on top of a chest.

312

313, 314

317

7. 6. Terminology for quilt-making

Before giving the actual words Vahaliai used to describe her work, I want to mention two expressions murmered by Vahaliai while working :

Mari ne jivade, reviving after killing; *marelane jivade,* reving the already dead.

These two phrases reveal that this work is looked upon as a creation after destruction, i. e. making the dead to live again. This is because old garments are torn apart and made into something new and useful.

The following terms are used by Vahaliai to describe the actual quilt-working process: *Katak ni taiyari,* preparation of the rags, is followed by *kataka otardya,* opening the stitches in the cloth, and by *kataka fadya,* tearing into pieces. The next steps are *kataka gothavya,* arranging the pieces, and *kataka hindya (sandhya),* stitching the pieces together. *Bharan karyu,* filling (the covers) up (with rags), *dhankan mukyu,* putting the covering, and *kantho valyo,* folding the hem, are the main processes in quilt-making. *Thigari mari,* stiching on the (coloured) rags, and *fantiya lidha,* making long running stitches, are the terms for applique work and for quilting.

7. 7. Applique ornaments

thigari, patch
Most of the coloured rags used for patchwork are of rectangular shape.

chopat, cross, game-board
Two rectangular patches intersect each other perpendicularly.

mandap, bower
On the corners of a large square, small rhomboid patches are stitched. – This design is generally appliqued in the centre of a quilt.

ful, flower
Under this term all ornaments are comprised which form a flower by joining four or more petals in or around a centre-piece.

ambo, Mango-tree
From both sides of a trunk an equal number of branches with leaves at their ends shoot out.

7. 8. Textiles decorated with applique work

The quilt
The quilt is rectangular, the outer covers of which are made of white patches stitched together. Between these layers of cloths, rags are distributed evenly. The entire piece is quilted by long running stitches except for the borders which are folded and hemmed. On both the outer coverings small coloured rags are arranged and appliqued with hem stitches.

318

quilt   dhadaki   *187*

The quilt is a multi-purpose article. It is used for sitting on the floor or on a cot where it is spread out. In the cold season it is used either as a blanket or as a shawl. While travelling it provides a comfortable seat in the bullock cart, or keeps the camel driver warm. It can be folded four times and made into a soft mattress for a child's cradle. The better type of quilts are stored in specially-made cloth bags called *mali* and piled up on the wooden chest.

The more ornamental quilts are taken out for use on festive occassions like marriages, family gatherings and religious festivals like *Divali, Holi, Dussera* etc. These quilts which form a huge pile on top of the wooden chest reaching up to the ceiling easily catch the eye of anyone entering the house. In some of the houses of Ratadi, as many as two hundred quilts may be seen. Periodically these quilts undergo an airing and are spread out in the sun-shine, after which they are again arranged in their special bags and placed on the chest. To keep these piles from toppling over they are tied with cords suspended from the round rafters. The size, number and splendour of quilts in a village house often indicate its wealth. It has a sort of prestige value.

Of such importance are the quilts that some idioms and proverbs are associated with them. Some of them were casually uttered by Vahaliai during conversation. I have noted down:

A to chuntha ni hobha chhe, this is embellishment with shreds, rags and tatters (of the quilt); *ani mane to mali nath*, mother has not found a quilt bag.

This is ment as a taunt by the bridegroom's family when the daughter-in-law has shown her goods. It means that the mother of that girl is a careless negligent women, or that the father of the girl is so poverty-striken that her mother could not even find one indispensable quilt-bag in her house. Another saying is:

Ma mane mali de, mother do give me a quilt-bag, i. e. keep all the taunts from the in-laws away.

It must be mentioned furthermore that men customarily never sit on a quilt whose outer covering is made of womens' coloured garments. Therefore, three different kinds of quilts may be distinguished: (1) quilts with white covering on which men or women may sit unhesitatingly, (2) coloured quilts which are only for ladies and (3) quilts with one outer covering white and the other coloured so that a male visitor may sit on the white side and the women may sit on the coloured side. When a sufficient number of rags have accumulated, but there is a shortage of white pieces, the women make a quilt with only one white covering.

However, all white quilts are decorated with coloured rags appliqued. In nearly all quilts, the centre has an outstanding motif. The prevalent motif is a square larger than the other appliques with four petals or four floral designs at each corner of the square. It may also be in the shape of a cross. In addition to this, many quilts have a rectangular border sewn all round or just two borders on the two long sides. These borders may be either plain or decorated with rags, shaped into triangles with their apex pointing towards the inner part of the quilt. Often patches of different colours are distributed over the plain white colour. The ornamental designs are often indicative of the community: f.i. patch-designs of Harijan-Dhed communities will have figurative motifs including figures of human beings, animals and birds. The most elaborate speciemens were produced by a lady called Rajiben, and are used in the household of Bhikabhai. On the other hand, a typical piece of a Mer household has only one flower-form stitched in the centre of the quilt, while simple rectangular patches are scattered all over the quilt.

The bolster

This is a small square mattress-like cushion. The white outercoverings are decorated with patch and applique-work on both sides, and generally the border-line is marked by a coloured applique band. Tassels of coloured rags ornament the four corners of the bolster. In the middle

319

of one of the border lines of the bolster a loop made out of rags is stitched for the convenience of hanging it on a peg in the wall. The stuffing may be cotton, wool or grass.

bolster	*chaklo*

Such a bolster is used for sitting either on the floor, on a small chair or on a stool while spinning or grinding grain. When a visitor comes with a baby, the hostess immediately takes a bolster from the peg and puts it either on the floor or on a cot to lay the infant on it. Furthermore, bolsters are spread out on the floor for visitors to sit on. A visitor even may help himself by taking a bolster to sit during a ceremony. The last but not the least, these bolsters have an decorative effect in the room, because they are hung in a row lining the wall. It may be mentioned that these bolsters are washed periodically. One side of the bolster is opened, the stuffing taken out and the cover washed. The stuffing is beaten with a beater to remove the dust, and then spread out for airing. Then it is once again stuffed and the side is sewn up.

The bolster generally has a symmetrical patch-applique designs on all four sides. Like the quilt, the centre is conspicuous by a flower-like form, whereas the border lines have the same patch-applique designs all around. Some bolsters have several lines parallel to the border. Each of these running lines forms a common base for appliqued triangles with the apex pointing to the central flower-like design.

In one house there was a special bolster which came from Porbandar. The coverings on each side were made of five square patches, dark coloured ones alternating with white, like a chess-board design. Each of the white squares had a tiny coloured rag in the centre on which was a coloured knot. This knot is made by piercing the needle on one side, pulling the thread out on the other where the thread is knotted. This design is not only decorative but makes a bolster more durable.

These bolsters sometimes occur as small flat round pads stuffed with cotton, grass or wool. They are decorated on similar lines as the square bolsters, and serve the same purposes. However, sometimes a pair of these round bolsters may be used to decorate a *ghorla,* horseheads, which form the ends of the door-beams.

round bolster	*gol*
(example in the possession of Rangmalbhai Karsanbhai)	
diameter	29 cm

The mattress
Rectangular mattresses are usually stuffed with grass and have a white covering with rough cloths stitched together.

The quilt-bag
Rectangular in shape, in the size of the length of a quilt, they have two drawers on either side, while the middle portion has a loose flap on the side to close the bag when a sufficient number of quilts have been arranged within. All round the two coverings, there is a broad braid connecting the two. These braids have patch work designs on them, generally triangles with the common base and the apex pointing towards the centre.

146, 147

quilt-bag	*mali*
(example in the possession of Jethabhai)	
length	175 cm

These containers of quilts are arranged length-wise on the wooden chests. They are used to avoid dust spoiling the quilts and mattresses.

IX. 8. The weft-twining of ornamental borders

8. 1. The informants

The weavers sell woollen blankets without ornamental borders. After the last pick of weft, a 276 roughly 12 cm stretch of warp is left free, one or two picks of weft being inserted after this to keep the ends of the warp threads from becoming entangled. The length of the woollen fabric is then cut out of the loom and either sold or handed over to the owner of the wool, who possibly sells it in his turn. A beautiful shawl in the possession of Rangmalbhai Karsanbhai in Ratadi had been acquired in Tukda, where it had been woven for a Rabari shepherd. He had heard about the shawl from his brother-in-law and had subsequently arrived at an agreement with the Rabari. The shawl had never been worn and had no decorative borders. It will be worn as it is, devoid of ornamentation, until Rangmalbhai finds somebody who has both time and inclination to work the decorative borders. The twining of ornamental borders is known as *kor bandhvi*; the part of the warp without the weft is called *okaryu*. This last is generally the occupation of the Rabari shepherds, who handle wool with dexterity and are pleased at the prospect of earning a little money on the side.

The teciturn Nathabhai, a Rabari from Ratadi, states :

// I learnt it by myself. // By watching. // Here is one more (man who practises this craft). In Degam are many Rabaris who know how to twine borders. // Generally all (villages have Rabari communities).

The other man in Ratadi who works decorative borders is Gigabhai Lakhabhai, a tuberculosis patient, about 27 years old. Gigabhai told me the following :

// I did not go anywhere to learn this craft. If someone comes and orders *kor bandhvi* and shows me the special design he wants, I will do it. // Customers always bring the blanket or shawl with them. // Should somebody desire a very special design, he must bring an old blanket as a sample. But usually the choice of the designs is left to me.

// It takes seven days to work two ornamental borders on a blanket. (Gigabhai works only in the morning.)

// I charge 15 Rs. for the wool and 4.50 Rs. for the labour.

/ Can you distinguish your work from that of Nathabhai? / (The sister interrupts from the kitchen calling: Let me make one *rotla*, bread, and let other women make some; put mine amongst the others and from far I will recognize which one is mine.)

// I work only during the winter. In the warm season there are no customers. // In the summer I stroll around. I posses some fields, but the doctor at the hospital has advised me not to do heavy work.

// *Bhagma,* I rent out the fields. // The yield is divided half and half. // Even in the case of irrigated fields. // I have given the fields to two persons, distant relatives of mine.

// When I am tired, I dislike the work. // I seldom have company.

// I start every morning at eight o'clock and sometimes I continue even after lunch up to three o'clock. But generally I work only five hours.

// The Luhana merchant Mohanlal was the first to give me an order. The border of my first blanket was plain and I only charged him five rupees, since it was the work of only two days.

// At first only one person knew that I could do this work, but later more customers came and work started. // The Rabari charges 18 Rs. for one blanket, but he takes 28 to 25 days before he finishes the work, whereas I finish within a week.

// There are different charges according to different designs.

// Every afternoon I go to the temple to read books. (He recites from them daily in the temple, listened to by old people.) // I like the *Ramayana* best, but I love all of them when they are about God.

// I started to read five years ago when I was in the hospital. I had only one year of Gujarati studies, but I taught myself more by reading books. Now I can read fluently.

8.2. The working procedure

So as not to expose himself to the morning wind, Gigabhai works inside his house. He sits on the floor on top of a woollen blanket. The spot he has chosen to work appears dark and somehow unhealthy despite its seemingly favourable situation just opposite the doorway.

The Rabari Nathabhai sits on a bedstead in his shady verandah, his legs curled under him. The blanket lies across his thighs. One edge is folded up so that the warp threads point away from him. The last few picks of weft after the strip of warp are cut away. The warp threads are already somewhat matted and have to be smoothed one by one.

285

Nathabhai keeps his collection of coloured yarns in a box. He untwists a piece of thick woollen yarn by holding it between his toes and separating the strands. He winds both strands of yarn separately into a coil. He first winds the yarn around two adjacent fingers und then draws off the coil. He now wraps the wool once around the middle and finally tucks the end into the loosely wound coil. He pulls out the starting end of the yarn and can now easily unwind it. He knots the starting end to the corresponding end of another coil and attaches the knot to the left outer edge of the fabric. He now threads both strands through the warp in such a way that after each warp thread the strands meet and cross. Nathabhai always works from left to right, that is, as soon as he has reached the other selvax he turns the blanket around and proceeds to pick the next weft, again working from left to right. An exact description of each individual manipulation and the various deft knacks employed cannot, unfortunately, be deduced from my notes taken on the occassion, for they succeeded each other with such rapidity as to elude minute observation. The most important point is that almost all ten fingers work equally actively passing the thread through, fixing it in place and dexterously plaiting the coloured yarn into the warp. All these movements follow each other with amazing rapidity and without confusion. A steady unbroken rhythm is maintained throughout.

The quantity of yarn required for each design is carefully measured. For instance, a length of yarn measuring two *vent,* handspans, is all that is needed for a simple triangle, whereas a length measuring two *hath,* ells, equal to the distance between the elbow and the fingertip, is required for a large double trapezium.

Next, the shape of the design is threaded through. Gigabhai also counts the number of warp threads through which the yarn will be twined, to make sure that the pattern will be regularly spaced. Both strands of yarn are knotted to the apices of the triangles and rhombus. All designs of one kind are first threaded into the decorative border before the shape outlined is filled in with different coloured yarns.

Should the thread finish while the work is in progress, a new length of thread is inserted by simply slipping it through near the end of the finished thread. Knotting it would result in a lump and is therefore avoided. A few simple lines of coloured yarn form the end of the decorative border. The warp threads are knotted in pairs and the ends carefully trimmed. As a final touch, short tassels of coloured woollen yarn bound together by encircling ties are hung in the loops formed by the knotted warp threads.

8. 5. Colours and designs

Woollen yarn synthetically dyed in brilliant colours is used to twine the designs. Nathabhai calls the colours he uses *karo,* or *tuto,* blue; *lilo,* green; *piro,* yellow; *lal,* red; *gulabi,* pink; *dhoro,* white or any pale colour. Remarkably enough, Nathabhai used the word *dhoro,* white, when alluding to the sky, a glaring blue.

All designs are geometrical. Triangles and trapezoids, both of which have sloping sides and are consequently easier to work, figure prominently. An oblong trapezium is known as *katkua*, three adjacent trapezoids in different colours are called *transiu*, and two vertically opposed trapezoids *machhali*, fish. A zigzag band with the central apices vertical is termed *deradiu*. Rhombs placed on end, with a similar central line drawn through in a contrasting colour are described as *badamada*. The tassels fringing the border are called either *fumka* or *sar*.

IX.9. Rope and cord making

9.1. The twisting of cords

Although nearly all farmers know how to make ropes from long jute fibres, they usually assign the task to specially dexterous friends, who either twist the rope themseves or supervise the procedure. In return they are paid a small sum of money. The payment very often is only an indirect one. Rope making, however, is no profession in the sense that it is not a full-time employment. Dahyabhai Nandiyabhai says:

// I am never paid in cash for rope-making. That is no business. If I am free, I will help. Nobody comes to call me.

In Ratadi it is chiefly the Rabari shepherds who have a reputation for being skilled rope makers. This is because they are accustomed to spinning thick woollen yarn. But when a long, stout drawing or hauling rope is required, most of the farmers solicit the help of Radiabhai Jivabhai, who possesses the necessary tools and makes an excellent job of it.

When the barber of Ratadi found that he required a strong rope, he enlisted the help of his Rabari friend Dahyabhai Nandiyabhai. It took Dahyabhai barely two hours to make a serviceable rope about one cm thick and five and a half metres long from a bundle of prepared jute fibre.

The basic material used for making ropes is jute fibre. The word for fibre is *santar*, while jute is called *ketki*. The barber says in this context:

// Generally all the farmers plant some *ketki*, jute, on the borders of their fields. Sometimes, the Harijans go and cut it where it grows wild now-a-days. The leaves are soaked in water until they are completely rotten. The residue is beaten with a stick or pestle. When dry, the resulting *ketki*, jute, can be used for making cords and ropes.

The work is carried out in the yard and varandah in front of the barber's house. As a sample, Dahyabhai first doubles and twists, with great rapidity, a metre or two of rope. He shows this trial piece to the barber, who determines the thickness of the rope to be made.

The Rabari sits on the ground. His left leg is curled so as to lie in a horizontal position, while his right leg is stretched in front of it. While working, he bows his head slightly over his work. He jams a few jute fibres between his toes and proceeds to twist them between his fingers to an s-shaped cord. As soon as the twisted portion has attained an appreciable length, he winds it round a short stick which he holds between his toes.

This cord is subsequently wound round the right foot, making the figure of eight. During twisting, the finished cord is held between the thumb and fingers of the right hand, while the thumb and forefinger of the left hand twist the fibre, the thumb being held above. After every second twist, the right hand is passed over the twisted portion. When one bundle of

fibre has nearly been used up he bifurcates about four cm from the end of the twisted cord.
Into this he inserts the thinned starting end of the next bundle of fibre and to firmly connect
the two and ensure an intertexture of the parts, twists it in with the left hand, while the thumb
and forefinger of the right hand press together from the side the fibres thus joined.

The fibre is taken little by little from the bundle and combed through with the fingers.
Rough and matted fibres are removed. When all the fibre has been twisted to a long cord,
Dahyabhai winds it round his right hand. He ties the starting end around the verandah post
with a simple slip-knot and stretches it across the yard. He now measures the cord in *vam,*
spans with outstretched arms. He discovers that the cord falls short of the required
fourteeen span measurement by half a metre. This deficiency is soon made up, for Dahyabhai
twists the necessary length of cord from the remaining fibre. He next winds the cord round a
stick, first in layers and subsequently only round the middle. He then carefully twists the
starting end, holding the bundle of wound cord firmly to the ground with his feet.

The bundle is once more unwound and the cord spanned taut. Any ragged ends and projecting
fibres are trimmed away with a large pair of scissors. Now comes the procedure of doubling
the cord to form a rope. This is effected by doubling and twisting it z - shaped.

About half the length of the cord is rewound on the stick. It is now tautly stretched. The cord
is held in the right hand, the thumb being underneath. The rope-maker now gives his hand a
twist and at the same time passes with his left hand the wound cord under the stretched one.
Thus the first twist is formed. The right hand now takes over the cord bundle, while the left
twists the cord. Two complete twists of the cord correspond to wrapping the cord once
around itself. When the left hand passes the cord bundle under the spanned length of cord,
the right hand lets go of the twisted cord and takes over the bundle until the left has been
drawn back. The work progresses at a brisk rate, Dahyabhai slowly advancing forward along
the spanned cord, which remains tautly stretched, while the finished piece is allowed to drag
on the ground.

By the time the post is reached, all the cord wound round the stick has been unrolled.
Dahyabhai returns and winds the finished doubled and twisted cord, now a rope, around the
stick. He unties the starting end of it from the verandah post and twists it carefully between
his fingers. During this stage, he sits on the ground with both legs outstretched. The stick
with the rope wound around it is held firmly on the ground between his two feet. He
meticulously inspects the entire length, bit by bit, to make sure there are no defects.

The final stage of work consists in shaping the starting end of the rope. This is done by doubling
back the tepering end and wrapping it around the rope, the last spirals being left loose.
Dahyabhai passes the cord end through these spirals, working once more backwards along the
length of the rope (this time obviously towards the starting end again) and gives it a final tug.
Through this the twist is tightened and a small loop is formed at the end of the cord.

The rope thus produced is termed *prau,* and is intended to serve as a *ras,* drawing or hauling
rope for the water-bag. When the barber measures it, he finds it exactly three spans in length
with outstretched arms. A simple cord is later twisted from the fluffy fibre waste, known
as *kucho.*

9.2. The twisting of cables

One evening I could by chance observe the process of making a *varat,* drawing cable, which is used to haul up the water-bag from the well. The following description is therefore merely sketched in rough outline.

The prosperous farmer Lilabhai Bhurabhai required a strong drawing cable. He engaged three young men from among his relations to join in the work and requested the help of maker. Radiabhai Jivabhai. This old man possesses a long-standing reputation as an expert rope Work begins in the late afternoon on the large, flat stretch of ground outside the village. The thick ropes are spanned between the stone stakes expressly set out for this purpose and free to be used by all the villagers. Some of the stones are rammed into the ground, while others are simply laid on the earth.

281

A rope twisted from several cords is wound around a wooden ring in figures of eight. The ring is in the shape of a pointed oval and is pierced through. The rim is slightly raised. The lower rope is halved. Each of the three ropes is tied to a branch that is broad at the end. The branch is first straight, then projects outwards at a sloping angle. After this it makes a gentle curve and ends in a point. These three branches, resembling sickles or antlers in shape are mounted in a row on a board pierced with three holes. This board is tied behind two stone stakes fixed in the ground. A similar but shorter board is mounted upon these three points, so that the three branches can be made to turn at an even pace.

An iron hook is passed through the ropes at their ends where they double back. This hook in turn hangs from two links of a chain. A revolving hook with a stout head is fixed into the edge of the latter, which is hammered flat. This revolving hook is anchored in a stone slab through which a hole is pierced. Several stone blocks are piled on the slab. A brake in the shape of a stick is temporarily inserted into one of the chain links.

Rags cut into ribbons are now wrapped around the three ropes stretched between the stone stakes. The help of everybody is enlisted for this operation. Radiabhai, however, reserves his skill and attention for the rope-ends at the point where they are doubled back.

The brake stick is removed. Now a wooden piece in the shape of a truncated cone is inserted between the three ropes at the point where they double back. This cone, technically called top, has three slightly curved grooves for the ropes be laid into. While two men rotate both outer branches at a uniform pace, whereby the ropes immediately near the top are twisted together in a z-shape, two boys pull back the top with the help of a wooden stick inserted between the ropes. To prevent the top from rotating as well, one of the boys firmly holds a handle of an antelope horn inserted through a nail shaped to a loop, which is attached on one side. With the progress of the twisting process, the length of the ropes, which now form the cable, may be seen to contract. It is therefore the duty of a fifth helper to slowly shift the heap of stones accordingly.

282

The twisted cable is next freed from the revolving branches. The three ends are tied together. The cable is rolled into a coil and carried away.

283

The old man packs together his rope-making kit, unbinds the boards from the stone posts, ties them up in a bundle and makes for home, without the word "thank you" being uttered a single time by any of those present.

284

9.3. The rope-maker's lingo

Rope-making is termed *nadu bhangava*, and the wooden ring *makdo*. The rotating chain is called *bhamarkadi,* and the braking stick *kamdi.* The anchor stone is known as *dhunia.* The transverse timbers are *patli,* in which the revolving branches – *kambadiu* or *vankia* – are fixed. The stone stakes are 40 cm high and called *khobia.* The cone-shaped rope-winder or top is termed *ful,* flower, and is fixed in place with a *singadu,* horn.

9.4. The uses of cordage

Cordage (that is cords, ropes and cables) in the "untreated" state is required for a variety of uses, the following being the most important : as drawing ropes and cables at the well, as harness, as a tie between the yoke-beam and shaft, to span across wagon loads, to suspend and tie tools, instruments and other articles, to tether animals, and for the network across the tops of bedsteads, stools and chairs.

An interesting point in this context is that sometimes a board pierced with two holes is used as a connection between two ropes, both ropes being tied to it by means of thick knots. The board is called *bhamarkadi.*

A thick wooden reel set in a rectangular wooden holder is often used to brace and span ropes. It is known as *garedo.* — Since the earth is mostly dry, loops of rope may be let into the ground and anchored there, the animals being tethered to them in the evening. These loops are termed *nadana.*

IX.10. The twining with a single thread

Only a few articles are made by twining ropes or cords to form a fabric. Techniques of knotless netting and even of simply knotting of textile fabrics practically appear to be uncommon. Besides crochet work (vide pg. 199), the only technique practised with a single thread is twining which occurs besides weft-twining in two variations, one is employed inthe making of yoke halters for oxen and for sling-beds, the other for making muzzles. The first articles are made from cotton cord, the second one from jute strings. Many men and boys are familiar with this craft; nevertheless, articles of this kind are usually purchased in the market at Porbandar.

Virambhai Ramabhai, the son of the Police Patel of Ratadi, showed me how a sling is made. Including the time taken to prepare the materials, he required about one and a half hours of work to complete the sling.

10. 1. The working procedure

Viram's mother gives him a bundle of coarsely s-shape-spun cotton thread, this being the basic material useed. He twists two threads into a long z-shaped cord.To accomplish this, he winds the long cord around his big toe, stretching it taut. He twists it between the thumb and forefinger of his right hand. When the right hand releases the cord to take position for the next twist, the left thumb fixes the fulcrum by pressing the cord against the forefinger of thesame hand. The end of the cord is knotted.

Next to Viram there lie 15 sticks. These are pieces cut from thick, nodeless millet stalks. Each piece is about nine cm in length.

Viram sits on the edge of the terrace in front of his father's house. He leans against the post and adopts a sitting posture typical of the Rabari - shepherds. He has his left leg curled under him, while the right leg is laid over it in such a way that the right ankle lies on the left knee. Later he allows his right leg to hang over the edge of the verandah. The work lies on his lap. When expeditious, it is pressed against his knee or chest.

Viram stretches the cord to ascertain whether all the meshes are even. He now untwists the first twist and inserts one of the sticks into it. With the same stick he dips into and picks up the second twist. Into the third twist another stick is inserted, on the right adjacent to the first stick. He now turns the work around and slips the fourth twist of the cord back on the first stick. A third stick is inserted adjacent to the first into the fifth twist. Once again he turns the work around and slips another twist over each stick, inserting a new stick on the outer edge of each row before turning the work and proceeding in the same way.

He holds the work with the thumb and middle finger of his right hand and untwists the cord   285, 286 with his left thumb and middle finger. The stick is pressed down with the middle finger of his left hand, while the same finger of the other hand is employed to draw the open twist over the stick, which is at this point pressed against the breast or the knee to better enable it to be inserted through the twist.

Should one of the sticks break, Viram pulls it out and replaces it with a new one. The sticks in the middle of the twisting, that is, those first set in must be longer and more stable than the others. He sometimes holds the work pressed between the thumbs and forefingers of both hands.

When thirteen sticks have been inserted, Viram pauses for a while and inspects the work. It appears to him of sufficient length. He now leaves out five twists and then commences to slip another row of twists on the sticks. On the opposite side he again omits a few twists before turning round the work. No fresh sticks are introduced. Instead, he cuts a four cm deep slit into the outermost stick with his penknife. Into this slit he jams the end of the cord and draws it together with the stick through the twine work formed by the twists. He then turns the work around and lays another row of twists over the sticks until he once more reaches the outermost of them. He now repeats the foregoing procedure by cutting a slit into this outermost stick, in order to draw the cord through the fabric. In this way, the sticks are one by one replaced by the cord. The end of the cord is knotted to the edge of the sling thus twined.

Finally, a cord is knotted to each of the two holes on either side and the sling is finished.

10. 2. Technical terms

Virambhai calls twining of this kind *bhangvu*. The materials used are *dori*, cord; and *saradia*, stalks of *bajra*, pennisetum and *juvar*, sorghum. The twists are called *sara*, the knots *ganth*, and the holes on either side *naka*.

10. 3. Twined articles

Beside slings made of leather thongs or pieces of cloth, there are also those made of twined   288 cord. Tho twisted cords are tied to the holes, the shorter of these ending in a noose.

sling	*gophan*
cords	*vaghia*

(example in the possession of Virambhai Ramabhai)

sling strap, length	13 cm
breadth	7 cm
cord, length	83 cm

The sling is manipulated with the right hand. The nose at the end of the shorter cord is wound around the little finger, the cord passing across the forefinger on its palm surface, while the second cord is held between tips of the thumb and forefinger. Momentum is gathered by holding the sling to the side and swinging it in a circle six or seven times. Now the cord in front is let loose and the stone is thus hurled forward in a wide arc.

The yoke halter
The yake halter is made in a shape similar to that of the sling strap decribed above, only on a much larger scale. The holes at the sides may be reinforced with leather strips sewn to the network.

yoke halter	*jotar*
(example in the possession of Rangmalbhai Karsanbhai)	
length	43 cm
breadth	16 cm

A loose twine-work can be produced by first forming a spiral with the twisted cord and then drawing it through across the twists of the spiral. However, only bristly material such as jute fibre or very strong cotton thread is suitable for this species of cord twining.

The muzzle

Muzzles may also be twined of cord. A muzzle of this kind is made in a hemispherical shape and has a reinforced border, either plaited or made from several thick cords twisted together. The cords forming the network branch off from this border. At their ends, alternate cords are taken up and twisted together.

muzzle	*shikla*
(example in the possession of Vajabhai Atiabhai)	
diameter	13 cm
length	18 cm

Kharero, cloth for rubbing down domestic animals may also be made in similar fashion from coconut fibre. These are known in Ratadi, however, no example could be found.

IX. 11. Primary textiles with two or more threads

11. 1. The knotting of cords and ropes

Since fishing and hunting nets are not to be found at all in Ratadi, there are very few articles made from knotted rope or cord. Indeed, the variety of goods of this kind is restricted to one basic type, the hanging net. Symmetrical knots are used as decorations on bridles and harness, and occur carved on wooden hooks serving as hanging devices. Special knots and loops were not noticed by me. I found that only a few old men knew how to form the special loop employed to hold in place on two sides the funnel mounted on the seed barrows.

The hanging net
Several cords, usually four in number, branch out from a base ring. The ring is reinforced,

being either double twisted or wrapped. At a few centimetres distance from the ring the cords
are tied together or fastened by an encircling knot, diverging thereafter once more to be tied
together again. This time each cord is knotted with its neighbour directly opposite. This short
net with wide meshes sometimes ends in loops to which four cords with knotted ends are
attached or else the meshwork itself finishes in four long cords, by means of which the net is
suspended from one of the roof beams. The size of these nets varies, depending on the number
and shape of the articles they are intended to hold.

hanging net	*hinka* or *hinkadi*
(example in the possession of Rangmalbhai Karsanbhai)	
length	83 cm
diameter approx.	17 cm

The commonest articles hung up in these nets are pots and vessels, which are stored in the net
one on top of the other. Sometimes a bottle may be hung in a narrow net.

11. 2. Basket plaiting

With the exception of the two types of basket and the cart fender, very few examples of basket
plaiting are in everyday household use. A piece of basket-work plaited paralled to the edges
may be placed over a corked bottle or may cover the shoulder of a bottle. Simple linen weave
is always used. The craft of basket plaiting is one practised solely by members of the Vaghri
or Harijan communities.

The basket tray
Stakes of bamboo are arranged radially one on top of the other. Broad strips of bamboo are
next plaited through the stakes parallel to the edge. Just before the edge, which is turned
upwards at a sharp right angle to form a rim, the broad strips are replaced by narrow bamboo
chips. The stakes are bent upwards along the rim of the cylindrical bamboo tray. The end of
the bamboo strip is tucked under the adjacent strip.

basket tray	*chhab*
(example in the possession of Parbatbhai Atiyabhai)	
diameter approx.	60 cm
height approx.	10 cm

The basket
Broad bamboo strips are used to plait parallel to the edge a hemispherical basket.

basket	*sundo* or *hundo*
(example in the possession of Bhurabhai Dahyabhai of Baradia)	
diameter approx.	50 cm
height approx.	15 cm

Baskets are used for the transport of working materials such as earth, sand, ash, etc. They may
also be used to hold grain, in which case they are previously cleaned. As a rule the baskets
are purchased in the Porbandar market or sold to the villagers by passing Vaghris.

The cart fender
When earth or manure is to be transported by bullock cart, the rear edge of the vehicle is
lined and banked with a piece of basketwork. The coarse diagonally plaited piece may be
worked from thick palm branches.

cart fender	*katarani*

One afternoon during my stay in the village, a big bullock cart laden with these basket-work fenders arrived at Ratadi. They had been made by a Bava and a Barot farmer, who now offered them for sale. The fenders were priced at five rupees a piece.

The carrying ring

These are rings filled with grass and wrapped with leaf fibres. The fibres are bound in place with cords, usually three in number, that are coiled around the ring. A short projecting length of plaited fibre is used to hang up the ring.

carrying ring	*indhoni*
(example in the possession of Samadbhai Karsanbhai)	
diameter	13 cm
thickness	5 cm

These rings, made by the Vaghri, prevail throughout Gujarat. They are used as pads when vessels are borne on the head or serve to hold vessels with rounded bases when these are not in use. There are also carrying rings ornamented with tassels and wound thread.

11.3. Ornaments made from cords and threads

Not only embroidery and applique work, but also multicoloured cords and tassels are used as ornaments to decorate oxen and horses. In the latter type of ornamentation, leather, cotton cord in various colours, pieces of mirror, silver threads, buttons, cowries and beads are employed. All these combined produce an extremely rich effect. Red, yellow, purple and green are favourite colours. The threads are twisted together and wound with coloured cord. They are tied in symmetrical knots and embellished with tassels. Through simple winding various effects can be obtained: the cords may be coiled or three strands may be interlaced to form a braid. Simple knots may be employed to produce a torus-like effect.

The different designs such as *mathavati,* a forehead ornament with tassels for oxen, *morado,* the same for horses, necklaces and bridles are made by members of the Vaghri or Malana communities. Rava Bapu, the Durbar of Pandavadar, has also made and sold several ornaments of artistic workmanship and design. A speciality is the tobacco bowls for water-pipes, which are encased in plaited coconut fibre.

290

tobacco bowl	*haijar nu bambu*
(example in the possession of Bhurabhai Dahyabhai)	
diameter	10 cm
hight	20 cm

11. 4. Crochet work

Working with a single steel needle to produce an interlaced network is a popular handicraft these days. Bags, cushion and pillow covers, and *toran,* lintel panels, are produced in crochet work. It is always the young girls of the village who devote their labours to this craft. I do not think that crochet work was known at all earlier in Ratadi.

Thick coloured cotton yarn is used to work plain surfaces, though sometimes stripes and open-work are introduced by way of variety. The most attractive piece of crochet work was a lintel panel in the house of the young shoemaker. It was made of thin white yarn. Swastikas, flower pots, small birds and large peacocks were arranged symmetrically on either side of the centre. The shapes of the designs were worked in closely spaced mashes, while an open network constituted the background. This piece of work is a clear indication that the artistic tradition maintained by the Mochi, shoemaker caste in Saurashtra is not extinct, and that the young girls are also capable of working with new designs and techniques.

297

IX. 12. Bead work

In traditional Mer villages such as Ratadi, bead-work as a handicraft is scarcely known. Amongst the very few examples of bead-work produced, fans, bead-covered coconuts and carrying rings are notable. Only in one house did I find a beaded lintel pannel and a rectangular wall hanging. These articles are either imported or made at home by the old women. They are regarded as show pieces and for this reason kept stored away in chests, to be brought forth on festive occasions.

The Ratadi bead-workers thread their beads according to the "monobead-system" or *eka moti nu guntham,* of which Dhaky (1966, pg. 76) says: "The beads are closely set in one row after the other". Only on the borders of the articles several beads may be threaded one after the other on a string to produce a fringe or a hem-stitched effect. White beads are employed for the background, the coloured designs being set against it. Sometimes small disc-shaped mirrors framed by pressed tin rings are set between the different designs.

As Dhaky (1966, pg. 89) points out that the designs employed may be taken to depict figures of gods and humans, animals and birds, plants, articles and geometrical forms. The deity most frequently represented is *Ganesha,* whom I found to be hardly ever absent, while *Shri Nathji (Krishna)* was shown on only one wall hanging. Among the human motifs is a woman with raised arms, a row of water-carriers, i. e. figures of women, each one supporting with one arm a water vessel on her head and finally, two women churning butter. As animal motifs are concerned, I observed with some amazement that cows and bulls appeared frequently, whereas elephants occured but rarely. Bird motifs show peacocks with both outspread and drooping tails, and parrots. Plants are always shown growing symmetrically out of a flower pot with long or rhombic leaves sprouting pinnately from the stalks. In a few rare cases, the stalks are crowned with circles of flowers in a variety of colours. Predominant among the geometrical designs is the swastika, the circle with a centre-point, the herringbone pattern and the zigzag border.

If the very limited number of motifs and examples of bead work at all allow classification, the style must be defined as being allied to the so-called "Coastal Mahajan School". However, I do not believe that the Mer possessed a large number of bead-work articles in former times. It seems more plausible that bead work as a decorative art has only recently developed.

The fan
The wooden cross-piece is fixed to the end of the handle by means of two wire rings. In most cases, the handle is lathe-turned and painted. The fan itself is usually disc-shaped or else in the form of a three-quarter circle with the circumference drawn in. Two pieces of coarse wire grating are fitted into this frame for the beads to be threaded through. The space between is stuffed with cotton. A frill of satin ribbon is stitched around the edge.

296

fan	vinjano
(example in the possession of Puriai)	
length of handle	40 cm
diameter	26 cm

The coconut
A large coconut is covered with a close network of beads. The naturally rounded end of the coconut serves as a basis. The designs are arranged in borders around the nut. Strings of beads bound together to form tassels are attached to both ends of the coconut.

294

coconut	*nariyel*
(example in the possession of Harbhambhai Rangmalbhai)	
height	17 cm
diameter	11 cm

These beaded coconuts are kept as decorative pieces and have a special function at weddings. For three nights before the wedding, the bridegroom rides through the village receiving gifts and blessings while carrying his sword in his right hand. In his left hand he holds the decorative coconut and a silver rupee coin. The coconut is deemed a symbol of luck and fertility.

The carrying ring

The carrying ring (vide pg. 199) plaited from grass and leaves is sometimes overlaid with a band of beadwork, the inside of the ring being left open or lined with red cloth. A band of bead work as broad as the ring hangs down on one side. In some examples of carrying rings thus adorned, a kind of fringe or hem-stitch edging may be observed around the borders, made by stringing several beads without interruption on a string.

carrying ring	*indhoni*
fringe	*kanthalo*
(example in the possession of Puriai)	
diameter	15 cm
length of band	11 cm

The lintel panel

Seven graduated triangular peaks of equal size hang from the base of an oblong panel, into which abstract designs apparently intended to depict animal figures are worked. The peaks are filled with geometrical tree motifs. In the central peak is a figure of a sitting *Ganesha*, with two arms stretched upwards.

295

lintel panel	*toran*
(example in the possession of Bhimabhai Avabhai)	
length	115 cm
breadth	21 cm

This decorative panel is hung below the lintel on three nails and adorns the doorway on festive occassions.

The wall hanging

A rectangular picture worked in beads is topped with glass and framed. The picture shows a border of cows, trees and swastikas enclosing a representation of *Shri Nathji*, a favourite manifestation form of the god *Krishna*, against a white background. The wall piece described here is in all probability the copy of a print. Various prints, showing figures of gods and being of the same size as the bead work picture, are hung on the wall beside it.

293

(example worked by Jitaben in Ratadi)	
height	39 cm
breadth	30 cm

X. Leather craft

by Eberhard Fischer

X.1. The shoemaker

1.1. The informants

There are at present only two shoemakers in Ratadi, uncle and nephew. The old cobbler
Keshavbhai Naranbhai assured me:

My family has been settled in the village for many generations. One of our forefathers came to Ratadı and
settled here.

Nevertheless the shoemakers are not so firmly rooted to the spot they have chosen to settle
down in. Keshavbhai himself lived for some time in the village of Bantua, while his brother,
the father of the younger cobbler of Ratadi, emigrated to East Africa leaving behind
his wife and small family in pitiful circumstances. The young man gave this information:

// My father is working in Africa. // He works in a shop and repairs shoes. // When I was five years old, my
father left for Africa and has stayed there ever since. // Most probably he will not return. //My mother has
always stayed here in Ratadi. She was here even at the time when I went out to learn the craft. // She lives
alone. // My father sends her the small sum of one hundred rupees for four months. Lately he has even stopped
sending this little sum. She goes out to work as a labourer at building sites and earns some money herself.
In this way she brought us up, all her children.

The younger shoemaker tactfully expresses the nature of his relationship with his uncle in the
following terms:

The other shoemaker is Keshav. He is my *kaka*, paternal uncle. We (my mother and I) are not on good terms
with him.

// I learnt the craft from my *mama*, maternal uncle. I don't own him (Keshavbhai) anything.

There are personal reasons for this discord between uncle and nephew. It is occasioned rather
by the quarrelsome disposition of the older shoemaker than by the consideration of professional
competition, for the younger cobbler makes mainly modern shoes, sandals, water-bags and
and leather harness for oxen teams, while his uncle only produces shoes in traditional
designs, waterbags and harness. The actual competitors of the young village shoemaker are the
cobblers at Porbandar, who have a large selection of ready-made shoes on display. The
competitors of the old cobbler are the workshops of Shrinagar and Kantela, where work is
conscientiously carried out, and the customers including many inhabitants of Ratadi buy
all their leather requirements from these workshops. The reason for this lies in the unpunctuality
and general unreliability of the old shoemaker who has a reputation in the village for being a
gossip-monger. The younger shoemaker on the other hand is reproached with inexperience in
various kinds of work.

1.2. The role of the shoemaker

The craft of shoe-making is the profession of the men belonging to the Mochi caste. Women
do not participate in the actual work. At the most they fetch the water required by the

cobbler or sweep away the waste leather from the floor of the workshop at the end of the day's work.

Since a shoemaker in a small village can expect only very few orders, large workshops with apprentices and paid assistants are extremely rare. The cobbler works mostly alone or with a family member whom he trains.

There is very little to be said about the apprenticeship. As a rule boys of the Mochi caste are trained by their fathers or one of their uncles, either maternal ot paternal.

When an apprentice feels he has mastered his craft, he either sets himself up independently at a suitable place or takes over his father's workshop. The young cobbler puts it in these words:

// I learnt the craft from my *mama,* maternal uncle. // When I finished, I returned to my mother in Ratadi and started my own business. First I had no customer. But after some time they came to me, one by one. The number of customers is still increasing.

No special devices to attract customers are resorted to. The young cobbler works above all for his personal friends. I am not aware of any prescribed ceremony taking place on the opening of a workshop. The tools are either purchased or taken over from the father's workshop.

Regarding religious rules for a shoemaker or his customer, Keshavbhai says:

// Two things are forbidden: (1) never sit on the *salari,* stone slab, and (2) never keep a *dhoka,* wooden hammer upright. This tool must always lie on the ground.

The shoemakers were unable to further explain these little significant regulations.

The dress of the cobblers is similar to that of the farmers. An old photograph of Keshavbhai shows him in a white turban, white waistcoat and wide trousers, also white. For going out he wears a white Gujarati cap, a white shirt with a collar and the traditional trousers, while his nephew wears a white or khaki-coloured outfit in Western style. The women of the Mochi caste are not in any way distinguishable from other craftsmen's women by their dress. Their attire consists of a colourful flared skirt and a head cover, generally printed and in a contrasting shade.

The shoemakers are generally poor, do not own land and are therefore held somewhat in contempt by the farmers. Theirs may be regarded as a transitional caste above the Harijans or untouchables. Some Harijans prepare the hides, while the Mochi works with the leather thus produced. It is probably because they work with cow-leather that the cobblers formerly lived outside the village.

The shoemaker Keshavbhai narrates the following:

// Formerly, we lived outside the village. But once all our houses burned down. My father moved to the house of one of his friends, who was of the Mer community. However, I settled for one year in Bantua because nobody gave me a house. Afterwards I stayed with Rangmalbhai. When he started to rebuild his house, I shifted over to this house. At that time this house had no backwall; it was broken down and in a very sad condition. I was told: "You can repair it and live in it without paying rent." The house originally belonged to a Mer who went to Africa.

// He will never come back. Some people of that family have already died in Uganda.

The cobblers use leather to make shoes of three different designs, large water-bags, slings and harness for oxen. Now-adays they also make modern shoes and sandals. They also carry out any subsequent repairs on their work. Taken as a whole, there is a very restricted range of leather articles to be seen now-adays.

These articles are made only on order and against payment. The shoemakers do not stock ready-made articles, but produce them only upon the order of a customer. Prices are fixed and payment is now-adays made in cash. A pair of tradional shoes of the best possible quality cost between ten and twelve rupees according to size. Women's shoes are simpler, the workmanship in addition being usually of poorer quality, and therefore cost only five rupees. Water-bags are far more expensive, for a greater amount of material is required for their production. An entire bag costs fifty rupees; the quickly worn-out tube can be renewed for twentyfive ruppees. The cobbler takes back the scraps of old leather to use as sole-filling for shoes.

The cobbler has a fixed clientele. He receives twenty *pali*, grain units, a year from his permanent customers as payment for keeping all their leather articles in repair. This agreement is known as *hath* and may be terminated at the end of the year.

The young shoemaker describes how such a payment takes place:

|| I have fifteen customers over here in Ratadi, and I take 20 *palis* of grain for *hath*. || The *hath* is paid in two instalments: I receive ten *palis* of *bajro* from the *Divali* crop (monsoon crop) and another ten *palis* at the end of summer. From the summer crop I get *sinar*-grain.

|| The other shoemaker here is my uncle. The amount given to him for *hath* is the same. The people give their work to the shoemaker they prefer.

|| The number of *palis* due to me by the terms of the *hath* remains fixed. I never get more, even if the farmer has had a very good crop that year. However, the same rule does not apply when the opposite is the case: in a bad year I get less grain from my customer.

|| Here *hath* in never paid in cash.

There is not much scope for earning, nor is there much by way of repair work. A rich farmer, for instance, generally possesses only one pair of shoes.

Very many people go barefoot and wear shoes only on special occasions. A prosperous farmer told me that he had ordered a pair of shoes from Keshavbhai two and a half years ago, which were the only shoes he wore. They were patched in many places, and the farmer said laughingly in the presence of the cobbler that he would have them patched until the patches themselves fell to pieces. In answering my question as to how long such shoes would last, he gently hinted at his prosperity by implying that he could afford to be at leisure in the village and therefore not wear out his shoes:

|| These who walk with shoes the whole day long (i.e. go to the fields) can use the shoes only about one year. I have been wearing these shoes for the last two and a half years in the village.

If he works at a brisk rate, Keshavbhai can make a pair of shoes in a day. He says that when he was young he could work twice as fast. As for the quality of the goods, the cobblers are quite capable of producing superior articles, although they sometimes indulge in bungling and generally slipshod work. To quote an instance of this, a pair of women's shoes of inferior quality were sold in my presence for four rupees. They were patched together from bits of waste leather; the uppers were blotched with unevenly applied colour, the seams were crooked and the cuts irregular. The woman accepted the shoes without a word of complaint.

The shoemaker Keshavbhai frankly admits that the quality of his work varies. He even said:

|| Today I am in a very good mood. The shoes will look very good.

However, when a pair of shoes were ordered for the funeral rites of a Brahmin from outside the village, the cobbler explained that the recipient of the gift was not one of his customers anyway. The quality of the work was therefore immaterial. He not only saved on good material, the workmanship of the whole was decidedly slovenly. The Brahmin also said that the shoes were quite useless and that he could not even hope to sell them.

The following defects in workmanship frequently occur. Because leather is worked when it is wet, it often loses its shape on drying. If the shoes are not completely dry before the edges are cut, the sole appears crooked. Another astonishing point is that even shoes that look presentable from the outside have old scraps of cracked leather for a sole lining. Once the sole is worn out, the entire shoe soon becomes useless.

X. 2. The tools

The tools described below are from the workshop of the shoemaker Keshavbhai in Ratadi. 322, 323
He says:

// I started my trade 35 years ago. If tools break, I have to order new ones. Some though, like the *krapli* and three of the *takna* I inherited from my father.

2. 1. Measuring and marking tools

Marking knife, *krapli*
This knife is made by the carpenter from *kher*, acacia-wood. It consists of a narrow, slightly convex blade sharpened on both sides and a small handle separated from the blade by an ornament of concentric circles. The shoemaker grasps the knife with his hand and presses it on the leather to mark lines.

Template, *takna*
The shoemaker uses standardised templates of leather for the different sizes. He lays the template on the sole leather and marks around it.

2. 2. Cutting and sewing tools

Scraper, *karpa*
This is a semicircular iron blade fitted with a tang. The edge is straight and only slightly sharpened. The blade is fixed in a cylindrical wooden handle. The scraper is used to treat the surface of leather.

Scraping knife, *rampi*
A long trapezoid blade with a straight edge is fixed into a cylindrical wooden handle. The blade is sharpened on both sides to a keen edge. This tool is used both to cut and to scrape off leather.

Large awl, *moti ar;* small awl, *nani ar*
An iron pin is fixed into a cylindrical wooden handle. Its point is hammered flat and the edge sharpened to a slightly convex shape. Awls in three sizes are used to pierce the holes on the seams.

Needle, *soi* or *hoi*
This is a common steel needle with a large eye threaded with a string.

Punch, *sumba*

This is a triangular iron with its base sharpened and bent. It is fixed in a wooden handle. With this tool, made by a smith at Porbandar, holes are punched into leather.

Large punch, *mota sumba*

The point of an iron pin of square section is flattened and bent to form a ring-shaped punch. The edge is sharpened. Holes are pierced along the edge of water-bags with this tool, which was made by a smith in Porbandar.

2. 3. Hammering tools

Hammer, *hathodi* or more exactly *singda vari hathodi,* horned hammer.
A short handle of *sisam,* rosewood, is driven through a heavy claw hammer head. This tool was made by a smith in Palakhda.

Iron beetle, *mogri*

This is a tapering cylinder with a broad head made of cast iron and partly ornamented with a punched-in herringbone pattern. It comes from Porbandar. The iron beetle is used to threat leather and to pound seams.

Wooden beetle, *dhoka,*

This consists of a simple cylinder of *baval*-wood with one end flattened. It was made by the local carpenter. The wooden beetle is used both to pound leather and as a support.

Iron eyelet hammer, *chukno*

This instrument is spherical. It is shaped into a pointed oval and fixed into a cylindrical handle. An eyelet passed through the leather is hammered flat with the point of this tool.

2. 4. Auxiliary and supporting tools

Stone slab, *salari*

A slab of fine crystalline sandstone from Bhuj in Kutch is used as a base or support. When moistened it may be used as a grindstone, too. The slab in Keshavbhai's workshop has served several generations.

Base, *kapi*

This is a slightly arched piece of buffalo horn used as a base when cutting leather.

Grindstone, *pathri*

A rectangular grindstone is attached on its narrow edge to a board by means of nails. It is purchased at Porbandar.

Water vessel, *kundu* or *sapnu*

A heavy black clay bowl with a double lip is three-quarters filled with water, which is used to wet leather and soften it. The bowl is the work of a potter in Shrinagar.

Stretching horn, *kol*

This tools is made from *bhens nu sing,* buffalo horn and has a narrow rounded base. At the other end it is broad. It was trimmed to shape by the carpenter in Ratadi and is used by the shoemaker to stretch the shoe uppers.

Stretching last, *kalbut*
Large last, *moti kalbut;* small last, *nani kalbut*
This rool is in the shape of a shoe, i. e. it swells from a point, contracts and broadens out again.
It is carved from *baval*-wood. There are three sizes, one for men's, one for women's and one
for children's shoes.

Stretching block, *gatho;* wedge, *fad*
The small stretching horn is used for the pointed front section followed by a cube, a wedge
and finally a halved cylinder for the heel. These four parts are placed inside the shoe and driven
in firmly by the wedge. The heel-piece and the wedge are made from *sag,* teak-wood and
are the work of the village-carpenter, while the cube shaped piece was picked up on the
beach. It had been a net float.

Polishing horn, *ladia*
The point of a buffalo horn is cut off and sharpened on both ends. It is used to polish leather
edges and corners and to give a shine to finished shoes. It was formerly used in place of
brushes.

2.5. Non-traditional equipment

Pincers, *pokar*
An imported pair of common pincers bearing the manufacturer's name 'Freytag' is employed
solely for the purpose of extracting nails.

Anvil, *pagu*
This instrument, used in making modern shoes, is of cast iron and imported from Porbandar.

All the tools are stored during the night in a small metal box standing in one corner of the
workshop. The box is used for no other purpose.

X. 3. The working materials

According to the shoemaker Keshavbhai, whose statements confirm my personal observations,
machine-tanned leather is used in Ratadi only for the manufacture and repair of modern
shoes. The quantity required is thus little. Keshavbhai declared that exclusively hand-tanned
leather may be used for making traditional shoes, and adds as explanation :

// "Machine-tanned" leather cracks when it gets wet. It is not durable in this place. It is smooth on both
surfaces and can only be used for making *but,* modern shoes.

Machine-tanned leather distinguishes itself from hand-tanned leather by being smooth and
polished on both surfaces and having the pores equally distributed, which latter characteristic
is doubtless to be attributed to its being evenly stretched. Its surface has a printed effect,
whereas hand-tanned leather is thicker in some parts than in others, while its surface reveals
unevenly spaced groups of pores.

Both types of leather are bought in small quantities by the village shoemakers. It is astonishing
to note that the cobbler Keshavbhai buys only enough leather for a single pair of shoes at a
time. This is probably because he is too much of a spendthrift to invest some part of his

earnings in stocking new material. The following is the cobbler's commentary on the subject of purchasing leather :

// The centre of leather-production is the village Vinjhrana; but in Visavada, too, some Harijan know how to tan.

// The leather merchants of Porbandar buy all the leather and sell it afterwards to us cobblers. We go to Porbandar to their shops. However, sometimes the people of Vinjhrana come to us directly to sell their leather. It also happens that I myself go to Visavada or even Vinjhrana to buy the leather I need.- These are the various ways of obtaining leater.

Leather is comparatively expensive. According to the cobbler, a large hide costs approximately 40 Rs. a smaller one about 20 Rs. Calf, cow or buffalo leather are priced the same according to the quantity bought.

These three types of leather are used for different purposes. The shoemaker says :

// For *kos*, water-bag, only that of cow and buffaloes is used. The hide of smaller buffaloes is used for shoe-uppers. Calf leather is used for laces and for the inner lining of shoes. The uppers of women's shoes can be made out of calfskin, too.

Other working materials:

Twine, *dori*
Double-twisted waxed cotton twine is used for sewing.

Wax, *min*
The twine is drawn several times over a small lump of beeswax in order to strengthen it.

Leather ribbon, *samano*
For specially strong or for decorative seams narrow ribbons of leather are used, which the shoemaker cuts chiefly from calf leather.

Nails, *khili*
Nails are not used in the making of traditional shoes. They are purchased at Porbandar.

Eyelets, *fudadi*
These are punched out of a sheet of bronze by machine and may be purchased at Porbandar. According to the cobbler they have but recently come into vogue as ornaments for shoes and were formerly unknown.

Dye, *hira kasi*
A white powder mixed with water is used to dye leather black. In Porbandar a small quantity of the dye may be purchased for one anna at a Gandhi shop, i.e. a chemist's shop. The powder is mixed with water and kept in a small red clay pot. The mixture is applied to the leather with a rag.

X. 4. System of measurement and workshop lingo

Shoes are nowadays generally marked according to their commercial sixes 5, 7, 8, 9, and 10. These are code numbers for particular foot sizes and cannot, in the opinion of the shoemaker, be readily converted into shoe measurements. He still finds it useful to measure with the *angar*, finger, as a unit. For each size, the cobbler has a template or sole pattern called *taknu*, the length of which is measured by placing the fingers adjacent to each other, omitting the pointed portion of the pattern. Women's shoes are always made 13 fingers long, corresponding to the commercial size 7, while for men's shoes the foot is measured and the shoe made roughly 15 fingers long, which corresponds to size 9.

A shoe is divided into *fana*, forefoot (sole) and *pani*, heel. Shoemakers distinguish between a *kevado* and a *sotalo*, the heel cap in men's shoes and the heel lobe in women's shoes. The inside leather of the heel is called *putia*. The shoe upper or vamp is known as *sajai*, the lining as *bevan* and the strip of lining under this as *pati*. The point of the shoe or toe piece is known as *chanch*, beak. The entire sole is termed *taliyu*, the insole *majara*, the stuffing *pati* and the inner removable sole *hagatri*. The lacing across the vamp is called *vadaliyu*, the leather under the lacing *pegadu* and the leather discs attached next to it *ankhiyu*, eyes.

The simple running stitch used for the seams is called *tebha*, while the twisted stich is termed *bakhia*.

The seam joining the shoe upper to the lining is referred to as *dubel silai* (engl. deriv.: double), while the seam joining the sole to the upper is called *tran silai*, triple seam.

Torn shoes are mended with *thigari*, patches.

X.5. The working techniques

5.1. Place of work

The roofed verandah of the shoemaker's house serves as the workshop. This is a raised   321
platform plastered over with clay and screened from the street by a loose network of broad bamboo strips. When the sun shines into the veradah in the afternoon, large pieces of cloth or leather are hung over this bamboo screen to keep out the heat and glare. An open wicket door patched together from planks leads into this verandah workshop. The shoemaker squats on the ground upon a folded gunny bag. He usually sleeps here as well, both in the afternoon and at night.

5.2. Working conditions

The cobbler is never too eager to start work, but once he has been persuaded to do so he will work indefatigably and diligently the whole day long. While at work, he chats uninterruptedly with his visitors without, however, looking up from his work or pausing even for an instant. He has a comparatively large number of visitors, for whoever wants his shoes repaired remains in the workshop till the work is done.

The old shoemaker Keshavbhai works alone. His only helper is his wife, who spins and twists the twine required, fetches water, sweeps the workshop and several times a day brings her husband *lal chai*, red tea, i.e. tea without milk.

5.3. Working schedule

In order to make a pair of solid and well-stitched men's shoes of traditional design from

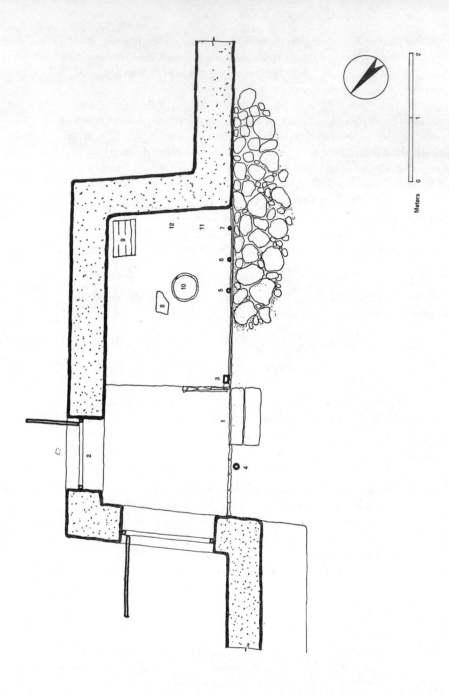

9. Plan of the shoemaker's workshop in Ratadi.

1 Entrance steps to the
workshop
2 entrance to the house
3, 4 roof posts
5, 6, 7 bamboo posts

8 stone for working
9 box for tools
10 water pot
11 large leather pieces
12 small leather pieces.

leather and cotton twine, the shoemaker requires approximately seven hours of work which
are divided in the following manner:

9.10 – 10.40	preparing the tools, cutting out and preparing both uppers and one sole
10.40 – 11.15	stitching together sole and heel of the first shoe
11.15 – 12.00	stitching together sole and upper
12.00 – 12.10	preparing the second shoe
12.10 – 2.00	interval for midday meal and afternoon sleep
2.00 – 4.00	stitching sole and upper of second shoe and stiching both these together
4.00 – 4.25	trimming the edges and stretching the first shoe
4.25 – 4.40	fitting the lacing into vamp of the first shoe
4.40 – 6.00	finishing the second shoe, including fitting of lacing.

5. 4. Working materials and tools

For the uppers, lining, heel cap and toe-piece the cobbler uses new, relatively thin cow or
buffalo leather. For the undermost visible sole layers and for the heels he uses strong new
buffalo leather, though inside the thick sole, is old leather cut out from worn-out waterbags.

Practically all the tools that make up the shoemaker's kit are employed in the making of   322, 323,
traditional shoes. What is not required is the large punch and all the non-traditional tools.

5. 5. Working procedure

Before commencing with the actual work, Keshavbhai takes all the tools he will require
out of the box and spreads them out on the floor, before him. He carefully whets the scraper
on the grindstone, rubbing first one side and then the other five times and finally flipping
the blade rapidly to and fro against the stone. He holds the scraper in his right hand, while   325
the forefinger of his left presses the blade on the moistened grindstone. He now tests his awls
as to their sharpness by passing the ball of his forefinger along the edge. Keshavbhai asks his
wife to bring some oil in a little bowl, from which he pours out a few drops on the stone
slab, using this to sharpen the awls.

Finally, he waxes the moistened twine. This he accomplishes by holding the lump of wax
between middle finger and thumb and pressing the twine against the wax with the forefinger,
at the same time drawing the twine several times over the wax surface with the other hand.

The shoemaker now searches around for a suitable piece of thin buffalo leather which he   324
moistens, rolls and pounds on the slab, using the iron beetle. He now scrapes the leather on
the underside, holding it in place on the edge of the slab with his toes and stretching it
with his left hand, while his right exerts pressure on the tool and simultaneously guides it
over the surface. He next turns the leather round and traces the desired outline with a
moistened scraper. He now lays the scraper on the slab with its edge projecting and cuts   326
the outline, passing the thin leather across the blade. He scrapes both strips again and then
stretches them lengthwise and breadthwise. This he does by placing the heel of his right
foot on the edge of the leather and jerking the leather with both hands towards himself.
By this operation the leather strip is unevenly stretched. After this he rolls the strips up and
pounds them with the iron beetle. Now he lays the inner longitudinal edge into pleats:

Applying heavy pressure, he guides the scraper across the leather strip, turning it sideways   *211* just before the edge is reached. This results in a pleat being formed in the moist leather. When the leather has been pleated halfway, he turns it around and works from the other side towards the middle. He now flattens out the pleats by pounding them with the iron beetle. The whole procedure is repeated, until finally he has a strip of leather curved in a hemispherical shape before him. This he folds in the middle in order to see whether the curve is symmetrical. Both shoe uppers are then laid aside.

The cobbler next selects a piece of moderately strong leather, moistens it, rolls it and pounds it several times with his iron bettle. He unfolds the leather and scrapes both upper and under surfaces. When necessary he holds the leather in place with his toes. The sharp scraper is used to cut the edges at a slant, all projecting fibres being removed. In the following operation he stretches the leather, holding it firmly to the ground with his heal. He pulls it towards him with all his strength, raising himself bodily at every jerk so as to use his weight as power. 329 Then the leather is rolled up once more and pounded with the iron beetle. During the pounding it is constantly turned round and round. Ultimately it is stretched once again.

Keshavbhai moistens the stone slab with a little water. He lays the point of the large template on the leather and traces along the outline with the moistened scraper. He stands the scraper on 327 one corner of the blade in such a way that the sharpened edge faces him. He cuts along the outline with a swinging motion, that is to say, the scraper remains rigid, while the leather is passed across the swinging blade. A small block of wood held in place with the toes of both feet serves as a base.

Keshavbhai now reaches out for another piece of leather, this time dark in colour. He turns the corners inwards, kneads it awhile and pounds it with the beetle. He lays the first sole on the leather, traces its outline with the moistened scraper and then cuts out the form. The leather is held in place with his right foot and left hand, the right hand being thus free to cut the leather. The shoemaker now takes a piece of old black leather, extracts from it a nail, soaks it a few minutes in water, pounds it and places it under the previously cut piece in order to cut it to the same shape. He presses the three sole layers between the soles of his feet and pierces them through with an awl. He next proceeds to sew them together. There are altogether three pairs of stitches, approximately in the point of the sole. A space is left and another double 328 stitch put into the sole centre.

For the heel, Keshavbhai prepares a large, almost rectangular piece of leather and in addition a second piece, similar in shape but somewhat shorter, and finally a small leather triangle. First of all he sews the two large heel pieces together with a few stitches through the middle. Now he applies the triangle in such a way that it projects beyond the larger heel piece. He next attaches the three-layered sole to the heel piece. The length of the shoe, that is to say, how far the sole may overlap the heel, is determined by measuring the sole with his fingers placed side by side, thumb excluded. With six double stitches the sole and heel are sewn together. So as to facilitate the twine being drawn through the leather with a steel needle, the cobbler pierced a hole through the leather pieces with his awl. The stone slab is beside him and on it there is a little drop of oil. Into this Keshavbhai dips the point of the awl before thrusting it into the leather, rubbing it an instant against the stone before dipping. When the threaded needle has been drawn through the hole, the cobbler gives it a powerful tug, so that the twine sometimes becomes invisibly imbedded in the leather between both holes.

When stitching, Keshavbbai has the soles wedged at a slant between his feet. His right leg, bent at the knee, is upright while his left, also bent at the knee, lies flat on the ground.

The needle is threaded in the following manner : a thread, lightly waxed and twisted, is drawn through the eye of the needle. The twine, which is twisted as well, is unravelled a little way, one end being twisted together with the thread in the neddle. The other end is pulled through the thread over this and twisted in the opposite direction. When the needle is pulled, the binding of threads is tightened without snapping apart. Should the thread finish during stitching, the end is drawn through the eye in the new thread, i.e. the end of it is pulled through the next hole in the leather and tightened. Odd ends of thread can be trimmed away later with the awl.

Keshavbhai now places the prepared upper upon the sole. He dips the edge of the upper for a few minutes into the water vessel and then trims it so that it is uniformly wide. Once more he methodically stretches the piece of leather in the direction of its length, holding it firm during this operation with the weight of his heel.

He uses the scraper to pare the blade of the wooden marking knife. To further sharpen it, he whets it on the stone slab. When marking designs into the uppers, the cobbler holds the wooden knife in the clenched fist of his right hand, while the thumb of the left guides the blade. First of all he marks out a close succession of zigzag lines. In the following process the left hand pulls the leather strip in jerks from under the knife blade, while the right foot gently holds the strip in place. The result is a longitudinal strip on the leather.- Keshavbhai then folds the strip in order to trim the side edges once more.

He next proceeds to prepare a strip of light brown leather with the help of the scraper. He moistens this strip with wet fingertips. Now he lays both leather strips together - the thin upper and the light brown lining - with their smooth surfaces facing. He sews them together with broad stitches. Only the centre of both strips, the point where the heel is situated, is left open. He later pounds the seam with the iron beetle, moistens it once more and turns both pieces of leather. With fingertips and palm he smooths over the leather, and, as a final touch, trims it even.

Having wetted his scraper, the shoemaker is ready for the next step. He marks roughly the triangular outline of the heel cap on a piece of thin leather of a light colour. He cuts out the form, scrapes it thin and prepares it by stretching, surface-treating and scraping. It is now folded to test whether the sides are of equal length. Lines are drawn on either side of the central axis, a few slanting lines being added as well. Twisting stitches are used to sew the heel cap to the outside of the upper. The finished seam is thoroughly pounded with the iron beetle.

An old sole, which the cobbler subjects to much pounding and scraping to make soft, does duty as the insole. He turns the rough side upwards and places a patch upon the smooth undersurface. The patch was formerly part of an old water-bag, the seams of which have been opened and plucked clean. He slants one side of the patch to fit and then soaks it in water for a long time. Keshavbhai next reaches for the sole and heel, which he has prepared and stitched together that morning, and places them before him. The pieces to be joined together are pierced through near the point of the shoe with an awl and thus held in place, a second awl being later used to perform the same function at heel end. The cobbler now sews the outer and inner soles together with strong stitches, following the outline of the smaller insole, which lies on top. With the same twine he sews along the centre triangular piece. With four final stitches the two layered undersole is sewn to the insole. All seams are pulled tight and then pounded. The awls are removed. - Keshavbhai now takes out the old leather that he has previouvsly soaked in water. From this leather he cuts many oblong pieces, the sides of which he slants. These pieces he now commences to dexterously stuff into the sole through one side. These scraps of old leather are intended to fortify the sole. He wedges the

330

sole between his feet, inserts the old leather scraps between the sole layers and pierces through the whole with an awl. He also attaches the upper to the sole edge, fastening it with another awl. This time, though, he lays a loop of twine around the point and handle of the awl. He next commences to sew sole and upper together, starting midway between point and heel. He places an additional piece of leather as lining against the heel before continuing with the sewing, which consists in piercing equidistant holes with the awl along the leather, drawing the twine through the hole, giving it a sharp tug after each stitch. A previously prepared piece of light-coloured leather, scraped quite thin, is next fitted into the v-shaped opening in the vamp. This leather inset is arched up with the right hand, while the left pinches the ends together. Keshavbhai cuts a narrow strip from the trimmings of the shoe upper, cuts it in half and sews both pieces as reinforcements on either side of the v-shape along with the leather inset. From the point of the shoe he pulls out some of the old scraps used as stuffing between the sole layers. These he trims to a slant and reinserts them in such a manner that the shoe point is pliable enough to be bent upwards.

332
342

333

334

Having completed this stage of his work, Keshavbhai for the first time changes his posture, maintaining the new posture for just a short while. He stretches out his right leg, the left remaining bent as before. The shoe lies in his lap.

The sole and upper being sewn together, Keshavbhai pounds along the edge with the iron beetle. During this, he presses down an appreciable portion of the upper. He turns the shoe on the stone slab, while his right hand deals short, sharp blows on the leather. The point of the shoe he pounds with the hammer. He inserts the hammer handle into the shoe, guiding it along the inside edge in order to lift the upper again and stretch it. He grasps the hammer head with his palm and presses against the seam with great force. He wets the point of the large last and hammers it into the shoe. He guides the stretching horn between the upper and the last, moving it to and fro, backwards and forwards in all directions, pressing it upwards against the leather or turning it. Lastly, he strikes the shoe with the infitted last several times against the stone slab, takes off the shoe and slips his foot into it for trial. He ascertains that the heel cap needs to be widened with the hammer handle. Having completed this, he lays aside the shoe to dry.

335

339
338

After a prolonged afternoon siesta, the cobbler makes a second shoe to correspond, following exactly the same method as for the first. He even changes his sitting posture at the right moment.

When the second shoe has been completed as far as the first, he puts it out to dry on the sunlit roof of the verandah while he gives the finishing touches to the first shoe. First of all, he wets the point of the shoe and cuts out a long strip from a piece of good-quality leather of a light colour. This he prepares and cuts into two long narrow strips. The shorter piece he stitches across the v-shaped opening, using four stitiches. The end of the strip is merely pulled under the seam and snipped off. He now takes the longer strip and sews it to the vamp as a border along the edge of the v-shaped opening. From the same soft leather he cuts a square patch, which he then divides in four, piercing each part to admit an eyelet, which is hammered down into place. Each of these four parts is then cut to a circular shape and laid on the floor beside the shoemaker.

340

Keshavbhai whets the scraper on the oiled slab, for he will now trim the sole edge smooth. Beginning at the heel, he cuts in five stages halfway through the thick projecting parts of the sole up to the shoe point. At the second go he cuts the sole right through at this point, and then trims the other side in the same way. In order to trim it smoothly, he moistens the edge slightly. The shoe is wedged between his soles. He holds the knife by the handle in his right hand, while the left thumb exerts pressure on the blade and guides it forwards. Last of all, he trims the point and polishes the edges with a piece of horn.

Now comes the turn of the heel cap, which at present consists of two pieces of leather attached to the upper. The shoemaker cuts out a piece of lining leather corresponding to the outline of the point of the cap, to which purpose he lays the cap upon the upright wooden beetle firmly fixed in place between his soles. Two prepared pieces of leather are inserted between cap and lining and prodded into place with the awl. A narrow light-coloured band of moistened leather is folded over the lining and stuffing and sewn to the inner cap edge. For this, a length of narrow moistened leather ribbon is used, which is threaded through the needle like twine. Finally, the seam is pounded from inside and outside with the hammer, the wooden beetle serving as a base.

337

Keshavbhai fetches the second shoe from the roof and sews together the cut-out v-shaped portion in front as for the first shoe. He now reaches again for the first shoe, stretching it once more over the moistened last before threading a lacing across the v-shaped opening. For this he uses a prepared length of narrow leather ribbon, which he halves right down its entire length, stopping just before the end, so that a forked ribbon is the result. Both ends are trimmed to taper to a point. Keshavbhai then pierces seven holes on either side of the v-shape. The end where the ribbon bifurcates, he inserts into the pair of holes at the point of the v. He now threads the lacing unsymmetrically across the opening. The holes near the point are threaded only once, while those in the middle are threaded twice. The holes at the widest part of the v are also only once threaded through. Shortly before finishing the lacing, Keshavbhai sews the two leather discs with their centre eyelets on either side of the widest part of the v. This is done with a leather ribbon for twine and a few stitches. The lacing is then also threaded through the eyelets. When the criss-cross lacing is ready, one end of it is stitched into the leather near the eyelet and the other tucked under the lacing.

341

Keshavbhai once more stretches the whole shoe, using the stretching blocks as well as the wedge. Between the wooden blocks and the shoe a few rags are inserted.

The shoemaker cuts another insole from a piece of thin leather. This he prepares and treats until it is soft and pliable. He lays the sole inside the shoe and trims the edge with the scraper. He takes out the sole again and cuts along the marked outline. He then replaces it and feels at the shoe point with his fingers to see whether the sole fits correctly. Having reassured himself on this score, he lays aside the shoe and turns his attention to completing the second one in the same way.

X.6. Leather articles

The articles made by a cobbler from leather are few in number. Keshavbhai informed me that he made only water-bags, oxen harness and shoes in three designs, which vary little in essentials. In deference to modern fashion, he has added sandals to his limited repertoire. His nephew is also adept in the art of making modern shoes.

The water-bag
The water-bag consists of a wooden frame with a hoisting device and a cube-shaped bag which on one side continues in an outlet pipe. The wooden frame (1) is made up of four stout battens, the two shorter horizontal ones being tenoned to the longer vertical pieces so as to

9

make up a more or less square frame. Two-thirds of the way up a transverse lath (2) is fixed to the frame, the tenons penetrating through the battens. A pair of small supports (3) are attached to the transverse lath, a small handle (4) passing through their top ends. The drawing or hoisting rope (5) and the wooden ring (6) are passed over this handle. Twenty holes are punched into the folded over edge (7) of the leather bag, a strong leather thong (8) running spirally through the holes around the wooden frame. In order to ensure the bag being always fastened in the right way, four triangular flaps of leather (9) are attached to the frame and indicate the centre of each batten. The ends of the thong are secured with a symmetrical knot. A weight (10) is tied to the upper horizontal batten of the frame. This weight is merely a common stone with a hole through it.

The leather bag (11) which is firmly tied to the frame, is shaped like a cube. Its surface is wrinkled. A pipe (12) tapering towards the opening projects from one side of the cube. It is stitched on with a strong leather ribbon, the corners being further reinforced with leather patches (13). A strip of leather is stitched across the unhemmed pipe opening, the ends of the strip being sewn over leather patches serving as reinforcements (15). The narrow drawing rope (16) is tied to this handle.

water-bag	*kos*
wooden frame	*machi*
(1) frame battens	*ada*
(2) transverse lath	*mas*
(3) supports	*dhingali*
(4) handle	*khili*
(5) drawing rope	*varat*
(6) wooden ring	*makdo*
(7) edge of bag	*var*
(8) leather thong	*setara*
(9) triangular flaps	*choti*
(10) stone weight	*nang,* lit. piece
(11) leather bag for drawing water	*kotho*
(12) outlet pipe	*sundh*
(13) leather patches	*galfi*
(14) cross strip of leather	*funkia*
(15) leather reinforcements	*naka*
(16) thin drawing rope	*varatadi*

During summer the leather dries overnight and is stiff and hard the next morning. If it is not rendered pliable at this stage, the weight of the water will tear the brittle leather. On arriving at the well, the farmer therefore immerses the leather bag in water and leaves it to soak. He then harnesses his oxen to the yoke and prepares the drawing rope. By the time he finishes this preparatory work, the leather bag is moist and elastic once more; the work can start. During the monsoon months, when artificial irrigation can be dispensed with, the farmer unties the wooden frame and removes it. He rolls the bag into a bundle and ties it up with the leather thong. The bag is hung up so as to protect it from the ravages of rats. Rangmalbhai Karsanbhai of Baradia stated that in former days bags were hung on *ankadia,* suspension hooks. He said that nowadays people were not so careful and simply suspended the bag under a disc by a rope. When irrigation is resumed, the bag is soaked in water for a few days. *Tel,* oil, is applied to the surface only once, when the bag is newly made. Subsequent lubrication is not customary, unless the bag has been left dry for a long time.

A leather bag with all its parts costs fifty rupees today. The outlet pipe alone costs twentyfive rupees. Hardasbhai Bhayabhai, the Patel of Baradia, explains :

// *Kotho,* leather bag for drawing water, is more durable and will last longer than the *sundh,* outlet pipe. By the time the season for irrigation is over, the *sundh* is always worn out. It is separated from the *kotho* and renewed.
// Because the *sundh* glides over the reel and the weight of the water presses on it, it gets spoilt every year.
// The *kotho* lasts longer. I can use mine for about two or three year.

// Shoemakers who can make water-bags live in Ratadi and in Shrinagar.

The oxen harness

Instead of a harness made of twined cotton thread, an oval leather plate may be employed. To this is affixed on one side a large leather loop and a smaller one on the other. The plate is frequently bordered by a leather belt, a leather ribbon being used for the stitching.

oxen harness	*jotar*
(example in the possession of Karsanbhai Mundiabhai)	
leather plate length	28 cm
breadth	18 cm
length of first loop	40 cm
length of second loop	50 cm

The leather harness is slung over the necks of the oxen when the yoke rests on their napes. The loops are fastened to wedges in the yoke. Since only leather of first-grade quality (and therefore hardwearing) may be employed to make this article, which is subjected to much wear and tear, a harness may cost up to eight rupees.

Men's shoes

Men's shoes may be divided into the sole with heel, upper with toe piece and the point. The heel is comparatively long and has rounded-off corners. Midway between point and heel, the sole is narrow but widens outwards to taper to a point at both ends. To this sole, made up of several layers of pieces of leather, is sewn the heel, which consists of two pieces of leather of different length. An unsymmetrical sole covering the outer edge of the shoe is sewn on under this heel; a small triangular piece of leather is sewn under the centre of the foot. The low upper, which is dark in colour and patterned with parallel lines, is sewn around its entire edge to the sole. It is lined with light-coloured leather, the inside seam being invisible. A heel plate made of light-coloured leather surmounts the sole and projects upwards in a point above the edge of the upper. This heel plate is lined and seamed. One sole layer is so cut that is tapers to and continues in a narrow band towards the point of the shoe. This band is arched up and curled backwards to form the point of the shoe. The upper is cut out up to the point and lined at this place with a toe-piece, into which six eyelets are clinched in a cross-formation. These eyelets are purely decorative. The cut-out portion is filled with lacing, a leather ribbon being used for the purpose. The narrow band forming the point is drawn under the lacing. On either side of the cut-out portion, a leather disc is sewn, an eyelet being clinched into the centre of each. Thin leather is used for the inner sole.

shoe	*pagarkha* or *mojadi*
(example made by the shoemaker Keshavbhai in Ratadi)	
length	28 cm
width	10 cm
height	6 cm
heel width	6 cm
thickness	1.5 cm
plate height	12 cm
shoe-upper height	3 cm

Women's shoes

Women's shoes may be distinguished from men's shoes firstly by their smaller size, secondly through the lack of decorative elements (the eyelets adorning the vamp being absent), and lastly by the lack of a toe-piece, which is replaced by a small triangular leather patch set into the upper. As a rule the cobbler takes less pains with women's than with men's shoes. The lacing is often dispensed with as well.

shoe	*savala*
(example in the possession of Bhimabhai Avabhai)	
length	25 cm
width	10 cm
height	5.5 cm

There is yet another shoe model, the light-weight men's shoe. Here the seam of the upper runs over the heel plate. The sole is thin. For this reason such shoes are not worn by farmers but by craftsmen who ply their trade at home. The modern cobbler also makes sandals, and other fashionable shoes.

Traditional shoes with their side opening are held to be healthy, although they are as hard as wooden clogs. Keshavbhai expresses this in the following manner:

|| *Pagarkha,* traditional shoes are very cool for the eyes.

He means that these shoes keep the eyes cool, that is to say, wearing them prevents headaches.

Comparing traditional shoes with modern ones, the shoemaker, referring to the quality, says:

|| *Pagarkha,* traditional shoes must be as good as those made by machine.

Traditional shoes have yet another advantage over modern shoes: it is not necessary to clean, grease or brush them. The wearers are resigned to the hardness of the shoes, and only before festive occasions take them to the cobbler, who polishes them with a piece of horn.

XI. Additional notes

XI. 1. The skin and hair decoration

by Haku Shah

Men's hair-cut and physical culture

The men wash their hands, feet and face every morning, but do not take a bath regularly except when they have time after the day's work is done in the evening. Sometimes they apply *tel,* oil, on their entire body and rub it into their hair.

Trajava, tatoo marks on the skin, are quite rare on men's bodies. One will find only a few motifs like *kankadi,* a chain like ornament around the wrist and *laduda,* dots. These tatoos are marked by professionals from Porbandar town.

Since the men always wear a turban, there is not much by way of hair styles. However, some boys get their foreheads shaved to a straight line which curves down at the sides of the ears. All hair cutting is done by the barber, who uses a simple pair of scissors for cutting and a razor without soap or oil for shaving. Formerly men wore large *muso,* mustaches, and even *katra,* full beards, were common. Nowadays beards are rare and seen only among poor people who cannot spend much on the barber. The full beard was often the mark of a *baharvatiyo,* an outlaw.

Women's hair and skin decorations

The women wash themselves perhaps more often than men do, but soap is a rarity. For washing their long hair, they use a grayish clay. Often they oil their hair and help one another rubbing it in. For beautifying the face, only *mes,* soot mixed with butter, is applied under the eyelids.

Trajava, tatoos, are common for the women. One finds tatoo marks from the neck down to the breasts, from the arms upto the elbow, the upper-part of the hand, the feet, and the lower part of the legs which are visible when dressed.

344

The most common tatoo-forms are:

panch kan, five dots
Five dots form the endpoints and the centre of a cross. There can be one or two dots in each corner as well.

ful, flower
Many small dots are arranged to form a star.

deradi, temple

On top of a massive triangle, a cross is placed to represent the flag on a temple.

bhim pachhedi, lit. Bhim's cloth

Four rhombs around a centrical dot form a large cross.

ambo, Mango tree

A vertical line ends in a small cross which bears leaves on both sides.

mor, peacock

This highly stylized figure consists of a horizontal bodyline which is crossed by two verticles, the front one longer and bending forward to give the shape of a neck. On top of this line a crown of dots is given.

Besides these ornaments animal figures like *havaj,* lion and *unt,* dromedary can also be seen.

XI. 2. Toys and games

by Eberhard Fischer

In the present chapter we shall describe toys made for children. It goes without saying that small children also amuse themselves with natural objects such as stones, sand, leaves and sticks, out of which they fashion playthings for themselves. These are not included in the present chapter. However, it may be mentioned that little girls play at cooking over imaginary fireplaces, using fragments of earthenware for pots and sand for ingredients. Little boys may be observed pushing pieces of broken pottery along furrows they have dug in the sand, imagining themselves driving bullockcarts. They also build small houses and entire villages with stones and fragments. When the game is over, everything is distroyed.

2. 1. Children's toys

The doll

Dolls made from rags and remnants of cloth are sold in the market for a few annas a piece.
They are made chiefly by the Vaghri women, although mothers sometimes stitch dolls at home for their daughters. The dolls have large spherical heads covered with white cloth, with lengths of black thread pulled through to represent hair. Eyes, nose and mouth are stitched with red thread. Short stumps for arms project from the ungainly body. The sausage-like legs are concealed behind a long skirt. - Wooden dolls are rare. They are sold at the trade-fair held at Madhavpur, and the villagers buy such dolls for their children to take home with them. These represent figures of clothed women standing on little pedestals.

345

doll	*dhingli*
(cloth doll in the possession af Kaliben)	
length	18 cm
breadth	10 cm

The cradle

Miniature cradles, in which dolls are rocked, are avaliable at Porbandar. These are small lathe-turned and painted stands with a transverse beam, to which the cradle-cloth is attached. The village carpenters make similar cradles from pieces of common wood.

| cradle | *ghodiyu* | 220 |

The wooden animals

I once saw a little boy playing with the wooden figure of a crouching monkey, which he had salvaged from among the ornamental carvings of a broken disused chest. However, these wooden animals are not specially carved as toys for children.

monkey	*vandro*
(example in Ratadi)	
height	10.5 cm

The wagon

Little boys sometimes draw small wagons behind them by a string. To the rectangular wagon is attached a tapering shaft and a rhombic crossbar. The whole is sawn out of one wooden board. A large wooden wheel is loosely nailed on each side. The wagon may be ornamented with designs in chip-carving.

347

toy wagon	*gadi*
(example in the possession of Lilabhai Bhurabhai)	
length	28 cm
bredth	18 cm

The paper bird

These are made from folded newspapers dyed in bright colours and from cloth rags. These bird figures are decorated with pieces of silver paper stuck on them and are hung on strings from shelves and cradles. These decorative toys are made and sold by the Vaghri women.

paper bird	*ghughar*, lit, rattle

2. 2. Games for grown-ups

Card games

The favourite game played by men is cards. The French motifs are used for the suits. These bear the following names: *lal pan* or simply *lal,* red for hearts, *chokedi* for diamonds, *karikit* for spades and *fulevar* or *fuli* for clubs. A trick is called *hath,* the word for trump being *hukam.*

The commonest game is a simple 'trumps-takes-the-trick' game for two parties played by four players with a complete pack of cards. The rule is for one player of the party that won the last game to select from among the first five cards of his hand which suit shall be trumps. The winning party is the one to make the first seven tricks.

There it a lot of cheating at card games. The system of signals described in the following is common and often used by all four players at once, so that the distribution of cards is more or less apparent from the very beginning of the game. Extending the tongue so that the tip is visible between the lips signifies hearts, the signal for diamonds is a shaking of the head, while a raising of the eyebrows means spades and a blinking of the eyes clubs. This game is never played for stakes. Gambling is forbidden in Gujarat and I have never come across it but once and that at a wedding in Bakharla. The game played was a variation of poker.

The dice

Though less popular than cards, a game known as *chopat* is also played. It is a rather complicated version of ludo, the game played universally in Europe. *Chopat* is a game for eight players, four partnerships of two opposing each other. Partners are neighbours. If there are only four players, the game is called *ata.* The board, in the form of a crosss, consists generally of a length of cotton cloth with patches in the different colours sewn to it. The central square is uniform in colour. The four arms of the cross, known as *par,* contain three rows of eight squares each. Three of these squares, the two fifth squares from the outside and the sixth square inside, are "safe" squares known as *ful* or flower. Four yellow, green, red and blue counters known as *sogath* are used and seven cowries, called *kodiu,* cast as dice. The players take turns at throwing the cowries, the shells which fall with their open face upwards being counted. The relation of the number of spots to the moves is a follows: $1 = 11, 2 = 2, 3 = 3,$ $4 = 4, 5 = 25, 6 = 30, 7 = 14, 0 = 7$. If a player casts 0, 1, 5, 6, and 7 he wins a second throw. However, if the same number is cast three times in succession, all three throws are invalid.

In order to start moving a counter, a player must first throw either 1, 5 or 6. Once all the counters of one partnership have "come out", that is, have started moving, an additional move to the adjacent square is allowed when the above numbers are thrown. This additional move is known as *pagada*. Each partnership has four counters, which are set out on the side of the arm of the cross pointing towards them, and travel along the entire cross, commencing with the inner row, then following the course of progress along the outer rows to return finally to their own base, their respective inner rows and jump at the end into the centre.

In *chopat* the object of the game is for each player to guide all his counters along the prescribed route, thereby attempting to capture, that is, replace as many of the opposing partnership counters as possible. This is only possible when the opposing counter all by himself commands a square on one of the outer rows, provided it is not marked as *ful*. A further rule is that one counter may capture another, only if all other counters of the capture's kind are in the game, that is, have "come out". In addition, it must previously have captured the opponent for the first time by means of the *pagada* move described above. It is not possible to return to base and therewith win the game without having captured at least one counter of the opposing colours. For this reason, high numbers in casting are only welcome when all the counters have come out and the opportunity to capture an opponent presents itself.

Games with checkers
The following games are for two players. The most popular is indisputably the one similar to the game of draughts common in Europe. The game is the exclusive form of evening recreation for some men, who are unsurpassable masters at it. The draught-board may be drawn with chalk on the floor or scratched into the clay floor of the verandah. Pebbles and pottery fragments serve as checkers. The only possessor of a set of ivory checkers and a set of chessmen as well is Darbar Hamir Sinhji of Baradia. This set is supposed to have originally come from Kutch.

Be kakani, two checkers, is the name given to a game in which each player has two checkers, which he moves in turn. The "board" is in the shape of a three-quarter circle with five points of intersection (two diameters). Once, if both the checkers have alternately "come out", the player moves his with the purpose of fixing or blocking the opponent.

Another game known as *char kakani,* four checkers, is played on a rectangular board with a cross in the centre. Each player has four checkers which are placed alternately on one of the nine points of intersection. As soon as all the checkers are out on the board, each player in turn moves one of his checkers one square forward. If two opposing checkers meet, neither can advance against the other; but if either has an empty square behind him, then the opponent at his next move jumps over the other which is to be removed from the game. The one to first forfeit all his checkers is the loser.

Yet another variation is *nau kakani,* nine checkers, which is played according to the rules prescribed for draughts. However, in the game I observed in Ratadi, each player started off with two checkers and the game ended as soon as one of the players succeeded in forming a *tran kakani,* an arrangement of three checkers in a row or a *panch kakani* an arrangement of five checkers in a double row. There is no rule which allows a player who has lost all his checkers but three to jump to any place.

Bhul bhulamni which means "make a mistake" is a game that taxes the patience; the object is to place nine checkers on the ten points of intersection of a pentacle (5-pointed star) in such a manner as to always start from a vacant square and jump over a checker to another unoccupied square beyond.

String figures
These games, called *dori ni ramat* are only rarely played. Two varieties are commonly known: 346
mor pag, peacock legs and *ramat,* trick. In the first game, a piece of string with its ends tied together is lifted in the middle so as to form two loops on either side, which are twined between the fourth and fifth fingers. In the second game, the string is laid around the two big toes and finally extricated by a process of inter-twining and transferring, the person to whom the trick is being demonstrated being permitted to place his hands on the toes.

Consulted literature

(a) Ethnographic literature on Saurashtra

MALKAN, J. M. (1958)
Adodias in Saurashtra. *Indian Journal of Social Work, Vol. 19, 29-38.*

MANKAD, B. L. (1940)
A sociological study of the Kolis in Kathiawad. *Journal of the University of Bombay,* Vol. 9, 224-269.

MANKAD, B. L. (1948)
A sociological study of the Mianas of Kathiawad. *Journal of the University of Bombay,* Vol. 17, 47-78.

MANKAD, B. L. (1952)
Rabaris of Kathiawar (A social study). *Journal of the University of Bombay,* Vol. 7, 31-71.

MANKAD, B. L. (1953)
A sociological study of the 'Mers' of Saurashtra. *Journal of the University of Bombay,* Vol. 22, 47-64,

MANKAD, B. L. (1957)
Waghers of Saurashtra. *Journal of the University of Bombay,* Vol. 26, 14-33.

SHAH, A. M. and R. G. SHROFF (1958)
The Vahivanca Barots of Gujarat: A caste of Genealogists and Mythographers. *Journal of American Folklore,* Vol. 71, 246-276.

SHAH, V. and SARLA SHAH (1949)
Bhuvel. Socio-ecomomic survey of a village. Bombay.

TRIVEDI, H. R. (1954)
Some aspects of kinship terminology among the Mers of Saurashtra. *Journal of the Maharaja Sayajirao University of Baroda,* Vol. 3, 157-168.

TRIVEDI, H. R. (1961)
The Mers of Saurashtra. An exposition of their social structure and organisation. Baroda.

TRIVEDI, R. K. (Edit.)
Census of India 1961, Village Survey Monograph: village Pachhatardi, Ahmedabad.

TRIVEDI, R. K. (Edit.)
Census of India 1961, Gujarat. Census Handbook 6, Junagadh District, Ahmedabad.

WATSON, J. W. (1875)
Sketch of the Kathis, especially those of the tribe of Khachar and house of Chotila. *Indian Antiquary,* Vol. 4, 321-326.

Gazeteer of Bombay Presidency, Vol. 8, 1884; Vol. 9, 1901. Bombay.

(b) Selected general literature on Indian handicrafts and Indian craftsmen

ABRAHAM, T. M. (1964)
Handicrafts in India, New Delhi.

ANDREWS, F. H. (1943)
The indian craftsman. *Indian Art and Letters,* Vol. 17, 44-52.

ARCHER, W. G, (1947)
The vertical Man. A study in primitive Indian sculpture, London.

BIRDWOOD, G. C. M. (1880)
The industrial arts of India, Calcutta.

CHATTOPADHYAYA, KAMALADEVI (1963)
Indian handicrafts, New York - New Delhi.

ELWIN, V. (1951)
The tribal art of middle India, a personal record, London.

FUERER-HAIMEN-DORF, CHR. V. (1958)
Asia South: tribal styles. *Encyclopedia of World-Art,* New York - London.

| GADGIL, D. R. (1957) | The decline of handicrafts. *Khadi Gramadyog*, Vol. 4, 53-62. |

KRAMRISCH, STELLA (1958) — Traditions of the indian craftsman. *Journal of American Folklore*, Vol. 71, 224-230.

IRWIN, J. (1954) — Arts and Crafts. *Marg*, Vol. 8, 112-120.

MUKARJI, T. N. (1888) — *Art manufactures of India*, Calcutta.

MOOKERJEE, A. (1957) — *Indian primitive art*, Calcutta.

MOOKERJEE, A. (1958) — Arts and crafts of Saurastra and Gujerat. *Art in Industry*, Vol. 6, 3ff.

REVEL, L. (1957) — L'artisanat familial et villagoise dans l'Inde. *France–Asie*, Vol. 60, 1282-1288.

SARASWATI, S. K. (1956) — The problem of rural arts. *Indian Folk-Lore*, Vol. 2, 22-25.

SHIVASHWARKAR, L. (1950) — Folk art of Kathiawar. *Art in Industry*, Vol.2, 1ff.

WATT, SIR G. (1903) — *Indian art at Delhi*, Calcutta.

(c) Handbooks and general works

BAER G. (Edit.) (1966) — *Metall. Gewinnung und Verarbeitung in aussereuropaeischen, Kulturen,* Basel

BAESCHLIN, A.-A. BUEHLER-M. GSCHWEND (1948) — *Wegleitung fuer die Aufnahme der baeuerlichen Hausformen and Siedlungen in der Schweiz,* Basel.

BOSER, R. and I. MUELLER (1968) — *Stickerei, Systematik der Stichformen,* Basel.

BUEHLER-OPPEN-HEIM, A. and CHRISTIN (1949) — *Die Textilien-Sammlung Fritz Ikle-Huber im Museum fuer Voelkerkunde und Schweizerischen Museum fuer Volkskunde,* Basel.

EMERY, IRENE (1966) — *The primary structures of fabrics,* Washington.

EXNER, W.F. (1873) — *Die Werkzeuge des Schreiners in China und Japan,* Stuttgart.

FORBES, R. J. (1955) — *Studies in ancient technology,* Leiden.

GILL, W.E. (1952) — *The shoemakers manual,* London.

GOETZ, H. (1929) — Beitraege zur indischen Waffenkunde. *Zeitschrift fuer historische Waffen und Kostuemkunde,* Vol. 3, 56-61.

HIRSCHBERG, W. and A. JANATA (1966) — *Technologie und Ergologie in der Voelkerkunde,* Mannheim.

KELSEY, W.E. (1954) — *Carpentry, joinery and wood-cutting machinery,* London.

LEROI-GOURHAN, A .(1943) — *L'homme et la matiere,* Paris.

LEROI-GOURHAN,
A. (1945)   *Milieu et techniques*, Paris.

LENO, J.B.
(1940)   *The art of boot and shoemaking; a practical handbook*, London.

LING-ROTH, H.
(1950)   *Studies in primitive looms*, Halifax.

MATSON, F. R.
(1965)   Ceramic queries. *Ceramics and Man*, Chicago.

RILEY, J. M.
(1960)   *A manual for carpentry and joinery*, London.

SCHEFOLD, R.
(1966)   *Versuch einer Stilanalyse der Aufhaengehaken vom mittleren Sepik
                          in Neuguinea*, Basel.

SHEPARD, A. O.
(1956)   *Ceramics for the archeologist*, Washington.

SOLHEIM, W.G. II
(1965)   The function of pottery in Southeast Asia : from the present to
                          the past. *Ceramics and man*, Chicago.

WALTON, J.A.
(1964)   *Woodwork in theory and practice*, London-Sydney.

WULFF, H. E.
(1966)   *The traditional crafts of Persia*, Cambridge, Mass.

ZBOINSKI, A. and
L. TYSZYNSKI (1963)   *Dictionary of architecture and building-trades in four languages,
                          english, german, polish, russian*, New York.

(d) Selected literature with reference to the chapters I - III

ADYE, E. H.
(1917)   *Report on the economic geology of the Porbandar State in the Province
                          of Kathiawar, India*, Bombay.

GODE, P.K.
(1940)   The indian bullock-cart : its pre-historic and vedic ancestors.
                          Poona-Orientalist, Vol. 5, 144-151.

HORNELL, J.
(1942)   Hero Memorial stones of Kathiawar. *Antiquity*, Vol. 16, 289-300.

KOPPERS, W.
(1941)   Monuments to the dead of the Bhils and other primitive tribes in
                          Central India. *Annali Lateranensi*, Vol. 6, 117-206.

KUMAR, L.S.S.
(1963)   *Agriculture in India*, Vol. 2, Bombay - New York.

MANNDORFF, H.
(1963)   Kulturpflanzen Indiens in Wirtschaft und Brauchtum.
                          Zusammenfassung der wesentlichsten Hauptergebnisse. *Wiener
                          voelkerkundliche Mitteilungen*, Vol. 1, 60-64.

RANDHAWA, M.S.
and PREM NATH
(1959)   *Farmers of India*, Vol. 1-3, New Delhi.

SHASTRI, H.
(1940)   An old Hero Stone of Kathiawad-Gujarat. In : *D. R. Bhandarkar
                          Volume*, 173-176. Calcutta

VAIDYANATHAN,
K.S. (1947)   Hero Stones. *Quarterly Journal of the Mythic Society*, Vol. 39,
                          128-138.

(e) Selected literature with reference to the chapter VI

BUNT, S. G. E.
(1927)   A note on Jali windows. *Rupam 29*

JAMES, H. E. M. (1894)	Notes on an Ahmedabad carved screen and bracket. *Journal of Indian Art*, Vol. 5, 38.
JAMES. H. E. M. (1916)	Wood carving in Guzerat. *Journal of Indian Art and Industry*, Vol. 18, 38ff.
MAFFEY, J. L. (1903)	*Monograph on wood carving in the United Provinces of Agra and Oudh*, Allahabad.
TREASURYWALLA, B. N. (1928)	Wood sculpture from Guzerat. *Rupam* 31.
TRIVEDI, R. K. (Edit.)	*Wood carving of Gujarat. Census of India 1961*, Vol. 4.
TROTTER, H. (1960)	*The common commercial timbers of India and their use*, Delhi.
WALES, J. A. G. (1903)	*Monograph on wood carving in the Bombay Presidency*, Bombay.
WIRZ, P. (1938)	Ueber den indischen Milchquirl und die Butterbereitung in Indien. *Verhandlungen der Naturforschenden Gesellschaft Basel*, Vol. 50, 221-227.

(f) Selected literature with reference to the chapter VIII

ADYE, E. H. (1917)	*Report on the economic geology of the Porbandar State in the Province of Kathiawar, India*, Bombay.
AIYAPPAN, A. (1947)	Handmade pottery of the Urali Kurumbars of Wynad, S. India. *Man*, Vol. 47, 57-59.
GAIT, E. A. (1897)	The manufacture of pottery in Assam. *Journal of Indian Art*, Vol. 7, 5-8.
GHURYE, G. S. (1936)	A note on Indian potter's wheel. *Man in India*, Vol. 16, 68-71.
GUPTE. B. A. (1887)	The Baroda Court. *Journal of Indian Art*, Vol. 1, 126-133.
NAYAR, T. B. (1931)	A corpus of Indian pottery (Summary). *Man*, Vol. 31, 139.
STARR, R. F. S. (1941)	*Indus valley painted pottery: a comparative study of the painted wares of the Harappa culture*, Princeton.

(g) Selected literature with reference to the chapter IX and XI

BRANDON, B. A. (1903)	Woollen fabrics of the Bombay Presidency. *Journal of Indian Art*, Vol. 10.
BRIJ-BHUSHAN, J. (1958)	*Costumes and textiles of India*, Bombay.
ENTHOVEN, R.E. (1903)	Cotton fabrics of the Bombay Presidency. *Journal of Indian Art*, Vol. 10.
HORNELL, J. (1932)	String figures from Gujarat and Kathiawar. *Memoirs of the Asiatic Society of Bengal*. Vol. 11, 149-164.
JAYAKAR, P. and IRWIN, J. (1956)	*Textiles and ornaments of India, New York*.
NANAVATI, J.M.-M.P. VORA-M.A. DHAKY (1966)	*The embroidery and beadwork of Kutch and Saurashtra*, Ahmedabad.

1

Village lane-bifurcation
2
House of a Mer-farmer
3
House under construction

2

3

8

9, 10

11

15

16

17, 18

19–20
Traditional cart
21
Manually operated
farming tools
22
Implements for threshing
thistles
23
Drill plough
24–25
Drill harrows

19, 20

21,22

23

24

25

26-27
Sinking a well
28-29
Quarrying stones
30-32
Masonary work

26, 27

28, 29

30

31

32

33

34

35, 36

33
Stone lintle slab and
consoles
34
Stone window
35-36
Small niches
37-40
Consoles

37, 38

39, 40

41
Old stone relief
42
Memorial stone with a
cart
43
Memorial stone for a
woman biten by a snake
44
Memorial stone for a
sati-woman
45-48
Memorial stones for men

45, 46

47, 48

49
Memorial stones on a
platform
50
Rows of memorial stones
in the village
51
Invocation of the
ancestors
52–55
Invocation of the
ancestors

56–62
Invocation of Vashhada
dada
63
Immages of Vashhada
dada

56, 57

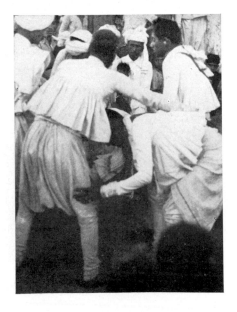

58, 59

64-65
Bringing clay for
wallreliefs
66-67
Preparing clay for
wallreliefs
68-71
Making clay relief wall
panels

68

69

70, 71

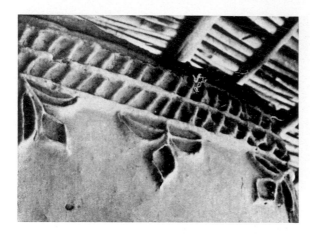

72
Clay decoration on
granery

73
Hand mill

74
Vertical clay panel

75
Granery receptacle

76-77
Larders from clay

78-79
Large niches decorated
with clay reliefs

73

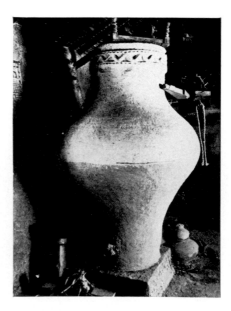

74, 75

80–82
Wall painting
83–85
Wall painting

83

84

85

90

91

92. 93

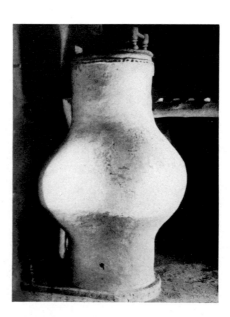

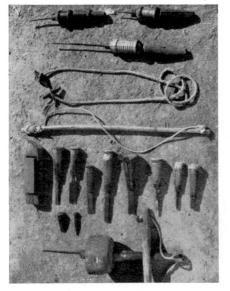

94–97
Carpenter's tools
98–99
Preparing a wooden board
100–101
Marking out the board

98, 99

100, 101

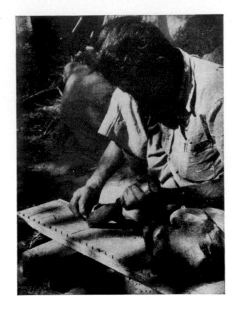

102–105
Carving ornamental
interstices
106–108
Carving figure reliefs

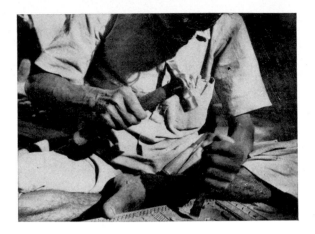

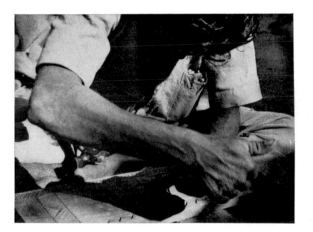

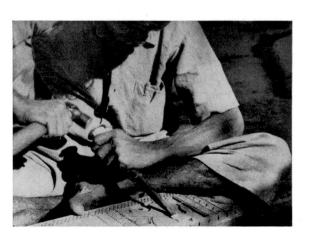

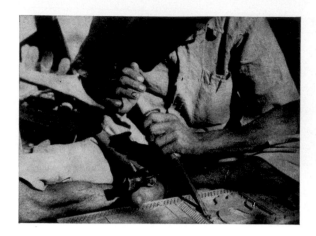

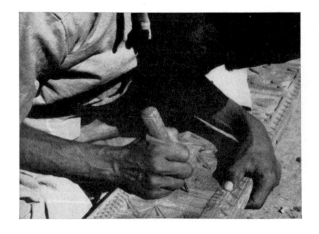

109-111
Carving figure reliefs
112
Sharpening the chisel
113-115
Preparing a wooden block

112

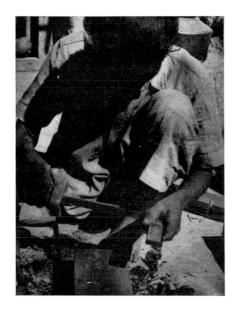

113 114

115

116–117
Teaching the apprentice
119–121
Carving the horse-head

119

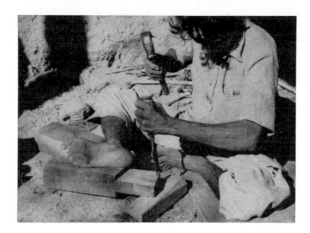

120

121

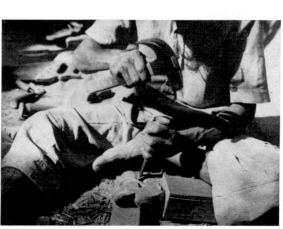

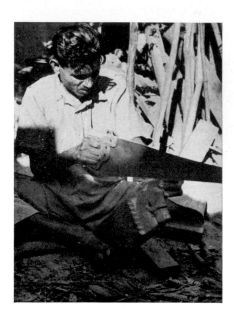

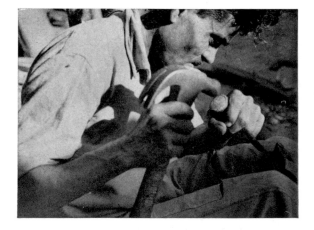

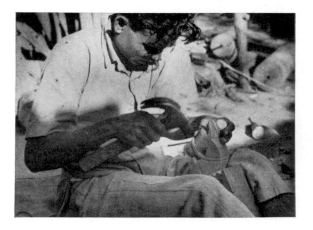

122-125
Carving the horse-head
126
Double winged door
127
Grated door
128
Door anchor beam
129
Anchor beam with
horsehead

130–132
Anchor beams
133–135
Lintel-boards

136–138
Reliefs from lintel-boards
139–141
Figurative reliefs from
lintel-boards

139

140

141

142, 143

144, 145

154, 155

156, 157

158
Four-legged stand
159
Table stand for water
vessels
160
Knee-prop
161
Stool
162
Chair
163
Small mortar
164
Hand mill
165
Salt container

173
Marriage lamp stand
174-175
Decorated water-pipe
176
Copper-alloy vessels
177-178
Potter's tools
179
Pile of paddles

180–181
Fetching clay
182–186
Preparing clay and temper

187-190
Preparing clay-mixture
191-194
Throwing and molding
vessels (red earthenware)

187, 188

189, 190

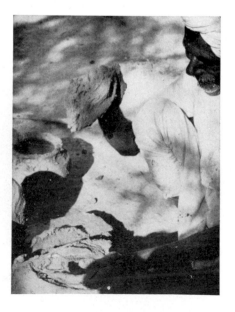

191

192 193

194

195–197
Throwing and molding
vessels (red earthenware)
198–201
Chasing

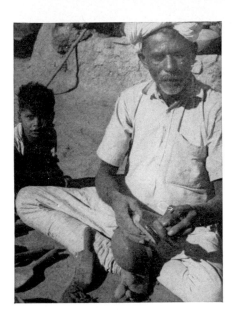 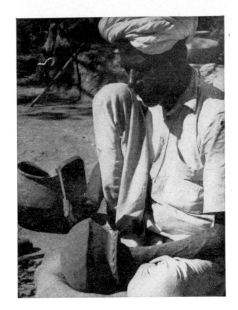

202

203

204

202
Preparing colours
203–204
Painting red earthenware
205
Polishing red earthenware
206–207
Firing red earthenware

208
Taking out fired vessels
209
Dipping vessels in water
210
Vessel-load ready for the
market
211–213
Throwing and moulding
of vessels (black
earthenware)

211

212

213

214-221
Throwing and moulding
of vessels (black
earthenware)

218, 219

220, 221

222–227
Chasing vessels (black
earthenware)

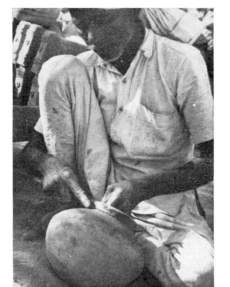

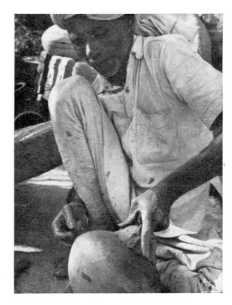

232, 233

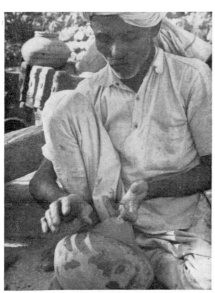

234, 235

236–238
Preparing vessels with a
narrow neck
239
Working in the courtyard
240
Ornamenting black
earthenware with a comb
241
Fetching ochre-clay

239

240

241

242
Coating vessels with
ochre slip
243
Polishing black
earthenware
244
Applying another layer
of slip on black cooking
vessels
245-247
Preparing kiln for black
earthenware

245

246

247

248-250
Preparing kiln for black
earthenware
251
The kiln is ready for
firing black earthenware
252-253
Opening the kiln and
testing the vessels

251

252

253

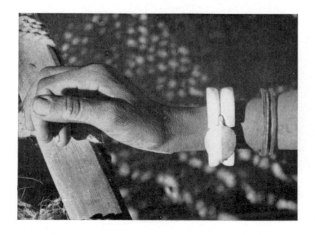

254
Black earthenware is
ready for sale
255
Taking vessel-load to the
market
256
Ivory bangle of a potter's
wife
257
Set of black earthenware
258
Small pot for storing
butter-milk
259
Flour receptacle

257

258

259

260

261

262

267-272
Mourning ritual of Mer-
farmers
273
Spinning cotton

272

273

274–275
Weaving at the cotton-
loom
276
Woolen blanket
277–280
Twisting of cords

275

276

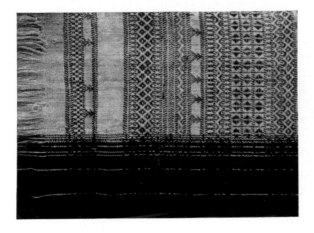

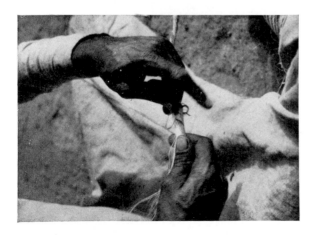

281–284
Twisting of cables
285
Weft-twining of
ornamental borders
286–287
Twining with a single
thread
288
Different slings

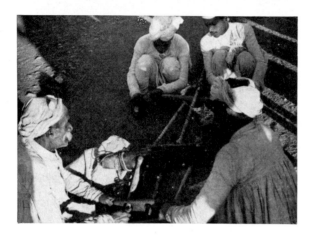

282

283, 284

 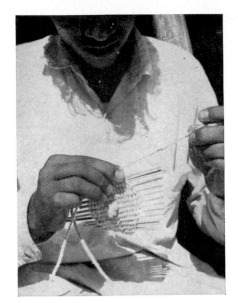

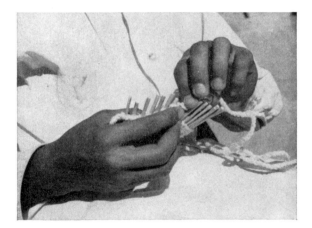

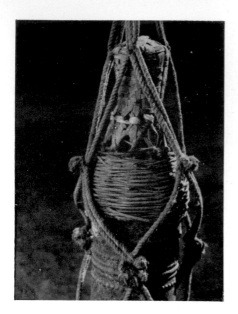

289
Plaited bottle-container
290
Tobacco bowl
291
Yoke halter
292
Twined muzzle
293
Wall-hanging of
bead work
294
Coconut covered with
bead work
295
Lintel panel of bead
work
296
Fan with bead work

297
Crochet work
298
Embroidered wall hanger
299
Wall decorated with
embroideries
300
Embroidered oxen-cover
with patch-work
301-304
Farmers from Ratadi

301

302, 303

304

305
Preparing rags for making
a quilt
306-308
Washing rags
309-311
Making a quilt

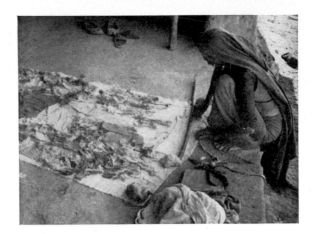

309

310

311

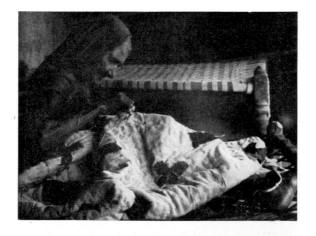

312
Stitching a quilt
313-317
Fixing applique work on
a quilt

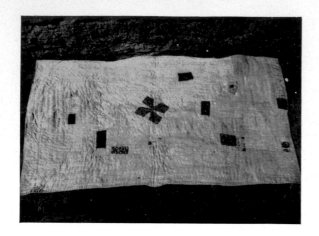

318
Quilt
319
Bolster
320
Saddle
321
Cobbler's workshop
322-323
Cobbler's tools

321

322

323

324, 325

326, 327

324-326
Preparing leather
327-328
Preaparing the sole
329-331
Fixing the upper to the
sole

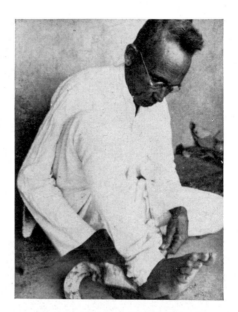

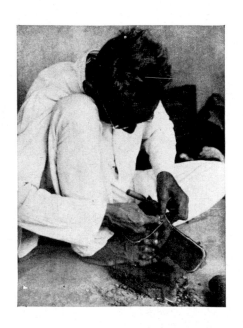

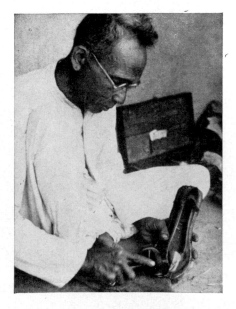

332-335
Fixing the upper to the sole
336-339
Trimming edges and stretching the shoe

336, 337

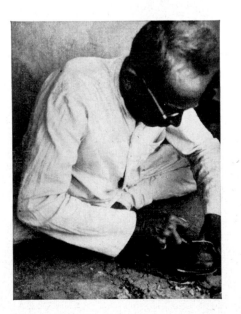

338, 339

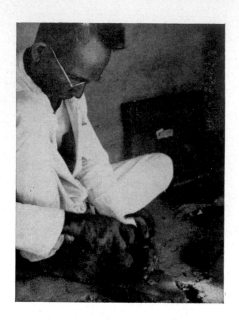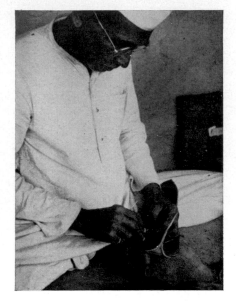

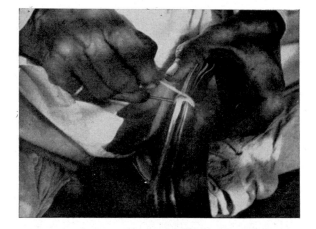

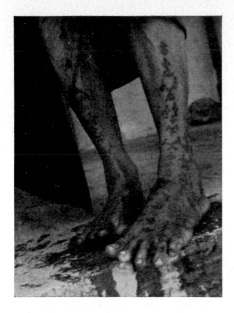

344, 345

346

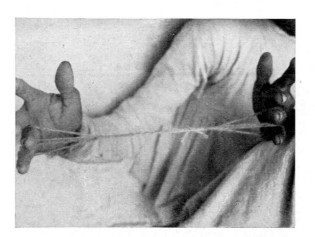

347

340–341
Fitting the lacing into
vamp
342
Tying sole and upper
343
Shoes for Mer-farmers
344
Tatoos on a woman's legs
345
Doll
346
String figure
347
Toy wagon